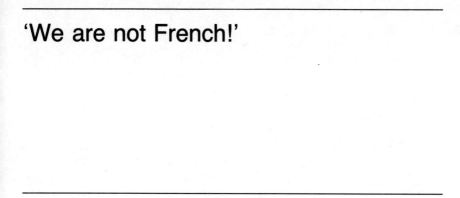

'We are not French!'

'We are not French!'
Language, culture and identity in Brittany

Maryon McDonald

Routledge
London and New York

First published 1989
by Routledge
11 New Fetter Lane, London EC4P 4EE

Simultaneously published in the USA and Canada
by Routledge
a division of Routledge, Chapman and Hall, Inc.
29 West 35th Street, New York, NY 10001

© 1989 Maryon McDonald

Typeset by J&L Composition Ltd, Filey, North Yorkshire
Printed and bound in Great Britain by Mackays of Chatham PLC, Kent

British Library Cataloguing in Publication Data

McDonald, Maryon
  'We are not French!': language, culture and
identity in Brittany.
  1. France Brittany Bretons Cultural identity,
history
  I. Title
  305.8'9168

Library of Congress Cataloging in Publication Data

McDonald, Maryon.
  'We are not French!': language, culture, and identity in Brittany
/ Maryon McDonald.
  p.   cm.
  Bibliography: p.
  Includes index.
  1. Brittany (France)—History—Autonomy and independence
movements. 2. Nationalism—France—Brittany. 3. Breton language–
–Study and teaching. 4. Breton language—Political aspects.
  5. Celts—France—Brittany—History. 6. Separatists—France–
–Brittany—History—20th century. I. Title.
  DC611.B855M43   1990
  944'.1—dc20   89–10358
                                                                CIP

ISBN 0–415–00632–5

Contents

Contents

Acknowledgements

I owe a special debt of thanks to members of Oxford University, in the Institute of Social Anthropology and in Wolfson College, for the important academic stimulus and moral support afforded me during the research on which this book is based; and to the Economic and Social Research Council (London), the *Centre National de la Recherche Scientifique* (Paris), the Taylor Institution (Oxford), the Oxford Women's Studies Committee, and the Royal Anthropological Institute (London) for the necessary financial assistance that made my work possible.

I give special thanks to Malcolm Chapman (a former student of the Institute of Social Anthropology, Oxford) for his reading of first drafts of this work and his helpful willingness to argue points with me; and to Dr Audrey Colson (formerly of the Department of Ethnology, Oxford) who supported me, academically and morally, throughout the early stages. I must give thanks, too, to Professor Ellis Evans, of Jesus College, Oxford, for finding the time and patience, early on in my research, to give some specialist advice to a relatively untutored adventurist into Celtic Studies. My greatest intellectual debt must be to Edwin Ardener (Institute of Social Anthropology, Oxford) who supervised the research which led to the original thesis, who offered me some invaluable insights, and whose scholarly encouragement allowed me to tackle some difficult problems. Edwin died suddenly in 1987. My debt to him is greater than any specific reference in the text might suggest.

There are many to whom I owe thanks for their help and encouragement when the thesis was put aside and the chapters of a book had to be constructed: to the Mistress and Fellows of Girton College, Cambridge, for the atmosphere of convivial wit and scholarship in which research and writing could proceed; and especially to Dr Marilyn Strathern (now Professor of Social Anthropology at Manchester University) for her interest and support; to my subsequent colleagues in the Department of Human Sciences, Brunel University, and particularly to Professor Adam Kuper for his support and comments; and to Professor Ronnie Frankenberg, of Keele University, who examined this work in its thesis form, who has offered many helpful suggestions for this book, and from whose critical insight and wit I have greatly benefited. At home, in the meantime, I must thank Colin Ross for his superhuman patience and his tolerance of my Breton ravings; and Angie Ashton for helping to introduce order into the text; and Heather Gibson of Routledge for her help and encouragement.

In Brittany, I owe thanks to the following for discussion and help in researching the position of Breton in the schools: to the *Rectorat* in Rennes; to the Academic Inspectorates of each *département* (and especially to Inspectors in Ille-et-Vilaine and Finistère); to the diocesan authorities in Rennes and Quimper; to the region's Technical Adviser for Breton at the secondary-school level; to the educational advisers for Breton at the elementary-school level, in Finistère and the Côtes-du-Nord particularly; and to the many headteachers and the teachers of Breton in the *Ecoles Normales*, the *Lycées*, the Colleges, and the primary and nursery schools in Brittany, public and private, who freely discussed issues with me, and who allowed me to be present in their classrooms. I also gratefully acknowledge the help of employees in the departmental and diocesan archives in Finistère; of MM. Gerard Jaffrédou (a former doctoral student of History at Brest University) and Armand Keravel (of *Emgleo Breiz*, Brest, and formerly of *Ar Falz*) for providing me with some specific references; and of both the French Embassy in London and Dr Lois Kuter of the International Committee for the Defense of the Breton Language in supplying materials I lacked.

For initiating me into the Breton language, and for accepting and encouraging my work on and with the Breton movement, I owe special thanks to the following: Professor Léon Fleuriot, of the Universities of Rennes and Paris, who was always ready to give me the benefits of his Celtic erudition; An Ao. Per Denez, of the Celtic Department of Rennes University, without whose skill and determination in Breton-language teaching I would never have managed to acquire the necessary competence in Breton to pursue my research; all the teachers and students of the Rennes Celtic Department for their help and tolerance; Bernard Tanguy of the Celtic Department of Brest University; Pierre-Jean Simon and Fanch Elegoët of the Rennes Department of Sociology and Ethnology; and Jean Gagnepain and Jean-Yves Urien of the Department of *Langage* in Rennes, whose seminars, lectures, or discussions were of great benefit to me. I gratefully acknowledge also members of the UDB party, of *Ar Falz*, and of the *Front Culturel Progressiste Breton* for their discussions, and for their acceptance of me at their meetings; and I thank *Skol an Emsav* members who helped me to learn Breton. A special note of thanks is due to Lukian Kergoat, Jil Kilivere, Yvon Le Gac, Yann Jegou, Gwendal and Herle Denez, Olier ar Mogn, Lena Louarn, Tangi Louarn, Anna-Vari Chapalain, and Herve Latimier, all of whom came to accept and support my efforts to understand the Breton movement and its cause, even if, in so doing, some of them had to overcome opposition and argument within their own ranks or to go against their own better judgement. I am very grateful to An Itron Vefa de Bellaing, of *Skol Ober*, and to Gilles Morin, of *Les Amis du Parler Gallo*, who never hesitated to give me practical help and encouragement.

I reserve a very special offer of thanks here to all the members of the *Diwan* organization, whether office staff, board, teachers, or parents, who gave me free access to their schools, their meetings, their literature, and, in many instances, their homes. Without the genuine friendliness of *Diwan*, and the desire of so many of its members to have a frank and open account of themselves, their own problems, and those of the movement generally, much of my work would simply not have been possible. I thank all the members of *Diwan* through their former presidents, Gweltaz ar Fur and René L'Hostis (Reun an Ostis). In the space available here, I can only single out a few of the *Diwan* parents to whom I owe a great debt of friendship and hospitality: Albert and Soazig Daniel, Louis and Chantal Lemoine, Helen Dausse, Guy and Anne-Marie Le Corre, Yvon Abiven, Marie-Jo Rivoal, Christian Jallais, Nadine Le Graet, and Yvette Laurent. Among the teachers and office staff of *Diwan*, I would like to thank especially Nannig ar Mee, Chantal Kervern, Denez Abernod, Kristina Roudod, Marcel Gorje, Line Gourvez, Jakez Bleunven, Maoris Jouanno, Daniel an Doujet, Maurice Guyomard, Annaig Gwiban, Yann Guillamot, Marie-Reine Jezequel, Kristina Jegou, Gerard Dantec, Yann-Ber Trousset, Patricia Le Bideau, Isabel Lucas, Fredy Salle, and Claudette Doucen.

In Plounéour-Ménez, I thank all those, far too numerous to mention, who showed me such hospitality, patience, and kindness, and especially in the hamlet of Le Relecq and the village of Kerguz. I owe particular thanks to Madame Thérèse Pouliquen and her son, Yves Pouliquen, in Kerguz. I gratefully acknowledge the help and kindness of M. Pierre Lachuer, mayor of Plounéour, and of all the members of the municipal council; also, Jean André, Théophile Le Gall, Jean Messager, Jeanne Pouliquen, Hervé Pouliquen, Martine Lautrou, André and Jacqueline Bothuan, Hervé and Hélène Pape, Maria Henry, Pierre and Anna Hélary, and Jean-Claude and Jocelyne Faujour, for their support and enthusiasm; similarly, all the staff, past and present, of Plounéour's public and private schools, as well as M. Le Recteur Tareau and An Ao. Person Troal, priests of Plounéour, for their willing contributions to my study; and Fanch and Yvonne Coat, Jean and Yvonne Kervern, Marcel Dourmad, Marcel Prigent, René Rolland, Hélène Lachuer, Jean-Luc Messager, the Goarnisson family, and Joël and Anne-Marie Kerne, for helping me to understand local farming practice and problems; and Yvon and Hélène Laouenan and Yann Crenn for teaching me about their arts and crafts. I am very grateful indeed to Madame Anne Jouan for renting me her house in Kerguz, and for entrusting me with its contents.

Acknowledgements

There are others in Brittany whom I should have liked to have thanked here, but to whom I can offer only a humble, memorial gratitude: Gwenola Abiven of *Diwan* who died in a tragic car accident in 1979; Hervé Laurent of Plounéour, who died in a road accident in 1980; Louis Pouliquen, former mayor of Plounéour, who died, after a difficult illness, in 1981; Henri Cosquer, mayor of Plounéour when I began my research, who died suddenly in 1983; Erwan Kervella, former teacher in *Diwan*, who died after a tragic accident in 1983, and whose unfailing good humour is much missed.

Abbreviations

ADF	*Archives Départementales: Finistère* (The departmental archives of Finistère, situated in Quimper; numbers and letters appearing after 'ADF' in the text are archival references, denoting the series or files of the archival system of classification).
ADI-V	*Archives Départementales: Ille-et-Vilaine* (The departmental archives of Ille-et-Vilaine, situated in Rennes).
AEB	*Amañ Emgleo Breiz* (Br.; in French: *Voice l'Entente Bretonne*; a militant journal printed in French, Breton, and, sometimes, English, for a national and international readership).
AM	*Archives Municipales* (The municipal archives of Plounéour-Ménez, containing the deliberations of the municipal council, and available in the town hall of Plounéour).
AN	Assemblée Nationale.
BAIP	*Bulletin Administratif de l'Instruction Primaire.*
BCD	*Bulletin de la Commission Diocésaine* (Quimper).
BEPC	*Brevet d'Etudes du Premier Cycle.*
BMSELF	*Bulletin Mensuel du Syndicat de l'Enseignement Laïque du Finistère.*
BN	Boucheron and Nonus (1889) 1890 (see bibliography).
BOSIP	*Bulletin Officiel et Spécial de l'Instruction Primaire (Département du Finistère)*
BPIIF	*Bulletin Pédagogique des Instituteurs et Institutrices du Finistère*
Br.	Breton.
BSAF	*Bulletin de la Société Archéologique du Finistère.*
CAF	*Conseil Académique (Finistère): Délibérations*, ADF (1 September 1850–8 April 1854).
CDD	*Conseil Départemental (Finistère): Délibérations*, ADF.
CDIP	*Conseil Départemental (Finistère) de l'Instruction*

	Publique: Procès verbaux des délibérations, ADF (vol. 1: 1854–65; vol. 2: 1865–80; vol. 3: 1886–8).
CELIB	*Comité d'Etudes et de Liaison des Intérêts Bretons* (see Chapter five).
CEN	*Commission de l'Education Nationale.*
CIRREES	*Centre Interdisciplinaire de Recherche et de Réflexion sur les Ensembles Economiques et Sociaux* (Rennes).
CLR	*Conseil de la République.*
CNB	*Le Canard de Nantes à Brest* (a left-wing, fortnightly paper; now defunct).
CP	*Cahiers Pédagogiques.*
CRDP	*Centre Régional de Recherche et de Documentation Pédagogiques (Bretagne).*
FB	*Feiz ha Breiz* (a Catholic journal, in Breton; now defunct).
FGDS	*Fédération de la Gauche Démocratique et Socialiste.*
FLB	*Front de Libération de la Bretagne* (Chapter five).
Fr.	French.
GERIB	*Groupe d'Etude et de Recherche des Influences Réciproques entre la Bretagne Orientale et la Bretagne Occidentale* (established by a member of *Les Amis du Parler Gallo*).
GIAB	*Geriadur Istorel ar Brezhoneg* ('Historical Dictionary of Breton'; Hemon 1959–78, see bibliography).
INRA	*Institut National de la Recherche Agronomique* (*Station d'Economie Rurale*, Rennes).
INSEE	*Institut National de la Statistique et des Etudes Economiques* (*Direction Régionale de Rennes*).
JAC-MRJC	*Jeunesse Agricole Chrétienne – Mouvement Rural de la Jeunesse Chrétienne.*
JASO	*Journal of the Anthropological Society of Oxford.*
JO	*Journal Officiel.*
LI	*Lois et Inscriptions*, ADF (1814–1864).
MAC	*Mémoires de l'Académie Celtique.*
MOB	*Mouvement pour l'Organisation de la Bretagne* (Chapter five).
O:II	Plounéour-Ménez: series O:II, ADF.
OU	*Orthographe Universitaire* (Chapter seven).
PB	*Le Peuple Breton* ('The Breton People'; French-language journal of UDB).
PCF	*Parti Communiste Français.*
PS	*Parti Socialiste.*
PSU	*Parti Socialiste Unifié.*
PV	*Pobl Vreizh* ('The Breton People'; Breton-language journal of the UDB).

RGA	*Recensement Général de l'Agriculture (Direction Départementale de l'Agriculture, Finistère).*
RTB	*Radio-Télé Brezhoneg* (a militant organization withholding full payment of licence fees).
SEMENF	*Société d'Economie Mixte d'Etude du Nord Finistère.*
SFIO	*Section Française de l'Internationale Ouvrière.*
SFRT-CGT-FR3	*Syndicat Français de Radio-Télévision – Confédération Générale du Travail – France-Régions 3.*
SGEN-CFDT	*Syndicat Général de l'Education Nationale – Confédération Française et Démocratique du Travail.*
SNETP-CGT	*Syndicat National de l'Enseignement Technico-Professionel – Confédération Générale du Travail.*
SNI-PEGC	*Syndicat National des Instituteurs et Institutrices – Professeurs d'Enseignement Général des Collèges.*
SNRT-CGT-FR3	*Syndicat National de Radio-Télévision – Confédération Générale du Travail – France-Régions 3.*
SV	*Skol Vreiz* ('Breton School'; a bilingual journal for teachers of Breton, produced by *Ar Falz*).
T:FIA	Series T: *Fonds de l'Inspection Académique. Rapports des Inspecteurs*, ADF.
THES	*The Times Higher Education Supplement.*
UBO	*Université de la Bretagne Occidentale*, Brest.
UCDP	*Union Centriste des Démocrates de Progrès.*
UDB	*Union Démocratique Bretonne* (Chapter five).
UDF	*Union pour la Démocratie Française.*
UNR	*Union pour la Nouvelle République.*
W.	Welsh.
'ZH'	The 1941 Breton orthography (Chapter seven).

Introduction

The subject of this book is the language and culture, the customs and manners of Brittany. That might seem like an innocent enough topic, but it positively bristles with political sensibilities. The chapters which follow attempt to make sense of the complex situation which engenders these sensibilities. A great part of the discussion will, in one way or another, be focused around issues of ethnic or minority identity; related questions, from feminism to terrorism, also impinge to varying degrees. It is rare for the parties directly involved in such issues to avoid the assumption of moral or political virtue. The following chapters make some attempt to hold up for reflection the worlds in which such virtue is assumed. In so doing, they take us via such apparntly diverse topics as the French Revolution of 1789 and wholemeal bread.

Britain and France, and France and Brittany

Brittany inhabits the wider context of France, and it is to this more general context that we shall look for the sources and structure of the culture of this north-western peninsula. First, however, it is important to stress that, within the context of *la France*, great indignation can be generated on the issue of Breton language and culture. According to the tenets of France's own history, modern France begins with the Revolution of 1789, but roughly two hundred years later France is still preoccupied with its own existence, which can strike outsiders as odd. Modern French politicians will commonly appeal to *La France*, and regularly declaim '*Vive la France!*', in a manner for which the only translation, within other contexts of very different sensibilities, might appear to be as comic melodrama or simple xenophobia. Certainly we have no easy equivalent in the UK (cf. Johnson 1986).

The bottom line of much anthropological writing about other countries or cultures must inevitably be some form of comparison with one's own country or culture. Comparison with the British context is here not only inevitable but informative to pursue. Brittany is but one of several indigenous regional minorities in France. These minorities are large, but the world has, until recent times, known relatively little of them in comparison with, say, the Welsh or the Scots in Britain. The majority contexts, and differences between the majority contexts which these minorities inhabit, are important for an understanding of the shape and status of the minorities constructed within them. Political events of the eighteenth century brought the Scottish Highlander on to the national and international stage just at a time when the intellectual world was beginning to look for the 'primitive' (Chapman 1978), and in the second half of the eighteenth century Britain was already in a position of constitutional security such that this 'primitive' within could be contemplated without fear. Across the Channel, France was only years away from revolution. Since then, when viewed from Britain and by some of its own historians, France seems to have been fighting a constant battle for its very survival. Occupied by foreign forces, enemies and allies, four times in the last two hundred years, France has also tried to define its way over the same period through two monarchies, one consulate, two empires, five republics, one definitive revolution, the Paris Commune, the Vichy regime, and May 1968. Faced with this succession of external threat and internal upheaval, Paris has never been sufficiently sure of the integrity of France to wish into existence other identities within it. On the contrary, France and the Jacobin State have given to the world a model of directive centralization (cf. McDonald 1986b: 164–5).

The political preoccupation of the State with its own centre has been consolidated by economic and demographic movements over the last two hundred years which have confirmed the pre-eminence of Paris as a source of organization and ideas. At the same time, France has retained large rural populations. France industrialized much later than Britain, and there has been no comparable shift of population from countryside to town. In the mid-nineteenth century, over 70 per cent of the French population was rural,[1] and it was not until the 1930s that this proportion fell to just under half, remaining still at 47 per cent in 1946. A marked shift of population from country to town came in the 1950s and 1960s, with the rural population falling, by the mid-1970s, to 27 per cent. In Britain, by the end of the eighteenth century, the self-sufficient small-holder was largely a thing of the past. It is only relatively recently, since the Second World War, that France has become conscious of a definitive dwindling of its large, 'rooted' *paysannerie*. At the turn of the century, almost half the total active population of France was engaged in (overwhelmingly small-holding) agriculture, and this figure was still well over a third in the 1930s. The dramatic 'rural exodus' of the 1950s and 1960s brought this proportion of the active French population down to 14 per cent by 1970. Even so, the corresponding figure in the UK was under 3 per cent, and the 'agriculture' of most of this 3 per cent cannot easily be translated, politically, socially, and economically, as *l'agriculture*.

Given these different contexts, the peasant could not, in France, be contemplated or regretted in the last century in quite the same way as in neighbouring intellectual traditions. Romanticism was largely the property of France's German and British neighbours, each reacting, in part, to the rationality of the French Enlightenment which fed into the 1789 Revolution. French romanticism flourished with vigour after the Napoleonic wars, but the divisions it helped to conjure up internally were muted on an international stage by the importance of French identity itself. International intrusion and pressure on a self-consciously fragile France had the effect of encouraging a tighter hold on the reins linking the old provinces to Paris, the centre of the nation. Many aspects of folklore studies as they developed in France followed a British model, but the metaphorical 'disappearance' of the folk-ways they depicted could not have quite the same resonance. Such ways were too real an obstacle to progress.

Some common images of France – including, for example, the idea that it has some very powerful intellectuals; that it is, at the same time, a quaint world of peasants and rurality, somewhere to go on holiday, and a country of well-established *cuisine* – begin to make sense within the comparative framework I have described. The particular status (and relatively non-pejorative image) of intellectuals in France derives, in part, from the importance of Paris and the relatively small urban élite which France has sustained but their position is also due to the active and effective involvement of intellectuals in important political events and issues (e.g., the Dreyfus affair) which have deeply affected France's development and self-image (see Reader 1984). The importance of France's intellectuals also derives from the fundamental place accorded to the education system in the construction and stability of the nation – a point to which we shall have ample cause to return. The issue of *cuisine* is not unrelated. The smallness of the urban population, the greater divide between the élite and the rural population, and the generally low esteem in which the gentry and the educated traditionally held rural life, all found expression in the medium of food in a way in which they did not in, for example, Great Britain (where urban/rural contact was greater and differences were not of the same order nor so extreme). In the seventeenth century, French food was something the English gentry scorned, but, by the nineteenth century, visible political, economic, and demographic disparities between the two countries and new structures for their expression meant that an élite mode of eating, still alien to the mass of the French population, was finding a new economic niche within France in the culture of the restaurant, and could be taken up as 'French' by urbane British travellers (for further details, see Mennell 1985; also McDonald 1985).

In many ways, Brittany has shared the political, economic, and demographic fate and the problems of France as a whole, but presents a somewhat later and intensified picture of some of the wider French trends.

By the mid-1970s, Brittany had a population of almost 2,600,000, or about 4.9 per cent of the population of France as a whole (INSEE 1980). Modern Brittany is an important fishing area, and there are growing secondary (particularly food processing) and tertiary (particularly tourism) sectors, concentrated mainly in the coastal areas. Brittany is also the foremost agricultural region of France, producing over 11 per cent of the national agricultural output. Most of Brittany's contribution comes from animal products (especially dairy products) for which, by the 1970s, Brittany already topped all the other French regions, producing 17 per cent of the national total (Houée 1979, 2: 90). Brittany has always been a pre-dominantly rural and agricultural area, and this rural character has brought both problems and glamour, backwardness and rural charm.

The population of Brittany grew steadily throughout the nineteenth century, at a rate faster than that of France as a whole, and with a larger rural sector. In the mid-nineteenth century, over 80 per cent of the Breton population was rural, and it was not until the 1960s that this proportion fell to under half, though still 46 per cent in 1975. In the early 1950s, over 50 per cent of the total active population of Brittany was engaged in agriculture; by 1975, this was just over 21 per cent (Daucé and Léon 1978). Throughout the nineteenth century, land was a more attractive investment than industry in most parts of France, and when native Breton capital *did* find its way into industry, it tended to leave Brittany to do so (see *Skol Vreiz* 1980: esp. p. 89). Much of the large, rural population was working barely viable family farms, smaller in Brittany than the national average (Houée 1979, 1: 38). Special government indemnities are now paid to those who retire and sell or rent out their land to form more productive units, and Brittany has participated in a general trend towards larger farms, intensified production, and contracts with agribusiness. Neverthe-less, most farms in Brittany, at the beginning of the 1980s, were 20 hectares or less, and small units are still typical of France in general, an image which has bolstered many a British farmer's concern about the Common Agricultural Policy.

When looking at France then, a visitor from a nation such as Britain can find a world that has only relatively recently been through processes of urbanization and industrialization, which we might term 'modernization'. In Brittany, the visitor can find that contrast drawn even more clearly. The traditional, rural, peasant world that meets the visitor can invite both condemnation of its backwardness and celebration of its unspoilt rural charm. There is much of this ambivalence, of condemnation and celebra-tion, in British views of France, and it exists too in metropolitan French views of Brittany. Generally, whatever France has seen, or wished to see, in its provinces, Brittany has been felt to have more of it. Brittany has been a great problem but is also, in many ways, a very attractive part of France. It is to Brittany that French folklorists went in the nineteenth century, and to Brittany that modern French social scientists, many of them pursuing France's 'disappearing peasant' (cf. Mendras 1970; L. Lévi-Strauss and Mendras 1981), have gone in great numbers since the 1960s. Moreover, Brittany is the second most important tourist area of France, after the Côte d'Azur.

A language fetish?

There is nothing in the British context to match the linguistic sensitivity of France. The French language and French national self-definition are deeply implicated the one in the other, and linguistic self-consciousness and political centralism have been closely linked features of the French nation. Both could be said to date from the Revolution of 1789. The Jacobin leaning to State centralism was one particular vision of France which triumphed over others (e.g., that of the Girondins), and was in part a heritage from previous monarchical organization and in part a product of the war emergency of the time. Similarly, preoccupation with the French language was neither new nor a product of solely internal factors. Previous interests were, however, given very different significance after 1789. Prior to the Revolution, there had been some internal administrative investment in the French language and considerable literary embellishment of it. The Villers-Cotterêts *ordonnance* of 1539, for example, had tried to make French, rather than Latin, the language of official acts, and the well-known *Académie Française*, founded in the seventeenth century, began a process of linguistic regulation and refinement. Neologisms and models of correctness and good taste were offered to the salons of high society. French was displacing Latin as the language of rational administration and of art and cultivation, and it was to such ends that the *ordonnance* and the *Académie*'s efforts were directed. There was no intention here that the mass of the people, the ruled and uncultivated, should actually speak French. The seventeenth-century Port Royal grammar confirmed an image of French as the natural expression of reason, and this fitting medium of logical and administrative clarity came, at the end of the eighteenth century, squarely on to the political stage. The 1789 Revolution politicized the French language, and did so with a new vision of polity. French has since been regularly invoked, internally and externally, as the face of France and of Frenchness itself.

French was clearly established as the international diplomatic language from the early eighteenth century to at least the Treaty of Versailles, and has been actively promoted in French colonies abroad. However, the economic conditions of the 1930s, the humiliations of the Second World War, growing nationalisms in the Third World, the collapse of old empires, and the emergence of new superpowers, all contributed to a decline in French internationally and strong competition from elsewhere (see Gordon 1978). Educated Frenchmen have shown considerable concern about the growing dominance of (some form of) English in the world, even if they use it themselves in many areas of international, scientific research. The French government has attempted to legislate internally against the use of English in certain domains (see Hayward 1976:7) and there has also been a manifest sensitivity to the influx of 'English' terms into French itself, for which the term *franglais* has been coined (Etiemble 1964). A major metropolitan French newspaper, *Le Monde*, has been known to devote whole pages to the issue of *franglais* and English dominance, as if debating the very existence of the French nation (e.g., *Le Monde* 15 July 1978:2; 9 September 1978:2; 24–5 September 1978:2). One of its journalists wrote in 1979, 'Beware! If the French language recedes, all we who speak it are threatened in our identity and being' (cited in Smyth 1979). If young people in France were turning to English in some areas and using *franglais*, then for them, he regretted, 'the language of liberty is no longer French'. It was the Revolution of 1789 that first declared French *la langue de la liberté*, and this is a description familiar to many educated Frenchmen.

Through the rise and fall of France's many regimes of varying degrees of stability (some of which are listed on p. 317), the French language and the 'Revolution of 1789' have frequently been drawn on to affirm, and represent, in defiance of the fluctuations of history, national unity and continuity. Some French commentators have argued that the result has been to make the French language a national 'fetish' (see esp. Bourdieu 1975). Many modern critical histories of France, generally written by Parisian scholars of left-wing sympathies, have focused on the Revolution of 1789 not as the glorious birth of the French nation which should ever be carried forward to vigilant unity but as the baneful source of an outmoded centralist government and national consciousness (e.g., Balibar and Laporte 1974; Calvet 1974; Certeau *et al.* 1975). Significantly, such modern histories have given considerable attention to the internal linguistic variety of the country.

The Celtic Breton language of the north-western peninsula shares the status of regional minority language with at least six other languages in France: Occitan (occupying almost the southern third of France, with several million speakers of one or other of its 'dialects'), Basque (with an estimated 100,000 speakers in France), Catalan (with about 200,000 speakers in France), Corsican (about 150,000 speakers), Flemish (about 200,000 speakers), and the languages or dialects of Alsace and Moselle (about 1,500,000 speakers) (for these estimates, see *AEB* 1981, 31). France's minority languages and dialects are now capable of carving up the entire national map, virtually isolating Paris and its central hinterland. Maps of internal linguistic variety have been produced particularly since the 1960s and, like the modern histories mentioned above, which emphasize the country's linguistic diversity, they have been a direct challenge to contemporary incarnations of national unity and centralist power.

It is generally estimated that Breton is spoken by about 500,000 people, mostly peasants, fishermen, and their families. This figure represents an overall drop, over the last hundred years, of about 62 per cent in the number of speakers (for the available figures, see Hewitt 1977:4; Kuter 1981:77–8). These estimates have been made chiefly by folklorists, Celtic scholars, and modern 'defenders' of the language. There are no official census figures. Unofficial estimates can vary according to context, but '500,000' is a common and easily memorable figure. The absence of official census statistics does not mean that there has been no enquiry within France into who speaks what (as we shall see in Part one). We have sufficient clues to judge the approximate demographic shape of the Breton-speaking population in Brittany. Breton, in common with other Celtic languages, is now often presented as having been in constant retreat, first before the invasions of the Romans and vulgar Latin, and then before the Germanic barbarians (largely Saxons, Franks, and Norse) right through to the invasions of, say, Giscard, Chirac, and Mitterrand. While Breton continued to contract socially and geographically within the French political context of the nineteenth century, the classes and areas within which Breton was spoken increased in population. It seems likely that the number of Breton-speakers reached its highest ever level in the twentieth century just before the First World War. Most of these speakers were geographically concentrated, then as now, in western Brittany. After the First World War, Brittany's population, rather than rising as it had in the nineteenth century, began, like that of France more generally, to fall or remain at much the same level – this demographic alignment being itself an index of the more general and pervasive influence of metropolitan values in the countryside at this period (cf. Weber 1977). After the Second World War, Brittany participated in the more general 'population explosion' but this new population growth, largely among those living in or heading for the towns and for the growing secondary and tertiary sectors of the post-war economy, was not in social or geographical sectors coincident with the transmission of Breton. We thus have a notional profile in which the number of Breton-speakers peaked before the First World War, then began a steady decline, and has fallen off more sharply in the decades since the Second World War. Playing an important role in these changes has been the education system. At the same time, in the towns of modern Brittany, some well-educated people who have been through this system can now be found discussing, in French at public meetings, the dire situation of Breton. Something must be done, they urge, to save the Breton language from imminent disappearance: 'Hardly anyone speaks Breton any more.' Meanwhile, just nearby, in the countryside if not in another corner of the same bar, Breton may well be in vigorous daily use. Some of the paradoxes, the problems, the assumptions, the motivations, and the aspirations involved in all this form the subject-matter of this book.

Nationalism and ethnicity

Nations are created

To understand Brittany, we need the national context of France, and an understanding of France entails, in turn, looking at a wider intellectual and international context. Modern France is one element alongside other like elements in a political taxonomy of nations. It might seem perfectly normal and natural that the political world map should be composed of nations. However, two world wars and the challenge of decolonization have produced a wealth of political and social science literature on 'nationalism' (e.g., Anderson 1983; Gellner 1983; Kedourie 1960; Kohn 1962; Seton-Watson 1965; Smith 1979), reflecting on the way in which 'nations' came to be constructed as apparently objective and inalienable units in this way. One important lesson to emerge from this literature is that there are (although the authors themselves might not put it this way) no 'natural' nations. Nations are units of identity and organization which found their modern form in the last two hundred years or so of European thought. They are creations. This applies as much to the relatively well-established nations of Europe as it does to those areas of the world to which Europe's ideas of nationhood have been exported more recently. Nations are not natural and self-generating units, or the emergence or re-emergence of atavistic forces of blood, soul, or territory. However, these are common features of the discourse in which they have been created, and in which claims to national identity – and to minority or ethnic identity also – have since been made.

Nation and education

One key historical pivot in the development of our modern idea of the 'nation' is generally taken to be the French Revolution of 1789, with France then launching the modern nation-state model. Various factors in Europe more generally, including quarrels within the Church, the development of print capitalism, and the important influence of liberalism and of Enlightenment philosophy, served to put in question the dominant allegiances and units of identification which existed prior to the eighteenth century, and to offer the possibilities of this new form of polity. In its political and philosophical assumptions and implications, the polity of 'nation' as it entered the nineteenth century had little in common with etymological cognates of earlier centuries (Peyre 1933; Zernatto 1944). As the nineteenth century progressed, the political ideal of internal popular sovereignty which the nation embodied took on a more obvious dimension of external self-assertion. Political unification, economic tariffs, and military conscription within the national mode of territorial organization, all gave the idea new substance and significance. German nationalism in the nineteenth century was to a great degree anti-French; French identity, which had long found its self-definition in conceptual opposition to the English (see Johnson *et al.* 1980), took on an obviously anti-German sentiment after 1870 with the loss of Alsace. Much of the blame for the French defeat was laid, within France, on the education system. The Prussians had won, it was felt, because they had better schools. Schooling was the major means by which a nation was created, and, in France, education was given new impetus by the Franco-Prussian conflict. The French Revolutionaries had always seen education as fundamental to the realization of their vision of a true nation, and the Third Republic, which began in the 1870s, did more than any other to institute a national education system. The opening chapters of this book try to give some sense of the importance of education in the creation of the French Republic. The French education system (the Ministry of which only recently dropped its 'National' epithet) is one area in which every French government seems to have wanted to leave its mark, in legislation and reform, and it has also been one obvious arena for the engagement of political combat.

Nation and language

For the French Revolutionaries, the ideal of a 'nation' had been, above all, a political ideal. Social strata hitherto excluded, within older systems of allegiance (and within older senses of the 'nation'), from political power were to become equally involved in the rational self-government of a common territorial unit. This ideal was informed and added to by other intellectual debates of the time, among them German romanticism and its associated philosophy of language (worked out by such thinkers as Herder, Humboldt, Schleiermacher, Fichte, and Grimm: see Kedourie 1960; Fishman 1972). This linguistic philosophy was born in a Germany which was, in other respects, fragmented and where French enjoyed a position of prestige. To speak another language, it was asserted, was to forfeit one's own *Volk* genius and originality. A proper nation had its own original language, in which its essential spirit or character found direct expression. Although partly formulated in opposition to French, there was much in this philosophy which appealed in France. It was a view of language which helped to harness the earlier linguistic rationalism (see p. 5) to the new political ideal of the nation. To speak a common language would mean a clear commonality of ideas and sentiment. There followed 'vast philological labours' (Kedourie 1960:67ff) throughout the nineteenth century and thereafter, accompanying nationalisms world-wide. The boundaries of a language, like those of a nation and a people, are socially defined, and national languages have had to be created.

Race and history

The classification of languages and that of races were closely linked endeavours; race was, like language, one of the important assumptions which nationalisms, in the nineteenth century, evoked and refined. The division of the world into races was encouraged by increased travel and by the development of 'science', through which the idea of race gained definitive and lasting credibility (in spite of the fact that, towards the end of the nineteenth century, the status of the phenotypical packages was already in question: see Banton and Harwood 1975). Europe exported 'nations' and also 'racialized the rest of the world' (Banton and Harwood 1975:9). Within Europe, nations and races were deemed by many to be properly coincidental. Each nation had a racial origin, even if, through invasion and conquest, it might now be mixed. In France, in liberal and republican historiography particularly, the Gauls, and the Romans who conquered them, and the Franks who conquered too, were ideally mixed in a single nation of free and equal citizens. Any of these historical, racial elements might be drawn on as the contemporary context demanded (especially Gaulish/Frankish conflicts to describe and explain contemporary French/German tensions or internal political troubles), but mid-nineteenth-century proponents of racial theories (such as the French thinker De Gobineau) in which a strict hierarchy of races was asserted, and racial purity exalted or racial mixing regretted, found few political followers within France. Such theories found more fertile ground in Germany, and in the advocacy of provincial and largely anti-republican identities which German romanticism encouraged. This is a point to which we shall return in Part two, in Chapter six.

By the end of the nineteenth century, 'nation' clearly implied a particular polity, with its own territory, language, common origin, and history. The nineteenth century has been dubbed both 'the age of nationalism' and 'the age of history'. The two went together. History, which developed as a distinct, scholarly discipline in the nineteenth century, was, above all, *national* history. The romantic historiography of the early decades of the century, strongly influenced by Walter Scott and Fenimore Cooper among others, was both appropriated and displaced by a 'scientific' positivist historiography which distinguished itself from the 'art' or *belles-lettres* history of earlier years principally by seeking 'proof' and 'truth' in written documentation (for a survey of these developments in French historiography, see Coornaert 1977). History had become one important medium of self-definition in which a nation both pursued a distinct origin and expressed its accomplishments. In the latter half of the nineteenth century, a proliferation of national institutions, from museums to school-texts to national holidays, organized and presented and 'commemorated' the histories so constructed. French history, like other national histories, had begun to gain its own definitive contours and trajectory, and one long struggle for national unity was read backwards from the nineteenth century to fifth-century Clovis (who – usefully enough – united Gauls, Romans, and Franks), and forwards again to the Revolution and the Third Republic; and thereafter this same struggle was carried on to the First World War and beyond.

Ethnogenesis

After the Second World War, there was a general moral, political, and sociological consensus that nations should no longer be threatened by other nations, that all were equal, and that, in the liberal melting pot of modernization, internal differences within nations would similarly be dissolved. At the end of Part one, in Chapter four, we shall begin to see some of the contradictions which different interpretations of liberty and equality could now pose.

These post-war years were a period in which the map of world power changed. Decolonization was important, and at the same time the labour demands of the post-war economies of Europe helped to draw increasing numbers of migrants, and there were civil rights marches in the United States. Liberal 'melting pot' theories were questioned. Rationalization and modernity, rather than spelling the disappearance of minorities, now seemed actually to create them. European nation-states found themselves challenged from without and within (Stone 1985: ch. 1). With increased communications, mass literacy, the growth of mass tourism, and the development of the 'mass' market generally came an increase in minority identities within the nation-state. These processes offered an intellectual do-it-yourself kit for the credible and persuasive construction and revindication of a distinct identity, and elements of nineteenth-century nationalism reappeared in new dress. Distinct peoples, with their own language, culture, and history, began to crowd the map of Europe.

Europe, with some American help, is now positively bursting with traditional folk-cultures. All have been through various stages of necessary or wistful disappearance as popular traditions, superstition, and folklore, but have thereby hung on long enough to be ripe for modern 'minority' or 'ethnic' sociologies. By the 1960s, modern schools of sociology, abandoning assimilationism, were attempting to explain the proliferation of 'ethnicities' all around them, and, since then, various explanatory theories have been put forward (for a survey of the major theories, see Smith 1981; Stone 1985; Vermeulen 1984). As theories of 'minority' or 'ethnic' identity have increased, and ethnic studies grown, so too has the number of ethnicities. Much of the persuasiveness and nitty-gritty feel of many modern ethnicities, and theories of ethnicity, lies in their conflation of different issues and problems from South Africa to Scotland, and in their combination of metaphors of the vital and basic (often drawing on domains we might classify as economic or biological). Some of these theories will be seen in action in this book.

Breton history

When the map of majority and minority identities was drawn up, not all parts of any one nation gained 'popular tradition', 'folklore', or, in later terminology, a 'culture'. A complex combination of historical, symbolic factors has led to a map of France in which areas such as Brittany have leapt forth, while other areas have remained as zones of conceptual silence. The Breton language has been an important factor in making Brittany a prime candidate for the map of traditions, folklore, or culture.

In this book, we shall be following the development, and the problems, of Breton culture, and the history of Brittany is important here – not simply as helpful or explanatory background but as part of that culture itself. One version of the earlier history of Brittany might run as follows:

Brittany was, in early classical texts, *Armorica*, or variations thereof, and inhabited by Gauls. Then Brittany was further colonized by Celtic-speaking peoples from areas of southern Britain. It is widely felt that these migrations of Christians from the British provinces of the Roman Empire gave rise to the close similarities between Breton, Welsh, and Cornish: all are defined as having descended from the same 'p-Celtic' language.

After the British migrations, and with the Gauls already present, Brittany became ethnically complete, with a Celtic 'origin'. Until the ninth century, however, Brittany had no political unity. In the early ninth century, Louis the Pious, son of Charlemagne, intervened to stop the quarrels and plunderings of the area's competing leaders and nobility. He appointed a supreme leader, a Breton called Nominöé, nominated 'envoy of the Emperor' by virtue of his proven loyalty to the Franks. On Louis' death, Nominöé swore loyalty to Charles and Lothair, Louis' brothers, but Charles invaded Brittany and Nominöé defeated him in 845. After negotiations, Nominöé gained virtual independence, with his leadership recognized by religious authorities. Brittany had now emerged as a relatively independent unit of the feudal structure. Nominöé marched into some of Charles's territories and claimed them as his own, but after his death in 851, the area became divided once more. Nominöé's son planned to marry his daughter to the son of Charles, to consolidate relations with the Franks, but was slain by his cousin, who had his own Frankish allegiances. In the midst of all this, both Brittany and the Frankish areas were troubled by invasions from Norse (or 'Norman') pirates. These were only stemmed in Brittany by an *emigré* count, Alain Barbe-torte, who returned from England (where he had been brought up) and defeated the Norse in a decisive victory in 939, and then claimed the Breton leadership. Barbe-torte was recognized as Duke of Brittany, and lived on good terms with his friend and co-*emigré*, Louis IV, the reigning king of the Franks.

Brittany was now clearly established, and was a Duchy. In the thirteenth century, the question of Breton Ducal homage to the French monarch was precisely regulated. The thirteenth and fourteenth centuries, however, were marked by the wars between England and France, and the Dukes of Brittany shifted their allegiance according to the fortunes of war and diplomacy. By the fifteenth century, with relative peace between England and France, the Breton leaders moved towards closer alliance with the French monarchy. They were, however, also concerned over their own feudal rights, and for the rights and privileges of the Duchy. The Breton Dukes had created their own Court, modelled on that of Paris, and sought to be competitive with it, in coinage, chancery, heraldry, and ceremonial. Breton scholarship of the Ducal Court and chancery depended, however, on training in the universities of the French kingdom – and the attractions of the French universities and of the Paris Court meant that the Dukes of Brittany often had difficulty keeping their nobles and scholars at home, and securing their loyalties. In the late fifteenth century, this degree of independence ceased. After two successive marriages of Anne, Duchess of Brittany, to French monarchs, in 1490 and 1499, Brittany became officially part of France. An Act of Union was drawn up in 1532, and the Duchy became a French province (for a general history here, see Chadwick 1969; Contamine 1976; M. Jones 1970, 1976, 1978; Spence 1978).

None of the sources cited for this history is the work of Breton writers. In modern histories of Brittany written by those keen to assert a Breton identity, the picture is less messy, and the contours and emphases of these periods slightly different. Nominöé is always an important figure, although his loyalties to the Frankish kings are muted. The competing Frankish connections of Nominöé's successors, important realities in their time, are not significant realities for those who would now chart Brittany's historical autonomy. The plan of Nominöé's son, to marry his daughter to the son of the Frankish king, receives no mention. The tenth-century invasions by the 'Normans' are emphasized, however, and the Normans invoked to be condemned, in part for having brought French to large areas of Brittany.

Alain Barbe-torte is the 'liberator', and his Frankish friend, Louis IV, often falls out of the picture. The period of the Duchy is presented as a time of glorious independence, politically and culturally, from France, with that independence inherited directly from Nominöe, the autonomous 'founder of the Breton State', into whose mouth Breton is placed. Subsequent events, notably the Union of 1532 and the Revolution of 1789, forced upon Brittany a coincident loss of prosperity and independence, and absorption into France (for some histories in this style, see Brekilien 1976; Gwegen 1975; Haas and Caouissin 1969; Markalé 1977, 1980; Poisson 1967). Although they might differ in scope and scholarship, all such histories are keen to emphasize Brittany's historical independence. With some justice, and with obviously sincere regret, they argue that Brittany has been assimilated into the wider French context and Breton identity virtually lost. However, the values and aspirations of these modern historians and the values and aspirations they accredit to the distant past have no necessary continuity beyond that which the modern writer seeks to construct. The largely aristocratic conceptions of provincial identity, all the earlier allegiances and aspirations, and any ideas, noble and plebeian, of linguistic and cultural differences have been given new form, relocated and restructured, within minority identity as we now understand it: of their earlier forms we have only shadows. It is, in many ways, only through Brittany's incorporation into the wider French world that the modern Breton identity came to be constructed, and it is only through the modern concern for the supposed 'loss' of this identity that there is any compulsion to seek, through history, the autonomy and independence lacking in the present.

From the tenth century to the sixteenth century then, Brittany was a Duchy. From the sixteenth century to the 1789 Revolution, it was a French province, with its own *Etats* and *Parlement* and with fiscal privileges greater than those of some other provinces (for some contemporary and archival accounts of this period, see ADI-V 1979; Rothney 1969). After the Revolution, all the old provinces of France were politically abolished, and the whole country divided up into *départements* (which we might translate as 'counties' or 'borough', but which have no exact political or administrative equivalent in the UK). 'Brittany' was now largely a folk category. At the beginning of the nineteenth century, each *département* had a Prefect (a top category of civil servant) charged with its administration, and centrally appointed from Paris. At the beginning of the 1870s, each *département* gained an elected 'General Council' (*Conseil Général*), the powers of which progressively increased, from control over budgetary decisions at the end of the nineteenth century to control over wider social and economic affairs by the 1950s. They remained nevertheless under the administrative *tutelle*, or guardianship, of Paris, with administrative guidelines and advice channelled through the Prefects. In recent decades, the *départements* have been grouped under the names of many of the old provinces, giving these names new political existence in the form of *régions* or 'regions', and 'Brittany' has become a governmental category again. In this new framework, the *départements*, their Councils, and the Prefects remained, and the Prefect of the principal *département* was promoted to a 'super' Prefect, dealing with the region as a whole.

This framework came into effect through legislation of 1972, by which Brittany became, officially, one of twenty-two 'regions' of France (see *Les Cahiers Français* 1973, 158–9, for details). The programme launched ten years later by the Socialist government enhanced the region's powers and gave direct election to its Council, but the 1972 law was the first major, if somewhat timid, step towards decentralization, creating regions as official 'public establishments' (*établissements publics*). Through this legislation, Brittany, like other regions, gained a Regional Council, concerned principally with the regional budget, and a consultative Economic and Social Committee. In 1978, Brittany also gained a Cultural Council, with a special budget (coming mostly from the State) to help save and promote Breton language and culture. Membership has overlapped with that of the Regional Council and the Economic and Social Committee, but has also included representatives from groups in Brittany directly concerned with the 'defence' of Breton culture (for details, see Keravel and Thomin 1981).

The Loire-Atlantique is not part of the official 'region',[2] although it was part of the pre-1789 province of Brittany, and Nantes, its departmental centre, was the old Ducal capital. Rennes, in the *département* of Ille-et-Vilaine, is the capital of modern Brittany and has had pre-eminence since the sixteenth century. Neither Rennes nor Nantes have ever been Breton-speaking.

Alongside its governmental structures, Brittany is divided into dioceses or bishoprics, which are the administrative structures of the Catholic Church. There are four dioceses in Brittany, just as there are, officially, four *départements*, and the modern diocesan centres are the same as the departmental centres: namely, the towns of Rennes, Vannes, Saint-Brieuc, and Quimper. State administration talks of the *départements* of Ille-et-Vilaine, the Morbihan, the Côtes-du-Nord, and Finistère, and Church administration now talks of the 'diocese of Rennes', the 'diocese of Vannes', the 'diocese of Saint-Brieuc', and the 'diocese of Quimper and Léon', respectively. Before the Revolution of 1789, there were nine dioceses in Brittany and, of these, four were considered Breton-speaking (in part at least). These were the Vannetais, the Trégor, the Cornouaille, and the Léon, with their centres in the towns of Vannes, Tréguier, Quimper, and Saint-Pol-de-Léon respectively (see the map on p. 322). The bishoprics of Tréguier and Saint-Pol-de-Léon were among those abolished during the 1789 Revolution: the Trégor became part of the diocese of Saint-Brieuc, while the Léon joined with the Cornouaille to give the modern diocese of 'Quimper and Léon'. The four old Breton-speaking dioceses are still associated with different dialects of Breton, however, and these dialects have been the focus of some argument, as we shall see in later chapters.

Brittany is further divided, in semi-popular usage, into the two areas known as 'Lower Brittany' (*Basse Bretagne*) and 'Upper Brittany' (*Haute Bretagne*). This division has no official administrative status, although *Basse Bretagne* seems to have emerged from a brief life as a category of fiscal administration in the fourteenth and fifteenth centuries. 'Lower Brittany' now generally designates the traditionally Breton-speaking part of Brittany, west of an imaginary line running roughly from Plouha on the north coast (between Tréguier and Saint-Brieuc) to the Rhys peninsula on the south coast (between Vannes and the mouth of the Vilaine). This area covers most of the old Breton-speaking dioceses of the Léon, Cornouaille, Trégor, and the Vannetais. The area to the east of this imaginary line is 'Upper Brittany'. In most parts of Upper Brittany, Breton has been little spoken, if ever at all (see Croix 1981:124–31; Kerhervé 1986). There are two universities in the region of Brittany, one in Upper Brittany and one in Lower. The first is at Rennes (the *Université de Haute Bretagne*), and the second at Brest (the *Université de la Bretagne Occidentale*). There have often been quarrels between the Celtic interests in these two universities. We shall see more of this tension in Part two, where we take up, in a modern context, the whole question of the 'origins' of Brittany and the problematic nature of its history.

So what kind of research is this?

This work is the result of several years' anthropological 'field-work' in France. The field-work tradition of anthropology became firmly established in the 1920s and 1930s, in the terrains of what later became known as the Third World. The method of 'participant observation' (see Ellen 1984; Frankenberg 1982) which developed is really a combination of techniques, but it evolved principally as a mode of intimate research, for the small-scale and the 'face-to-face' community, and it still carries, for some, an image of 'going native'. This idea was, in its own time, revolutionary; it took the anthropologist out of the armchair of evolutionary comparativism into the 'field' and the world of the 'natives', a venture which came to mean trying to understand 'the native's point of view' (e.g., Geertz 1973, 1983). Such an ambition remains highly problematic, but it has become, in some form, a common aspiration in social anthropology. This book shares, in its own way, this general ambition, but its terrain, assumptions, and results cannot, within the same tradition, be taken for granted. There follows a brief summary of the contents of each section of this book, after which I return to a few relevant features of my own theoretical approach.

The four parts of this book

The book is divided into four parts. Part one takes us straight into
French nationalism, the world of the National Assembly and the self-
consciousness of the Republic. The central focus is on education, especially
on the place and images of Breton in educational debates and legislation
and in the schools. Part one is not, I should stress, a full history of French
education (for which see, for example, Anderson 1975; Halls 1976), and it
is not the only history of the subject that might be written. It is,
nevertheless, one that has not hitherto been attempted. Its sources are
partly archival and partly modern, in the schools and administrative offices
of Brittany. The proportions of Brittany's total school population in
private and public education are 41 per cent and 59 per cent respectively.
Private or church-run education is organized within the modern dioceses
(see p. 15), while public or state education is organized in the *départements*.
The national Ministry of Education, the regional *Rectorat*, and then the
departmental *Inspections Académiques* form the major tiers of educational
administration. There is now formal co-operation between private and
public authorities (and a system of contracts giving state and public funds
to the private sector) but quarrels between the two – between private and
public, between the *écoles libres* and the *écoles laïques*, and between
Church and State – are well-known in France, and have been lively in
Brittany.

Part two deals, as its title suggests, with 'The Breton Movement', and
takes us into a world which, in contrast with the self-consciously French
world of Part one, is that of people who have made it their business to
create and assert a distinct 'Breton' identity. This book draws on field-work
which began in 1978 and continued uninterrupted until 1981. I spent over a
year based in the regional capital of Rennes, living, studying, and working
with members of the Breton movement. This involved travelling widely
within Brittany, attending their meetings and learning Breton with them.
When, in late 1979, I then moved my field-work base and emphasis from
the regional capital, Rennes, to the rural heart of Lower Brittany, I still
maintained contact with the Breton movement. Research among different
sectors of the population continually overlapped, although the conceptual
overlap of these worlds is not, as we shall see, a simple matter. This
research was first written up as a thesis (McDonald 1982), from which this
book derives. In the Conclusion we return to the vigorous reaction which
this work has already generated within Brittany. Although I returned to
Brittany for further field research after this period, and later periods are
included here, much of this book concentrates on the years 1978–81 – a
period which might now be deemed to have been a hey-day of political
counter-culture in France. Situated between the vigour and ebullience of
the 1960s and the relative sobriety of the 1980s, between the Fifth Republic
of Giscard and the Fifth Republic of Mitterrand, and between the

enthusiasms of urban, educated people and the world of peasants in Lower
Brittany, the ethnography of this period which these chapters contain has,
I think, an interesting story to tell.

The overriding emphasis in the chapters of Part two then is on the recent
enthusiasms of the Breton movement – and there are some enthusiasms
here which many readers may well recognize, in other contexts, as their
own. Within this modern emphasis, however, we do not lose sight of
history. Apart from histories of itself as a 'movement', the Breton
movement also has its own history of Breton, of French education, and of
Breton's place in the schools. The histories which the Breton enthusiasts
construct are drawn up in the context of modern preoccupations. Such
histories are not thereby 'wrong', but they are different from those that
might be written by other generations or other interests. In this book, I try
to give some idea of other histories, of how they were born, changed, or
forgotten. Ethnographically, history as it is written, imagined, highlighted,
and neglected is always part of the present. I write as a social anthropologist, and my task as such might be deemed to be to understand the
'ethnographic present'; I make some attempt to understand that 'present'
therefore, whether it be in the distant past, or in the modern day. There is,
in this book, no divorce of anthropology and history, or of ethnographic
and historical reality. We are dealing throughout with 'peoples' from a
nation with a long, strong, and well-documented historical tradition. There
can be no question here of ignoring history because 'In the primitive
societies that are studied by social anthropology there are no historical
records' (Radcliffe-Brown 1968:3). Nor can there by any question of
ignoring history on the grounds that it can be doctrinally excluded from a
synchronic analysis. History, for the people I have studied, is alive in the
present: it is used to justify, authenticate, and criticize the present; the
present self-consciously incorporates history, to re-enact it, refuse it, or
redeem it. This book combines, therefore, *historical anthropology*, in
which categories and voices from the past are granted their own historical,
cultural context (allowing for all the caveats and limitations which such an
exercise entails: see, for example, MacFarlane 1977), with an *anthropology
of history*, giving some account of the way in which the people studied
construct the past, and of the moments or situations in which that history is
told, written, or comes alive.

In Part three, entitled '*Diwan*: Breton schools', we stay with the modern
Breton movement and see, through an ethnographic account of one
important practical venture of the movement, how very difficult it can be to
assert an independent Breton identity. The definitional process, of the
Bretons as of any ethnic group, can result in a peculiar short-circuiting of
the minority aspiration to difference. While Part three may appear to be
specifically about schools, and offers, I hope, some insight into issues of
language and education, of bilingualism and pedagogy, its chapters also

offer, along with those of Part two, some more general comment on ethnic or minority identity in action.

In Part four, we arrive finally in a rural, Breton-speaking commune in Finistère. Finistère has always been considered the most solidly Breton-speaking *département*, and Plounéour-Ménez, the commune to which we are led in Part four, is situated on the northern slopes of the *Monts d'Arrée* range in the centre of this *département*. These 'mountains' reach only about 250–350 metres for the most part, but their name underlines a social geography of isolation. A *commune*, which I translate here (as is conventional) by the term 'commune', is the smallest unit of governmental administration in France (*not* the 'commune' of alternative living). A commune has its own municipal council, and its reality is also maintained through various social activities and the *associations* or 'societies' established for anything from hunting to fund-raising for the local schools. The commune lives its extension in space in a way that the English village does not. The commune is often, as it is here, a parish also: the two are geographically congruent (since the commune structure of the Revolution commonly appropriated the old parish map), but a 'parish' is the unit of the Church, not the State. Plounéour-Ménez (total population: 1245, in the 1975 census) has a lay-out typical of rural communes in Brittany. Its largest agglomeration and main social centre is the 'bourg' (*bourg*), which more easily evokes an English village. In the bourg (population: 530) are concentrated the main social services, with the parish church, the town hall (*mairie*), schools, bars, shops, and a post-office. Surrounding the bourg is the agricultural land making up the rest of the commune, with peasant 'villages' (or *villages*: groups of farmsteads and houses) scattered across it up to a distance of about two miles from the bourg. Two of these villages receive special mention here. One is Le Relecq (population of about 30), which is, in fact, the site of one of the Breton movement's earliest Breton schools (see p. 324 for a map of the *Diwan* schools, and p. 326 for the commune of Plounéour-Ménez). The other is Kerguz (pop. 32, including myself, when I first moved there in 1979) which is just next door to Le Relecq and which is, after the bourg, one of the largest villages in the commune. The villages, in their modes of settlement and livelihood, are tending now to change from the agricultural focuses they once were, but they continue to have an existence in the organization of social life, in loyalties (especially at funerals and weddings), and gossip.

It will become clear, when we talk thus of different villages, communes, dioceses, and so on, that there are many units of social identification, other than the region of Brittany, which might have claimed more of our attention. However, it is Brittany as a unitary entity which stalks through the pages of this book like a giant, and it does so largely because there are many educated Breton enthusiasts who would place Brittany in the same political taxonomy as France. The four parts of this book thus tell the story of the implication of the Breton peasant in two different, and in many ways opposed, struggles: to establish the French Republic and to defend Breton language and culture. We begin, in Part one, at the heart of majority self-definition, with the Revolution of 1789; and we end, in Part four, with the roots of modern minority identification, in a peasant household in the rural and isolated interior of Breton-speaking Brittany.

Stereotypes

At the beginning of this Introduction, I tried to suggest that there were readily available structures of ethnographic interest which might lead the British to France, and both the British and the French to Brittany. Indeed, very few anthropologists have been tempted across the Channel in the opposite direction. Wrapped up in this are theoretical issues to which it might be helpful to make explicit allusion here. In the following chapters, such points will then be left, to a great extent, to make themselves.

There are three simple aspects of what we like to call national or ethnic identities which it might be useful to bear in mind. They are points which can serve, I think, for an understanding of the 'character' or reputation of any group or category. First of all, such identities are clearly dependent on the social and political maps of the time, on the categories available for the marking of us/them boundaries, and the particular salience of any one set of these categories. Second, it seems likely that what we might term cultural mismatch or a critical 'lack of fit' (see Ardener, e.g., 1982) between any codes or systems of behaviour, linguistic or otherwise (and which are all, in priority, conceptual and classificatory), will be picked up particularly at that boundary of us/them, evoking it and giving it expression and empirical confirmation. Third, the apprehension of mismatch, or a lack of fit, will commonly have a dominant discourse (or genre or systematized way of talking about it) in which to find ready expression. (Some people might like to talk here of 'stereotypes'.) These three points, I would stress, describe a common simultaneity of experience for many of us, rather than any stages, conscious or otherwise, of thought. Let me give one example. The categories of 'France' and 'England' are a fairly salient part of our contemporary social and political map, and may well be the categories of identity which some readers of this book might themselves occasionally assume. Now, the self-consciously rational Englishman often 'knows', within a now very common discourse of representation, that Frenchmen are emotional and passionate; differences of verbal and body language, in which the French can appear to get very excited with their words and tone, and wave their arms about, and, good heavens, kiss each other, readily confirm the imagery and its distribution between the two halves of the English/French pair (the us/them boundary operative in this instance). In this brief example, my first point about having to have the categories available and salient is perhaps obvious enough, and my second point about cultural mismatch is one to which anthropology is well accustomed. It is well known that one set of cultural practices, when observed or heard through the structures of another, can make its practitioners seem volatile, unpredictable, irrational, inconsistent, capricious, or even dangerous. My third point is merely to do with the socio-historical contextualization of this apprehension. That critical 'lack of fit', an apprehension of indeterminacy, easily becomes confirmation of a rational/irrational dichotomy, and of the various systematized versions of this, in 'reason/emotions' and so on, which the twin discourses of 'positivist' reasoning and romanticism, accompanying the construction of nations and their peripheries, have left us in legacy. The common image of the excitable, fun-loving, soulful, and sexy or passionate French held by the self-consciously rational English should come as no surprise. It should come as no surprise either perhaps, if we now take the points of this paragraph together with the points made earlier, in the first section of this Introduction, that the English should be attracted to France. In a taxonomy of national self-definition, where nations define themselves in contradistinction to other nations, the French readily reproduce versions of this imagery of themselves and turn it to virtue. When, however, metropolitan France turns its face inwards to its own peripheries, it does not claim this imagery, but attributes it instead to its margins and re-situates itself on the other side of the dichotomy, as structured centrality or order and rationality. Many of the preoccupations and the problems of the French intellectual, whether in his centralist or minority-enthusiast guise, which are set out in this book, illustrate and implicate common recensions of these same us/them distinctions, and spill out of the modes of their expression and confirmation.

It may seem at times, when I talk of images of the French or the Bretons, or any other such category of identification, that I am dealing merely with 'stereotypes', a term carrying social and epistemological denigration. In the different parts of this book, we see the views which some members of the French government and administration hold, and have held, of Brittany, Breton, and the Bretons; and some of the images which Breton enthusiasts have of both the French and the Bretons; and the views which some people in Finistère hold of all these categories. At every stage, it might be countered that these views are 'just stereotypes' or 'stereotypical views'. What, after all, do French government ministers really know about Brittany? And what do members of the Breton movement know about the French government? And what do a few people in Finistère really know about the Republic or the Breton movement? Or what do any of these people really know about Brittany or about France and the French, for that matter? To call their views 'stereotypes' might seem to salve our consciences about the problematic statistical accuracy of such images, and the implication has often been, within social science, that more rigorous research methods, properly sampled and quantified, might give us a truer view of the ideas held, and of national or ethnic 'characteristics' (see e.g. Peabody 1985).

I do not wish to list here the academic caveats about such an ambition or about sampling or quantitative techniques, but some of the basic problems may, in the following chapters, become obvious. The very categories of 'French' and 'Breton' slip and slide, and might move away as fast as the researcher runs in pursuit. More important to stress here perhaps is that the images of the French and the Bretons, or of France and Brittany, set out in the following chapters, whether they be images entertained by government ministers or Breton militants or peasants in Finistère, are not some kind of quirky distortion of a reality which exists in its properly realized, objective form elsewhere. Neither France nor Brittany (nor any other such category) exists in any tangible or objective form other than in the ideas which people have of it. Some of these ideas may feel more concrete than others but they are none the less conceptual for that, and when we look at what ministers, militants, or peasants say about French or Breton, or about Brittany or France, we are not studying some elaboration on the *real* entities of French or Breton, or Brittany or France: we are studying these realities themselves. There is no problem posed here by the fact that 'France' or 'Brittany' appear to be 'large-scale' or 'macro' entities. Categories such as 'France' or 'Brittany' do not have, on account of their size, different conceptual statuses either from each other or from the smaller units of identification, largely at village level, with which the anthropologist might be more familiar. We shall be looking at different realities of French and Breton, and France and Brittany, and at how, when, and why these and other categories of identity recruit people into them, and appear to demand the behaviour that they do. It is the way in which these identities are constructed, their capacity to persuade or repulse, the ideas and actions they evoke, which interest us here; and identification with, or opposition to, a group or category, whatever its size, is a social fact whose objective reality does not vary from the small to the large.

Real anthropology

This book is a contribution to European anthropology, while at the same time containing an ethnography of aspects of that anthropology itself. Anthropology, when it first came as close to home as Europe, tended to continue to choose 'primitive', 'backward', or 'peasant' corners to study, minimizing thereby the break with previous anthropological practice (on this, see Davis 1977). This book to some extent follows this emphasis, in as much as it deals with a peasant village in a backward and isolated area.

Any reader seeking a traditional account of Brittany and Breton culture might be surprised that my work did not properly begin among the Breton-speaking peasants in Lower Brittany, where an authentic and traditional Breton culture might seem more readily to present itself. Although the peasants, and their views, are implicated throughout, it is not until the last part of this book that we arrive, firmly and unequivocally, among them. On the way there, whenever we pass through historical or linguistic detail, it should be borne in mind that both history and linguistics have been enormously important to the definition of the minority, and to the creation of its simple and wistful status as a 'disappearing world'. There might be some impatience to get on to the 'real people' and a 'real' anthropology. I do not decry this impatience, but I do find it interesting, for in many ways the traditional structures of anthropological interest are very similar to those of minority-language enthusiasm. It is perhaps no coincidence that there are, within the ranks of the minority-language enthusiasts I have studied, some who might, in other contexts, call themselves ethnologists or anthropologists (as well as historians and linguists, and many who professionally fill other categories of social scientist – psychologist and sociologist included). Most metaphors of traditional anthropological expression run counter to the inclusion of intellectuals in the ethnography, whether in the guise of administrator, tourist, activist, or academic. For social anthropology, urban and educated people have not seemed sufficiently traditional and 'native', or sufficiently and authentically real, to constitute a fit object of study. The journey to peasant authenticity that the Breton intellectual makes is parallel with the journey to the same peasant which I, as an anthropologist, made myself. It is, in part, the persuasiveness and the problems of such a pursuit which we see in this book.

Part one

Politics and pedagogy: a history of Breton in the schools

Chapter one

The Revolution of 1789

In this chapter, I concentrate on the period surrounding the Revolution of 1789, and suggest the relative images of French and Breton in legislation and debates concerning education in France at this time. There were four main laws explicitly concerned with language in education in the first Republic: two in 1793 and two in 1794. It should be borne in mind that these were only a small part of Revolutionary legislation.

French for French citizens

Much of the Revolutionary legislation was directed against what became known as the *Ancien Régime*, a regime marked by feudal, aristocratic, and clerical privileges. Everyone was now to be a 'citizen', fully educated in Republican ideals. This ambitious project brought a flood of educational laws and decrees. A 'Republican catechism' replaced that of the Church, and education became, for the first time, the responsibility of the State. Bills and projects of law railed against the 'abstract' education, theology, religion, and Latin of the church-dominated schooling of the *Ancien Régime*. Several Enlightenment thinkers from Brittany had contributed to Revolutionary sentiment on these issues. In the 1760s, for example, the Breton La Chatolais, parliamentarian, philosopher, and friend of Voltaire, had openly said that he could not see what relevance the study of 'a foreign language [Latin] and monastic procedure' could have for the agents of rational government (cited in Rothney 1969:76).

Such thinkers had generally seen no necessity to educate the peasants. For the Revolutionaries, however, the education of all levels of society was important. A law of *30 vendemaire an II* (21 October 1793) stressed that everyone should learn their new citizens' rights; children would therefore need to 'learn to speak, read and write the French language' (article 3). Additional decrees (26, 28, 30 October 1793) barred nobles and ecclesiastics from teaching, and stated that public education was to be everywhere conducted such that 'one of its prime benefits be that the French language become, in a short space of time, the language familiar to all parts of the

27

Republic' (art. 6). Moreover, 'in all parts of the Republic, instruction is to be given only in French' (art. 7).[1]

Breton education before the Revolution

Before the Revolution, the wealthy had hired tutors for their children, and others sent their offspring to elementary schools (*petites écoles*) organized by the clergy. These were prospering by the seventeenth century. They were, in principle, free for the poor (*indigents*), although it is not clear that broad sections of the peasantry benefited from them, and little is known of the teaching they offered. Catholic, moral doctrine seems to have been stressed, as were the rudiments of Latin. It is likely that Breton was used, and that some learnt to read. In more advanced education, Latin was the language of learning in Brittany as throughout France. Breton colleges, which explicitly copied the 'Paris model', taught theology as a main subject, with only Latin allowed for lessons and discussions (see Durand 1912–13; Ogès 1936; Schlemmer 1936).

Even as early as the tenth century, however, many of the educated and the nobility, in both Lower and Upper Brittany, knew not only Latin but also some form of 'French'. By the time Brittany became officially part of France in the early sixteenth century, French had been the language of power and nobility within the province for a few hundred years. The learned in Breton-speaking areas sought knowledge of French, and Breton texts of the Middle Ages show heavy French borrowings (see Piette 1973). The earliest existing Breton 'dictionary' (the *Catholicon* of 1499) was trilingual, offering French and Latin translations of Breton terms and expressions, for Breton-speaking Bretons with educational and commercial ambitions. By the eighteenth century, Breton–French dictionaries and *colloques* (or phrase-books) abounded.

In the eighteenth century, catechism remained the basis of education, but we now find more lay teachers offering tuition outside the ecclesiastical system. In Finistère, they boasted such titles as *'grammariens'* and *'maîtres-ès-arts'*. French tuition was prized (Ogès 1937:22), and French closely associated with schooling. One *colloque* of the period offers, among its translation pieces, a conversation between a visiting parent, a pupil, and the pupil's mother, part of which runs:

(visitor): Does he not go to school?
(mother): Yes, he is learning to speak French.
(visitor): Ian, can you speak French?
(pupil): Not very well, but I am learning.[2]

This *colloque* went through at least seventeen editions from 1626 to 1759 (see Le Goaziou 1950). Such *colloques* were widely used in the schooling of young Bretons, and the conversation cited above seems aptly to have expressed the values and ambitions of those involved.

Reading in the eighteenth century began with Latin, and then moved on to French; only last, if at all, did pupils learn to read Breton (see Ogès 1937:29). Breton had a place in religious education, but often only in oral recitation. In general, it seems that Latin and French were competing for pre-eminence in many schools before the Revolution, with French already beginning to win. An especially popular teaching order (the '*Ignorantins*') dispensed with Latin, and concentrated on French. Surviving exercise books of Finistère pupils indicate that arithmetic was gaining in importance, with problems written out in French (Ogès 1937:30–3).

Then, just before the Revolution, an interesting development occurred at the lower levels. Influenced by the French pedagogue Rollin (1681–1741), an enterprizing lay schoolmaster from the Léon asserted (in French) that it was by 'the mother tongue' that education should begin, and that the 'knowledge of one language serves as an introduction to the study of other languages'. He produced a school textbook, beginning with the known (that is, Breton) and moving on to the unknown, instead of starting with Latin or French. The aim was not to dwell on Breton, however, but to move to French as soon as possible (Ogès 1937:36–8).

This approach, using Breton as a teaching aid, turned out to be broadly compatible with the educational legislation of the Revolution, and this Breton schoolmaster's books continued to be used into the early nineteenth century. The legislation of *an II* (1793) had stressed that only French was to be used in the schools; another law of *27 brumaire an III* (17 November 1794), however, put it slightly differently: 'education will be given in French', and 'the local idiom can only be used as an auxiliary means' (art. 3).

Reaction, isolation, and superstition

In matters of language, Latin was clearly not the only problem in the task which the Revolution had set itself of providing education for all in French. In 1790, a nationwide enquiry into the idioms of France had been launched. This enquiry ultimately revealed that only one-fifth of France could confidently speak French, under two-thirds understood it, and over one-third knew no French at all (see Chervel 1977:24). The National Assembly had decreed, at the beginning of 1790, that its texts were to be translated into the local idioms, including Breton, and this was duly carried out, although it was not easy finding people who could write Breton, and resultant texts show considerable improvization. In 1789, both the Breton nobility and the bourgeoisie had used some Breton in competing propaganda directed at the local populace (see, for examples, Bernard 1911–12). As the Revolution wore on, however, it was increasingly counter-revolutionary propaganda that appeared in Breton, emanating from the nobility and clergy. After *an II* (1793), no more official Revolutionary texts were written in Breton: the new Republicans were against it.

The years 1790–3 were particularly troubled in Brittany, and came to dominate and confirm the policy-makers' image of the former province. The clergy and nobility, who had dominated in the *Etats* and the *Parlement* of the old province, had surrendered their old fiscal privileges unwillingly with the passing of the *Ancien Régime* (see Déniel 1976:16–19; Meyer 1966). Then, during 1790 and 1791, over three-quarters of the Breton clergy refused to swear the civil oath, and there were some popular demonstrations in their support and clashes with government forces (see *Skol Vreizh* 1980:24–8). There was widespread incomprehension, at the popular level, of the persecution of the priests; many of the latter fled, some of them to England. From 1791 to 1793, there were royalist plots of reaction from some of the threatened Breton aristocracy, who made monarchy and religion a single cause against the new Republic. At the same time, during 1792 and 1793, some Republican Bretons sided with the Girondins, and several were executed under the triumphant Jacobin regime. In 1793 came the beginnings of the *chouannerie*, which continued intermittently until 1799. The *chouannerie* is a misleadingly singular name for a variety of insurrections in which economic conditions, royalist sympathies, resistance to enlistment, and support of the priests mingle as likely causes and motivations (*Skol Vreizh* 1980:28–43; Tilly 1976). The *chouan* uprisings were particularly marked in areas to the south-east, bordering the Vendée, but parts of western Brittany also participated (see F. Roudaut 1975). The *chouan* uprisings were not linguistically marked: they were not against French, and their leaders were French-speaking. Moreover, the *Club des Jacobins* had originated in Brittany, and some major towns of the newly established *département* of Finistère were strongly Republican. In the face of sustained insurrection in Brittany, however, the new regime came to associate Brittany and Breton with the forces of reaction and counter-revolution.

In this context, the limited extent of French-speaking and the prevalence and diversity of 'local idioms', as revealed by the enquiry, began to appear as a positive menace to the Republic. Two replies to the linguistic enquiry came from Brittany in the early 1790s, both penned by Bretons apparently sympathetic at least to the early aims of the Revolution. One spoke of the situation in the old dioceses of the Léon and the Trégor (incorporated into the *départements* of Finistère and the Côtes-du-Nord): he reported that most of the existing literature in Breton was religious in nature, and that it had the sole merit of 'maintaining moral purity by facilitating a knowledge of religion' for the few who had at least received 'a basic education' (cited in Gazier 1969:282–5). A taste for education in French was growing fast, he reported, but schooling in the countryside, where it existed at all, still consisted mainly of catechism in Breton. The picture he offers includes the hardships imposed by landowners on their tenants; he congratulates the Revolution for having taken steps to end this situation, but says that he can offer no real indication of the 'political and religious import' of any project that might aim to 'destroy' Breton, or of how the Revolution might effect this. The staunchly Republican Abbé Grégoire, from the east of France, who had instigated the national enquiry (and who became a noted member of the National Convention, promoting, among other things, the abolition of slavery), had explicitly asked for suggestions on this point.

The second reply from Brittany, claiming to speak for the *départements* of the Côtes-du-Nord, the Morbihan, and Finistère, blamed the 'isolation' and 'ignorance' of the Breton countryside on the dominance of the Breton *'patois'* (Gazier 1969:287). Both reports pointed out that the towns and some coastal areas spoke French, but that in rural, inland Brittany, it was mainly the nobility and clergy who knew French and acted as inter-mediaries.[3] The second reporter was more confident than the first about what might be done to ameliorate the peasant condition through language policy. Better communications were already helping, he said, but clerical dominance, Breton, and reaction were all linked, and he had little doubt that the 'political and religious import of entirely destroying this *patois*' would be to teach the population to 'abandon superstition' and 'to know the truth about religion'. Teaching the people French would 'give them a political existence which they do not feel and which they know nothing about' (Gazier 1969:288). Similar sentiments came in, about other local idioms, from elsewhere in France.

Barère and Grégoire

By 1794, the attitude of the Republic to all local *'patois'*, 'idioms', and 'dialects' was clear. In January of that year (*8 pluviose an II*), Barère presented a report and bill of law to the National Convention, in the name of the Committee of Public Safety (or the *Comité de Salut Public*); its subject was 'Foreign idioms and the teaching of the French language'. This Committee already knew of Grégoire's findings, and, by this time, was quite ready to associate 'reaction' and Breton. In contrast, Barère des-cribed French to the Convention as:

> the most beautiful language of Europe, the first to have consecrated the rights of man and the citizen, and the language which is charged with the role of transmitting to the world the most sublime thoughts of liberty, and the greatest political speculations. (Barère 1794:2)

He also stressed that there should be a single and uniform language now, without 'hierarchy' or 'affectation' in a new egalitarian world. The variety of difficulties which France was facing, both internally and externally (for the country was intermittently at war with other nations in Europe), now began to seem linked to the issue of language, which provided one arena both for their expression and for their possible solution. 'We have observed,' said Barère, that

> the idiom known as *bas-breton*, and the Basque idiom and the German and Italian languages have perpetuated the reign of fanaticism and superstition, and assured the domination of priests and nobles ... [they have] prevented the revolution from penetrating into nine large *departemans* [sic], and can favour the enemies of France.

In Brittany:

> ignorance perpetuates the yoke imposed by the priests and nobles; there citizens are born and die in error: they do not even know yet that new laws exist.
>
> The inhabitants of the countryside only understand Breton; it is with this barbaric instrument of their superstitious ideas that the priests and the intransigents hold them under their sway, direct their conscience, and prevent citizens from knowing the laws and from loving the Republic. (Barère 1794:3–4)

Barère's concerns were founded in obvious fears of counter-revolution and in the knowledge that demands for betterment of the Breton peasantry's condition were not being met.[4] The Committee wished to liberate the countryside through legislation and education, and expressed sadness that three years of projects, laws, and discussions had failed to realize their vision. 'The enlightened ideas', said Barère, 'that have been carried to the extremities of France at such great expense, die out on arrival, for our laws are not understood' (ibid:7). Local idioms, however, could not readily be used in pursuit of this understanding, for as Barère said, in his now famous description:

> Federalism and superstition speak Breton: emigration and hatred of the Revolution speak German; counter-revolution speaks Italian, and fanaticism speaks Basque (ibid:8).

Much had been spent on full, written translation ('as if it were for us', the Committee complained), to maintain idioms that 'can only serve the fanatics and the counter-revolutionaries' (ibid:10).

It is worth bearing in mind that this was still the period of that response to insurrection and counter-revolution known as the Terror (marking especially mid-1793 to mid-1794). The likening of linguistic diversity to everything counter-revolutionary and despicable, and the equation of linguistic and national loyalty, were emotive and persuasive conflations. These were serious matters, and feudalism and federalism, with which local idioms were linked, were, in this context, objects of loathing. In June

1794 (*16 prairial an II*), just a few days before the institution of the Law of Suspects and some of the toughest times of the Revolution, Grégoire presented his report on the nationwide enquiry to the National Convention. It was now year II of the 'single and indivisible Republic' and France had 'no more provinces' (for the provinces had given way to the new administrative *départements*); and yet, Grégoire went on, 'we have still about thirty *patois* which remind us of their names'.[5] He expressed concern about these 'feudal idioms', fearing that the nobility might resume their privileges if the people were not quickly educated in French to be able to participate as citizens of the Republic. He also felt that a common knowledge of French would offer access to advances in agricultural practice and to meteorology, elementary physics, and the like. French was thus 'the language of liberty', and pursuit of 'unity of idiom' was an 'integral part of the revolution' (see Gazier 1969:293–305). A unity of language, it was now felt, would create a unity of ideas and sentiments, and both express and shape a common patriotism.

I have quoted these two reports, by Barère and Grégoire, because they stand as the clearest, and now the best-known, statement of the Revolutionary period on the language and idioms of France. They provided a definitive framework for many subsequent discussions through the Third Republic and on into this century (and have been much cited, with new significance, in debate since the late 1960s, as we shall see in Chapter five). These reports were also directly concerned with education in Breton-speaking Brittany. Appended to Barère's report was a bill of law, which the Convention accepted. The law instituted special teachers of French in Breton-speaking areas, as well as in frontier areas of the rest of France where a manifestly 'foreign' link existed – in the Rhine (German), in Corsica (Italian), and in the Catalan areas near Spain. Unlike other teachers, these new teachers, who were specifically to teach French, were to be given, in theory at least, a fixed salary from the State. A decree soon followed (*15 messidor an II*) which clarified their obligations. They were to give extra lessons in French over and above any teaching required by previous laws, and were to teach *civisme*, or Republican citizenship. Moreover:

> The French language teacher must, everyday, teach the language and the Declaration of the Rights of Man to all citizens of both sexes, and every *decadi*[6] read out to the people the laws of the Republic, translating them orally. (cited in Ogès 1940:111)

These teachers, then, were clearly to be agents of the Republic, bringing its ideals and laws to all citizens. Some of the clergy – even if they had sworn the civil oath – resented these newcomers taking over the churches (renamed 'temples of reason' at one stage) for their proclamations. Sometimes, where no other building was available, churches were used as schools, cleared of their altars. The local population did not happily accept such sacrilege, and some skirmishes resulted.

There does not seem, however, to have been opposition to the specific institution of 'French language teachers' as such; rather, their free teaching in French was widely welcomed and often drew pupils away from other teachers (Ogès 1940). The new French language teachers were required to know Breton, in order to translate orally, and local recruitment bodies were firm on this, following government directives. The Archives of Finistère hold letters of application from several Breton candidates, one or two of them evidently impoverished by the Revolution, but all of them manifestly able (if only perhaps for the income) to summon up enthusiasm for the Republic's project. They all emphasize that they know Breton well, and while most of the letters of application are written in French, I have found at least one which, with the explicit aim of proving the author's suitability for the post, had been laboriously written out in both Breton and French.[7]

The law instituting the special post of an extra teacher of French seems soon to have been overtaken by the second law of 1794, in which 'local idioms' were to be used as an auxiliary means for the teaching of French. There is no clear information on what happened to the post of extra French teacher, but it seems that, in Finistère at least, most of the extra language teachers were absorbed into the new regime, becoming ordinary teachers in the schools (see Ogès 1940). By the end of the Revolutionary period, any notion of a fixed salary for the teachers had gone. A principle remained that one quarter of the pupils could attend free of charge, but without a large contingent of paying pupils a teacher could not survive, and many gave up (see Ogès 1942).

Revolutionary legislation chased the clergy out of the schools and dismantled the old system of schooling, but the funds were not available for a full replacement. Few rural areas could maintain regular schools, and the idea of formal education was still alien to much of the peasantry. The practice of popular education was, therefore, limited and sporadic. In theory, however, by the end of this troubled decade, from 1789 to 1799, French was established as the national language, and as the language of education, and Breton was an aid to its teaching. French and education were not new in Brittany, but neither 'French' nor 'Breton' were to be quite the same again, and education was now a national enterprise.

Chapter two

After the Revolution

The Consulate and Empire

It was under the Consulate and first Empire that the Jacobin model of political centralization became a national reality, and an administrative framework was established that has lasted until modern times. The new bureaucracy demanded secondary education for its 'army' of *fonctionnaires*, or (in qualified translation) 'civil servants'. The famous *Lycées* came into being, with French now the undisputed medium of instruction at this level; mathematics, grammar, and (a secular) Latin were important subjects. Standard grammatical texts, with a rationalized French sharing the categories of Latin grammar, also passed into the lower levels of education (see Ogès 1945–6).

Elementary education, however, was relatively neglected by the Consulate and Empire. The *Concordat* of 1801 partially mended the rift between Church and State, and a law of 1802 tried to make local communes financially responsible for elementary schools. Most could not afford this, and parents were still expected to contribute if possible. (For it was not until very much later, in the 1880s, that public and private education became distinguished as free and paid education respectively, and public schoolteachers became (in 1889) themselves *fonctionnaires*, wholly paid by the State.) In Finistère, however, the combined efforts of the Bishop and Prefect encouraged the communes to stretch their resources, and, by 1812, at least one-fifth of them had well-established elementary schools, with others providing some intermittent schooling. The common cause of Bishop and Prefect here was not based upon unity of ambition. The Bishop was seeking to increase recruitment to the clergy, while the Prefect was worried about the lack of literate municipal functionaries,[1] and about poor housing and health education. Under the alliance, however, of Bishop and Prefect, Finistère acquired a steadily increasing number of both elementary and secondary schools, and by the end of the Empire had more secondary schools than any other Breton *département* (Ogès 1945–6:80).

35

In rural communes, with poor roads, widely scattered hamlets, and the demands of work on the land, the establishment of elementary schools faced and posed many problems. Moreover, those who did aspire to education, and who might have been the instigators of elementary schools in these areas, persistently sent their children to schools in larger bourgs or the towns. Smaller, rural municipalities could not open viable schools when local peasants sought education in areas where, in the words of one rural municipality, 'they learn French and they all say that they cannot learn it here' (cited in Ogès 1945–6:38). The authorities were informed by many of the Breton-speaking communes that those 'who are in a position to give their children some instruction, send them to town to learn French, which they regard as the basis of their education; even then, it is only during the winter'.[2]

Teachers by this time were supposed to hold a qualifying certificate (*brevet*). However, many rural teachers remained unqualified, offering only rudimentary instruction, and some used only Breton (Ogès 1934:105). Even where teachers *were* qualified, some rural communes provided no more than elementary religious instruction wholly or mostly in Breton; in 1863, in Finistère, for example, thirty-three rural schools (or 6 per cent of its total number at this level) were still teaching only in Breton in this way.[3]

The 'Loi Guizot' and the 'Loi Falloux'

From the beginning of the nineteenth century, when the Catholic catechism had come back into the schools under Napoleon, until the Ferry laws of the 1880s, when all religious instruction was banished from the schools again, the need to learn the catechism in preparation for one's First Communion was a powerful incentive for sending children to school, even if only for a short time. The authorities often exploited this incentive to encourage attendance. This policy was not without its contradictions, however, and conflicts arose between clergy and government in Brittany which have an important bearing on the position of Breton.

Between the 1830s and 1850, educational administration was secular, although religious and moral instruction figured highly in the curriculum. The broad framework for the period was given by the *Loi Guizot* of 1833. Communes were obliged to open a boys' school, and it was assumed that the learning of French was a paramount aim of education, although the text of the law did not explicitly stipulate that French was to be the medium of instruction.[4] A later circular, in 1838, urged teachers to avoid any 'mechanical' teaching of French, and to be sure that pupils understood what they were hearing, reading, and writing; it advocated 'translation into the local idiom' where really necessary, echoing the 'auxiliary' role accorded to 'local idioms' in previous legislation. The same circular also asked teachers to try to 'purge pronunciation and the language of anything that recalls the time when the same instruction and the same language were not common to all Frenchmen'.[5]

One source of tension between the clergy and the state authorities was the 'mutual' system of schooling, which was actively encouraged by Guizot, the Minister of Public Instruction. This system, influenced by contemporary English projects, involved using older pupils to help the teachers in their work. Many 'mutual' schools were established in Finistère but they were not welcomed by the clergy, who saw them as Protestant-inspired. Guizot himself was a Protestant. Although, in Finistère, very few 'mutual' schools were actually Protestant, further tension resulted between mayors and priests in several communes (Ogès 1931:76–124). By the 1840s, 'mutual' schools were rare in Finistère, and in 1850 came a new law, the *Loi Falloux*, which again accorded the clergy some say in school administration.

In general, the legislative texts of the Revolution had been interpreted in terms which we might see as pragmatic – translation into Breton was permitted and practised in order to ensure understanding of the French. Under the Guizot regulation, this practical 'auxiliary' role remained, but the *Loi Falloux* did little to clarify matters thereafter. The clergy now had greater control over education, and religious instruction an even more prominent place. This raised the question of what language religious education should be given in, for the Breton-speaking area had four well-established catechisms written in Breton, one for each of the old dioceses that had existed before the reorganization according to *départements*. Preaching and catechism in the churches of the Breton-speaking areas were in Breton, and the Breton clergy argued that, since many children were at school only to learn their catechism, then catechism in the schools had to be in Breton too.[6] They did not feel that this was against the text of the new law in any way. The educational authorities felt that it was, but they knew that catechism was a strong incentive to schooling. This dilemma occasioned a flurry of official correspondence.

The ambiguous articles of the *Loi Falloux* seem to have been the following. Religious instruction was given pride of place (articles 13 and 23); the 'basics of French' remained important, with a footnote added by the Academic Council of Finistère (which now included religious authorities) stating that: 'In the rural communes, to facilitate the study of the French language, teachers will be invited to exercise their pupils in the translation of Breton into French' (ADF:CAF:7 October 1852:art. 13, footnote).[7] The earlier 1838 circular had implied only translation from French into Breton. Article 28 of the new law concerned 'writing', and mentioned that 'useful' texts might be employed to copy and practise from, including, for example, texts dealing with 'the dogma and precepts of religion, the fine traits of the Holy Scripture, and the history of France'; article 29 then went on to deal with 'orthography and grammar', and here stipulated that 'only French is to be used in the schools'. There was plenty of room for conflicting interpretations and confusion, and room for Breton texts under articles 13 and 28, if not under article 29.

In 1846, prior to this regime, there had already been correspondence between the Academic Inspectorate of the Côtes-du-Nord and the Bishop of the diocese about the fact that prayers and catechism were done in Breton in the schools. The secular authorities saw this as 'prejudicial to the propagation of our national language'. The Prefect had written to the Bishop reminding him that 'Our schools in Lower Brittany have the particular aim of replacing Breton with French and this would already be a great benefit'. He explained that he understood about problems of comprehension and of continuity with church practice, but asked the Bishop to consider producing a catechism in both Breton and French (cited in Durand 1912:81–2).

In Finistère in the 1860s, enquiries and reports by local Inspectorates revealed mounting tensions. The Inspectorate for the area around Brest reported, in 1863, that some of the clergy were explicitly equating Breton and faith, fearing that a perceived 'invasion of French' would weaken the Catholic faith of the peasants. The same report warned the higher Inspectorate, however, that simply to switch to a French catechism might result in deserted rural schools in some areas.[8] A letter in the same year from the Morlaix and Quimper areas, involving large sections of Breton-speaking Finistère, reported that about one-tenth of the total population, mostly *fonctionnaires* and outsiders, knew only French, that about half knew both French and Breton, and the rest knew only Breton. This report suggested that more translation exercises in the schools might help, but urged that the church authorities should be consulted directly by the higher Inspectorate on the issue of the language of the catechism.[9]

The Third Republic

With the 1870s came the Third Republic, strongly influenced by the optimistic positivism of Auguste Comte, himself attracted by the ideas of the eighteenth-century *philosophes*. Ideas which had often been invoked in the first Revolution were now translated into a new context – a context with its own tensions between clergy and Republic, and with the apparent realization of Enlightenment and Revolutionary rationality through modern science. Comte's positive reason was state rationality, and French and education the means of realizing France, a nation now faced with ever more powerful national units at its borders, as well as continuing threats within. The *Ancien Régime* re-emerged as an internal metaphor of opposition. Jules Ferry, who became Minister of Education at the beginning of the 1880s, was determined to chase out the old order for ever: 'my aim', he said, 'is to organize humanity without God and King'. A secular and 'neutral' school – an *école laïque* – was to be the means to realize, in Ferry's terms, an 'egalitarian nation, a nation animated by that spirit of unity and that confraternity of ideas' (cited in Zeldin, 1973 I:625–6). The Republic has emerged four times since its first appearance, each time as an apparently continuous ideal, relived in self-conscious continuity. In the Third Republic, in particular, the contours of French history, or the 'History of France', and '1789' with it, took definitive shape (see p. 11). The textbooks of Ferry's schools were to make it clear that the 1789 Revolution, *the* French Revolution', was the rightful 'heritage' of every child.

Tensions of the 1860s and 1870s were the immediate history informing Ferry's vision and his legislation, and, in a period of developing republican radicalism, the very existence of catechism in the schools was questioned. With Breton and religious instruction firmly linked, a battle ensued over the ambiguities of articles 13, 28, and 29 of the Falloux regulations. Both church and secular authorities in Finistère cited some or all of them, either for or against Breton catechisms in the schools, according to their respective commitments.

In 1876, the Finistère Inspectorate and the Prefect received complaints from local Breton republicans (including the mayor of one commune[10]) that local teachers were using Breton texts. The Prefect of Finistère then entered into direct correspondence with the Bishop over the possibility of a bilingual catechism, such as had already been produced in the *département* of the Nord, he said, for the Walloons. The Bishop replied that catechism in Breton was not against the law, and was, in any case, still attracting children to the schools. The Prefect had suggested that bilingual catechisms might be useful for translation exercises, but the Bishop argued that, since word-for-word translation of the Breton was not possible, then even this use for the proposed text was not evident. Statements such as this served to confirm the view of those who felt that members of the clergy were not simply introducing Breton texts in the interests of translation, which the Finistère footnote to article 13 of the national regulations had at least provided for. The Bishop added that there were four Breton catechisms (one for each of the old dioceses) and an attempt to reduce them to one had failed, so it would be ultimately too expensive to produce bilingual texts, as this might effectively mean eight catechisms in all.[11]

With battle lines being drawn in this way, the Ferry laws of the early 1880s[12] instituted free, compulsory, and secular (or, ideally, politically 'neutral') education – the *école laïque* – and attempted to resolve such issues by simply excluding all religious instruction from the schools. In 1880, an educational decree ruled once again that 'only French is to be used in the school'; in 1881, the Finistère 'Departmental Council for Public Instruction' accepted this, without any footnote this time about Breton or translation.[13] Towards the end of the 1880s, new educational legislation (under Goblet) reiterated much of the earlier regulations, and article 14 stated once again that 'only French will be used in the schools'. In the same year, 1887, the Finistère authorities once more accepted this ruling without additions, the only difference being that the departmental regulation numbered it as article 13.[14] This same 'article 13' remained to be quoted occasionally in correspondence in educational journals and was variously cited, according to context and commitment, to suggest a role for Breton, or no Breton at all, or to imply flexibility.[15] The 1887 ruling thus offered a new focus for argument, but by no means closed the debate.

Breton and French in the churches

By the turn of the century, the clerical/republican battle was fierce, and although many Breton-speaking areas were strongly republican, Breton and republicanism seemed clearly opposed at some levels, including that of national debate in the Chamber of Deputies and the Senate. Until 1905, with the separation of Church and State, priests were paid a basic salary by the State, and the Ministry of Public Instruction and Worship was a single body. In 1890, Fallières had tried to prohibit certain dialects of France in religious offices. In January 1901, Waldeck-Rousseau had asked the Prefect of the Nord to request certificates from mayors to affirm that local priests were not using solely Flemish for catechism and preaching in the churches – otherwise the priests would get no state salary. In September 1902, under Combes, it was the turn of Breton, with a similar request and threat made in Brittany. In a few cases Breton priests did have their pay withheld (see Jacob 1981). However, this 1902 circular had little general effect and was, it seems, withdrawn – but not before arousing heated debates among both Senators (in 1902) and Deputies (in 1903). A very brief glance at these two debates will show how current political opposi-tions were stacked around Breton and French.

A debate in October 1902 in the Senate, ostensibly about another ruling of 1901 which had involved the closure of many schools run by religious orders, discussed also Combes's circular of September 1902, regarding the use of Breton in the churches. The two issues were easily conflated, especially by anti-republican Breton Senators, who debated the issues as if wanting French in the churches of Brittany meant wanting local teaching nuns thrown out on the streets. In general, these right-wing Senators saw both measures as a single attack, for, as one declared, Breton 'is the sister of faith'. The left of the Senate was generally *for* the government measures, although one Breton republican was hesitant. He pointed out that the majority of the General Council (or *Conseil Général*) of Finistère was, for the moment, republican, that Bretons had started out now on the republican path, and that such measures might seem like government provocation and could swing many back to the right again. The rest of the left, including Clémenceau, reminded the Senate that the Church had long taught a 'hatred of progress, of modern civilization and liberalism' and was becoming all too powerful; there was no intention of prohibiting Breton altogether, it was said, but rather of making at least part of what went on in the churches complement the work of the schools. Combes insisted that he was merely against the clergy's 'premeditated exclusion of French', and suggested that High Mass could perhaps offer its sermon in French, with Breton remaining in any preaching at Low Mass. The Senate voted in favour of the government ruling on the closure of the religious schools, and it was clear that this was also a vote in support of French in the churches of Brittany.[16]

In 1903, the Chamber of Deputies then debated the 1902 circular explicitly, and similar arguments reappeared. Breton right-wing Deputies (including well-known Deputies such as Lamy and De L'Estourbeillon) were against it. Lamy argued that there were still an estimated 743,000 monolingual Bretons, most of whom were old people, women, and small children; Bretons were taxpayers, and there was nothing in the laws governing priests' salaries that demanded preaching in French; to threaten Breton was to threaten the Catholic faith. Combes, also present here, retorted that the clergy were deliberately keeping French out because of all the 'ugly and detestable republican ideas' it bore. Moreover, while both Breton and French catechisms were now available, the Breton versions obliged the faithful to consult the priest before voting.[17] Indeed, Breton catechisms of the early 1900s in Finistère taught that it was a sin to vote for the left or for those who did not support 'religion' (Singer 1971:42). One republican Deputy from Brittany, Louis Hémon, tried to speak out against the overt equation of Breton and anti-republicanism upon which the debate turned. If the 'reactionary' party was using Breton, then perhaps the republicans should do so: 'with the help of French', he said, the Breton vocabulary could speak republican ideas. However, he felt that the best solution would be simply to build more schools, for there were still not enough in the Breton-speaking areas; this would be better, he argued, than launching into a ferocious anti-clericalism that risked becoming a new state religion in itself.

The Chamber voted in favour of Combes's circular, and the debate ended with a right-wing Breton Deputy, the Duc de Rohan, thanking the Minister ironically, for now he said, Bretons might see the 'folly' of the republican path. Then De L'Estourbeillon exclaimed: 'Vive la Bretagne!' This was met with the jeers of the left.

In spite of all this, the religious-run schools did open again in Brittany and flourished, with a great increase in the years 1906–11 (Singer 1971:65); Breton also continued in the churches, in hymns, catechisms, and sometimes in the preaching, until the Second World War in some areas, although French was already taking over well before this time. The main result of the debates outlined above was to convince the higher authorities of the continuing menace that Breton presented to the Republic. In 1924, the Minister of Education, François Albert, issued a circular saying that only local idioms of 'Latin' origin could help the teaching of French, and that Breton and Basque, for example, were of doubtful use (see Guieysse 1925:23). His successor, Anatole de Monzie, took this up in tougher mood in 1925, and, explicitly placing himself in a direct line from the 'Revolution of 1789', declared that the teaching of any *patois* was a luxury, and that (citing the French writer Musset) 'The only one who is truly French in heart and soul, and from head to toe, is he who knows and can speak and can read the French language.'[18]

Girls and the 'écoles libres'

Breton could still have a place in the private, church-run schools – the *écoles libres*. Their 'liberty' was invested mainly in religious instruction, which they had always dispensed (and still do). Virtually all the schools for girls that had existed in Brittany in the first half of the nineteenth century had been run by the Church, and generally offered only exercises of piety and devotion in Breton. It was only after the Falloux law of 1850 that the government obliged local communes to set up girls' schools, and many of these continued with only Breton and the most elementary instruction. Breton women, with less education, and not subject to compulsory military service, continued to know only Breton far longer than their menfolk.

The authorities began to fear that the girls of Brittany were in danger of being linguistically isolated and in the power of those clerics who feared the 'invasion' of sin and French together. In 1850, over two-thirds of Finistère's girls of school-age were receiving no education at all, but three and a half times as many girls as boys were in private, religious establishments.[19] This was a situation that secular authorities in Brittany were keen to change, principally by opening more public schools for girls – girls who were destined, it was felt, to have great influence as wives and mothers. For Jules Ferry, one important motivation in bringing free and lay education to both sexes in the 1880s was to get women, and thereby husbands and children, away from the influence of the clergy.[20] Young girls thus entered the political and linguistic battleground, and Church and State fought over them.

Church schools in Brittany continued to offer catechism lessons after the Ferry laws, although the very existence of the schools themselves was threatened from the 1880s to at least 1906. A few of these schools also offered intermittent lessons in Breton (some of the domestic education lessons for girls, and some agricultural lessons for both boys and girls) until the 1930s; this practice was very limited, however, and most church schools were as hostile to Breton by that time as were the state or public schools (see Le Berre 1935:25, 35–36; Taldir 1935). The events of the turn of the century especially had made any lingering attachment to Breton in the private schools seem like an invitation to persecution. Moreover, the private schools were dependent on a paying clientele. By the First World War, even religious instruction was given in French in many of these schools.

At the beginning of 1930, the Bishop of 'Quimper and Léon' (or Finistère, in secular terms) found it necessary to issue a circular to remind teachers in the diocesan schools that they should be doing at least the catechism in Breton in Breton-speaking areas. He also stipulated that there should be some study of the geography of Brittany, with visits to farms and local monuments; such a study, he felt, could help 'to slow down the rural exodus'. Bretons were noticeably leaving the land[21] and, so it seemed, abandoning Breton and religion at the same time. The Bishop advocated teaching young Bretons the 'History of Brittany', to help make them 'proud of their race and their faith'. To keep alive the Breton language, and the tradition of family prayers and readings of pious works, he suggested that oral Breton, at least, should form part of the *certificat d'études libres* examination, and that the reading and writing of Breton should also be encouraged.[22] Few, it seems, took any notice, for in 1935 the Bishop reissued the circular, adding that diocesan inspectors would be checking up this time on observance of its measures.[23] It is not clear that there was any uniform application of these measures, although members of the clergy actively produced suitable texts and it seems that many pupils came out of the private schools of the immediate pre-war period able to read at least some Breton, principally the catchism and devotional works.

Chapter three

Breton or no Breton in the schools?

Montalivet: bilingual schooling

It is clear that political ideals and the tensions between clergy and Republic, or between Church and State, largely determined the relative positions of Breton and French in the schools from 1789 until at least the Second World War. There was always enough ambiguity in the texts to allow for different interpretations, however. There was never any clear legislative framework totally banishing Breton from the schools nor any relentless governmental fight against Breton for purely political reasons. Pedagogical considerations were not absent from national debate, and local representatives had influence in the determination of policy at both national and local levels. Moreover, there were those at the national level who were in favour of Breton in the schools, and those at the local level who were against it.

In 1831, for example, there was an official project for a fully worked-out programme of Breton-language education in the initial years of the elementary schools. A government-sponsored enquiry of that year seemed to suggest that at least half the population of rural communes in Finistère knew little or no French.[1] Many teachers, however, were apparently giving entirely French books to children who could speak only Breton. The Minister of Public Instruction, Montalivet, therefore circulated suggestions to the Prefects of Finistère, the Côtes-du-Nord, and the Morbihan, asking them for their views on a teaching programme in which the study of Breton would have a place. Montalivet's suggestion was that *only* Breton should be used in the first year of schooling, with the pupils then moving from the local Breton dialect to the other dialects, and also beginning to learn French, only in the second year.[2] The response from Finistère to this proposal is of special interest, not only for its own content, but also because it seems to have influenced the replies from the other areas.

The Prefect of Finistère decided to ask the local *Comité d'Instruction Primaire* in Quimper for their views on the proposal; this Committee produced a full report, and it was this that the Prefect returned to the

Minister as the Finistère reply. The Prefect pointed out that he was not from Brittany, and so had asked the Committee for their views because they were all born in Brittany, many of them spoke Breton, and they all knew the area and the locals better than he did. The Committee was firmly against the project.

The Committee claimed that there were not really four dialects, as Montalivet's project assumed, but as many dialects as there were communes, and that 'the Breton of Finistère' was as different from 'the Breton of the Morbihan' as was French from English. Moreover, the Léon dialect predominated in writing, and was the only one that had 'grammar'; otherwise, they said, Breton was, in comparison with French, 'capricious', with more exceptions than rules. The Committee was echoing here a common view of Breton (and one which we might expect to fall out of the juxtaposition of two incommensurate systems; see the point about cultural mismatch on p. 21). Some version of 'capriciousness' was a widely expressed description of peripheral languages and 'idioms' when perceived from the self-defining, ordered centrality of national languages (see Henson 1974). The conclusion here, for the Committee, was that Breton was no fit medium for schooling. The Committee argued that most children, in order to read and write Breton, would need to learn the Léon dialect. They also had to learn French. This would effectively mean that they would be learning two new languages at school. Since many children went to school for only about two years, there was, the Committee argued, a danger that pupils would leave knowing only how to read and write Breton. French would then penetrate the countryside even later than it otherwise might. The Committee suggested, therefore, that instead of any Breton-French project of this kind, more stringent measures should be taken to make sure that the children learned French rapidly. Far from treating Breton as a language fit for the schools, the Committee said: 'Should we not, on the contrary, encourage, by any possible means, the impoverishment and the corruption of Breton, to the point that, from one commune to another, mutual comprehension would be impossible?'[3] Then, said the Committee, all peasants would be obliged to learn French. The Prefect of Finistère sent this report to the Minister, with a covering note saying that he relied on the Committee's authority and agreed with their conclusions.

The Prefect of the Morbihan also received a copy of the Finistère report, however, and disagreed strongly with it.[4] He pointed out that he, too, was a Breton. The Vannetais had a well-established written form, he claimed, and the differences between Breton dialects were not nearly as great as those between French and English. There would not be the necessity of learning two new languages, therefore. Although a 'positive' mind (for which we would now say 'positivist') might find him 'romantic', he said, he believed that Breton was a proper or 'regular' language, but also full of 'primitive' simplicity. The Prefect thus sought to find, within Breton, both rational order and unfettered expressiveness. Whereas, for the Quimper Committee, the irrational 'capriciousness' of Breton confirmed an image of the uncultivated *sauvage*, for the Morbihan Prefect the indeterminate feature of Breton yielded confirmation, not of savagery, but of an unspoilt 'primitive' spontaneity (these two images being, of course, but the negative and positive sides of the same coin; on the nineteenth-century French genre of the *sauvage* more generally, see Weber 1977). Furthermore, for the Morbihan Prefect, a language was a 'people', and any attempt to destroy a language was therefore 'murder'. In the 1830s, the associated ideas of nationalism and romanticism were fast becoming the common intellectual equipment of the cultivated. The couplet 'positive' (later 'positivist')/'romantic' was part of a system of metaphorical associations within which the adjective 'primitive' was no longer employed in simple denigration. The Prefect of the Morbihan could manifest his good taste, and his French *Lycée* education, by expressing this confident, sophisticated evaluation of Breton. Even the Secretary of the Quimper Committee could not match this; he was a teacher, but only at local college level. Other members of the Quimper Committee included tradesmen and landowning members of the peasantry.

The Prefect of Finistère, using a self-consciously rational expression of the romantic/positivist dichotomy, added to his covering note that the view from the Morbihan seemed to be based more on 'sentiment' than on any concern for 'veritable progress'. The Prefect of the Côtes-du-Nord, himself not a Breton, seems to have relied on the local Finistère view, and replied in like manner.[5] Montalivet was left with apparently contradictory views from Bretons about Breton, and, with two of the three Breton-speaking *départements* giving negative responses, the project was dropped. In the meantime, the Prefect of Finistère actively encouraged translations into Breton of important government texts (such as Louis-Philippe's Charter of 1830) and offered prizes for books in Breton giving useful advice on general topics of agricultural and health interest for the Breton-speaking countryside (see Bernard 1917:9). Under Guizot, such books were further encouraged and, along with translations in Breton of well-known French texts, were distributed in the schools (see Ogès 1934:82).

The symbole and Carré

In 1836, the local Education Committee for the *arrondissement* of Brest took the matter into their own hands; they voted that, in their own local public schools, 'the use of Breton is forbidden' (cited in Ogès 1934:85), thus going further than any government ruling had ever done. It is also from the Brest area, three years earlier, that we find what seems to be the earliest report of a practice used for the teaching of French which was, in one form or another, common to many parts of France. An Inspector, M. Dufilhol, wrote in 1833 of a pedagogical method which 'involves the children watching each other' for a word of Breton. Anyone who inadvertently uttered a word of Breton had to hold 'quite a heavy piece of wood', he said, and 'cannot take part in the games until he has heard one of his friends speaking Breton'. The piece of wood was then passed on to the next child caught in the act, and so on. He reported that a 'few teachers' were using this method to encourage the use of French, and that 'the children carry out their watch in a very active and gay manner'.[6] In some instances, it would seem that this practice involved a *jeton* (or token) of moderate size, also held in the hand (and sometimes, it is said, a wooden peasant clog tied round the child's neck, although I have seen no inspectors' reports of the use of this last item).

This device is now generally known as the *symbole*, although Dufilhol did not use this term. The use of the *symbole* does not seem to have been the subject of any official directive from central government, and its origins are obscure.[7] It was briefly encouraged in the 1860s by one inspector covering the area of Quimper and Morlaix,[8] but it was not widely approved in official circles. In 1889, a General Inspector by the name of Carré, who came to Brittany to help out following the 1887 legislation, explicitly and firmly condemned the practice in a discussion with an assembly of teachers from all parts of Finistère; a local educational bulletin reported that Carré had told the teachers 'above all, not to make any use of the *symbole*, should this practice still exist anywhere' (BN 1890:38; cf. an earlier condemnation, in a national pedagogical journal, Carré 1888:232).

Carré's comments on the *symbole* were part of a more general discussion of teaching methods in this period. Education was expanding, and 'childhood' ideally constructed as a special time set aside for learning and education. There was increased production of children's literature and, with the advent of compulsory schooling (from six years of age), pedagogical studies were of growing interest (see Crubellier 1979). The more educated ranks of society were accustomed to the already well-established category of 'childhood'.[9] Among the peasantry, however, children were commonly at work in the fields from an early age. To the educated, this seemed to be uncaring neglect. Peasant children appeared to be denied their childhood, and to be locked into a senseless, uninventive traditionality. One result of this was a new attention to nursery education (see Chapter ten). When Carré spoke to the Finistère teachers, compulsory primary schooling was making manifest the disparities between children of different backgrounds, and between children's backgrounds and school. The language issue in Brittany became part of a general discussion of what kind of knowledge, if any, children brought to the schools, and what relationship this had to the content and aims of schooling.

When Carré came to Brittany in 1889, he offered a self-consciously progressive method for the teaching of French, which we might now call the 'direct method'. He offered a manual of explanations and exercises which would guide teachers in a careful progression from the oral to the written word, from classroom and local vocabulary to wider discussions and compositions, from the naming and counting of objects to the structures and relations of both grammar and basic mathematics, and which would use everyday relations of time and space in the classroom (e.g., before/after, up/down, and so on) to aid acquisition of the structures of French.[10] The idea was that the children would learn French effortlessly and gradually.

Where, however, did Breton figure in all this? Breton was, after all, still the language of the majority of the children, and it was Breton they knew when they came to school. In his published article, and in his talk delivered to the assembly of Finistère teachers, Carré was careful to explain why he had chosen this method, and not others where Breton figured more obviously. In a series of rhetorical questions, he outlined and discussed other possibilities, beginning with the totally hypothetical. Could teachers not simply teach solely in Breton, for example? No, he argued, because this would mean abandoning the 'national language' in Brittany, and that was not at all in the spirit of the educational legislation (BN 1890:36–7). In any case, he pointed out, Bretons needed French for wider commercial and social relations of all kinds. He emphasized, throughout his discussion, that he had absolutely no desire to 'destroy' Breton or any of 'the particularities of Brittany' including 'the language, customs, costumes, traditions, etc.' If his suggested method were ever shown to be 'destroying' Breton, then he would be 'the first to renounce it' (BN 1890:36–8; Guieysse 1936:180).

Could there not be a bilingual method then, teaching both Breton and French? Here we find Carré aware of established counter-arguments, such as those from the Quimper Committee in its report of 1831, and of the views of a number of Celtic scholars. Breton had four dialects, he said, and many variations, and no fixed orthography. He cited, on his last point, the remarks of a Breton grammarian of the early nineteenth century, Le Gonidec, who had found 'chaos' in the modes of writing Breton. More-over, Carré went on, popular Breton was said to be 'corrupt', using more and more French terms. A combination of French and English would be far more useful to the children than that of French and Breton: Breton offered no possibility of external relations, and its only interest, he concluded, would be for '*savants*', with Breton literature kept in museums or libraries and studied in Rennes University (where some courses had already begun). In the meantime, Breton would, of course, continue as a daily language for many – something that no one, he stressed, could ever stop or had ever tried to stop (Carré 1888:221–2).

Could Breton not have a place at least as an auxiliary means for the teaching of French? Some inspectors were keen on this. Carré emphasized that he realized that, since most children (especially girls) knew no French when they came to school, there were arguments in favour of using some Breton. However, there might be a tendency to translate all the time. It was now felt that children should enquire for themselves – asking a friend when they did not understand, perhaps – and should try to think in French as far as possible. Experience of foreign-language teaching at the *Lycée* level, he explained, showed that learning words for their own signification was more effective than word-for-word translation between different languages. Carré also reported that an Inspector from Vannes, by the name of Poitrineau, had informed him that Breton children were neglected and left to themselves, barely fed and clothed, put out in the fields in all weathers and barely spoken to; the children barely spoke even at home, it seemed, except 'a few words of prayer, morning and evening; and even then, it is rare ...'. Poitrineau, Carré continued, had said that the net result was that the children were intellectually retarded and 'taciturn'; this last judgement was, he added, a common assessment of the Breton peasant. Carré cited other inspectors with similar views of peasant children, and quoted a headmaster of a Quimperlé school who had estimated that the Breton child had a vocabulary of only about '500 words' in Breton when he came to school. (This was, at the time, a common assessment of the lexicon of 'primitive' languages in general.) Carré felt, therefore, that the value of the Breton that the child knew when he or she came to school should not be exaggerated. The teacher could proceed as if the child were virtually beginning, all over again, to learn about the world and to speak (Carré 1888:222–6; BN 1890).

Breton could still be used in the classrooms, however, in 'a restricted and well determined way', in order to help teach vocabulary in the initial stages (Carré 1888:230); and Carré stressed that, in the playground, children should be allowed to play freely in Breton, since they would otherwise become too tired (BN 1890:38). French, however, was to dominate in the schools. This was fully in keeping with the 1887 law, which, although it had made no mention of Breton or method, Carré felt had to be translated into this rational methodology. Some of his views were considered progressive for his time, and he had, in principle, abolished the *symbole*.

The teachers who heard Carré's views in Finistère in 1889 mostly agreed with him, it seems, with the exception of one from Normandy, married to a Breton woman, who had learnt some Breton himself and wished to carry on using some Breton in his school; Carré let him go ahead, and took particular interest in this school thereafter, visiting it whenever he returned to Brittany (Guieysse 1936:108). In the 1890s, there was a continuing debate in educational journals and official bulletins in Brittany on the ideas that Carré had put forward; the teachers who contributed generally agreed with Carré, except one who found Carré's method too optimistic in practical terms and too stringent an interpretation of 'article 13' (Le Gac

1896:301–3).[11] The very existence of debate of this kind suggests flexibility in the interpretation of the texts of the law.

In 1897, however, one member of the higher Inspectorate of Finistère, by the name of Dosimont, ended the debate to his own satisfaction. Basing his views on those of teachers in Brasparts, in the region of the Arrée mountains of central Finistère, he affirmed that there was no longer any question of carrying on with the old translation methods, since the method of Carré, the *méthode maternelle* as it was called, was proving much more effective; as a result, he said, the general and 'inviolable' rule now was to be: 'Not a single word of Breton in class, nor in the playgrounds' (Dosimont 1897:362). Dosimont thus went much further than Carré, and gave yet another interpretation of the 1887 law. In 1934, the Minister of Education, still subject to the 1887 law, announced nevertheless that he had never heard of any teacher being reprimanded for using Breton to aid his teaching in French.[12]

Debate continued until the Second World War. Some argued that using Breton would help the learning of French; others argued that using any Breton would lead to a 'mixing' of the two languages, turning French into a 'jargon', a *'charabia'*, or a *'patois'*, and weakening French national allegiance.[13] Many of these debates drew explicitly on the ideals of the 1789 Revolution or on the common ideas of nineteenth-century nationalism, and clarity of language definition remained a figure for clarity of national, political allegiance. Most argued that the direct method produced the best and purest French; others argued for the use of both languages to produce the same end.[14] There were those, too, who began to argue the cultural and intellectual advantages of bilingualism,[15] a view which at least one Minister of Education, Anatole de Monzie, felt was mere 'polemic' disguising other motivations (De Monzie 1925:207). There were also those, particularly on the Breton right-wing, who wanted the use of the two languages to protect the purity of Breton.[16] Linguistic and political issues were firmly entwined, and there was no possibility of purely linguistic or pedagogical debate.

Chapter four

After the Second World War

Tolerance and equality

Following the Second World War, ideas embodied in the United Nations, UNESCO, and numerous international conventions[1] actively involved France in an international movement of opinion that sought lasting peace through cultural tolerance and equality. France, as the self-conscious origin of secular philosophical tolerance and the Rights of Man, was keen to confirm to the world its support of such ideas. However, ideas of equality and tolerance can lead to very different conclusions when applied to the relationship between France and other nations and when applied to the internal structure of France. The new international tolerance that stressed the equality of all cultures, languages, and peoples was ripe for translation into an *internal* socio-linguistic and socio-cultural relativism – and, within such an internal relativism, all the 'local idioms' and *patois* of France could claim equal status with French.

Usually, internal and external contexts do not meet and contradiction can be ignored. Breton-language enthusiasts, however, have sought, exploited, and published such apparent contradictions and inconsistencies in modern statements made by France's political leaders on the question of local languages. For instance: in 1969, Pompidou declared himself wholly favourable to public support for the languages and cultures of 'our provinces and *pays*'; in April 1972, however, speaking near the German border in the Lower-Rhine, he then said that there was 'no place for regional languages in a France destined to make its mark in Europe' (cited in Gwegen 1975:40, 54). Giscard d'Estaing tried to bring the arguments together coherently in 1974, in reply to Breton enthusiasts who were demanding an assured place in the schools for Breton, and who were citing international conventions as internal obligations; Giscard declared himself fully aware of these ideas of 'the modern world' in which France stood before other nations, and then he went on:

> The diversity of cultures, of men, of characters and landscape is, in fact, one of the riches of France; it is obvious, however, that respect for this

diversity can only be realized in the context of a full and clear awareness of the fundamental postulate of National Unity. (cited in Gwegen 1975:52)

The 'Loi Deixonne'

The position of Breton in the post-war schools was first clarified in a law of January 1951 devoted to the question of 'the teaching of local languages and dialects'. This law began in 1949 as a report presented by a Socialist (SFIO) from the Var, Deixonne. Deixonne was reporting on three bills of law presented earlier during 1947 and 1948. Two of these had concerned Breton; one had been tabled by a Communist from Brittany, by the name of Hervé, and the other by a mixed group from all parties. After a complex process of discussion,[2] a final text was voted by the National Assembly in December 1950 and declared law on 11 January 1951. It had much the same content as Deixonne's original report of 1949 in spite of much debate, curtailment, and re-addition.[3]

During the debates, political divisions of right and left were more confused than previously. All sides were still prey to the fear that opening schools to any 'local speech' would mean officializing *argot* (or slang) and that the whole business would spell the end of education itself. And education was not to be taken lightly, for as one Socialist Senator, Lamousse, who opposed much of the bill, explained:

If there is, indeed, one institution that should only be touched with trembling hands, it is surely our University – which has been building French civilization for a thousand years – and our schools, which, for the last three quarters of a century, have made the Republic. (Lamousse in CLR 2 March 1950; see note 3)

Others went back, for their arguments, beyond the Third Republic and Ferry to the Revolution. However, the Minister of Education himself, M. Delbos, always stepped in to try to save the original text as far as possible.[4] 'Local languages' could now be defended in the name of the integrity of France.

The final text of the law allowed for some Breton at all levels of education, although there was some trouble about the higher degree level. The local languages were to count as parts of a more general degree (article 8), and when the *Conseil* at one stage (in March 1950) tried to add a clause to the effect that they would not count towards a degree valid for teaching, Deixonne himself got this clause struck out (in July 1950) and it did not appear again. However, a special Commission, set up in July 1951 to discuss how to put the law into effect, reported in September to the *Conseil Supérieur de l'Education Nationale* with a fully worked-out project which did not include local languages in degrees valid for teaching. To have included them, they argued, would have meant going beyond the actual text of the law (see *Ar Falz* 1951 (November–December):25). During further debate on this issue, in 1963, it was, significantly, a right-wing politician, Madame Ploux (born in the South of France and married to a Breton), representing the Châteaulin area of Finistère, who voted against any inclusion of the languages in teaching degrees (see *Ar Falz* 1963, 5:8, 14). She was later reminded that there were already Breton courses at Rennes University which, since 1958, had been officially recognized as part of a modern language degree, valid for further teaching qualifications.

Article 1 of the Deixonne law aimed to 'favour the study of local languages and dialects'. Article 2, in the 1949 text, stated that 'rules at present in force will be modified' to allow teachers to use 'local forms of speech' where they might aid in the teaching of French. The Minister of Education pointed out that this was, in fact, already practised, and so the final text began 'instructions will be addressed' to education authorities to 'authorize' this. In spite of manifest confusion, this article at least gave positive official sanction to the practice, where it existed, of using Breton to teach French, and silenced any surviving followers of Dosimont in the Inspectorate. One argument behind this article 2 was that Breton was still, for many, the 'mother tongue'.

When some senators in the *Conseil* tried to limit the law, in the name of the 'Republic', Deixonne retorted: 'Shame on the man who scorns his cradle and forgets his mother!' (see CEN:28 July 1950; note 3). Education had brought men from rural backgrounds to Paris and Deixonne advised them not to forget their origins: these languages were their 'mother tongues'. One member of the *Conseil*, in March 1950, had talked of 'the native tongue' in this context, but another had quickly retorted that 'the native tongue of Frenchmen is French'. The term 'mother tongue', however, was allowed to pass (see CLR:23 March 1950; note 3).

This was not the first time that 'mother tongue' had been used of these languages, but any moral persuasiveness of the metaphor to their advantage had been muted by political conflict. Earlier uses of the image had in any case been confused by Carré, who had based his direct method for French teaching on mother-tongue acquisition, confirming an ideal association of the term with French.[5] Carré's method, often known as the 'maternal method', had, by 1973, been largely discredited, as 'anti-pedagogical' (*AEB* 1973:36). What, however, were the languages of home and of school to be called? In 1975, the Minister of Education, M. Haby, talked flatly of 'the mother tongue, French'.[6] In the meantime, in bills of law, Breton and other languages, which had once been *patois* or, at best, 'local idioms', had become 'local languages' (1949–51, Deixonne law) and, ten years later, 'regional languages',[7] and then (in a Socialist bill of 1974) 'minority languages'.[8] The values ascribed to these languages were changing at all levels, and especially so in the post-war years and after the

1960s. The mother-tongue concern informing article 2 of the 1951 law had officially become, by the end of the 1970s, a recognition by teachers of 'Bretonisms' or regional expressions in French.[9]

Other articles of the 1951 law were similarly caught up in different interpretations and changing educational frameworks, but some definitive change was effected at all levels. Article 3 of the law instituted one hour per week, optional for teachers and pupils, of Breton language (oral and written) and literature in the primary schools, in the context of time already set aside for general 'directed activities' (or *activités dirigées*).[10] Article 4 of the law encouraged teachers to seek information on the 'culture and folklore of their region' for use in the schools. Article 5 instituted 'optional classes and courses' for student-teachers in their final year at the *Ecoles Normales* to study the local language and the 'folklore, literature and popular arts'. Article 6 then dealt with the secondary Colleges (11–15 years) and *Lycées* (to 18) and here, as at the primary level, optional Breton was to be offered in the 'directed activities' slot, although no time-limit was placed on it. In fact, Finistère had already received official authorization for optional Breton at this level in the *Lycées* of Quimper and Brest in 1948 (and Quimper offered it in that year to a few pupils who volunteered; see *Ar Falz* 1949 (October):1; 1949 (December):2). By 1950, this had already been officially extended to all Colleges, *Lycées*, and *Ecoles Normales* (final year), although a total of only twelve establishments were reported to have taken up the possibility.[11] After the law, in 1952, nine *Lycées* were said to be offering some optional Breton at the higher levels (*Ar Falz* 1952 (March–April):17). In general, two hours per week were offered. There was never any question of these classes being anything but optional (as *facultative* or an 'extra', external to the normal syllabus); in the debate on the text itself, it had been stressed that they should not replace any part of the official programme (see CLR: 2 March 1950; note 3).

The Deixonne law also instituted, against some opposition but at the Minister's insistence, an oral examination in Breton, again as an 'optional extra' at the *baccalauréat* level. The status of this examination varied over the years.[12] Candidates for Breton at the *baccalauréat* in Brittany rose over the decade 1965–75 from 150 to 933, and continued to rise, with Breton available for the major series of the *baccalauréat* from 1976 onwards.

Dissent in Finistère

The official entry of Breton into the schools, which the Deixonne law so clearly offered, by no means interested or pleased all teachers in Finistère, even when Breton-speakers themselves. Post-Second World War Breton was not attractive to all. In 1954, a Breton *instituteur* (primary school-teacher) published his dissent, in the name of a local commission of the

National Primary Schoolteachers' Union.[13] He objected that Breton was coming into schools and examinations without teacher consultation, at a time when 'fewer and fewer children are coming into the infants' class knowing no French' (Thomas 1954:31). He reminded readers that it was 'Pétain, Abel Bonnard, Carcopino and Co.' who had first instituted optional Breton in schools and examinations (ibid:30–1). The association of Breton in the schools with the Vichy regime, and with the humiliations of Occupation, was an important social fact for many who, after the war, were keen to recover local and national dignity; not all local Breton Communists agreed with men such as Hervé, the proposer of the 1947 Communist bill which had sought a solution in national recognition for the Breton language in the schools of a new France (see, for one published example of disagreement, Trellu 1954).

The Deixonne law was not a simple replication of the measures of the Vichy regime, but was sufficiently similar to let the ghosts of Vichy walk again. In January 1941, a Prefectoral circular had officially authorized the free use of Breton to teach French, and Carcopino appointed a Commission to write a school 'History of Brittany'. At the beginning of 1942, Carcopino instituted the optional study of regional languages, for up to one and a half hours per week, outside the official school programme. Then in June, his successor, Bonnard, gave financial assistance for these hitherto unpaid classes, and introduced optional Breton in the *Ecoles Normales*. Most teachers and student-teachers either ignored all such measures, or were hostile to them.[14] Hostility to Breton in such a context was also hostility to the Occupation.

With the end of the Occupation, all these measures lapsed.[15] For many, however, Breton retained associations of Occupation and imposition, and it was in terms of an apparent revivification of those earlier times in the 1951 legislation that the Finistère teachers published their dissent. The Second World War had been made an event of the 1950s, with history thus, as ever, constructed and brought alive in the present. More was involved, however, than simple opposition to Breton or to the Breton of the war. These teachers, as upholders of *laïcité*, also opposed private education and this, too, was associated with the Vichy regime.

The Vichy regime had given financial aid to the private schools. This had led to an increase in the number of private schools in Brittany, which was already ahead of the rest of France in this respect (see Halls 1981:62–102). On average, over the four *départements* of Brittany, there was an increase of 8.3 per cent in the proportion of schoolchildren in private establishments from 1939 to 1943.[16] Breton in the schools, an increase in private education, and the Occupation were all easily associated, such that the new proposals for Breton in the schools appeared, to many, as a continuing threat to French, to education, and to *laïcité*.

The Deixonne measures tried to institute a new secular Breton by associating Breton with a continuing French tradition of liberty and equality – from the Revolution to the laws of Ferry to the new post-war ideals. This was not easy, given the intrusions of the war and its associations. Debates both determining and following the 1951 law had continually to stress the dignity, unity, and unthreatened liberty of France in order to conceive of any Breton in the schools at all. It was ultimately in debate about the self-image of France, and in the construction of an apparently unbroken French tradition, that Breton won a place in French schools.

Changing values of Breton

National debate about regional languages has always been politically entangled, and the image or value of Breton has changed according to its changing function in the political and moral debate woven around it. During the twentieth century, especially with the new international context of the post-war years and then new right/left oppositions of the 1960s, Breton has moved from being a broadly right-wing cause to one attracting the sympathies of the political left (and we shall see more of this in Part two).

For the moment, it is worth reflecting briefly on the changing image of Breton in national debate in order to note how, although Breton's political and moral associations have shifted considerably, persuasive continuities have nevertheless been constructed. As far back as 1870, three philologists – the Count of Charency, Henri Gaidoz (the founder of the *Revue Celtique*), and Charles de Gaulle (the great-uncle of the future President) – had circulated a petition from Paris, principally to learned friends, notables, and top-ranking clergy, asking the government for the teaching of 'provincial languages'. This text explicitly presented 'provincial languages' as a means of keeping the peasants on the land and 'at the plough', and as a form of 'intellectual decentralization' which would, said the petitioners, involve using these languages in the schools in order better to teach French and responsible suffrage to the menfolk of Imperial France. The idea was formulated in the context of a fleeting interest, on the part of the Imperial French government of the time, in the possibilities of decentralization, an interest that swiftly disappeared when war broke out with Prussia. The petition remained in the form of manuscript correspondence, soon forgotten even by the few who knew of it. In 1903, however, the text was published (Charency *et al.* 1903), with the help of the clergy, in a new context and with rather different significance. It appeared now as a defence of Breton particularly, at the height of the Republic's anti-clericalism. Breton's association with clericalism and anti-republicanism was regularly given new life and confirmation in texts or requests of this kind, and the dominant republican tradition found little sympathy with it.[17]

A modern and nationally respectable post-war 'Breton' was laboriously constructed, however, and history shaped according to the demands of contemporary argument. Many earlier requests were cited in debates leading up to the Deixonne law, placing the law in a seemingly long tradition of worthy French support of its local languages. Deixonne's supporters were careful, however, to cite only the least clerical and least anti-republican aspects of earlier proposals. In the mixed-party report informing Deixonne's own project, for example (see Vourc'h *et al.* 1948, note 3), the 1903 petition was redated to 1870, and emphasis placed on the philological and literary interests of its authors. Their politics, and the politics of the 1903 publication, were forgotten or ignored.

Communists, perhaps more than others, have had to perform acrobatics in pursuit of political consistency since, for most of them, the priorities of the class struggle have long taken precedence over regional considerations. Other structures have intervened, however, to modify these priorities. In the late 1930s, Communists, both nationally and in Brittany, were generally against Breton because they were against 'reactionary' forces. After the war, however, it was a Communist, M. Hervé, who proposed one of the bills that led to the Deixonne law. Hervé argued that Bretons, and especially Breton Communists, had been active in the Resistance, and the teaching of Breton in the schools of France would be a recognition of Brittany as truly and patriotically French (see Hervé in *Ar Falz* 1947 (December):2–3). Other bills or proposals, including the Deixonne report, pleaded this last aspect, too. The special poignancy of this plea will become clear in Chapter seven.

In post-war national debate, 'Breton' has moved with the changing alignments of party politics. By the 1950s, as we have seen, the left was arguing with itself about regional languages in the schools: Lamousse and Deixonne (see p. 52) were from the same party, now considered part of the history of the modern *Parti Socialiste*. By the early 1960s, the right-wing was tending to argue against Breton (see Madame Ploux above, for example); thereafter, arguments in favour of Breton came more and more from the parties of the left. In 1975, even the Communist Party, keen to keep up with the other opposition parties, proposed a further bill for Breton (and other regional languages) in the schools.[18] Breton in the schools was put forward here as part of a wider project for the 'democratization' of education and of the 'cultural means of expression'; Hervé's bill was cited in this new bill, as if it had been a project of the same order, although the original had spoken of the very different values of the years immediately after 1945. This 1975 bill was the closest the Communists came to citing Breton within a vision of decentralization. The Socialist Party, born in the context of post-1960s politics, has, at the national level, been much more forthright in its espousal of regionalism, decentralization, and Breton.

Facts and figures

With increased discussion of regionalism and decentralization in the 1960s, and with the growing clarity of new left/right political opposition over these issues, came a need to clarify the history of legislation concerning Breton in the schools. By the mid-1960s, ministerial authorities were trying to do just this.[19] More recently, educational authorities such as the regional *Rectorat* (see p. 17) in Rennes have collated the most recent documentation, impelled by increased interest in the subject (of which I was one manifestation) and by further reports and circulars. The changing political value of Breton, and the complexity of previous legislation, gave the task growing urgency. As we have seen, some articles of the Deixonne law effectively allowed things already practised or permitted. Those involved in national debate did not always know what was allowed and what not. The 'macro' level of national debate is (as any macro level inevitably must be) its own 'micro' level. Reports and recommendations have often been formulated not on the basis of what previous documents actually allowed, but on the basis of what was popularly thought to be allowed. After the Deixonne law, faced by further demands for more Breton in the schools, the government itself was often unsure whether further measures required new laws, or simply additional decrees, circulars, regulations, or instructions (cf. note 19).

During the twenty-five years from the Deixonne law to 1976, there were twenty more bills and reports, some of them simple re-tablings, and including at least six explicitly from the Socialists (PS), one from the Communists (PCF), one from a left-wing alliance of Socialists and Radicals (FGDS), one from the Centre (UCDP), and three from the right (UNR). There were also several meetings between local and national levels, plus eleven ministerial or rectoral circulars and decrees. After all this, the situation was as follows. Primary and nursery schools could, with teachers' and parents' consent, teach Breton for a total of one hour per week. The Colleges (11–15 years) could use some of their extra-curricular 'directed activities' time to teach Breton; two hours a week was normal. The *Lycées* (up to 18 years) could do likewise and, since 1971, teachers at this level could claim full overtime payments for any extra work involved. Up to three hours a week of Breton-teaching could be offered. The *Ecoles Normales* (for student-teachers) had similar possibilities, and short in-service training courses for all teachers were beginning. The universities became the responsibility of a separate ministry, but Breton continued there also, counting towards a wider range of degrees. The regime of the state schools also applied, in principle, to those private schools which had opted for a contract with the State. These contracts, which involved at least state payment of staff, had been negotiated principally by the right-wing Debré in 1959; they were further promoted by a right-wing Breton Deputy from Finistère, Guermeur, leading eventually to legislation that bears his name (the *Loi Guermeur* of 1977).

How many pupils, however, have taken up the possibilities offered? Statistics of pupils studying Breton in Brittany have gained significance in recent years, and have been the subject of some debate. It has not been possible to come by any simply 'correct' figures, external to such debates and their associated interests, for the numbers of educational establishments offering Breton in Brittany, or of numbers of pupils actually studying Breton within these. It is an ethnographic commonplace that figures and measurement of any kind are subordinate to the categories and context in which the counting or calculations are done. The fact that any such figures for Breton exist is itself significant. The figures I offer here derive from a variety of oral and written sources, official and unofficial. Numbers have varied according to who provided them, their function, and the context of the discussion they were invoked to serve. Some of the themes which organize the statistical facts include the state/private opposition, an assumed contrast between Upper and Lower Brittany, proof of compliance with new values and fashion, statement of continuity or assiduity of study, and interest in the growth or decline of pupil numbers over time.

Neither diocesan nor state educational authorities had paid much attention, in the past, to the numbers involved in Breton-learning in their own domain. However, since the late 1970s, ostensibly objective statistics have poured out from different sources, and have been progressively centralized, for both private and state schools, in the rectoral and prefectoral offices of Brittany. Scraps of paper bearing casual jottings, in official offices or amateur studies, have been sprucely typed up into respectable estimates, and have come to be generally accepted as statistical fact.

A more vigorous official interest and centralized collation have no doubt swollen the figures in many schools, state and private; teachers thus present a dutiful face to heads of schools, and heads of schools to the higher authorities. I consistently found that estimates for 'Breton classes', from whatever source, were informed by some external interest in Breton – and were often, internally, somewhat hollow categories. A 'class of twenty-one', for example, in a large state College in Rennes, with 660 pupils in all, turned out to be a group of six regular attenders, plus the headmistress and two other interested members of staff. This was by no means untypical, except for the presence of the headmistress herself. She was very keen to promote Breton, and her school was in an area in the south of Rennes where a large number of the families are from Lower Brittany, and the parents, she told me, 'Breton-speaking'. This figure of twenty-one had been established both for higher authorities and for explicit self-definition in the face of a neighbouring *Lycée* of fierce ambition, with whose authorities there were frequent tensions and arguments. The headmistress of the College was from Lower Brittany, or the 'Breton-speaking' area, while the *Censeur* of the *Lycée* (who was in charge of the timetables) was a lady of some means, with a second home in Lower Brittany, and a relation teaching Breton at a university. Since Breton was encouraged in the *Lycée*, the College was not to be outdone.

In another Rennes College, a 'class of at least ten' turned out to be an embarrassed teacher waiting for a single, late pupil; elsewhere I was positively discouraged from visiting classes because there could be no guarantee, the teachers said, that anyone would be present at the 'Breton class' apart from the teacher himself. Such classes nevertheless had a reality, passed on in figures to higher levels. In official statistics, all *Lycée*-level optional classes must have a minimum of ten pupils; such a class is unwillingly reported to be fewer, by *Lycées* or Colleges. It often seemed that I arrived in the *Lycées* and Colleges on the wrong day, for 'last week' or, more often, 'at the beginning of the year' there had been too many pupils for an effective language class. The 'class of twenty-one' that I mentioned, however, was visited in the first term of the school year, and six pupils counted as twenty-one for the entire year in official, tabulated 'fact'. (Similar points could be made, it should be stressed, for certain optional classes in other subjects, but their numbers have never gained the significance or politicization which those for Breton have received.) During my first year of field-work, I visited several secondary-level establishments, public and private, and found that attendance at Breton classes was often irregular, and that the largest consistent group was in a noted private school, where Breton was something of a crusade; otherwise, 'twelve' was a favourite estimate all round. This was perhaps an accurate head-count in cases where the teacher was enthusiastic, the teaching effective, the weather rainy, or examinations far away.

The schools I visited during this time were mostly around Rennes, and there I was told by many teachers that in Finistère, at least, classroom attendance and official figures would tally. In official estimates from both rectoral and diocesan sources, there is certainly a greater proportion of pupils studying Breton in Finistère than there is in the traditionally non-Breton-speaking *département* of Ille-et-Vilaine where Rennes is situated. For example, figures gathered for 1978–9 for the Colleges would give the following proportions:

Percentage of pupils at College level learning Breton

	State schools	Private schools
Ille-et-Vilaine	1.1	0.1
Finistère	2.5	1.5

These proportions do not seem contentious, since it is felt to be only natural that a Breton-speaking area should have more interest in Breton learning. Those learning Breton may well not be from a social milieu in which Breton is actually spoken, but the two can appear, nevertheless, to be associated.

As yet the relative numbers of pupils learning Breton in Ille-et-Vilaine and Finistère have not occasioned much public debate. The state/private relationship, by contrast, is the focus of persistent argument. The state authorities now collaborate with the private schools and diocesan authorities to produce officially agreed statistics. There has been much mutual suspicion and disagreement nevertheless,[20] and Breton has again become something for the two factions to fight about, but this time with each accusing the other of not doing enough.

Evidence of this can be found in Finistère. Finistère has about 31 per cent of the population of the four-*département* region of Brittany.[21] In 1978–9, it had 29.6 per cent of the total school population of the region; 60 per cent of this school population was in state or public schools, with an estimated 2.2 per cent of these learning *some* Breton at least – involving about 2408 pupils aged between 2 and 18 years.[22] In the same year, at the secondary level (Colleges and *Lycées*), 32 per cent of Brittany's state schools were estimated to be offering some Breton. In Finistère alone the proportion was higher, at 42 per cent. In the same year, 43 per cent of Finistère's private secondary schools offered some Breton. It is at the secondary level especially that Breton is taught and has assumed importance and been heavily politicized but these are figures that are generally agreed.

Figures for elementary schools have been of less public interest, and so are either less available or non-existent. My figures suggest that 2.7 per cent of all Finistère's state elementary classes (nursery and primary) offered some form of Breton teaching during 1978–9; no precise comparable figures are available for the private sector. However, one private sector source had estimated during 1977–8 that 7.7 per cent of their Finistère elementary classes were offering some Breton (see *Ero Nevez* (Br. 'New Era'), 1978:2), involving 7.1 per cent of pupils in the private sector at this level. In 1979 other private sector sources gave a much higher estimate, 17.6 per cent, for the same year (1977–8), and stated that the proportion was increasing. These sources were keen to stress that the private elementary schools of Finistère were doing better than the public schools. In 1978–9, the public schools could only muster a figure amounting to just over 1.6 per cent (or 1100 pupils) of their elementary school population. The state sector had produced its own figures in 1979, following enquiries by teachers and inspectors during the school year itself.

During these enquiries, one state inspector for the Brest area wrote to me with the information that, 'alas', only one class in his area was regularly offering some Breton at the elementary level, involving thirty pupils, or only 0.7 per cent of the pupils in his *circonscription*. He was upset that 95 per cent of the teachers in the state elementary schools in the area were 'absolutely not interested'. However, estimates in the private sector were 'too optimistic', he stressed, and he challenged their figure of 7.7 per cent for 1977–8. He was doing so in 1979. It was also in 1979 that private sources boosted this same figure to 17.6 per cent. The year 1979 was an important time for Breton-teaching generally, especially in the upper levels, with much public discussion and media coverage of controversies.

The Cultural Charter and the 'second modern language option'

To find out why 1979 was such an important year for Breton in the schools, we need some more figures. The following are for pupils learning Breton in the state sector for the whole of Brittany[23] and show changes over the period 1977 to 1979–80:

Pupils	Colleges		Lycées	
	nos	% of total	nos	% of total
1977–78	1498	1.6	1603	2.9
1978–79	1695	1.8	1442	2.6
1979–80	992	1.0	1206	2.1

These figures became the 'facts' of debate concerning them, although the figures for 1978–9 onwards did not always tally when produced by different official sources such as the *Rectorat* and the *Préfecture(s)*. In every case, however, I have given the most generous figure, which was also the one generally deemed the most 'realistic' by the end of 1979–80.

At the *Lycée* level, these numbers are taken as an encouraging rise over, for example, a figure of barely 100 students estimated for the year 1951–2. They are also still above an estimated 1184 students for the *Lycées* and 1047 for the Colleges for 1973–4. Available past estimates thus assumed importance, and some have argued that 1978–9 was a good year for Breton at this level. Between the school years 1978–9 and 1979–80, however, the number of pupils taking Breton in the Colleges declined, quite suddenly, by 41.5 per cent. From one year to the next there was a drop of 703 pupils – and an apparent loss of about seven Colleges doing any Breton at all.[24] Amid heated controversy following this drop in the numbers, new figures were produced that narrowed the gap, but even the most generous estimate suggested that at least one-third of College pupils studying Breton in 1978–9 decided not to continue in 1979–80. This was generally agreed to be related to a major intervening event, a 'Cultural Charter', which had given Breton a new status.

In February 1978, a unique 'Cultural Charter' for Brittany was signed by central government and local representatives. This Charter was, I was told, the result of many years of petitioning central authorities for 'recognition of Breton linguistic and cultural specificity'. The final document emerged from numerous local and national debates, and was voted by the Regional Council of Brittany in January 1978.[25] Many aspects of the Charter relating to Breton in the schools confirmed promises already made by the Minister of Education in 1975.[26]

What exactly did this Charter introduce? The text recognized the 'cultural personality of Brittany', with the Breton language as 'one of its fundamental constituents'.[27] A major section dealt with 'The Teaching of Breton Language and Culture', much of it expanding on earlier legislation and circulars. The teaching of 'Breton culture', in French, was to be encouraged. This had already been advocated in the 1951 Deixonne law, for the higher levels at least, although it was linked in that text to 'folklore' (see p. 54). In subsequent circulars this had gained the weightier name of 'regional civilization' and was for all levels. Now 'Breton culture' was to be taught at all levels, but with more 'serious', mainstream status at the secondary level, where it might form part of the normal periods of history, geography, economics, literature, and art (*Charte Culturelle*, *Titre 1*, art. 1). Other articles put emphasis on historical research, and promised an increase in courses for future teachers of Breton (art. 5). At the elementary level, 'Educational Advisers' for Breton were introduced (art. 4), becoming a reality in 1979. At the secondary level, the Colleges, and not just the *Lycées* as previously, were to include Breton teaching-hours in the normal service of the teachers, with full overtime payments where necessary, instead of the smaller payments given to the extra-curricular 'directed activities'. As far as possible, Breton was to be part of the normal time-table and not an after-school or lunch-time 'extra' as under the old regime (art. 2).

The existing oral Breton test would remain as an optional extra at the *baccalauréat*, but a full and separate 'Breton language and culture option' was also to be created, consisting of both written and oral examinations, as for other languages at the *baccalauréat* level (art. 3). This new option was to start at the College level, beginning in the third form (*4ème*) in 1979–80, leading to the first full examination when these students reached the *baccalauréat*. Breton, therefore, had a new status in the Colleges from 1979–80. It was to become a full 'second language option', part of the normal syllabus and not just an 'extra'. The text made it clear that this new option would 'benefit in all respects from the regime of second modern languages' (art. 2). In other words, Breton was to be considered on a par with, for example, English, German, or Spanish (still the most popular languages studied in this way).

French schoolchildren generally select a 'first modern language' (usually

English) at the beginning of their secondary education. In the third form
(the '*4ème*' of the Colleges), they then choose a second 'option' from a list
including Latin, Greek, extra study of their 'first modern language', extra
French, technology, or another modern language not hitherto studied.
Breton was to be added to this list, with the extra advantage of the
possibility of studying it in the two earlier years (*6ème* or first form and
5ème or second form) as a *facultative* option as before, along with aspects
of 'Breton culture'. However, when the new 'second modern language
option' of Breton became a real possibility in 1979–80, only thirteen (or 6.5
per cent) of Brittany's state Colleges opened Breton-option sections, with
a further six (or 14 per cent) of the private Colleges doing so. Only about
0.8 per cent of Brittany's state College students at the *4ème* level chose to
do the option, and it was clear that Breton's new status was itself a major
cause of the sudden decline in interest.

Breton was now to be treated like any other subject, an important point
to which we shall return. The apparent lack of interest in Breton which
followed the Charter was blamed on the educational authorities by the
Breton movement, and the authorities became increasingly defensive. The
movement argued that information concerning the new option was slow to
arrive in the schools and that some Colleges did not even know about it
until after the 1979–80 school year had begun.[28] The authorities denied
this, arguing that they had sent out clear information early in 1979. In
February 1979, at a meeting of the 'Cultural Policy Commission' of the
Breton 'Cultural Council' (itself an innovation of the Charter, and including members from cultural associations of the Breton movement), a
Rectorat representative had claimed, in response to accusatory discussion,
that the Colleges were being informed for the coming year. During 1978–9,
a 'Technical Adviser' for Breton (another of the Charter's innovations)
visited all the Colleges and personally informed them of the possibilities.
This 'Technical Adviser' was a committed enthusiast and a member of an
organization devoted to the promotion of Breton. He probably did his job
well.

Lack of information was not the only or major constraint, therefore.
One College in Rennes had distributed 165 forms to pupils in the *5ème* year
(or the second form) in 1978–9, asking them if they wished to do the new
option for the coming year; fifty-one of these forms were never returned,
and only thirteen trickled back with a qualified 'yes'. When the year 1979–
80 began, only two were ready to do the option. No Breton option section
was opened here, since a minimum of ten students was required. Elsewhere,
sections with less than ten pupils did open, and the authorities gladly
claimed that they were turning a blind eye, informing me that they 'did not
want to be accused of stopping people learning Breton'.

The provision of teachers for the Breton option was also contentious.
Most teachers of Breton teach it along with another subject, often another

language which was their main degree subject. In the context of the new option, amateur outsiders were excluded (as they were in other subjects). The anomaly remained, however, that there was still no degree in Breton, and the Minister of Universities had not been a signatory of the Charter. This meant that if a teacher of English, for example, who also taught Breton, were to leave, then continuity of Breton teaching could not be guaranteed. (Such a problem occurred in one Côtes-du-Nord College a year after the option scheme started.) The *Rectorat* was anxious to point out that a full post of 'Breton teacher', teaching only Breton, would be possible if there were sufficient demand.

Against this, however, some argued that there was not the demand because there was no full post of Breton teacher. The *Rectorat* recommended a grouping of state establishments for this purpose, thereby building up enough hours for a full service (a normal teaching service or post being eighteen to twenty-one hours per week). However, grouping establishments is not always easy, especially in some rural areas of Finistère. Itinerant teachers were asked for, and this remained a possibility under discussion. The Cultural Council of Brittany argued, in February 1979, against another possibility, that of employing *vacataires*, or temporary teachers; they did not want to see Breton leading to job insecurity, without insurance or pension rights. Everyone agreed, therefore, that full-time Breton teachers were desirable. In the meantime, enough pupils had to be found to justify this. At the same meeting of the Cultural Council, one ageing right-wing politician, an ex-teacher from a private school, suggested that perhaps private and state schools in the rural areas could collaborate, with one teacher moving between establishments to teach Breton. Everyone present gasped and then fell into nervous laughter at the thought of openly transgressing the boundaries of *libres/laïques* in this way. For a brief moment, all other debate subsided. 'That will just have to depend on the teachers', said the *Rectorat* representative finally and nervously, before bracing herself for the swiftly renewed onslaught from 'Breton culture'.

Debate continued between the Breton movement and the educational authorities, with a definitional divide between the two becoming more and more marked. Breton enthusiasts sought to defend 'Breton culture' against a world that was, even if promoting it, apparently not part of it. Those who worked to promote Breton in the higher levels of the *Rectorat* had to change hats regularly or resign themselves to exclusion. I saw some well-intentioned officials changing, over a period of a year or more, in the eyes of the Breton enthusiasts, into definitional enemies of 'Breton culture' and, in the face of further onslaught, losing enthusiasm and becoming dismissive of their accusers. When it came to sending out information for the second year of the new Breton option's existence, 1980–1, the authorities sent out several circulars to the schools, almost, it seemed, in a spirit of revenge. At the same time, enthusiasts had flooded the media with accusations and more statistics; there was little chance this time of remaining ignorant of the Breton option. The numbers did go up in the Colleges, to 1471 studying Breton (according to the highest estimate); this was still 13.2 per cent down on the figure for 1978–9, before the new option was introduced. A total of 189 pupils elected to start the Breton 'second modern language option' in the third form (or *4ème* level) in 1980–1, or only just over 0.8 per cent of the possible total at this level; 150 had chosen it the year before.

Work and fun

It may well be that neither lack of information nor lack of full-time Breton teachers were major factors determining pupils' choice or rejection of Breton in its new status.

One headmaster of a College in Rennes explained that only children of a 'certain milieu' chose Breton, and that no child who was already struggling at school would 'risk his career' by using precious time to 'study something as useless as Breton'. Among children and parents, it was generally felt that Breton had been useful only in giving additional points to help children through the *baccalauréat* if other subjects were weak. Now, however, there was a risk of failing the Breton examination (not a consideration under the old purely *facultative* regime) and of jeopardizing the whole *baccalauréat*. Breton examiners I met insisted that no one would fail the *baccalauréat* simply because of a poor Breton paper, but when I relayed this information to a group of College pupils, they shrugged their shoulders and all agreed that 'well, it wouldn't be the same as before, anyway'. I pointed out that they could perhaps do the old optional course still, but this, under the new regime, seemed to some like a poor second; the new value of Breton devalued the old, and at the same time made all Breton classes seem like a new order of activity. Many pupils wished that Breton had stayed solely and clearly in its old status. They all agreed that they had lost enthusiasm, and that they would have carried on doing Breton if it had remained an 'interesting extra' and 'just good fun'; now, however, as one girl put it – 'we'd have to work hard in Breton lessons like everything else'.

The new status of Breton in the schools turned it into 'work', where before it had been 'fun'. Breton was definitely 'not like other subjects'. When I asked pupils if they had never worked hard in Breton, responses were hesitant. 'Yes, in a way', was a common reply, 'but it didn't feel like being at school.' Schooling and Breton evidently do not mix easily, and 'being at school' is, by definition, not 'fun'. However much pupils might enjoy school, a clear and self-conscious statement that 'school is fun' can easily seem like symbolic contradiction. During my discussions with College pupils, one 13-year-old boy dared to protest, in the midst of a group of pupils, by saying 'but I like being at school'. His class-mates jeered.

In retrospect, of course, school can change its value or meaning and seem like the 'fun' years before the demands of working life. In August 1979 I visited an old rural, public, primary school at Tregarvan, in southern Finistère. This school, opened in 1875, was closed in 1974 due to a lack of pupils, and is now a museum. Since 1976, it has been open to the public every summer, and houses a class-room apparently unchanged since at least the 1930s. It thus stands as one modern, symbolic reconstruction of what schooling was like during earlier periods. Whatever used to go on in that school, it is now a showplace for modern contemplation of a long tradition of government efforts to provide schooling in rural Finistère. The museum's visitors' book is full of congratulatory comments; some are from ex-pupils delighted at the 'fond memories' that the school now evokes. There was not a word about the language question from such sources, and nothing in the museum that suggested any linguistic problem in the past, although Tregarvan was a rural Breton-speaking area.

We should not imagine that schooling was only a battle to teach French, or that debates have been about nothing but the language issue. Certainly, the spread of education and the teaching of French have often seemed to be one and the same thing, but the teaching of French has been a battle on several fronts at once. The brief history of French education which I have presented is focused on Brittany, and on Finistère particularly, and concentrates on the position of Breton. In its focus on the minority language question, however, and on Breton in the schools, my history is a statement of modern concerns. I have picked out past discussions that bear on the present, and I have tried at the same time to give some idea of what Breton meant to those involved, in the past, in creating the content and objectives of French education.

One important source whom I have cited for earlier periods, the scholar Louis Ogès, was himself from Lower Brittany and a primary schoolteacher in a rural school in a Breton-speaking area of Finistère; he was also a committed *laïque*. He taught and conducted much of his research in the inter-war years, particularly in the 1930s. I have had to comb through his work to find the details that now appear relevant to the position of Breton in the schools. Ogès is felt to have been a conscientious teacher who took careful account of the fact that his pupils were from peasant and fishing families, introducing relevant topics into his teaching.[29] The language question was not a great problem or a significant preoccupation. Ogès' only known treatment of the issue was in an article written in 1919, in the particular circumstances after the First World War (of which more in Chapter seven). The need for French was particularly apparent at this time, and the place of Breton in elementary schools, he argued, was only to help children learn French, and to help get rid of 'Bretonisms' (Ogès 1919).

Ogès produced at least nine solidly researched articles on the history of schooling in Finistère, and these show a much greater concern with the spread of education than with Breton. As both teacher and researcher, he was concerned with the rivalry between clergy and *instituteurs* and with the struggles of Bretons to get any regular education at all.

The Tregarvan school-museum has drawn heavily on Ogès' work; archival research has made up the rest. The Archives of Finistère, at Quimper, have recently started a special, and growing, file on Breton in the schools. The contours of history are thus being redrawn according to modern interests, and the Archive staff are now well used to people seeking information about the language issue. I have made frequent reference to their resources. Inevitably, there is some collapse of past preoccupations into those of the present.

In the turmoil of modern debate about Breton in the schools, and the heated discussions following the Charter and 'second language option', it is perhaps not surprising that a new comment should have appeared in the late summer of 1979 in the visitors' book of the Tregarvan museum. A confident script in French accused the museum administration (made up, in part, of state educational authorities) of one important omission: they had not given details, it said, of the situation of Breton in the schools in the past, and of the 'terrible punishments' inflicted on children, especially 'the *symbole*'. When I returned to the museum a year later, the authorities had made their reply.

Pinned to one wall was a full photocopy of Carré's 'method', including his remarks on the '*symbole*' (see Chapter three above). Next to this was a recent manuscript letter from a local Breton, a *Lycée* teacher whose father had been a Breton-speaker and an *instituteur* in rural Finistère before and just after the First World War. The letter tries to situate the father's work, when he had occasionally reprimanded children who used Breton at school; the son calls his father an 'old revolutionary' and explains:

> Economically and socially, the French language, spoken or read, was liberating. ... The Church of the time, profoundly reactionary, saw a fundamental virtue in the resignation of the people, and fiercely defended Breton against French. Why?
>
> In one Finistère commune, certain country squires reprimanded their tenants for using French to their children. Why?
>
> And in opposition to this, there were the *instituteurs*, almost all of them progressive, and devoted body and soul to the emancipation of the people, and extolling French. Why?
>
> And then there were the poor ... who wanted French taught to their children, always and above all French. Why?[30]

Such questions, posed in the 1980s, do not necessarily bear their own answers. It does not seem to have occurred to the young commentator who wrote, with comfortable outrage, of 'terrible punishments' and of the '*symbole*' to pose the problem in this way. As the son of the 'old revolutionary' continued:

> Such questions sound a tune rarely heard nowadays. He who sounds it braves the critics for the sole purpose of re-situating certain facts in their time.

Part two

The Breton movement: a 'Breton' world

Chapter five

The Breton movement

The manuscript letter in the Tregarvan exhibition, cited at the end of Chapter four, argues that French education in Brittany was inspired by a vision of popular emancipation. The writer of this letter, however, clearly expected little sympathy for his views, and he would get little from what is generally known as 'the Breton movement'.

In this chapter, I try to give some idea of the nature of this movement, its size and shape, and its major organizations and preoccupations. The movement is not a mass movement, but the power and influence of any group have no imperative relationship with size. The movement's members are often skilled in the use of the media, and thereby exert an influence beyond their numerical strength. They also have, as we shall see, some powerfully persuasive arguments in which many modern metaphors of educated, moral right are stacked on their side.

The movement

First of all, who and what are we talking about? There is not, it should be emphasized, any one organization that is 'the movement'. The term is sometimes used to describe a wide range of cultural, linguistic, economic, and political activities in Brittany and applied to an ever-changing array of societies or groups, united only by a common commitment to some aspect of Breton language, culture, or politics. As a *self-ascription*, however, it tends to be limited to those fighting for a specifically 'Breton' world in which the Breton language figures prominently. The terms which this self-defining 'movement' uses to describe itself are of interest. In French, *le mouvement breton* might be used to outsiders and by other people; within the movement, however, the Breton word *emsav* is used, and has stronger connotations. *Emsav*, a literary neologism, has connections with the French *se lever* (or the Breton translation, *em sevel*). Modern Breton/French dictionaries translate *emsav* as *soulèvement* ('uprising'), *révolte*, or simply *mouvement*. The word *emsav* is little known or recognized outside the movement, and its political semantics are perhaps more significant in

French than in Breton. I will speak here of the 'movement' and refer to its members, as they do themselves, as 'militants' (*les militants*, Fr; *an emsaverien* or *ar stourmerien*, Br.). For some militants, the term 'activist' (like *activiste* and *activisme*) has pejorative connotations, suggesting, for example, mindless bomb-throwing.

Most of my field research on the movement has been carried out among Breton language enthusiasts who see themselves as 'militants' involved in a 'struggle' to 'defend' and save Breton. There are others not directly involved in language militancy who might also consider themselves to be part of a 'Breton movement', and there is some tension between broadly 'political' and broadly 'cultural' definitions of the cause, as also between those who actually speak Breton and those who do not. However, it is primarily the language issue which has the capacity to unite the movement, and groups of folk-musicians and folk-dancers have been known to make strong political statements in defence of Breton, and thereby maintain some credibility in the eyes of committed *emsaverien*.

A 'militant' defence of Breton clearly has political connotations, although the great majority of groups in the movement are not established as political parties. Most are clubs, societies, or cultural 'associations' established according to legislation dating from 1901 (for some details of the legislation, see *Ministère de l'Intérieur* 1979). Just how many groups there are in the movement is difficult to say, and its exact size and shape are elusive and changeable. The Breton/French language difference lies at the heart of a very general system of oppositions through which militants define a 'Breton' world in contradistinction to things 'French'. The definition of the 'Breton' movement itself, therefore, shifts and changes according to who or what might be deemed 'French'.

In 1977, an American researcher, William Beer, tried to count the groups in the Breton movement, and found thirty-four clearly named groups, forty-four relatively vague groupings, and a further sixteen that seemed to have been formed between his research and going to press (Beer 1977:147–8). Groups can form and disappear in a matter of weeks, and an organization calling itself a 'federation' of other groups may turn out to be one or two devoted individuals producing cyclostyled sheets of information in defence of Breton (in French and English) and sending them round the world, claiming the recipients as a following of thousands. At least three of the thirty-four groups that Beer managed to name are federations containing several groups; at least ten of the thirty-four no longer exist, or have split up and regrouped; two of the names he cites are different names for the same (now defunct) group; and some are discrete groups within federations of which he also gives the name. Others are either unrecognizable or unknown in the mainstream of the modern movement, and some may well have existed only on paper.[1] I do not make these points in order to suggest that Beer's work is 'wrong', but only to show how complicated the picture is. Beer seems to have consulted, by questionnaire, a wide range of enthusiasts in Brittany, including folk-singers, poets, folklorists, periodical writers, and novelists, as well as those with more avowedly political ambitions. The movement is acutely aware of the power of the media, and replies to any questionnaire are likely to reflect this. Breton periodicals can be counted as distinct groups (as in Beer's listing), even if the same few individuals are involved in several publications at once. Subscribers to the journals, however far away, can also be listed as members of the movement, and huge sum totals then produced.

The movement is not, therefore, a 'countable' phenomenon in the conventional sense. Here, as so often in social anthropology, the empirical problem is one not of enumeration but of definition and self-definition. Such definition depends, moreover, on the context within which it is carried out, and certain events in particular have changed that context in recent years. One such event was 'May 1968', the effects of which will be considered later in this chapter. Another, ten years later, was the Cultural Charter (p. 62), which provided some funding for the movement's activities (for details, see Decaux 1979). This Charter, according to militant lore, had its origin in an election visit made to Brittany by Giscard d'Estaing in 1977: Giscard asked for some musical entertainment to greet his arrival; a group of Breton musicians relayed the request to their larger and more militant federation; music was then offered, in return for the Cultural Charter. A figure such as Giscard was capable – in the past or in its narration – of uniting the whole of the movement in opposition, and stories such as this are told as evidence of the movement's unity and solidarity.

Through the Cultural Charter, combined state and departmental funding was offered which would potentially cover nearly half the total estimated expenditure of Breton cultural associations. Estimates of necessary expenditure shot up in consequence. It was the self-consciously 'militant' members of the self-defining 'movement' who negotiated the Charter, and they were the first, but not the only, people to claim funds. Less than half of the fifty or so groups receiving money in the first round had direct connections with the movement, as defined by the militants. Some militants expressed regret and disgust that archaeological digs and church restoration, for example, should benefit under the Charter. Meanwhile, museums, exhibitions, ballet and drama groups, musical, literary, and cinematographic interests began to file their claims. The Cultural Council of Brittany had difficulty defining what was, and what was not, 'Breton culture'. When finance was distributed for the second time, about eighty groups shared the funds, only a third of which had recognizable connections with the established movement. Some groups were rejected because, to the embarrassment of at least one of the movement's own representatives in the Council, they had obviously sprung up in recent months at the hint of finance.

An important point here is just how difficult it can be for militants to limit 'Breton culture' and to define their cause without external opposition. The figure of Giscard d'Estaing had created, in a sense, a unified 'movement'; both unity and definition then disappeared.

A history of oppression

The movement is united, at least in public avowal, in struggle over the language issue. For this reason, the schools and educational authorities always figure prominently in the histories of Breton that are written and lived by the movement. Militants regard French educational policy since the eighteenth century as a continuous 'cultural genocide'. One influential militant manual, to which the neophyte militant is regularly referred, has a title which translates as 'The Breton Language in the Face of its Oppressors' (Gwegen 1975). The 'oppressors' are primarily all those who have thought out and directed French education. Gwegen's book contains much excited citation of past educational policies, with the ironic epitaph 'may Barrère [sic], Abbé Grégoire, and Jules Ferry rest in peace!' (Gwegen 1975:41). Other figures, such as Carré, Dosimont, Poitrineau, and de Monzie, are also scorned. Such histories, cataloguing denigrations of Breton by French authorities, are common in militant literature.[2] Two hundred years of French educational policy are collapsed into a single oppression of Breton, and all its leading figures, long dead as they are, are cited as if they were speaking today.

A favourite subject in modern militant literature is the *symbole* (which I mentioned in Chapter three). The cover of Gwegen's book shows an imaginative sketch of a glum child with a clog (the *symbole*) slung around his neck, and three pages are devoted to the subject (Gwegen 1975:38–40). Such accounts of 'that infamous badge of oppression' (*CNB* 1981a:8) are common. In the 1970s, it was discovered, to militant excitement, that the *symbole* had still been in use in two or three schools, public and private, in Lower Brittany, in the late 1950s and early 1960s.[3] The *symbole* is usually assumed to have been a government-instigated measure. The modern movement has little to do with the Church, and, although the French government is ultimately blamed, militants do not scruple to accuse the church schools of 'collaborating' with it.

In the early 1980s, the education authorities of Finistère organized courses for teachers and interested parties to discuss the position of Breton in the schools of the Third Republic. The authorities seemed to have two hundred years of unmitigated genocide to live down. Our attention was eventually drawn in one class to Carré's prohibition of the *symbole* (BN 1890; Carré 1888; cf. Chapter three). A young militant present immediately reached for his bag and, pulling from it a text giving a standard, militant history of Breton, began to recite the familiar catalogue of oppression.

Confidence was further regained when we turned to the texts of the Ferry and Goblet laws, with their articles 14 and 13 (which I mentioned in Chapters two and three, see pp. 40 and 49). 'There we are', exclaimed another militant, with apparent relief, 'Breton was definitely excluded!' Amid mutual congratulation, the mantle of oppression was resumed.

In militant historiography, the realities and the progressive ideas of the past are forgotten or traduced in the preoccupations of the present. Even the bilingual project of 1831 can figure in the modern inventory of oppression. Indeed, this project, like the *symbole*, is a favourite subject in militant literature. The rejection of the project is attributed primarily to the Prefect of Finistère, and the ideas of the local Quimper Committee (see Chapter three, p. 45) are attributed not only to the Prefect but also to Montalivet (the Minister of Public Instruction). It is the former, for example, who is said to have urged that Breton should be 'corrupted' to stop Breton-speakers understanding one another.[4] Sometimes Montalivet himself is quoted as having said that he wanted to 'destroy' Breton, although his ambition was wholly contrary (see, for example, Olivier *et al.* 1978:35). Such misreadings are not due to wilful intellectual dishonesty. Militant texts simply copy one another in their citations and look no further. For the movement, the Breton/French divide is an opposition that runs through all their readings of history. The facts are constructed from premises and preoccupations organized around a Breton/French opposition in which language difference is given morally and politically compelling dress. This opposition, to which complex events and histories are reduced and from which they take their meaning, is read back into the past, becoming a structure for its interpretation. Histories written independently of this opposition easily appear messy, complicated, fail to interest or convince, or they may be read through those very same structures and placed in the opposing camp. The movement requires external opposition against which to define itself, and that opposition is sought wherever it is to be found, in the past or in the present. The result is a picture of unrelenting historical foul play.

Groups in the movement

The movement is diverse but with some overlap in the membership of its groups. There are numerous clubs and societies enjoying 'Celtic' dance and music (especially the many *Cercles celtiques* with a collective membership of thousands), and others principally concerned with the collection of 'folklore'. Societies with militant language interests are more prominent in the self-definition of the movement and range from Breton theatre groups to language-teaching organizations. I leave aside, for the moment, any discussion of *Diwan*, perhaps the most important such group in the movement, and which is treated in Part three.

The journal *Al Liamm* ('The Link'), which has appeared regularly since 1946, is the best-known and most learned Breton-language periodical (although Beer's list omits it, surprisingly: see note 1). As a publishing house, *Al Liamm* produces a literature of hard-line linguistic militancy. At the beginning of the 1980s, the journal claimed about 1200 subscribers, and its editor reflected that it was the events of 1968 which had boosted its following so that 'in a short space of time' the journal had 'gained more subscribers than in all the fifteen years before'. There had, he felt, been 'a political phenomenon, a certain liberation' (see *PB* 1980:6). The many militants who have since struggled through the journal, with the aid of their dictionaries, are evidence of how strong a commitment can be commanded by Breton, through its definitional status as 'liberation'.

Another important organization is *Ar Falz* ('The Sickle'), which produces an eponymous bilingual journal and other educational periodicals. Beer (1977:148) records the founding date of *Ar Falz* as 1945; although *Ar Falz* was in fact first founded in 1933 and gained a small following in the post-war period, its modern form might more accurately be said to date from post-1968. By 1980, it claimed about 300 members, although only 180 of these seemed to be paid up, with voting rights, and only just over half of them attended its annual General Assembly. It was pointed out to me, rather wistfully, that things were much better in the early 1970s.

Ar Falz campaigns for a greater place for Breton in state schools, and although most branches of the movement also do this, it is *Ar Falz* that produces many of the necessary, practical teaching materials. Under the name of *Skol Vreiz(h)* ('Breton School'), members have also written histories of Brittany for use in schools.

Skol an Emsav is a very well-known group in the movement, founded in 1969. It is, as its name ('School of the *Emsav*') suggests, primarily concerned to recruit and train language militants, to which end it organizes a variety of courses and publicity campaigns. Members are very conscious that *Skol an Emsav* owes its birth to the events of 1968 and that membership has fallen in more recent times. By the beginning of the 1980s, it had only about fifty paid-up members, but its militant following and its influence in the movement have been greater than this figure would suggest. Those prominent in *Skol an Emsav* keep a close watch on other activities of the movement and are felt to make shrewd use of the media, calling their own press conferences and producing their own 'press book' of newspaper cuttings.

The movement also includes card-carrying politics, principally in the form of the political party known as the *Union Démocratique Bretonne* (or the 'Breton Democratic Union'), founded in 1964. The party also has a Breton name, translated from the French: *Unvaniezh Demokratel Breizh*. It is generally known as the 'UDB'. This is the only serious 'autonomist' party in Brittany, although it has affinities with the nationally organized

PSU (*Parti Socialiste Unifié*), with which it ran a joint campaign in the 1981 elections. The autonomy that the UDB seeks wavers between regional autonomy and separatist nationalism, in either of which the Breton language is a means of awakening the 'Breton people' into self-conscious definition. They will then become a 'nation', and, ultimately, a 'state'. It was in terms of these three stages that the party's strategy was commonly presented to me by UDB members. The party's internal journal is called *An Emsaver* ('The Militant'), although it is largely in French; political commentary and the party line are also published in *Le Peuple Breton* ('The Breton People') and its Breton-language sister edition, *Pobl Vreizh*. The UDB, like other groups, saw its membership increase greatly after 1968, and then fall. Membership rose again in the 1970s, however, and from 1975 to 1980 the UDB claimed to have anything between 500 and 1000 militants. It has not so far gained great electoral support, and militants have regarded 3 per cent of the vote in any 'constituency' as a great success.[5]

The UDB is always anxious to distinguish itself from the much better-known 'FLB' (the *Front de Libération de la Bretagne*, or 'Breton Liberation Front'). If the reader finds these abbreviations confusing, it might be of some comfort that FLB and UDB are also regularly confused by the Breton public at large. The UDB finds little joy in this, however, for the FLB is an openly 'terrorist' organization (albeit a necessarily shifting and nebulous one), outlawed since 1974. The FLB seems to have been created out of the fusion of at least four groups who discovered each other by accident when they learnt of bombings that their own group had not carried out. There have been further internal divisions, but the generic title remains (see Berger 1977:170; J. and M. Dayries 1978:95; O'Callaghan 1983:89–96). The FLB has carried out sporadic bombing attacks on government offices and buildings since 1966 (with a notable increase after 1968). Heavy prison sentences were meted out for some of the more recent bombing attacks, and these sentences, taken as solid evidence of 'oppression', served to unite even parts of the movement normally unsympathetic to its activities. The FLB, although criticized for its politico-economic naïvety (or *activisme*) and for the bad publicity it brings, nevertheless brings a certain glamour to the movement's image of itself, and most of the movement has pleaded on the FLB's behalf in court hearings. Only the UDB has stayed aloof. While condemning the FLB for the sake of party distinction and credibility, however, some UDB members have been happy to cite the FLB's activities as evidence of a shared and threatening opposition to central government (e.g., Morvannou 1980:10–11).

The UDB is currently the most active group in bringing an 'economic' aspect into the Breton militant cause. Other post-war organizations have worked towards economic improvement in Brittany but these did not, as is the modern fashion, always tie their economic analyses to questions of linguistic and cultural specificity. As a result, their position remains ambiguous in the movement's history of itself.

Perhaps the most important such group was the pioneering regional pressure group known as the 'CELIB' (or *Comité d'Etudes et de Liaison des Intérêts Bretons*). This group, formed at the beginning of the 1950s and uniting left and right, was composed of Breton notables, politicians, and union and commercial representatives. It aimed to produce a plan for the development of Brittany's industrial and transport infrastructure[6] and became a model for similar regional groups elsewhere in France. Its influence was great in the 1950s and early 1960s; by 1954 it had official government recognition, and ten years later it was co-opted into a Regional Economic Development Committee. From the mid-1960s, its influence declined. Not only was it no longer a body distinct from official committees, but its own internal divisions of right and left became more marked, and other more militantly 'Breton' groups began to eclipse it. Some subsequent histories of the Breton movement have dismissed the CELIB as part of the 'French system' or as an aberration that can be 'left aside' (see, for example, Olier 1972:45–6).

Nevertheless, the CELIB promoted a 'regional' consciousness that was credible at both local and national levels, and in this succeeded where most groups of the movement had failed (cf. Berger 1975:*postface*, 1977). By the end of the 1960s, agricultural unions, inspired by the CELIB, were (in Finistère at least) beginning to see their problems in the context of an overall under-industrialization of the region, rather than in a national but exclusively agricultural context. By the early 1970s, some CELIB members were working for the development of Brittany through local sections of the Socialist Party.

A predominantly right-wing group called the *Mouvement pour l'Organisation de la Bretagne* (MOB) had been formed in 1957 in imitation of the CELIB, largely to supply political and cultural elements the CELIB was felt to lack. This group, unlike the CELIB, entertained ideas of political autonomy and cultural nationalism and sought to be a united 'Breton' front, wanting no part in 'French politics' (see Fouere 1977; Olier 1972; R. Roudaut 1973). The MOB broke up in the late 1960s, giving rise to a myriad of new groupings, most of them now defunct; some of its members are now in other groups already described. A few went on to establish an increasingly nationalist Breton party, called *Strollad ar Vro* (or 'Party of the Country'), along with various other self-consciously 'dissident' groups, some of them now reduced to daubing anti-French graffiti on walls and bridges. Others, more left-wing if not always less nationalistic, had formed the UDB.

The movement and the left

It is part of the radical lore of the UDB that it was formed by a split in the MOB over the question of French involvement in Algeria. Future UDB members sought to vote a motion condemning the French government's involvement, but the motion was not passed, on the 'no French politics' principle. The defeated proponents broke away to form the UDB, and were already sharing a platform with the French left by 1965. This meeting of the Breton movement and left-wing political causes merits consideration here, for the modern Breton movement, at least in its dominant self-image, is almost entirely left-wing. The modern movement has taken much of its definition and vigour from opposition to the political majority of France in the Fifth Republic, which, until 1981, had been fairly unambiguously right-wing (*pace* Giscard d'Estaing's claim to the centre). There is now, in consequence, a well-established symbolic collusion of the political left and the cause of Breton language and culture. As we have seen in Part one, however, this is by no means historically self-evident, and is not without its modern contradictions.

The modern Breton movement has been active in producing, and structuring, histories of itself as a unitary entity. For its origins, the movement defines the relevance of nineteenth-century history, and tells us where to look in that crowded century for events now judged pertinent to, even homologous with, the modern cause. Those nineteenth-century figures now looked back to as founders of the movement were largely, in their own time, Catholic and legitimist (and, through their works, it has been possible to read Breton nationalism right back into the Dark Ages, of which more in Chapter six). Similarly, those who co-ordinated *an emsav* in the inter-war years of this century occupied, in their own time, the political right-wing. Since the late 1960s and especially the 1970s, some historians of the movement have tried to find and add, in a reconstruction of the movement's past born of different preoccupations, some left-wing sympathies and sympathisers to their pantheon, however transient or marginal these may have been.[7]

The modern association of the left and regional causes dates from the 1960s,[8] and particularly from the events of 1968. 'May '68' stands as a metaphor of origin for many radical trends in France, and we can discuss the modern movement using '68 as an historical pivot, for it brought together a range of linguistic, political, and educational issues. In the 1920s and early 1930s, Communist internationalism had briefly drawn attention to internal 'autonomist' causes in France, eliding them with a wider struggle against 'imperialism'. For the most part, however, left-wing studies of imperialism and colonialism restricted their attention to overseas territories, and did not include internal French regions in the analysis. Internally, class analysis prevailed as the dominant discourse, with regionalist and autonomist sentiments a reactionary sideshow in the larger class struggle. In the 1960s, however, interest was growing in regional affairs, and workers' strikes were also claiming attention. In 1968, class, colony, and regional minority all became implicated, in radical sociology, in a common debate; the struggles of colony against metropole, of periphery against centre, of proletariat against bourgeoisie, and of peasant against the urban, educated élite, all became as one with that of the region against the machinery of the centralized State. By the early 1970s, a well-known Parisian radical journal, *Les Temps Modernes*, was talking of the common cause of the lower classes, regional minorities, and all colonial victims of imperialism (see Person 1973a). Discussion of the cause of regional languages and cultures became couched in the rhetoric of the left. The peasants and the proletariat of Brittany were seen to be the speakers of its language and the carriers of its culture; they were also the 'base' of the Marxian economic edifice, on which all else stood or fell. The politics and the economics of the left thus joined up with regional 'culture' in a full epistemology of opposition. Political parties of the left discovered regionalist causes, and upholders of regional languages discovered the politics of the left and took on a socialistic definition of their cause. In Brittany, a sociological journal called *Pluriel* was launched for nation-wide consumption, offering studies of the Bretons, and all the other 'ethnicities', 'minorities', and 'colonies', internal and external, that might be found to share the platform.

Many of those now active in the Breton movement were students in May 1968. They are part of that generation often referred to in France as *'les soixanthuitards'* ('the sixty-eighters'). Some were behind the street barricades or in the sit-ins in the universities of Brittany or Paris, and others were in the *groupuscules* of the *Lycées*. In general terms, May 1968 was a protest against 'the system', or so it lives on in ageing but still youthful historical memory. Student protests and workers' strikes were coincident in May 1968, and are remembered by some as a single protest against dominant bourgeois rationality. The schools and the universities, in particular, came under attack from teachers, pupils, and students: they were cut off from the realities of local life, too centralized, selective, and class-orientated, dispensing 'bourgeois culture' and capitalist rationality. An easy coherence was found between a hierarchy of knowledge or culture and the class structure, and many sought the bottom layer of these hierarchies in the regions, among those speaking regional languages. Regional cultures and languages were called out against the schools, against the 'system'. For the Breton movement, the events of May had already become a 'Breton' cause in these terms by October 1968 (see Broudig 1968), and every peasant protest or industrial unrest was then appropriated by the movement to its cause: the 'system' was French and bourgeois, and Breton a radical alternative. When Beer published his research article in 1977, he stated that, of an estimated ninety-four groups in the Breton movement, only eighteen were founded before 1968 (Beer 1977:147). We have already seen that many of the groups in the movement boosted their memberships after 1968 and through the early 1970s. All in all, '1968' was a good year for Breton.

In a Republic which has, since its inception, made the French nation and the French language synonymous, the cause of a regional language such as Breton offers a ready stick with which to beat the government. The national parties of the left no doubt saw, in the causes of decentralization and of regional languages and cultures, the possibilities of an alternative power-base and a new constituency (although these causes were not, as it turned out, the great vote-winners they were expected to be: see Safran 1984). The PSU (*Parti Socialiste Unifié*), the only party to support the students in '68, also supplied movements such as the Breton movement with some important themes and slogans (e.g., *autogestion* or 'self-management', formulated originally for the factory). The PSU has, in some ways, acted more as a pressure group than as a political party, and some of its ideas were also taken up fairly rapidly by the PS (*Parti Socialiste*), with a number of PSU members physically moving over to the new Socialist Party, formed in 1971. When the Socialist President, François Mitterrand, came to power in 1981, he took for himself the heritage of the Revolution and of the old left of the Third Republic, but then showed how far the political left had moved since. 'France needed a centralized power to come into being', he asserted, 'and she needs a de-centralized power to avoid falling apart' (cited in Smyth 1981).[9]

The relationship between the movement and the left must inevitably be affected by the clear Socialist victory in the elections of 1981 after more than two decades of right-wing rule, and by the less clear victory of 1988. While the left's accession to power presented the left-wing movement with definitional, and therefore practical, problems (to which we shall return), there has not, for the core of the Breton movement, been any simple coalescence of identity. Most of the young people in the movement voted for Mitterrand's party in the 1981 elections (in the second round, at least) but, as militants often told me, this was no unqualified vote for the 'PS' (as the *Parti Socialiste* is usually known). Few members of the movement belonged to the PS, and known members were commonly teased for belonging to a 'French' party. At a gathering of Breton militants a year before the critical elections of 1981 it was stressed that 'you can't trust the PS' because they were 'French'. A small group of PS members who came along, party literature at the ready, were virtually ignored. Not long after the election results were known, however, a *Skol an Emsav* member addressed a rally of the movement and emphasized, with some pride and jubilance, that the movement had 'helped to put the Socialists in power'. They were left-wing allies. Certainly the PS and the movement had shared for the elections a common opposition to the majority right. In a sense, however, the opposition of the PS to the government was because it was right-wing; the opposition of the movement to the government was because it was the government and 'French'. The PS then became the government in its turn, an ambiguous and dubious ally.

Economic realism

With the coming together of the left and the Breton movement, the 'economic', as the 'determinant' of left-wing theory, firmly entered the regionalist debate. The economic is now an important part of every 'real' analysis, as every educated Frenchman knows. When I left Brittany to come home to write, one militant said farewell with the reminder 'and don't forget the economic aspect!' Ethnographically, the economic intrudes as part of the theory that people have of themselves, and it is as such that we can consider it here.

France shares in the European tradition of thought that opposes the 'economic' to 'culture' as mutually exclusive and mutually defining entities. This is a mode of thought common to a broad political spectrum, from left to right. Given this opposition, it is clear that the cause of, say, local culture or language would not have seemed self-evidently linked to economic issues. In the immediate post-war years, maps drawn up by architects of France's post-war industrial boom were indifferent to the boundaries drawn up by philologists or folklore and regional culture enthusiasts. This was not simply because post-Vichy France was keen to rid itself of all traces of war-time provinces. For the economic planner, Brittany was not recognized as distinct, but was incorporated into a large region called the West, whose problems it was implicitly made to share (see *Les Cahiers Français*, 1973, 158–9:6–7). Other maps of economic contours continued to ignore Brittany's specific claims.

Now, however, the assumption of oppression, informed by a left-wing interpretation of economic problems, has become important in large sections of the movement. The UDB, in particular, prides itself on its 'realism' in this respect. Keen to demonstrate that Brittany is economically oppressed, exploited, and underdeveloped by the French capitalist system, the UDB has appropriated the Algerian image, and views Brittany as a 'colony' of France. A UDB pamphlet entitled 'Brittany=Colony' (*Bretagne= Colonie*) lists the disadvantages imposed on Brittany by a colonizing France. These include under-industrialization, agricultural problems (with Brittany peripheral to the developed regions of France and the EEC), rural exodus, demographic imbalance, alcoholism, and military installations (UDB 1972: esp. 5–7). Other regions of France share these problems, it is recognized, but, taking into account 'linguistic oppression' also, 'it is only in Brittany', we are told, that aspects of each exist (UDB 1972:7).

Not only May '68 and the realignment of the left, but also the successful Algerian war of independence, and decolonization more generally (cf. p. 11 above), were important in the construction and development of modern minority nationalisms within France. Throughout the nineteenth century, France's experience of colonization overseas had provided some comparisons for certain areas of metropolitan France: carrying French and 'civilization', development and schooling, to certain uncivilized, 'wild' parts of *la France obscure* easily found expression in the metaphors of colonization.[10] From certain French provinces, including Brittany, requests and recommendations for help sometimes came back in the same form: why send *colons* elsewhere to cultivate the land when help is needed here? Give us new agricultural techniques and railways, and speculate here with your capital, as in the colonies (see Bouët and Perrin (1844) 1970:267; Weber 1977:487, 489). In a post-imperial, well-educated milieu, and with the benefit of hindsight, it is easy now to read the modern damnable associations of 'colonialism' back into the rhetoric of an earlier time, and forward again to make a recognizable and effective discourse of the oppressed: the modern Breton movement collects, and cites in its modern history, all the past comments made by 'French' authorities in which Brittany is likened in some way to a colony.[11] Relocated in this way, from one era and discourse to another, figures of the past who may have held concerns as well-meaning as those of the modern movement are credited instead with malicious denigration and a wilful maintenance of economic differentials.

In equating Brittany and Algeria, the UDB finds in Brittany a peripheral, agricultural, underdeveloped region, providing a reservoir of raw materials and cheap labour for the more prosperous and industrialized areas, especially Paris. Such industrialized areas are not, however, since the recession of the mid-1970s, without their own problems, which the UDB has appropriated. Brittany suffered like an underdeveloped colony, but also like an ageing industrial giant. In 1979, the problem of unemployment in industrial Lorraine was gathering attention and media-conscious UDB militants began calling Brittany 'Lorraine', with the covers of their journals announcing in large letters, as an advertisement to Brittany, 'Welcome to Lorraine'. A reader from Lorraine was moved to write in to protest at so shameless a misappropriation of the sufferings of others, and the UDB editorial staff duly apologized (see *PB* 1979 (August and September); *PV* 1979, 114).

I do not wish to seem to suggest that Brittany is, or has been, without its economic problems. The indices used sometimes tell us more about the values of those who do the measuring than about the worlds they claim to describe. Different political commitments, moreover, will always be capable of producing wildly diverse analyses from the same mundane statistical realities. Economic argument put forward by the movement contrasts Brittany unfavourably with other parts of France over such issues as capitalization, investment in industrial and transport infrastructure, emigration, subsidy levels, living standards, unemployment, per capita incomes, and so on. Brittany is by no means alone in this, and other areas suffer similar or worse problems.[12] Outside the movement, there are several writers who have sought in Brittany an 'internal colony' of France, and who, through their writings, actively create and contribute to the very phenomenon of ethnicity which they claim to be analysing (e.g., Reece 1979). Given the moral and political persuasiveness already weighting the minority cause, their enthusiasm is perhaps not surprising. More complex, and less common, are studies which examine the requirements of an 'internal colony' thesis and find the model inapplicable to Brittany: no institutionalized or lasting economic deprivation is found in Brittany in the intensified relations between 'core' and 'periphery' resultant on increased modernization and industrialization; on the contrary, disparities have decreased and some quite dramatically so (see, for example, Rogers 1984).

The picture is, as we might expect, an uneven and messy one, and it is not easy to find, or to write, analyses that are independent of the structures of minority enthusiasms. The question of right and wrong in economic terms is, even at its simplest, far too complicated to go into here. It is not, in any case, primarily economic 'realities' with which we are concerned here, but rather the use to which economic argument is put. The 'colony' image is obviously of some moral and political importance. More generally, in the 'economic', the movement has a readily and popularly understood measure of oppression, a metaphor for dissent, and an anchor on reality. In a sense, however, economic arguments are brought in to provide an apparently secure underpinning to a movement whose concerns are, in priority, elsewhere. Although the UDB, for example, concerns itself to a considerable degree with economic matters, there is no doubt that the language difference in Brittany provides a structure around which other issues can crystallize, and through which they can be posed. Without the language, analysis of the other issues might never be made, as witness the many other areas of France that share Brittany's economic problems but do not have the linguistic claim to specificity, and do not have their 'movement'.

Part of the appeal that the left-wing economic argument has for the movement lies in its power to explain many of Brittany's problems by reference to the larger 'system' of centralized France and international capitalism. An autonomous Breton world of full employment and prosperity can then be imagined outside this, in a political fulfilment as appealing as it is imaginary. When we turn to philology in the next chapter, we shall see that the structure of the economic argument is part of a more general tendency, in the thinking of the movement, to construct models of interpretation that locate outside Brittany the source of all Brittany's problems.

Salaries have been, and still are, lower than those of the Paris region,[13] and this is often cited as a measure of the willed underdevelopment of Brittany. At the same time, Paris and its industrial areas are not seen, by members of the movement, as a desirable place to live or as offering conditions that they would be prepared to tolerate. Some militants have commented, after periods visiting or working in the capital, that they would 'have to be paid a lot to stay there'. It is a requirement, however, of the way militant argument is constructed that they deny Parisians a right to higher salaries. The UDB has proudly published a letter from a distant and wistful reader in the capital, and I quote it here, hoping that some of the ambiguities of minority resentment, both moral and economic, will speak for themselves:

> Bravo to your journal, which I sometimes manage to get hold of and read. Personally, I am unfortunate enough to come from the Paris area. I am, however, doing my best to make known to those around me the movements or associations militating for the recognition of regional rights and cultures (this is relatively easy for me as I run an ecology club). . . . Could you let me know of (and send me if possible) some kind of literature (books, photocopies, etc.) so I can teach myself Breton? As I said at the beginning of this letter, I was born and bred in the Paris region and 'suffer', too, from having no regional claim in my ancestry. However, it is not too late – as I am only twenty years of age – to get myself integrated into a specific regional context (I would willingly do this, and friendship will mean a lot in the process). (*PB* 1979, 184:39)

Language and education

So far, we have seen some of the dominant features of the modern movement: it is self-consciously 'militant', predominantly left-wing, and united by an assumption of common oppression, articulated by some through economic arguments and by all as a defence of the language and culture of Brittany. Since the Breton language is of prime importance, learning Breton is an important part of becoming a Breton militant. You may learn Breton dances (in a *Cercle celtique*) or blow up the palace of Versailles (like the FLB) and call yourself part of the Breton movement; you will not always be taken seriously, however, by those who now dominate the movement, if you do not speak, or at least seriously aspire to speak, Breton.

Skol an Emsav tends to be the most hard-line proponent of the Breton language in the movement, and regularly condemns *Ar Falz* and the UDB for their failure to conduct their meetings and produce their literature exclusively in Breton. Many of the militants of *Skol an Emsav* are recruited in the Celtic Department of the University of Rennes, where teachers and students, even if not paid-up members, often espouse the ideas of *Skol an Emsav*. These ideas are sometimes referred to as a 'Rennes' position. Very briefly, this involves an ideal in which the Breton language would do everything: the individual 'Breton-speaker' (*brezhoneger*) would use it in all contexts and for all purposes. In the fullest realization of this ideal, all Bretons would be *brezhonegerien* (Breton-speakers) in the militant sense, using always and only Breton. It is acknowledged that this is a far-off ambition, and the proximate aim is to gain official recognition for Breton, so that *brezhonegerien* will be able to use it where and when they choose, and ideally all the time.

In a bilingual world, the two languages can offer a powerful structural divide. For the Breton movement, with its minority enthusiasms, bilingualism vibrates with the structural and moral values through which the majority and minority worlds are seen to be opposed. In the 'Breton' world of intellectual creation, French is associated with oppression and imposition, and Breton with liberation: it makes obvious moral and political sense, within such logic, to wish to speak Breton in a Breton-speaking Brittany. To realize such a Brittany, however, requires that those who do not know Breton be taught it, and that those who do know Breton be taught to use it all the time. The Breton movement is, in its militant aspect, an educational and linguistic enterprise, dominated by, and largely made up of, educated and sophisticated people. Virtually all the leading members of the movement, now as in the past, have expressly learnt Breton, having been otherwise well-schooled in French, often to university level. William Beer's research, which I have already mentioned, is indicative of this: he found that the overwhelming majority of Breton 'activists' (his term) were in professional, white-collar, or generally 'intellectual' occupations.[14] The Breton movement is, in more ways than one, a product of French education.

The importance of the Breton language in the definition of the Brittany for which the movement militates inevitably derives much of its force from a French tradition, with the French language far more critically involved in the definition of the French people and nation than, say, the English language in the definition of Britain and the British. The moral unity of language, people, and nation is wholly credible in France; by seeking unity within Brittany through the pursuit of Breton linguistic unification, the Breton movement is, in many ways, throwing back at the authorities some important moral and political equations from the French world in which the militants have been educated. From the structures of a wider debate, the French nation-state, its identity, and its resources of persuasion and commitment were forged from the late eighteenth and nineteenth centuries onwards. Now, through French education, the oppositional structures out of which 'Breton culture' has been, is, and can be forged have been learnt. It should be no surprise that the modern regional identity boom, and the greatly increased education and studentification of the population of post-war France, have been coincident.

The Breton militants, with an earthiness at once romantic and left-wing, look to the soil of Brittany and its humble people for the foundation of the world on whose behalf they militate. In many ways, however, their 'Brittany' is a metaphorical reality, anterior to the innocent social and geographical object that is Brittany, and this metaphorical reality, and the image and persuasive values it gives to 'Breton' and 'Brittany', are a product of wider French debates, rather than a natural growth from Breton soil. It is a 'Breton' world created in the nineteenth century and politically re-created, with the greatest metaphorical force, after 1968, that the modern militant now inhabits.

A united front

Some of the ideas, successes, and problems of the world which the modern movement inhabits are exemplified by an organization known, in French, as *Le Front Culturel Progressiste Breton* ('The Breton Cultural Progressive Front'; *Progressiste* here means politically left-wing). Formed early in 1977, on the initiative of *Ar Falz*, the Front brings together several groups, although its meetings have been dominated by representatives from *Ar Falz*, *Skol an Emsav*, and the UDB, three of the most powerful groups in the modern Breton movement. I attended meetings of the Front from mid-1979 to mid-1980, and the remaining sections of this chapter briefly outline some of the preoccupations and internal discussions of the Front during that busy period of Breton militancy. We now enter the ranks of the movement, but in its public relations mode.

United opposition

The Front has special interest for two main reasons. First, it has been an important platform for public statements of the Breton cause, making a self-conscious effort to woo the Breton population at large. Second, it is a body which managed to gain formal adherence from organizations from outside the traditional bounds of the 'movement', or *emsav*.[15] The Front's meetings were attended by representatives from co-opted organizations such as teaching unions, media groups, and the Socialist Party, with such organizations being co-signatories of much of the Front's propaganda. This was the first time that such support had been publicly rallied to the movement's cause. Those co-opted to the Front, however, did not necessarily see, or want to see, themselves as members of 'the Breton movement' and were not always sympathetic to those who did. It was more the case that the Front, as a whole, represented a united opposition to the right-wing then in power nationally, with the cause of

Breton language and culture providing one ready platform for opposition of this kind.

Talbenn and Front

Some of the difficulties facing the Front are implicit in its Breton name: *Talbenn Sevenadurel Araokour Breizh* (or, word-for-word, Front/Cultural/ Progressive/of Brittany). This neologistic title would not be understood by anyone lacking competence in modern, standard, literary Breton. The *Skol an Emsav*, *Ar Falz*, and UDB representatives, who had given the Front its Breton name, possessed this competence and were the only regular attenders of the Front who did so. The *Talbenn* is usually spoken of as *le Front* in its own meetings and in its press releases and tracts, all of which are usually in French. In my brief presentation here, I sometimes distinguish between *le Front* and the *Talbenn*. The French term *le Front* is used to denote individuals in the Front who were not members of established groups of the movement. I use the Breton term *Talbenn*, on the other hand, for those Front members who were members of *an emsav* or who would generally be considered hard-line enthusiasts of the Breton language. It was usually on this axis that internal differences and problems arose. The Front, as *Talbenn* and as *le Front*, could find unity in a left-wing cause, but the Breton/French opposition often threatened to disrupt this unity, intruding and dividing the Front itself.

'Brittany, Socialism, Laicity' ('*Breizh, Sossialism, Laikelezh*')[16] are notions that do not easily go together in the history of the movement. This, however, is the slogan of *Ar Falz*, and one it emphasized in the Front in order to unite Brittany, teaching unions, and the opposition parties. The *Parti Socialiste* was represented in the Front by a former teacher, who had been promoted in the employ of the *Rectorat*, and who also occupied, simultaneously, two positions as elected politician. A very busy man, he only occasionally came to Front meetings. *Talbenn* members lamented this absence and criticized him for pro-Breton stands taken by his Party nationally without consulting their own forum. This PS representative often helped me with my research, and we spoke French together. In the presence of the *Talbenn*, however, living down his 'French' connections, in job and politics, he spoke Breton to me and to other *Talbenn* members.

The *Talbenn* was particularly pleased to have co-opted some union representatives. These included members of a technicians' union from the section of the state television company dealing with Breton (and French) programmes on the regional network (known as FR-3). Breton is little used on radio and television,[17] and these union representatives wanted more hours of Breton, more funds, better working conditions, and more local involvement in programme-planning. For them, support of Breton and local culture was a general protest against control of the media by

Paris. They were as much interested in local control of the French-language media as they were in Breton-language programmes, and not all of them spoke or understood Breton.

A 'real popular culture'

Also adhering to the Front was a small group that withholds the full payment of TV and radio licence fees in protest at the meagre Breton-language content of radio and television. In a meeting of the Front, this group's representative explained in French (he did not speak Breton) that theirs was a fight for 'pluralism' and 'freedom of expression'. He was against the 'mass media' because of both the 'consumerism' and the 'suffocation' of local languages that resulted. His group wanted, he explained, a 'real popular culture' on television and radio. This idea was important in the ambitions and discussions of the Front. It did not mean 'folklore'. *Talbenn* members were anxious, in the presence of union members openly wary of an apolitical 'cultural' stand, to show that they represented advanced sections of the Breton movement. The UDB member declared that folklore enthusiasts were of a 'low intellectual level' and at a 'low level of consciousness'; their activities were 'empty nonsense'. This attack was explicitly directed against 'Celtic circles' who parade in Breton costume and dance for tourists in *fêtes folkloriques*: the 'prostitution of Breton culture', it was said. In many ways, it was a nineteenth-century vogue for 'folklore' that created and sustained Breton culture, as all that rational modernity was not (see Bertho 1980; and Chapter six) but fashions change and new oppositional values are now required.

The *Talbenn* also criticized Hélias, whose immensely popular works (especially *Le Cheval d'Orgueil*, Hélias 1975) militants see as defeatist, apparently content to present a picture of a disappearing past in folkloric tradition (for the best-known such criticism of Hélias in print, see Grall 1977). Hélias has explicitly condemned, through fiction, the language movement (see Hélias 1975:ch. 8), and actively supports 'folkloric' events of the kind that the *Talbenn* despise. He displays no obvious sign of the political commitment which the movement requires in historiography and epistemology. The UDB representative in the Front, who was always to the fore in dismissals of 'folklore', urged that 'people have to be persuaded that Hélias is no good'. This was to be part of the struggle to rid people of their 'alienation'. All in the Front could agree here: there was a 'real popular culture' to fight for, and 'alienation', and other equally general wrongs, to struggle against.

Teaching unions

Within a decade after 1968, all the major teaching unions independently expressed some support for 'Breton culture' in terms of anti-capitalism, anti-dehumanization, and anti-uniformization (see, for details, *Galv* 1969: 39–40; *AEB* 1979, 22:8–10). Not all these unions, however, joined the Front or supported its aims. For most of the time, representatives from only two teaching unions were present at the Front's meetings. A teacher in a *Lycée d'Enseignement Professionel* represented the technical sector. He spoke no Breton, but his support of Breton language and culture was linked to the fact that many of the pupils in this sector of secondary education are said to be from Breton-speaking, rural homes. The technical sector is widely considered to be second-best to the more academic streams of *Lycée* education. *Talbenn* members, with their own high-level *Lycée* education, soon made conscious efforts to speak French to this union member. The other union representative, who did know Breton and taught it, was from a union referred to as the 'SGEN-CFDT'. This union claims to represent all levels of mainstream state teachers, but it is not numerically the most powerful union in Brittany and is mainly of College (11–15 years) bias. These two union representatives were welcomed by the *Talbenn*. Even more welcome, however, would have been a representative from the SNI (or *Syndicat National des Instituteurs*), the more influential National Primary Schoolteachers' Union, which now also represents (as the SNI-PEGC) some teachers in the higher levels, especially in the less academic streams and rural Colleges. Having the SGEN-CFDT in the Front, but not the SNI, was likened by one *Talbenn* member to 'having nationalist China [Taiwan], when what we want is popular China'.

Within the SNI in Brittany, the Morbihan section has expressed the keenest support for Breton in the schools, and showed some interest in the Front – although it did not, for many months, commit itself formally to membership.[18] The Finistère section, however, refused to join. This was a bitter disappointment to the *Talbenn*, for Finistère is their most cherished 'Breton-speaking' area. The Finistère section of the SNI-PEGC pointedly published an article attacking the movement. It condemned the claims of 'those who pretend to lead the struggles for Breton' and asked: 'Is the enemy Paris, French, or France?' The SNI supported the teaching of 'Breton language and culture', and would oppose centralization in Paris, the article suggested, but did not oppose French and France (see *Bulletin du Syndicat National des Instituteurs*, 1979, November: 9). The opposition between 'Breton' and 'French', or 'Brittany' and 'France', through which militants define most clearly their world and their cause, here works against them when they try to enlist public support.

National culture

Related difficulties arose in Front discussions over the question of Breton nationalism. One *Talbenn* member, who came from a strongly nationalist family of the older movement (of which more in Chapter seven), took great care to avoid using the terms 'nation' and 'national' when talking of Brittany in the Front. The UDB member, however, regularly used the terms 'nation' and 'national' as an indication of his own advanced Breton consciousness, with the evident conviction that all the 'people', including *le Front*, required education in their true identity. Front members objected to the terms 'nation' and 'national' on several occasions, sometimes interrupting and feigning miscomprehension, pretending to have understood France as a whole, rather than Brittany. This only confirmed the *Talbenn*'s conviction that *le Front* members needed their consciousness raised – especially when one of the union representatives stated that he would prefer the Front to speak publicly of 'the Breton dimension of culture' rather than of 'Breton culture'. He was sharply overruled, and the propaganda of the Front, finalized by *Talbenn* members, stated in capital letters that there was 'NO BRITTANY WITHOUT BRETON CULTURE'. *Talbenn* members would go further, firmly holding the view that there is no Brittany and no Breton culture without the Breton language, although they did not insist on this to a French-speaking Front.

Serious work

In the summer of 1979 an event occurred which brought into focus a good deal of discussion, both inside and outside the Front, on the subject of Breton. A young militant of *Skol an Emsav*, and a close friend of the *Talbenn* members, became national news in France. This young man was Jil Kilivere (or, in French, Gilles Quillivéré), in his mid-twenties, who comes from a farming family in the Léon. Jil was brought up in French, but had learnt Breton through *Skol an Emsav*. In the summer of 1979, Jil took his *baccalauréat* examination, which he had already failed in the past, but this time he wrote all his papers, on all subjects (with the exception of the French paper), in Breton. This was no mean achievement, for although he took one of the technical series of the *baccalauréat*, considered by many to be easier, he had had to put in considerable extra work in order to provide the necessary Breton vocabulary. Jil's papers were examined by a jury and he passed.

This venture and success were unprecedented. Nobody had ever written full *baccalauréat* papers in anything but French, although there was nothing in official texts that explicitly forbade this. Although Jil was interviewed on national television and in the press, the *Rectorat* seemed to have no fear that this flurry of attention would lead to a rush of *baccalauréat* papers in Breton. Most candidates, they maintained, even committed Breton-speaking candidates, found it much easier, after all, to write their papers in French. Nobody has yet repeated Jil's achievement, or tried.

While the movement was thrilled at Jil's success, it soon became clear that not everyone thought so highly of it. Already in July 1979, *Talbenn* members reported having seen unfavourable reactions in the local press. They reported readers' correspondence saying that Jil would have done better to have learnt English, or any other modern language, rather than Breton. The UDB representative regretted that Bretons were still 'at that stage' of consciousness, and it was decided that the 'Breton people' needed to be 'conscientized' with some urgency. The *Talbenn* decided to formulate tracts for distribution in the schools, and to parents, in order to persuade them of the 'real value of Breton'.

In meetings of the Front that followed, it became clear how difficult this would be. Everyone was agreed on the importance of focusing in the tracts on the second language option (see Chapter four, p. 62). For *Talbenn* members especially, this was an important step for Breton. It was evident, however, that it was a step that few Bretons were willing to take. Few had taken up the option in its first year (1979–80), and it was obviously going to be a hard task promoting it for the coming year. Teachers in the Front reported constant 'resistance' and 'hostility' from Breton-speaking colleagues and parents. The cause of Breton was being 'sabotaged'.

Militants had been asking for the second modern language status for Breton for over a decade (see Le Menn 1975), but now it was obvious that there had been a miscalculation of public support. The *Talbenn* wanted to integrate Breton into the normal school day. They wanted Breton to be responsibly taught and learnt, and they wanted Breton to be taken seriously like other subjects. They had no conception that such an aspiration, while appealing to them as an oppositional, political ambition, might run counter to pupils' evaluations of their own Breton classes and be a controversion of much of the more jolly dissent that has animated post-1968 enthusiasms. 'Breton' is always contextually, and oppositionally, defined – and, unless the context of definition is unambiguous, different oppositional values or realities can be brought into conflict. This happened in the schools between 1978–9 and 1979–80, when 'fun' and 'serious' Breton met, and enthusiasm for learning Breton declined as a result (see Chapter four, above).

Mental blocks and complexes

The *Talbenn*, like the movement more generally, held a firm conviction that if Bretons did not want to learn Breton, then this was due to their 'alienation', and if they did not want to speak it, in the militants' own image of 'Breton-speaking', then this was due to 'mental blocks' and to a 'complex' they had about their Breton. How could the Front make popular appeal in its tracts to people with 'blocked' minds and 'alienated' values, and do so without sounding like a privileged 'urban élite' (a risk of which all Front members were very aware and constantly warned each other)? It was decided that some appeal had to be made to popular values, and it was obviously required that Breton should seem 'useful'. Perhaps it could be argued that learning Breton could help pupils to learn other languages? There was a risk, however, of thereby making Breton part of the 'system', which equated usefulness with 'capitalist *rentabilité*' (or 'profitability'). It was decided therefore that people might be persuaded that a child's education could not be measured in terms of 'utility' or 'profitability', and that, for Breton as for art, music, physical education, and the like, more 'human values' were involved – 'well-being', 'roots', and the 'inner man'. In keeping with this, some utility could then be boasted in such humane areas as care of the old and the dying, and in psychiatry. It is known that some Bretons, when very old or very ill, sometimes speak Breton in contexts where French would normally be used. Such a fact serves to confirm many militants in their view that all 'Breton-speakers' are prevented from speaking Breton all the time, in the normal course of things, only by unnatural 'inhibitions' and 'mental blocks'.

Tolerance and equality

Front members also argued that Breton could encourage 'concrete respect' of family and local milieu, and a 'rooting in popular culture', as opposed to an 'élitist and abstract vision of culture'. Breton similarly stood in opposition to 'abstract book-learning'. All such ideas were debated at length, and the viable ideas written into the tracts. For these tracts directed at the schools, attacks on past and present 'oppression' by the schools and educational authorities were deliberately played down. Emphasis was given instead to citation of international conventions that treated of racism, and ethnic, religious, cultural, and linguistic discrimination (for a list of the conventions cited in the Front's tracts, see Chapter four, note 1). Breton was promoted, therefore, within the general ethic of cultural and linguistic tolerance and equality. One problem arose, however, over the Front's emphasis on *laïcité*. Was this to appear on tracts which might go into all schools, public and private? The *Skol an Emsav* representative in the Front, although himself a supporter of *laïcité*, was from a family of the older movement that equated Breton and faith (a common conflation that we have seen in Part one). He did not mention this to other Front members, but pointed out that the Church and private education were still strong in many parts of Brittany, and might provide the most fertile ground for the growth of 'Breton consciousness'. The radical image of 'Breton' held in the Front, however, would not allow any compromise with the Church or the 'privatization of education': union representatives were especially firm about this. The *Skol an Emsav* member, aware of the danger of schism, did not press the point. Breton culture was declared *laïque*.

Economics and culture

The unions and the UDB were the first to point out that if the Bretons were alienated, then they could be fully de-alienated only by restoring an economic base in Brittany. The slogan *'vivre au pays'* was used to express this. Since the 1960s, this has become a common slogan in French regionalism generally (see Quéré and Dressler-Holohan 1978 for details of its development). It does not readily translate into English, since *pays*, although often translated as 'country', can mean anything in size from a few parishes to a nation, depending on the context. Since the mid-1970s the UDB had developed the slogan into *vivre* (live) *et travailler* (work) *au pays* (and later *décider au pays*, too), with the *pays* in question intended as Brittany or localities within it. All in the Front were agreed that more work in Brittany was a good thing, but rifts came again when a *Talbenn* member then insisted that the 'Breton people' needed 'Breton culture' if they were to live in the area, because they could not be expected to live in *'la merde'* ('the shit') of the 'French culture' imposed on them.

In the Front's discussions, union members were sometimes quite obviously more concerned about economic issues, and *Talbenn* members feared that their 'Breton culture' was seeming ephemeral. However, the UDB representative solved the problem to the satisfaction of all. There was a 'dialectic', he explained, between the 'economic' and 'Breton culture': if people regained their cultural 'specificity' and their 'Breton identity', then they would be unwilling to leave to find work elsewhere, and there would thus be more demand for jobs in Brittany. At the same time, a local economic infrastructure would recreate a specific 'Breton culture' for all, and a 'Breton consciousness' in the area, and encourage a relative autonomy, and so on. This was accepted, and the tract which the Front finally produced for the schools in January 1980, began with the words: *'VIVRE ET TRAVAILLER AU PAYS: QUEL PAYS? PAS DE BRETAGNE SANS CULTURE BRETONNE'*.

Unity lost

All the months of discussions in the Front, the tracts, and the multiple press releases helped to produce a small rise in the number of pupils newly taking Breton as a second language option (in the year 1979–80, 150 pupils had enrolled; in 1980–1, there were 189 new enrolments; cf. Chapter four, p. 66). Many familiar post-1960s arguments were, as we have seen, appropriated in the Front to the cause of Breton, and we shall see more of this. The Front was most active in the period leading up to the 1981 elections. After the Socialist victory, activity subsided. Within months, the Front had all but disappeared. Internal divisions, along the lines I have outlined, became paramount once the unity forged of external opposition was lost.

Chapter six

Celts

History and ethnicity

Breton, Welsh, Cornish, Manx, and Irish and Scottish Gaelic are all 'Celtic' languages. For the modern Breton movement, the Breton world is Celtic, and the Bretons Celts. The definition of certain languages as 'Celtic' is widely taken to imply a distinct category of people, the Celts, who share a common origin in language, culture, and flesh and blood. They are also felt to share a common external subjection which has largely destroyed their language and their culture and the people themselves. This model of a people and its history shares the structure of other areas of the modern Breton movement's historiography. It also exemplifies historicist and essentialist assumptions that are very common as a view of what ethnic identity involves.

Identity is forged out of the structures of the present, and turns to the past for self-derivation. The present is understood by reference to the past, and the past made to generate the present. This doubly historicist mode of argument is not, of course, limited to minority claims. We have already seen in Part one how the majority French nation-state has been moved, over two hundred years, to construct its own continuities. In this chapter, we will be concerned with the 'Celts' and 'Celtic Studies', but I should stress that much of what I say here could apply also to other ethnic categories – not exempting the 'Anglo-Saxon' – and to other concentrations of interest, 'French Studies' included.

In the history which the Breton movement writes for Brittany, the Celtic origin of Brittany, its language, culture, and people is important. The language movement has its counterparts in Celtic countries on the other side of the Channel, and close contact, with regular meetings and informal gatherings, has been established between the various Celtic movements. In Ireland, Scotland, Wales, Cornwall, and the Isle of Man, there are also 'Celtic' revivalist ambitions, with enthusiasts who are trying, with varying degrees of militancy, either to revive or to save their Celtic, minority language. Breton is the only minority language in France that is formally

Celtic, and (leaving aside the Welsh colony in Patagonia) it is the only modern Celtic language spoken outside the insular context of Britain and Ireland. Breton's insular link is important but controversial, as is the ethnic kinship that goes with it. In the political arena, Breton's Celtic kinship becomes especially significant. If Brittany can be placed within the same political taxonomy as the insular Celtic areas, then it becomes, not a region of France like any other, but a 'Celtic nation' and has at least the conceptual possibility of rightful autonomy, or of separation from the majority world, with a different history and ethnology drawn up in support.

My work with the Breton movement brought me, inevitably perhaps, into close contact with members of insular Celtic movements. These self-conscious 'Celts' feel that they have, or ought to have, something in common – an idea that is becoming more and more widespread as it appears in school textbooks in the Celtic areas. The major series of history texts now produced by the Breton movement for use in the schools is entitled not simply 'The History of Brittany' but 'The History of Brittany and of Celtic Countries' (these other 'Celtic Countries' being Wales, Scotland, Ireland, Cornwall, and the Isle of Man). The texts show what are, in many ways, rather different cultures, and, given the disparate majority contexts they inhabit, the differences are inevitably the most stark between Brittany and the insular Celtic areas. Nevertheless, all the modern Celtic countries are deemed to have something in common, from Galway to Rennes and from John O'Groats to Nantes, and then notions such as 'ethnocide' and 'cultural genocide' are included in the texts in a glossary of significant historical concepts (see *Skol Vreiz(h)* 1974, 1975, 1978, 1980). The model at work here – by which something is first posited in common and then ideas such as 'cultural genocide' are invoked to explain any differences, or the loss of this commonality – is important in militant argument, and it is an important theme in much of this chapter.

Nobody likes to identify with 'oppressors' or perpetrators of 'genocide', and anyone of any social conscience likes to feel that he or she is on the side of the oppressed. This simple but none the less compelling moral structure is but one aspect of the powerful symbolism that the Celts have working for them, and helps to explain the otherwise bizarre characters that one can sometimes come across in the circles of the Breton movement. I will just cite one example. There is, for instance, one lively, young student character who chooses to call himself by a common Breton name. We will call him Yann (a not uncommon name). Yann likes to speak only Breton or Welsh (both of which he has learnt) and he has been variously introduced, or introduced himself, to me as Cornish or Welsh. A rather different truth came out one evening when he was drunk at a militant Celtic gathering in Brittany. Yann had the temerity to argue with, and even to mock, a hardy Scot who was struggling with Breton, who could speak no

Welsh, and who, alas, did 'not have the Gaelic'. As Yann began to dance rather wildly, apparently in mockery of the Highland Fling, the angry Scot chose to reveal that Yann had, in fact, been born and brought up in Northampton. Yann, it seemed, was really 'English'. There are perhaps many Celts who might want to join in here, against a figure such as Yann, and perhaps point out that their own Celtic movements are often given a poor public image due to the antics of people in them who are really English. I sympathize but, in one sense, whether Yann was born in Northampton or not is neither here nor there. It is the revelation and the definition that are interesting, and (to use a linguistic analogy) the structural arbitrariness of the definition is specially interesting to note. It is common, I have found, for self-conscious Celts suddenly to declare someone 'English' who is otherwise quite accepted as a Celt but who might momentarily embarrass, annoy, or disappoint them. 'English' is (along with 'French') one ready categorical dustbin for those whom the Celts might choose definitionally to reject. It is perhaps understandable, or will become so, I hope, by the end of this chapter, that any figure such as Yann might not willingly choose to come out (as we might say) and call himself 'English'.

Celts: from Gauls to Welshmen

But who, first of all, are the 'Celts' and how were they invented? The category 'Celt' travelled a long and rather complicated road before finally leaping forth as this ethnic self-ascription on the north-western edge of Europe. I am not going to attempt to set out here any full story of the Celts, or their real or imagined cognates, but a few aspects of the Celtic tale might help to explain one problem of definition that the militants of the Breton movement face, but which their insular Celtic counterparts do not. We will also see some of the different contexts through which the Celtic category has moved, changing meaning accordingly.

'Celts', in one form or another, have long been hovering on the edge of, and used in the self-definition of, the civilized world, and as centre and periphery have shifted in the history of Europe, 'Celts' have moved westwards accordingly. They began their recorded life as part of the ethnological bric-à-brac of the classical world (along with Phaeacians, Scythians, and others). From potentially filling the entire space of everything odd, barbaric, or different, they eventually became most clearly pinned down, geographically at least, in Gaul. This is largely because the *Celtae* made their best-known classical appearance as one of the three peoples of Gaul, in Julius Caesar's *Bellum Gallicum*. References to them thereafter are slight and obscure (see Dumville 1983) until what we like to see as the 'Renaissance', and its own rediscovery of European classical antiquity. A late fifteenth-century Italian monk, Annius of Viterbo, brought the Celts out of the biblical flood as the descendants of Japhet (born of Noah) and peopled the entire map of early Renaissance Europe with them. Soon afterwards, the Celt was claimed by French scholars (looking back to Caesar) as French property, and the Celtic Gaul was then used, through the sixteenth and early seventeenth centuries, in expressions of French monarchical self-definition and expansionist ambition.

By the end of the seventeenth century, France had a tradition over 150 years old of tracing its ancestry to the Celt (see Dubois 1972; Piggott 1967). Brittany, although a part of France, had no particular part in this lineage. Indeed, it was not until the beginning of the eighteenth century that Brittany definitively entered the story. In an influential work published in 1703, the Breton scholar Pezron drew up, for the prestige of his province in France, a lineage from such ancestors as Gomer, son of Japhet, plus Jupiter, Saturn, and Titan, coming down through the Celtic Gauls to Brittany and contemporary France (Pezron 1703). He thus gave his province of Brittany an important place in the French lineage. There was an important linguistic dimension to his work, too. Wider scholarship had already noted the existence of Breton and claims had been made for its similarities to other languages, including Gaulish, Welsh, and, of course, Hebrew (Droixhe 1978; Dubois 1972:126). Pezron tidied this up into a scheme whereby Breton and the tongue of the 'Welsh of *Angleterre*' [sic] became surviving evidence of France's Gaulish heritage (Pezron 1703:17–19; 329–30). It was as yet undecided in eighteenth-century France whether French should be considered Celtic or Latin in 'origin'. Following Pezron, several scholars pleaded the Celtic case, using Breton as surviving proof of France's Celticness and claiming for it the status of the original 'mother tongue' (Pezron 1703:330; see Droixhe 1978:142–56 for details). In general, however, taste was moving towards Latin, and the Celtic exponents earned themselves the title of 'Celtomaniacs' and the mockery of self-consciously rational men such as Voltaire (see Droixhe 1978:154).

This was not, by any means, the end of Celtic France. In the political ethnology of the Revolution, for example, it was the Gauls who took the Bastille, and the Franks, the old regime nobility, who were overthrown (see Duranton 1969). Celtic France triumphed again under Napoleon, with his 'Celtic Academy' (*Académie Celtique*) established in Paris in 1805. Once again, the juxtaposition of different Celtic maps, the Gauls in France, and the Celts all over Europe, gave support to French expansionist ambition. The Academy's members (one-ninth of whom were Bretons) set themselves the task of establishing the old map of Celtic Europe as historical precedent for the modern territorial claims of the Napoleonic Empire. In this search for Celtic France, and Celtic Europe, Breton now held a privileged place, and its insular connections were noted.[1] This was not to derive Gaulish or Breton from the insular languages, however, but quite the reverse. The Academy knew that the British were beginning to take an active interest in things Celtic, and, although much of the appeal of the Celt under the Napoleonic Empire derived from British sources, such as Macpherson's Ossian, the Academy was nevertheless scornful of any British claims to original Celticness. Britain (which was called *Angleterre*) was, it was said, jealously seeking to 'usurp the Celtic primogeniture' and the title of 'mother of nations', both of which were felt to be the rightful claim of France, as Napoleon was showing. Britain could not claim such glories, said the Academy, for her 'mountains would still be uninhabited if it had not been for the children of Armorica' (*Mémoires de l'Académie Celtique* 1808, 1:15). (Armorica, the old Gaulish name for Brittany, is still an alternative, if rather folkloric, name for the peninsula.)

Before we go any further, there are three things worth noting about the Celtic story at this point. First, the whole of France was felt to be Celtic, and Brittany, in this framework, supremely French. Second, there is a clear notion that the Gauls had peopled ancient Britain. And third, there is a developing (and sometimes competitive) interest in things Celtic on both sides of the Channel.

It had been clear to Pezron, and later to the Celtic Academy, that the Gauls had peopled ancient Britain, and this history, drawn from classical texts, had received some attention from British scholars. With Pezron's work, interest increased, and it was through a translation into English of Pezron's work, by a Welshman, that the ancient Britons first received the appellation 'Celts' (Piggott 1967:11). Pezron had written of 'Celts otherwise called Gauls', which in English was translated as 'Celtae or Gauls, taken to be Originally the Same People as our Ancient Britains' (see D. Jones 1706). The Britons were thereby made to share the prestige of the Gauls. In the meantime, the Welshman Edward Lhuyd was working, in Oxford, on his own theory of Welsh and Gaelic descent from Gaul. Lhuyd knew of Pezron's work and liked the Celtic prestige it gave to Welsh, even if he did find the biblical edifice fanciful (see Lhuyd 1703 in Gunther 1945:489–92).

Lhuyd's own published work (1707) stimulated interest in Scotland (where educated Scots were keen to assert their own Gaulish, Celtic lineage) and, by the middle of the century, Celtic Druids had taken over Stonehenge, and the Welshman Edward Williams later invented, and practised, on Primrose Hill in London, the druidical rites of the Welsh *eisteddfodau* (see Heppenstall 1958). It was from 1760 onwards that the British Celt really took off into public debate, after the appearance of James Macpherson's Ossianic poems (in 1760, 1762 and 1763). These gave rise to a fierce and long-running controversy over their authenticity, within which the categories 'Celt' and 'Anglo-Saxon' (alias Goth, Teuton, and Saxon) were summoned into existence as moral contraries (see Chapman 1978). The 'Anglo-Saxon' category had long had a place in the study of Old English, and had served as precedent and authority for the Protestant establishment of post-Reformation England (see Piggott 1967). As England, in the eighteenth century, took off into industrialization and scientific progress, so the Anglo-Saxon came to embody progress, civilization, and materialism; the Celt, by contrast, swathed in druidical and Ossianic mist, retreated into a primitive, peripheral, and 'natural' world. A creation of primitivism, of the cult of sensibility, and of an often fanciful archaeological theory, the British Celt was never more than a marginal minority, an oppositional counter to the 'Anglo-Saxon' of majority self-definition.

In the nineteenth century, the British Celt came quite clearly to inhabit, and to represent, that 'idealist half-world' which has been described for the Scottish Gael (Chapman 1978). The work of Matthew Arnold was perhaps the most decisive in giving to the Celt his most enduring metaphorical form. In summary, Arnold defined the Celt as all that Victorian, industrial, utilitarian, male-dominated society was not, and made him, in the process, peculiarly spiritual, imaginative, irrational, and, in many respects, feminine.[2] We are all now familiar with the wonderfully artistic and poetic (etc.) Celt constructed in this way, who has, in brief, all the qualities that the majority world is felt to lack. (Such relative images, metaphorical and arbitrary, can easily receive empirical confirmation of a kind, and are quite commonly positivized into essentialist argument about what, say, the 'Celt' or the 'Anglo-Saxon' are *really* like.) Arnold's imagery owed much to French sources, notably Amédée Thierry, Henri Martin, and Ernest Renan, and to the image of the French Celt which such writers were active in establishing, and which served (among other things) to define France in symbolic opposition to Germany. Much of the Celtic ethnological imagery (or 'stereotype', cf. p. 20) with which we are now so familiar, and which we associate with the Celtic minorities, was first used by nineteenth-century French Celticists to distinguish the true Celt (the Gaul) from the German (where claims to Celticness were also being made): to distinguish, in other words, all of France from Germany. This symbolic opposition of Celtic France and Germany came to have a long political life (the statues of Vercingétorix, for instance, put up at the time of invasion from Prussia, being but one of its manifestations). Aspects of the Gaul/Teuton opposition neatly corresponded with the Celt/Anglo-Saxon duality in Britain. However, for our purposes here, there is one particularly important difference to bear in mind: while, in Britain, Celticists knew that when they talked of the Celt they were talking about the marginal minorities and not the majority English, in France, on the other hand, Celticists could be talking about not just the Bretons but all Frenchmen.

All this leaves something of a problem for militants of the modern Breton movement – who want to be a Celtic minority, while the very majority world against which they take their most convenient definition (France) can also, if it so chooses, claim to be Celtic. The insular Celts just do not have this problem: the majority English have not chosen to be Celtic, and have generally been content to be 'Anglo-Saxons' in a way that the French are not content to be, say, Franks, or the Germanic invaders of Celtic Gaul.

The Bretons have, however, been able to find a solution to their definitional problem, and both to be Celtic and yet distinguish themselves from majority France. The solution was developed for them through the political divisions of nineteenth-century France and the works of men whom modern militants would now look back to as founders of the Breton movement. These founding fathers were mostly noblemen, priests, and scholars strongly opposed to a Republic increasingly anti-clerical in its commitment to the ideals of the 1789 Revolution and to a progressive, 'positive' philosophy. Prominent among them was a young Breton noble- man named Theodore Hersart de la Villemarqué (1815–1895) who prod- uced in Paris, in the late 1830s, a work entitled *Barzaz Breiz*, which became in some respects (albeit in more muted form) the French literary equivalent of Britain's Ossian. La Villemarqué's work went through several editions in his own lifetime, especially in 1845 and 1867; contro- versy about its authenticity reached a head in 1870, and continues to the present day, having followed much the same path, and raising many of the same issues, as the Ossianic controversy.[3] In France, however, the controversy has always been politically entangled. The 'Poetical History of Brittany', the *Barzaz Breiz*'s subtitle, pretended to stretch back, through popular poesy and song, to the Dark Ages, and symbolic figures such as Arthur, Merlin, and Nominöé were all thrown on to the nineteenth- century stage, pitted against Saxons, Franks, and others. Whatever dress the French were given, as Franks, Normans, or whatever, they could be read as nineteenth-century Republicans.

The *Barzaz Breiz*, or readings of it, not only helped to define and locate Brittany on one side in national political battles, but also relocated whatever local traditions of song existed in a single new tradition, on a national and international stage, of popular lore and lyricism. This image is important and its congruence with the 'Celt' not fortuitous (cf. Chapman 1978 for the cohabitation of folklore and the Celt in the different political context of Britain). It is worth emphasizing that the discovery and creation of this popular world, in its shape and substance, in its ethnology, and in its location in Brittany, was a process in which the self-definition of positivist rationality played a definitive role. The politics, of Church and Breton alike, which opposed this rationality were working within the same structures, taking up the metaphorical space which that rationality offered to describe and define its own conceptual frontiers. It is no coincidence that what we now see as the romantic movement appeared with the consolida- tion of national boundaries, or that in France romanticism should have been enmeshed with religion in the provinces. With the definition of national units had come the definition of what the nation was not, and the construction of national peripheries. We have seen the 'Celt' appear and shift as definitional counter to the classical world, then to the French and Anglo-Saxon. The dominant rationalities of Europe had, in contemplation of themselves and in definition of their own characteristics, long sought and constructed upon their boundaries their own contrary, but to this definition of self and other, positivism and romanticism gave enduring expression within the world of modern nations. The national minorities appeared conceptually with the majorities, and a loss of identity – whether as an inherent feature of their romantic construction and attraction, or as part of the necessary trajectory of positivist, rational history – was always a primary feature of the identity which the minorities were later to assume. The 1789 Revolution and Napoleon's Academy (and its successors) had launched an interest in 'popular tradition', constituted by all that was curious, irrational, or uncivilized and bound to disappear. Civilized and uncivilized, rational and irrational: the mutually defining images of majority and minority were born together, and the minority born as disappearing. Brittany was already ripe to be the 'other' of rationality in the contemporary distribution of centre/periphery, order/disorder relations. Certain events of the Revolution (see Chapter one) had fed into, and confirmed, an image of the volatile, uncultivated, or recalcitrant in the far west distance, where Brittany – whether named as such or not – was ready to serve European thought as one obvious site for the location of barbarians, savages, and oddities. Brittany was explicitly one such metaphor for the French educated world by the eighteenth century, and in the nineteenth century, with the consolidation of the modern national map, this picture of Brittany, carrying all its ambiguities of the uncivilized and unaffected, gained coherence, and was systematized through romanticism and the development of literacy and schooling. Folklore and the Celt were two faces, in knowledge and ethnology, which the contrary of positivist rationality (or 'positive' reason) then came systematically to assume. Within all this, it was largely through the *Barzaz Breiz*, in the light of which other works came to be read, that Brittany became fixed as a peculiarly expressive land of folk-custom, mystery, ritual, song, and lyricism (see, for example, *La Revue des Traditions Populaires* 1855–1916, in which Brittany regularly figures; Brittany also occupied a far greater space than other areas in France's developing ethnological museums, with ethnology and anthropology the direct heirs to folklore: see Cuisenier and Ségalen 1986). From roughly the middle of the nineteenth century, the tortured desolation of an earlier romantic wash (e.g., in Chateaubriand) had become, in the imagery which Celtic Brittany could gather about itself, a more feminine and lyrical, ritual and spiritual world (see Bertho 1980). It was not difficult for any of this imagery, and especially the easy symbolism of the peculiarly spiritual, religious Celt, to be used to oppose the Republic itself.

In Britain, the minority Celt was a metaphor for all that the dominant rationality was not, and so, too, in France, the Celt was now becoming, in the hands of some, a figure of opposition to certain prevailing intellectual trends. The chronology is not simple, but, very broadly, through cross-Channel exchanges in the eighteenth and, especially, nineteenth centuries, an oppositional symbolism that distinguished the French, the true Celt, from the German, had been to Britain and helped to distinguish the minority Celt from the Anglo-Saxon, and then returned in various guises and could effectively distinguish the Breton from the French and the Anglo-Saxon alike.

But what about the Gaul? Were the Bretons not after all, Gauls in origin? In the political divides I have mentioned, the Breton was uncertainly poised between kinship with the Gaul, a figure of majority France, and opposition to things 'French'. The Breton as Gaul was less and less politically apt.

At this point, we have to mention one discipline that has been, and still is, enormously important in the whole Celtic story, and in nationalism more generally: comparative philology, or historical linguistics. Those now regarded as key founding members of the Breton movement had been in touch with German philologists, especially Zeuss and Grimm (themselves creative in, and influenced by, German romanticism). From their work, it was plain that if French was a 'Latin' language, then Breton, by contrast, was 'Celtic' and closest among living languages to Welsh. The Bretons then became, through philology, blood relations with the Welsh, and, in a new historiography, a key emigration began to change direction. It was now a question not of Gauls peopling ancient Britain, but of Britons peopling Armorica; the British Celt was not, in this new framework, the scion of the Gaul, but the origin of the Breton. Political divides found new expression to the point that, by the end of the nineteenth century, Breton and Gaul were, in the eyes of some, totally independent figures. The Gaul lost his place as the 'origin' of the Breton, an origin was sought instead in Britain, and earlier histories that had talked of Dark Age Britons coming to Armorica now gained a significance they had never had before. Several possibilities were available, but the chosen history was the one of greatest metaphorical and political aptness: a fifth-century arrival of Britons fleeing their homeland before the invading Saxons. As the nineteenth century progressed, so the number of fifth-century Britons increased dramatically and the number of Gauls they encountered diminished. The Gauls were slowly slipping out of the distinctly 'Breton' or unFrench world that was required, and they were even, for some, obliterated altogether from the Armorican map. One of the neatest of such solutions was put forward in the 1860s, in the ebullient days of the Second Empire, by an aristocratic Breton scholar, a friend of La Villemarqué, who decided that the Britons had come to Armorica, in the fifth century, with what amounted to a fierce nineteenth-century nationalism in their hearts, and had slaughtered the Gauls they found there.[4]

The Gaul has managed to survive, however, as the ancestral figure of France. In the French school history books of the Third Republic and onwards, the French Celt has served as a regular reminder of how Celtic unworldliness, volatility, or lack of organization have, at every moment in French history, invited invasion and conquest (see Duranton 1969; Gendre and Javelier 1978). *Nos ancêtres les Gaulois* (the traditional historical cliché of school textbooks), and *Gauloises* cigarettes (the cigarettes of the national, state-owned tobacco company), and Astérix cartoons are just a few instances of the ancestral Gaul in French consciousness. The Breton, meanwhile, while sharing the Celtic metaphoric, has taken it over, for the Breton movement at least, in its insular, British form. For the majority of Breton militants, the Bretons are not Gauls and have no relationship with them.

Students in the Rennes Celtic Department, for example, and militants associated with it certainly do not want Gaulish origins. Several times, in courses or discussions, the leading Breton-language lecturer in Rennes warned that to assert any kind of Gaulish origin for Breton or the Bretons was to make 'Breton and Brittany the patrimony of the French Republic', something clearly undesirable. In the Celtic Department of Brest University, on the other hand, there has been active interest in the Gaulish origin of Breton, and social and linguistic arguments have been drawn up in support (see especially Falc'hun 1962a, 1962b, 1963, 1970). Hostility between the two departments, and between those who espouse aspects of one view or the other, has become legendary in the movement, and no one studying Breton and Brittany can fail to come across at least its more benign by-products in one form or another (including conflicting local scholarship and different forms of the language, of which more later). The main Breton-language lecturer in Rennes was born over sixty years ago into a French-speaking family in Upper Brittany, while those in Brest who draw up a Gaulish ancestry for Breton, alongside its Brittonic element, are from Breton-speaking families of Lower Brittany. Those in Brest can, and do, declare the Rennes faction 'French'. On the other hand, because Brest tolerates the Gauls, militants in Rennes regularly define the Brest scholars as 'French'. The division between the two camps is coloured and confirmed by other differences, not least of which is that while Rennes leans to a Breton nationalist position, there are members of the French Communist Party in Brest. Both departments have their own internal differences, but 'Brest' and 'Rennes' have commonly been cited as metaphors of two clearly opposed viewpoints in the movement, and the metaphorical Gauls and the metaphorical Welsh have been known to insult and denigrate each other, usually from the relative safety of their respective ends of Brittany.

This mutual hostility has been known to take rather serious forms, but the story also has its more amusing and relatively amicable manifestations. This was evident when, early on in my field-work, I attended a one-week 'crash course' in Breton at Rennes University. The Rennes Celtic Department and its followers organize such courses every year. On this occasion, each class was expected to produce a brief sketch for the last evening, and one particular sketch met with great approval and applause. Two angelic-looking 'Bretons' were seen wearily rowing to the shores of Armorica, fleeing the terrible Saxons. Finally they arrived, with some relief and delight. Seated on Armorican soil was a single Gaul. The two Bretons approached the Gaul and, in a post-1968 era of peace and love, one of them extended his arms in greeting. The Bretons were left alone to people Armorica, however, for the Gaul, crouched like a monkey, ran away, grunting incoherently.

Descent and the Dark Ages

Language, we know, has long been important in argument about national and ethnic definition of the kind I have been discussing. This has been particularly true, however, since the early nineteenth century, and I have already mentioned the romantic philosophy of language which informed the definition of peoples and nations. This was also the period when comparative philology came of age as a discipline, and a linguistic taxonomy was established (with elements such as Celtic, Romance, Indo-European, and so on) that is still largely unquestioned in our own time. It was more or less tacitly assumed throughout the nineteenth century that descent and differentiation of languages were congruent with, even con-substantial with, descent and differentiation of people, race, culture, and polity. As biological evolutionism made itself felt, philological arguments about the development and origins of language were paralleled by ethno-logical and biological arguments about the origin of peoples. Ethnology used the categories of philology, and philology then re-appropriated the findings of ethnology, and so on. A category such as 'Celtic' was a language, a race, and a culture all at once.

It is still a widely held view, in popular and in certain academic circles, that 'ethnic' groups are defined by their descent, that a name is attached to every mass of humanity, and that every such mass is positively defined by birth, language, and culture. This is still very much the unquestioned, if largely implicit, orthodoxy in many areas of Celtic studies. The ethno-logical map of modern Europe came into being in the eighteenth and nineteenth centuries, and there is always a temptation, in trying to understand any 'people' on that map, to write the history of that people, in flesh and blood, back to the year dot. Modern anthropology, in the hands of some of its exponents, has shown that 'identities', 'ethnicities', and so on (call them what you will) are semantic and definitional in essence. This means that the history of any one of those 'peoples' marked on the map – for example, the Celt – is the history of a category, and the meaning of that category, whom it designates and how, is always to be found in the contemporary context. We have to separate the category from the hordes of flesh and blood, or a supposed genetic history, with which we might be tempted to fill it. At the same time, we have to bear in mind that people may move from one category to another as a matter sometimes of external definition, sometimes of self-definition. People can and do change their definition, the categories themselves shift, more across the globe, change dress, or disappear altogether. Recruitment, exclusion, and movement are achieved as much through definition and change of definition as through death, birth, migration, and massacre (see, particularly, Ardener 1972a, 1974). There is no reason to suppose that this was not true in ancient Britain and Gaul (as true as it was, for example, in the Southern Sudan (Evans-Pritchard 1941) or West Africa (Ardener 1967) or Asia (Leach 1954) in the mid-twentieth century).

Such a perspective would find few friends in popular Celtic enthusiasms, and consideration of the semantic and definitional fluctuations of categories such as 'Breton' or 'Celtic' is scarcely ever attempted. For most, such categories have the same logical status, in continuity and delimitation, as biological species. If we were to look, however, at the problem of the Gaulish/British origin of the Breton from a semantic, definitional aspect, we might find that the problem, in such terms at least, largely dissolves. I cannot pretend here to offer any thorough study of what *really* happened, in the lived and active social definitions of the time, between Britain and Gaul during and after the Roman period. Any such study would demand a very sensitive use of meagre sources (with any real ethnographic basis for sensitivity necessarily absent) and a fairly comprehensive confession of ignorance, only the latter of which could properly be brief (for fuller details, see Chadwick 1965, 1969; Fahy 1964; Fleuriot 1980).

We might note just a few major points, however, from the flimsy evidence available. Relations between ancient Britain and Gaul appear to have been frequent and easy, and their languages were thought by some to be similar (according to Tacitus, for example, in the first century AD: see Fleuriot 1980:14). Nineteenth- and twentieth-century oppositions of Briton and Gaul, conflated with 'Breton' and 'French' respectively, are inappropriate in the context of the different and common ties (which we might call religious, scholastic, economic, and political) of those times. There was a two-way traffic between Gaul and Britain. Gaul and Briton were against Caesar, then united by the Roman Empire and, after the fall of the Empire, by common interests of defence again. In such a context, and whatever the active, social definitions or self-ascriptions lived locally on either side of the Channel, it is clear that the question 'Are you a Gaul or a

Briton?', while potentially pertinent in some form, might equally well have appeared either inconsequential or senseless. It seems likely that invasions from 'Ireland' (the 'Scots') in the island of Britain in the fourth and fifth centuries AD, together with threats to the Roman Empire on the continent, encouraged recruitment to organized military embarkations from Britain into Gaul.[5] A consolidation of 'British' interests in Armorica occurred between the fourth and the seventh centuries AD. This was due as much to a continuing attraction of defence and of politico-economic and religious colonization of the peninsula, as to any 'push' from the island, whether from 'Scots' or, later, 'Angles' or 'Saxons'. The apparent consolidation was also a matter of external definition, and pro-Roman interests, industrious land-settlement activities, organized learning, and religious commitments, or a combination of these, could no doubt have encouraged recognition of a 'British' presence in Armorican Gaul and recruitment to the social categories or definitions supplied by this recognition, or which immigrants brought with them. Evidence suggests that, probably in the sixth century AD, a number of immigrant scholars (the *sancti*), with a perhaps not dissimilar vernacular and a prized Latin learning, helped to define a 'British' presence in the peninsula and to set up religious centres of learning. This, together with military pride and conviction, could have generated a world of *Britanni* or *Brittones* in Armorica, by external recognition and contextual self-definition, without any need for the majority of the people so defined ever to have seen Britain, and without need of any mass migration or massacre. It is the category or definition, and recruitment to the definition, that are important. (And, of course, the values that might, long ago, have encouraged recruitment to designation as *Brittones* (Latin, pro-Roman, colonization, and so on) are quite different from those which now encourage recruitment to the self-ascription of *Bretoned* (Br.) or *Bretons* (Fr.) in the modern 'minority' world.) The relationship between the ancient *Brittones* and the modern *Bretoned* or *Bretons* is to be found in philology rather than biology; and between the Dark Ages and the present day innumerable definitions and re-definitions have occurred, historically and contextually, which this philology does not show.

Self-consciously 'Breton' and 'Celtic' scholarship, seeking to establish the security of a biological rather than a merely semantic or structural lineage, has tended to focus on a single, mass 'emigration' or 'flight' of Britons to Armorica, and to date this in the fifth century. The most popular tradition in the Breton movement is still that of 'Anglo-Saxons' forcing great numbers of defenceless 'Celts' over the sea (any 'Irish' involvement and any 'Roman' or Latin interest or definition being thereby excluded). The nineteenth-century oppositional metaphoric of Celt and Anglo-Saxon is used to make luminous the politics of the Dark Ages. When Anglo-Saxons came to Britain, Celts, naturally, left.

When the category 'Celtic' first entered philological debate in its modern sense, in the works of Zeuss and others, it was as part of a genetic scheme that supposed its existence in real time and in real history. When the origins of Breton, Welsh, and Gaelic were traced back to a common 'Celtic', it was supposed that this hypothetical 'Celtic' was indeed a language that had once been spoken, by a people called 'Celts'. Since language, race, and culture were coextensive categories, modern self-conscious Celts feel they share, in every sense, a common origin, traced through philological lineage. This one-time linguistic solidarity implied political and cultural solidarity, and nineteenth-century intellectuals set themselves the task of restoring the fullness and unity that history had, apparently, taken away. As so often in the scheme of nationalist and ethnic argument, the posited one-time autonomy has been overlain with external intrusions or accretions, and an essentialist image of a people, required to identify with particular language and culture, is used to argue away the events of history and to reassert the autonomy that time has apparently failed to conserve. Once Breton was no longer French or Gaulish, a few Breton scholars set about consolidating its links with Welsh, as we shall see in the next section, and invoking political, moral, and racial ties as well. The modern movement exhibits many examples of the same ambition. The 'Celtic' countries have immensely varied histories, however, of changing allegiances and self-definition, within the general political context of what we might call Britain and France. At no time in this history was there a self-defining 'Celtic' solidarity until nineteenth-century intellectuals began to work towards this.

The emphasis which I place on understanding identity as a product of the contemporary context is not invalidated by the reality of that context containing some idea of the nature of history and its trajectory. The contemporary context is always changing, and theories of continuity with the past may be one important factor in its change. The meaning of a term such as 'Celt', in linguistics and ethnology, is always, in a strict linguistic sense, arbitrary. A continuity for such categories is sought in history, but the contemporary context determines where and how continuities in the past will be charted.

Now that the definitive structure of lineage has been drawn up, it is widely felt that all the essential continuities run through it. Where Celtic solidarity is not manifest in the present, linguistically, politically, or culturally, it is felt that this is so because external and fortuitous events have 'interfered' with the proper course of history. This idea of undisturbed lineage and original unity has an important moral dimension, with integrity and purity invested in the imagined original unity, the undisturbed autonomy of theoretical history. Certain modern categories, especially 'English' and 'French', then enter as interference, disruption, impurity, and everything else undesirable. This theme can be found in the economic, linguistic, and political arguments of the Celtic movements, and it is one that runs throughout.

The categories and lineage around which such definitional argument rages are philologically established, and it is the linguistic model that is the security for the entire cultural and political edifice. The 'Common Celtic' language of nineteenth-century philology is no longer accorded the real and unproblematic historical status it once had. For modern historical linguistics, the evidence of texts and of the modern Celtic languages, and rules of sound change, are used to establish a hypothetical, original 'Celtic' form; this form will then, according to the rules of its own establishment, in perfect tautology, regenerate rule-right modern forms (see Ardener 1971b). The original Celtic form is now, as an unattested form, an hypothesis only: it is not a word, nor a part of a language, but a device to make sense of the present; it has no status in real history and no date in real time. As such, it is accompanied in modern linguistic analysis by an asterisk, */thus/. The asterisked form is a theoretical utility, a formal emptiness in historical linguistics. Because the Celtic starred or asterisked form represents 'Common Celtic', however, it is often accorded, by the various Celtic movements, an implicit historical reality that is at once – in nineteenth-century style – linguistic, political, cultural, and racial. The asterisk could be seen as an apt metaphor, therefore, for the hollow unity, theoretical and abstract in origin, that is pursued by the Celtic enthusiast, and which he fills with words and deeds, with birth, copulation, and death.

Pan-Celticism and the Breton language

The minority 'Celtic' definition has had some self-fulfilling effects in the linguistic sphere. From the nineteenth century onwards, Breton has been progressively unified and standardized. This modern process was first launched under the auspices of Napoleon's Celtic Academy, resulting in a Breton grammar (in 1807) and a learned Breton-French dictionary (Le Gonidec 1821). Pursuit of purity and archaism were, at that time, part of the desire to demonstrate that Breton was the original *langue-mère*, anterior to French. In the mid-nineteenth century, in a new political context, La Villemarqué re-edited the dictionary and further 'purified' Breton of French, adding many Welsh terms, along with some Gaelic and Cornish (La Villemarqué (1847) 1977; 1850).

Attempts to popularize this new Breton, largely through the translation of Catholic journals, brought complaints of incomprehensibility from the clergy (see Tanguy 1977). Common ground was readily found, however, in opposition not only to the Republican ideas and secular materialism associated with French, but also to the general immorality assumed to be carried by the schools which the reign of Louis-Philippe encouraged. By the 1840s, La Villemarqué and the priests were agreed that Breton could be a 'boulevard against corruption and impiety' (cited in Tanguy 1977: 162–3). The 1848 Revolution further confirmed, for many, the republican dissoluteness of schoolteachers, and the Church and (for some) Breton seemed the means to counteract this. Linguistic purification was purification of republican immorality. The debates described in Chapter two, about the catechism and church services, were very much a part of the context in which a Breton of new, un-French, Celtic dimensions was actively developed. Although none of the catechisms actually adopted the 'purified' Breton of La Villemarqué, the Bishop of Quimper and Léon gave symbolic official approval to his efforts.

In 1867, La Villemarqué held the first of many 'Interceltic Congresses' in Brittany, inviting 'compatriots' (or simply 'kith and kin') from Wales, 'brothers' from Cornwall, and 'cousins' from Ireland and Scotland (cited in Tanguy 1977:343, 389ff). Such pan-Celticism, furthering Breton's un-Frenchness, has not always served Breton well. It was noted in the early years of this century, for example, that some Bretons appeared to have developed 'autonomist' and 'separatist' ideas at such meetings.[6] The potential transposition of the political structure of Great Britain (and more particularly of the 'Irish question') into that of France haunted some national debates about Breton. Support from non-French Celts sometimes worked against Breton in a Republic anxious for national unity.

However, separatist groups of deliberately anti-French and pro-Celtic sentiment have been most prominent in militating for Breton. Particularly important in the inter-war years was *Breiz Atao* ('Brittany For Ever'), a small group of educated young men (mostly from Upper Brittany or Paris), formed soon after the 1914–18 war. This group, which constructed a lineage for itself directly from La Villemarqué and the *Barzaz Breiz*, was nevertheless disappointed in the Church for its failure wholeheartedly to promote Breton, and became the pioneer of secular Breton nationalism (see Déniel 1979:24). To counteract the perceived 'decadence' of post-war France, its members suggested that Celtic women from Britain and Ireland should immigrate to breed pure Celts in Brittany, thereby replacing 'Latin and Saxon dross' and restoring 'Celts, like our illustrious ancestors at the time of Arthur and Nominöé' (cited in Le Sann and Férec 1973:41–2, 54–6). *Breiz Atao* produced a political journal of the same name, which was mostly in French. Alongside this was launched a Breton-language journal called *Gwalarn* ('North-West'), which lasted from 1925 to 1944, and in which the term *emsav* (see p. 73) began to be used. The editor and main contributor was Roparz Hemon, a one-time teacher of English, who was born Louis-Paul Nemo in Brest, in 1900, of an Italian father and mother from Upper Brittany. Hemon was the main author of modern, standard, literary Breton, and he took much from earlier work, including that of La Villemarqué. Like his predecessors, and the few contemporary Celtic scholars who helped him, Hemon learnt most of his Breton from old dictionaries and texts, and went on to write new dictionaries, journals, and texts, which, in their turn, have been the major source for modern learners and scholars, virtually their only readership.

Breiz Atao's concern with a dwindling purity of the race (of which more in Chapter seven) was given its immediate parallel in the dwindling purity of the language, and *Gwalarn* was concerned to refashion Breton as it ought to be. For this, a 'pure' Breton lexicon was again created, according to three main recipes: one Welsh, one ancient, one domestic.[7] Borrowing from Welsh seemed to be the surest method, although there could be problems here, as Hemon himself later realized; for example,

> One sees the word *modern* so often in our journals of the last few years, and it has come to us from Welsh. Our writers have seen it in Welsh journals. To borrow a Welsh term borrowed by the Welsh from the English, and by English from French, is an astonishing thing to do, don't you think? (Hemon 1964:71)[8]

Borrowings from Welsh, the favoured recipe, were effected with or without a hypothetical phonological evolution. Such terms included the word for Wales itself – *Kembre* (cf. Welsh *Cymru*), for which the complete set of derivations now exists in standard Breton.[9] The same has happened for the term for Ireland. La Villemarqué had added *Iverdon* ('Ireland') and *Iverzonek* ('Irish language') and Hemon, from these and the Welsh (*Iwerddon*), came up with *Iwerzon* ('Ireland').[10] Both La Villemarqué and Hemon and his colleagues forged a Breton 'history' for this, in phonological change, and a complete derivational paradigm of *Iwerz(h)on* has been installed. Scotland and Cornwall have also been fitted out with Breton nomenclatures. Breton thus achieved a modern linguistic paradigm productive of its Celtic history. The Breton *Kembre* ('Wales') speaks direct descent from the Welsh *Cymru* in a way that *Wall* or *Oual* (the already existing Breton terms) or, indeed, *Galles*, could not.

Seeing themselves as an 'intellectual élite' whose task was to 're-Celticize' Brittany (Hemon and Mordrel 1925; Hemon 1928a), the scholars of the 1920s and 1930s also felt it necessary to create an 'abstract' and 'scientific' lexicon for a secular Breton of the twentieth century. There were rarely native Breton terms for the new technological world, and, amid quarrels and competing creations, they came up, Humpty Dumpty fashion, with an often unstable vocabulary that meant what they wanted it to mean. Hemon later felt that earlier enthusiasms had perhaps gone 'too far'[11] but he remained convinced that this 'linguistic purification' (*ar c'hlanyezhegezh*, another neologism), meaning principally 'getting rid of French terms', was the only way to 'ensure the future of the language'.[12] The result has been, in one modern researcher's view, not Breton but a 'Celtic esperanto' used only by learned enthusiasts (Hewitt 1977:13). Certainly Hemon's own attempts at popularization failed miserably: on his own admission, all his 'popular' literature, children's books, and magazines were read only by the intellectuals themselves (see Morgan 1979).

A Celtic language for the Celtic people

Modern standard Breton now appears in one of its most learned and 'purest' forms in the journal *Al Liamm* ('The Link', see Chapter five, p. 78), the link in question being that between Brittany and the insular Celtic countries. Until his death in 1978, in voluntary exile in Ireland, Roparz Hemon regularly contributed to *Al Liamm* as well as producing several other journals to further Celtic unity (among them *Ar Bed Keltiek*, 'The Celtic World', a title that still survives). Hemon aspired not only to a standard Breton but also to a standard Celtic for all Celts. He had always stressed the importance of Celtic unity and of Brittany's link with the insular areas, by which, he hoped, the Bretons might rid themselves of their Frenchness and become a proper Celtic nation again. However, it was clear that all this was going to be no easy task, even in the circles of the most committed enthusiasts. At a Celtic Congress in Dublin in 1925, Hemon had heard Celts talking English and French between themselves, and was dismayed. In an open letter to the Celts, he said it was 'laughable' to hear the 'Welsh talking English with the Scots' and the 'Irish talking French with the Bretons', while complaining about the 'invasion of English and French in their countries' (Hemon 1928b:77). Other members of the Breton movement at this time quite keenly entertained visions of a single inter-Celtic language that would allow the Celtic race to communicate without English or French (see Le Sann and Férec 1973:55ff). In the 1930s, Hemon began, as a second best, a short-lived publication in Esperanto; Esperanto, while not common Celtic, was at least felt to avoid the unhappy symbolic resonances of English and French (Hemon (1931) 1972:135–6).

In the establishment and maintenance of a unified, standard Breton, it has been argued that Breton is 'one language', and this unity has been pursued into a theoretical past before the modern dialects had diverged. In the same pursuit of a hypothetical (or asterisked) form of original unity, but climbing still further up the philological family tree, certain nineteenth-century Breton scholars had said that not only all Bretons but all Celts could understand one another, including Bretons and Gaels, because they all spoke 'dialects' of a common 'language' (see, for example, La Villemarqué (1847) 1977:9–10). Edward Lhuyd, without quite the same ethno-philological axe to grind, had found, on a visit to Brittany at the beginning of the eighteenth century, that spoken Breton was incomprehensible to him, and one prominent Breton-speaking member of Napoleon's Celtic Academy had asked Welsh contacts to send only Welshmen who knew French to visit him (see Dujardin 1949; Gunther 1945). Since the nineteenth century, however, there has been an exaggerated notion of the easy mutual comprehensibility of Welsh and Breton. Scholarship has created philological unity as an asterisked form, and enthusiasts have set about making this asterisk an historical reality, in writing and in speech. Celtic students in Brittany now know that, philologically, they are supposed to understand their Welsh kin, and, through a few common terms and expressions, will feel able to do so. Some, to make sure, go further, and many Welsh students now come to Brittany to learn Breton and Breton students return to Wales to learn Welsh. They may encounter serious difficulties in learning, but explain these away by saying that Welsh has been 'Anglicized' and Breton 'Frenchified' – and Celtic commonality thus fractured. Young Breton enthusiasts often set off from Roscoff in Brittany, bound for Wales or Ireland, clutching copies of the *Mabinogion*, or Welsh and Gaelic learning manuals, in pursuit of their 'roots'. The 'Brittany Ferries' cross-channel ferry company undoubtedly owes some of its success to the empty spaces of philological logic, now filled with fare-paying passengers.

Hemon reported in the 1950s on fresh attempts being made to create a single 'Celtic language' for Celts to use among themselves (Hemon 1953). There were disagreements, however, and English dominated the meetings. Attempts have continued to create a 'common Celtic' as enthusiasts recoil from French and English and at the same time tire of the effort of learning the separate Celtic languages (see, for example, *Carn* 27 (autumn 1979):13, 23, 24). No solution has been found, however.

Some readers may now be wondering if Breton is, or is not, a Celtic language. The point I would make in response has been expressed in other ways in this chapter, and would apply, I think, to other linguistic/racial/ ethnic classifications of the modern ethnological map. Since Breton is, through historical linguistics, a 'Celtic' language, scholars looking for similarities of a Celtic nature between Breton and the other Celtic languages will find them; these similarities are already built into the formal definition of the languages as 'Celtic'. Differences and discrepancies are then 'loans', corruptions, or intrusions, from outside the Celtic model. Such is the *definitional* reality of Breton, through which its relations with Welsh are systematic, and its relations with French random and fortuitous. Where is the *historical* reality of Breton, however? If we were to look for similarities between Breton and French, we would easily find a very long list indeed, and Breton would be firmly placed in its French context. Even the most committed comparison of Celtic languages is bound to point out that Breton shows a very significant 'French influence' (see, for example, Gregor 1980). The historical reality of Breton might well be said to be French. In this connection, a telling point was made some time ago, in rather different terms, for the relationship between Welsh and English:

> In the case of some modern spoken Welsh it can be said to be, at the level of phrase and sentence, a calque upon English: a one-to-one code.

In the terms of generative grammar the 'deep structure' is shared in part with English. Here the findings of the modern descendant of 'synchronic linguistics' clash with those of the traditional historical linguistics. For what is more 'historical' about Modern Welsh? Its English connections? Or those with Irish, Breton and epigraphic Gaulish? (Ardener 1971b:221)

Language and ethnicity

The minority is a creature of the majority context it inhabits, and for Brittany this means especially the French national context which came into being with the 1789 Revolution. An autonomous minority history has been constructed and identity pursued into a distant past according to the preoccupations and images of the present (whether those of nineteenth-century royalist Catholics, say, or of post-1968 radicals). If we try to look back into the past, however, with a modern anthropological gaze, the categories of modern debate and the context in which the Celts now understand themselves (including the entities of France and Britain) are not there. I do not say this to adjudicate on the historical authenticity or inauthenticity of modern Celtic identity or ethnicity but, on the contrary, to stress that its validation is always to be found in the present, in the contemporary context in which self-definition is sought.

The 'Celtic' idea now extends far beyond philology, into politics, race, economics, culture, and morality. A live and robust category of 'Celtic art' has been created out of the muddling and uncritical employment of archaeology and philology, and there is now also 'Celtic music', 'Celtic literature', and much else besides. All such pursuits can and do feed, in turn, on the appeal and persuasiveness of other argument, political, moral, or economic. In educated discourse, modern Celts have tended to appropriate the morally privileged half of whatever contemporary oppositions have presented themselves, and they are now self-defining minorities. As such, they are morally opposed to the majority world, and since part of the privilege of the self-consciously 'Celtic' movements is to assume oppression and manipulation at the hands of this majority, they are morally exempt from responsibility not only for the actions of the majority, but also for their own (violence included). Post-war sociology and events such as 'May '68' in France have given the modern Celts a secure place in the relations of majority/minority, centre/periphery, colonizer/colonized, exploiter/exploited, and so on. The symbolically marginal, spiritual Celtic world can now also claim modern political subjection through 'ethnic' studies. Modern militants do not use the term 'race' any more, for racialism is now old-fashioned and reactionary; within the uncritical positivism that marches language and culture and blood kin back together into history, however, 'ethnicity' is no more and no less than racialism, and can breed the same resentments.

The Breton movement is fond of 'historical' maps, showing the oppression of the Celts. Maps that might attempt to show the shifting complications of external definition and self-definition show, instead, Celts of flesh and blood wandering across Europe. In a book of which the title translates as 'Breton, Celtic language', there is a map entitled 'Celtia, 25 centuries ago', in which Celts are shaded in from Asia Minor to Hibernia (Brekilien 1976:13). Some pages later comes a map called 'Celtia now', where the shading is limited to Brittany, Cornwall, Ireland, the Isle of Man, Scotland, and Wales, each given its name in its respective Celtic language (ibid:29). In between is a chapter called 'The Assassination of Celtia', the assassins being chiefly Romans, Saxons, and Franks. Modern Celtic enthusiasts are thus offered the righteousness of 'twenty-five centuries' of bloody assassination, in spite of which, or perhaps because of which, we can safely say that there have never before been as many self-conscious 'Celts' as in recent decades. Maps of the modern 'Celtic countries' are commonly produced by the movement, and these show little respect for cultural history or contemporary reality. On such maps, all of France except Brittany is a blank. Brittany itself is all 'Celtic' west of a line from Mont St Michel to the mouth of the Loire. The Breton/French language duality is not, and never was, socially or geographically congruent with the duality Brittany/France, but it is thus made to be so. French is thus in Brittany only as an intrusion, an external interference. On these same maps, all of Ireland is labelled 'Eire' and shaded in as 'Celtic'; Belfast is given the sole name of '*Béal Feirste*' (see Gwegen 1975:171). Maps of this kind do not show the end result of centuries of 'assassination' of 'Celts' but are, if anything, the maps for which bombs are exploded. Interceltic congresses of all kinds make use of such maps, and the most innocent of 'Celtic Studies' must share some responsibility for the highly charged contours that philology traces, and for the enduring and dangerous naïvety with which philology is allowed to assume 'ethnic' flesh.

Celts now meet in various kinds of congress and festival, sharing their origins and their oppression. Similarities between them are taken to be evidence of common heritage; differences are blamed on the majority worlds that have wrongfully 'assimilated' them. Just as, in the philological model, 'Celtic' elements are evidence of continuity and 'non-Celtic' elements seen as interference, so in the historical and political model, majority histories are external to the Celts, who have their own history, a single and independent trajectory, skewed and distorted only by majority intrusion.

Since the Second World War, the Cornish have secured a place in the youthful and non-academic 'Interceltic Congresses', which are now held annually at a series of Celtic venues. There had been some misgivings about the Cornish since they no longer had the Cornish language but, at the beginning of this century, it was already being suggested by Breton enthusiasts that the Cornish, even though they had no living Celtic language, should perhaps be present at Celtic gatherings since they shared the racial soul of the Celt (see Le Goffic 1902). Some Cornish have, of course, since begun to revive the language in earnest, and now use Cornish among themselves as a means of communication. During my field-work, I was invited to a Cornish-Breton wedding in Brittany. The bridegroom was a Cornish boy who has learnt both Cornish and Breton, who has made frequent trips to Brittany, and who considers himself part of a movement in both Cornwall and Brittany. The bride was a Breton girl who has been active in the Breton movement and who has learnt Breton. The wedding was held in a cathedral in Lower Brittany, and the priest had been persuaded to perform the service in Breton. Several Breton militants were present, as well as some Cornish nationalists, and the parents and families of bride and groom. The service included a reading of the scriptures in Cornish. As families stood uncomprehendingly, many younger guests looked delighted. The whole service was charged with a youthful symbolism of language difference and Celtic unity, although the priest, in his sermon, was more concerned with the fact that the groom was a Protestant.

As we left the cathedral, the Celts danced behind bride and groom, through the streets of the town, to the wedding reception. The young Cornishmen sported kilts and played bagpipes. Enthralled local shoppers and shopkeepers hurried out to see *les Ecossais*' ('the Scots'). During the wedding breakfast, I found myself sitting between a Cornish nationalist and a Breton militant, and conversations were conducted across me, comparing the Breton and Cornish languages. It was made very clear to me that English was not to be spoken. Some of the Cornish were keenly learning Breton to aid their own Cornish lexicon. Opposite me sat a young Cornish enthusiast, who is bringing up his children in Cornish; he would not speak English to me, and his Breton was extremely elementary. It was a very long meal. In the meantime, the bride's parents, native Breton-speakers, were speaking French with their own age group, and the bridegroom's parents were valiantly coming out with school French; all around them, the room buzzed with learnt Breton and Cornish. In a jovial interlude, the braver guests entertained us with songs. Breton militants stood up and sang in Breton, and the Cornish in Cornish; they applauded one another vigorously. Then one young Breton couple, relatives of the bride, took their turn at the microphone. They apologized blushingly for knowing no Cornish or Breton and sang a popular French song, to the applause and encouragement of the older guests. The bridegroom's parents then stood up, and explained, in French, that they were going to sing a song in Esperanto, which they did. It was the only language that no one else in the room understood, but which all could comfortably applaud. Militant hands stopped clapping, however, and groans of despair were heard when the groom's mother gaily shouted 'Vive l'Entente Cordiale!'.

She was cheered by the older guests, who faced each other as French and English. The younger language enthusiasts faced each other as Breton and Cornish, however. The Anglo-French unity which the mums and dads were celebrating was the very opposite of the Celtic unity which the whole ceremony seemed to have been designed symbolically to seal. The bridegroom casually explained to me afterwards that he had invited me to show his friends and family that someone else from 'the other side' of the Channel (he did not say England) had learnt Breton and was using it in Brittany. I had also supplied the 'English' presence by which a new Cornish identity can, by opposition, be summoned up.

The problem of being English

In the modern scheme of Celtic ethnicity, the 'English' category is important. The ethnography I present here is neither irrelevant anecdote nor a question of the vagaries of personalities; rather, it is an attempt to present the fine ethnographic detail of contexts in which ethnic identity comes alive and of a situation in which the identity of the ethnographer can become very much a part of the context under study. An 'English' ethnographer is categorically part of the structural context in which the modern 'Celts' find their definition. Sociologists would commonly talk here of problems of 'access' in research.

In my own field-work with the Breton movement, my identity was usually ambiguous. By definition, an 'English' person studying Breton could be up to no good. Very early on during my stay in Brittany, a militant had exlaimed: 'English? What are you doing learning Breton?' This was a question often posed to me during my work with the movement, with varying degrees of hostility. I soon learnt that the 'English' were 'imperialists' and 'fascists'. A Welsh friend was not asked why she was there learning Breton, for it was taken as only natural that she should be doing so. I often explained my work in some detail to militants, and they showed interest. Some urged me to write articles about them and their oppression, and others were keen to get hold of my archival research, with a view to picking out any new citations of historical oppression that they might have missed. (Some of these would be scrawled in large letters on posters regularly stuck up on the walls of the Rennes Celtic Department.) A few were keen to classify me as a political 'spy'. Police and spies were regularly conjured up as the opposition in their midst, and as 'English' I was an easy figure of suspicion. (The fear of informers was not always without justification, but the structures of the militant world are such that members of the movement would be unlikely to suspect actual culprits, swathed as they would be in 'Breton' authenticity, and their attention is turned instead towards easier categories of opposition.) I supplied the movement with some archival references and with other details of interest, such as figures for the numbers studying Breton in the schools. This, together with the fact that I obligingly spoke Breton, and only Breton, in militant circles, gained me some defenders. However, I always remained 'English', contextually, for some members of the movement, as the occasional and readily available focus of militant outrage.

Recruitment to this Celtic world involves more than a commitment to language-learning or to the values of the movement. It involves also a biological model of kinship, and notions of ancestry and descent. Usually, descent from Breton, or better, Breton-speaking parents or grandparents is an adjunct to political militantism; it is invoked by individual militants to explain their initial interest in Breton or to boast the peculiar authenticity of their standing in the 'Breton' world. In my case, my being 'English' was in symbolic contradiction with the Breton I learnt and spoke. Many times, especially in the initial weeks, I wondered if my being 'English' made my work with the movement in Brittany impracticable. I was deliberately made conscious of my 'English' identity and made to feel uncomfortable. Moreover, Welsh and Breton enthusiasts would deliberately speak Welsh in front of me, even if we all knew Breton, English, or French better: their choice of language said more in such contexts than their conversation, which was often hampered by an elementary knowledge of Welsh. On many occasions, I have approached Welsh and Breton enthusiasts happily speaking English to one another, only to find that my presence, as 'English', immediately re-defined the context and changed the value of the language. The Welsh would then begin to condemn the 'English', and take on an exaggerated Welsh accent. When the Celts had no common medium of communication other than English, French, or Breton, the fact that I knew all three muddled their world, and a clear boundary was drawn up in insult. However, I gained an alternative identity during my first few months in Brittany, and it was this that enabled me to work with greater ease and credibility.

First of all, in a class in Rennes University on the 'History of Celtic Languages', the lecturer decided to use my surname as a comparative example. My name was declared more truly 'Celtic' than those of the other students in the class, who, said the lecturer, had 'French' or 'Frenchified' surnames. Students began to take more interest: so I had a 'Celtic' name. Not long afterwards, my identity attracted further interest in a meeting of militants, outside the university, after a language class. The militants were weighing up whether the Breton language was suffering more from French than French was from English. Some cheerfully declared that it 'served French right' that English was in dominance, but a few argued that Breton was the cause of the oppressed, and that Bretons, therefore, should fight all forms of 'oppression'. English-language dominance emerged as the worst form of 'linguistic imperialism', and a Welsh girl present, who had recently learnt both Welsh and Breton, pointed out how Welsh was 'suffering' because of English. There were murmurs of sympathy. One militant noticed that I was saying nothing in the discussion. 'Where are you from?' he asked, eyes slanted in suspicion. I replied that I was from England and, in my nervousness, let slip that I was born in Oxford, a fact which apparently made my fault even more grievous. A militant friend, however, rescued me from what threatened to be a nasty burst of hostility. 'But where is your father from?' said the friend, nudging me with a knowing and kindly smile. My father is, in fact, from Wales, and a native Welsh-speaker. This was clearly the required information. 'Oh well, then you're Welsh,' said the militant, relaxing from accusation into acceptance, and raising his arms in surprise at my error. 'Don't worry,' said my friend, reassuringly, 'you're not English really.' In other discussions, it also came out that my mother is from Ireland, and knows Irish Gaelic. The re-definition was simple. On this, and many similar occasions, I was declared a 'Celt', and, as such, united with the ranks of the oppressed, where life was, in many ways, distinctly more comfortable.

Chapter seven

Wars and petitions

'Brittany For Ever': the Second World War

In this chapter, we look at how the First and Second World Wars have been incorporated into militant history and into militant self-definition. We will pay greater attention to the Second World War because it is more alive in popular memory, and still alive within the movement, organizing some of its own internal differences. This is so largely because of perceptions of the war-time activities of *Breiz Atao* ('Brittany For Ever'). Long dead as an organization, *Breiz Atao* (introduced in the last chapter, p. 112) is still alive in associations of fascism and the war, and presents an awkward passage in the history which the movement constructs for itself. The most popular histories of the movement, oral or written, mention *Breiz Atao* only in passing, if at all. The subject is generally taboo in militant discussion.

We will examine three aspects here concerning *Breiz Atao* and the war: first, 'collaboration'; second, links between *Breiz Atao* and Breton in the schools; and last, the way in which the war is alive in present internal divisions in the movement. There is no room for a full treatment of any one of these issues here, but no account of the modern social value of Breton can ignore them.

Collaboration

Relations between *Breiz Atao* and the French Communist Party (which, in spite of some initial ambiguities, came, after the war, to represent the Resistance) are of special interest. In the 1920s, *Breiz Atao* was proclaiming support for the external colonies of France, including those of North Africa, as well as for the internal 'minorities', notably in Alsace. The young French Communist Party, then in its strongly internationalist phase, was arguing along similar lines. In the 1930s, however, *Breiz Atao* began to slide from anti-imperialism to political racialism. Members of *Breiz Atao* – notably its leader, Olier Mordrel (born Olivier Mordrelle, in Paris, in 1901) – began explicitly to praise Germany and to move the Breton and

Nazi cause together (see Déniel 1976, 1979; Denis 1977; Le Sann and Férec 1973; Simon 1979). The Celtic state they envisaged was to be protected from the 'contamination' of Jews, Negroes, Arabs, and Latins (including, in the last, the Occitans and the rest of France). By 1936, the Communist Party was supporting the left-wing Popular Front government and sharing its fears about *Breiz Atao* and Breton sympathies. In 1932, when an off-shoot of *Breiz Atao* had blown up a new commemorative statue in Rennes of the Duchess Anne kneeling before France, the Communist Party had seen this act as an apt symbol of the fight against 'imperialism'; continued bombings, however, which had always been condemned in the local and national press, came also to be condemned by the Communists, who, by 1938, saw not anti-imperialism but a 'German fascism' in Brittany (see Déniel 1976).

Members of *Breiz Atao* – or of groups which grew out of this focus of militant activity – attempted to sabotage early mobilization of the French war effort; attempts were made to ship arms from Ireland for this purpose and to aid the construction of a Breton State. Visits were made to Germany and, when France was defeated and occupied, the Breton movement enjoyed German support before being left to the Vichy regime, from which the movement successfully gained official sanction for Breton in the schools. Some have felt that the Breton movement was at its most powerful during the years 1941 to 1944 (see Morgan 1979:ch. 6), and Hemon himself said that a 'breath of liberty' had blown over Brittany during the years of the Occupation. *Al Liamm* seems to have had no qualms in publishing this statement in 1950 (*Al Liamm* 1950, 20:31), although many now wish that this had neither been said nor published.

The term '*Breiz Atao*' is now often used (especially at the popular level) as a general term for all the broadly right-wing groups, small and changing, that made up the Breton movement of the 1930s and 1940s. Fights between *Breiz Atao* and the local Resistance in Brittany, especially the Communists, were not uncommon. Some Bretons will tell tales of torture at the hands of *Breiz Atao* followers, of how some Resistance fighters died at the same hands, and of how a group of *Breiz Atao* associates donned German uniforms in 1943 and actively hunted out Resistance members. Such tales are largely oral history (although not undocumented) and can be elicited in detail from certain Resistance veterans and Communists who were personally involved, and who would clearly not like this history forgotten. More generally, we are dealing here with common modern social fact in Brittany: *Breiz Atao* 'collaborated'. A group which no doubt saw, in the German victory and Occupation, a chance of independence from France was required, after the war, to represent that notoriously impenetrable 'collaboration' of which France has sought, and sometimes still seeks, to purge itself.

In 1944, when Frenchmen were 'liberated', many a self-conscious

'Breton' was imprisoned or in hiding. Several took refuge in Germany briefly, including Hemon and Mordrel. Hemon was condemned to ten years' *indignité nationale*, but soon left France for Ireland (*via* Wales), and never returned. Such a pattern, of refuge in Germany and then in one of the Celtic countries, especially in Ireland, was not uncommon for such Bretons after the war. A few now appear in 'Celtic' gatherings or Breton-language courses, and have connections with the modern movement.

Breiz Atao offers a particularly striking example of the problems of minority identity within a nation-state as fragile as France has felt itself to be. France's chronic instability has brought several crises of majority self-definition, offering little of that security of opposition on which minority self-definition depends. Conceptual opposition to France itself has enabled the construction of a distinct 'Breton' identity, but conceptual opposition is also political opposition here and, when France has been threatened in its very existence, the political arena has not been a safe place to be. *Breiz Atao* members and sympathizers discovered this at great cost to themselves and others. Since the war, France has been faced with the difficult task of reconstructing its identity and a history in which the nation emerges free and proud from victory over the barbarism of German fascism; there has been no place, in this historical memory, for collaboration other than as an evil limited to a small minority – of which *Breiz Atao* has provided one convenient metaphor. Every memory and telling of the events of the war is structured by the necessity of the tale ending with teller and friends on the right side of history. This is true in all milieux, including that of the Breton movement itself. A few individuals from the movement of the war period expect a young movement that has 'sold out' to France and its politics to recall them one day to lead the fight; others have simply taken on post-1968 values, and then (as in one prominent case) might declare themselves to have been 'ill' during the entire war. Innocence of 'fascism' and 'collaboration' has now to be asserted somehow. The young organizations of the modern movement have been founded in an entirely new political world, when France has been an apparently stable and largely right-wing Republic against which a left-wing rhetoric of separatism and minority rights has been relatively safe and easy to assert. Whatever they did or did not do, the Breton enthusiasts of the war period are treated with some ambivalence by militants of the younger generation, but open accusations of 'collaboration' are unusual, partly because a few prominent younger militants are related to those older members and partly because the issue of collaboration is still capable of tarnishing the whole movement. Many people in Brittany choose to see *Breiz Atao* revived in the modern movement, to the horror of the latter, and throw the damning label *Breiz Atao* at any autonomist, separatist, or self-consciously Breton activity. In public, therefore, younger militants will generally limit themselves to an occasional teasing of militants of the war period, and it is only in very much more discreet conversation that active discussion of collaboration appears. (Interestingly, it has been one area in which the necessity of some form of historical relativism has been explicitly argued in militant meetings.) We shall see, however, that there is one axis of relations within the movement where accusations of collaboration fly freely, both across and within generations: in the relations between Brest and Rennes Universities. Brest is concerned to lay the whole collaboration image on Rennes, and some in Rennes, as a retort within this structure of relations (but not to the public at large), simply assume this as the more robust militant tradition.

Ar Brezoneg er Skol

The activities of *Breiz Atao* had, in the long term, a malign effect on the image of Breton in national educational debate. In the mid-1930s, however, although Breton and the activities of *Breiz Atao* were acquiring an undesirable, autonomist, and 'fascist' image at the national level, at the level of local municipalities this association was not at all clearly made. Between 1934 and 1938, the movement achieved what militants now regard as a monumental 'victory', in a 'plebiscite' of local opinion. This was an ambitious petition mounted by a group of Breton students and enthusiasts (who had mainly forged their plan in Paris), who had links with *Breiz Atao*, but took the name of *Ar Brezoneg er Skol* ('Breton in (the) School'). Through a clever use of men of respected social standing (notably scholars and doctors) who took cyclostyled voting forms to local municipalities, many in Lower Brittany and some in Upper Brittany were persuaded to vote for some Breton in the schools (for details of the campaign, see Fouere 1935 and 1938). As municipal councils voted, new forms were circulated, on which the number in favour was exaggerated, and more encouraged to follow suit. (These circulars can be found in the departmental archives in Quimper, ADF:T:1:79.) During the campaign, a priest named Desgranges presented a report in the Chamber of Deputies in favour of Breton in the schools, citing the local votes, and the campaign circulars then began to point out that, at the impressive level of national debate, a priest was arguing for Breton. They were also careful to argue the value of Breton in secular, pedagogical terms. Municipalities of all persuasions could thus be encouraged to vote in favour. It is now claimed that, by 1938, about 48 per cent of the communes of Lower Brittany, with a large proportion in the Léon, were in favour of some Breton in the schools (see Gwegen 1975:46). This result has pride of place in histories of a movement that seeks to rally the 'people' to its ranks.

Over 40 per cent of the communes did not vote, however, and about 10 per cent actively voted against. (These votes against seem to have been registered mainly in 1938, when bombings and *Breiz Atao* were becoming known locally, and condemned by all parties.) There is some evidence of organized hostility in the votes against[1] and the votes *for* Breton involved disparate values and allegiances. In most cases, it was a vote for a minimal pedagogical aid to the teaching of French. This was not a vote for the definitionally un-French 'Breton' world which the results of the campaign are, in modern histories of a 'plebiscite', now often claimed to voice.

Three major petitions for more Breton in the schools are commonly cited in this way in modern militant literature: one from 1870, one from 1919, and this one of 1934–8. The petition of 1870, penned largely by Celtic philologists and eminent clergy, has already been mentioned in Chapter four (p. 56); it disappeared when war broke out with Prussia. The 1934–8 *Ar Brezoneg er Skol* petition, the first and only one with popular signatures, began to disappear nationally not simply because of growing concern about *Breiz Atao* but more generally because of the Second World War. The 1919 petition, to which I shall return at the end of this chapter, was penned by a right-wing politician, the Marquis de L'Estourbeillon, and had suggested that more Breton in the schools might help France better to resist the German might in the future: the German strength was in their race, it was argued, but France still had its 'Celtic corner' and, in promoting this, might achieve its own Aryan supremacy (see L'Estourbeillon 1919). This was an evocative argument, but not successful. This 1919 petition was addressed not solely to the French government but to the Versailles Peace Conference, and President Wilson had declared (in innocent ignorance, some would say, of the possible implications for certain European nation-states: see Cobban 1969) the necessity of self-determination for all nations. The war of 1870 had cost France Alsace-Lorraine, and, through the war of 1914–18, at bloody expense, it had just been regained. The French government was not about to contemplate another division of the Republic (and the now atypical power of the Church in Alsace and the presence of some separatist sentiment there encouraged this view in many milieux – not least in the Radicaux party and, later, the *Cartel des Gauches* which, in the face of both 'Bosche' laws and 'reactionary French legislation' (i.e., *Loi Falloux*), explicitly redeclared 'the Revolution of 1789': see Berstein 1977). The 1919 petition was ignored, therefore, buried in the political results of the First World War (which included this revivification of 1870 and then 1789) and buried also, along with its successor, *Ar Brezoneg er Skol*, in preparations for the new conflict which became the Second World War.

After the Second World War, debates about Breton in the schools were haunted by collaboration and *Breiz Atao*. The cause of Breton was further hampered by those who had fled into exile in Celtic countries, whence they avidly produced anti-French propaganda, and have continued to do so. Meanwhile, in France, those in favour of Breton, from the Communist Hervé through Deixonne and on to subsequent proposers of bills of law for Breton in the schools (even into the 1960s), had to plead, in order to win support, that not all Bretons were collaborators (see especially the texts referred to in Chapter four, note 3). Moreover, when, in the 1950s, the Finistère teachers published their disapproval of Breton in the schools (see Chapter four, p. 54), they were objecting to the collaborationist associations of the Breton movement as much as to the Vichy regime. Breton's official place in the post-war schools had to be gained through a counter-image of Brittany as a stronghold of the Resistance, which men such as the Communist Hervé deliberately stressed. Such an image of Brittany, as fighting with and for France, is anathema to much of the modern movement.

Dialects, one language, and the 'orthographic war'

The Second World War and the Breton movement are remembered in sections of the Breton public through ideas like '*Breiz Atao*' and 'collaboration', but, within the movement, the war lives on more vigorously in linguistic and orthographic struggles. Orthography, a subject one might expect to be dry and technical, has important moral and political investments, and Breton orthography is certainly no exception. Indeed, many visitors to Brittany, and other interested researchers, linguists, and participants in Celtic conferences, have been variously puzzled and shocked by the strength of feeling that can be generated in intellectual Breton circles by different Breton spellings. To understand some of the sentiments evoked, we need to return to the work of Roparz Hemon.

French has long been considered, by grammarians and politicians, the symbol of national order and, as such, the only properly ordered language of France: French is *la langue*, and everything else *patois* and disorder. This, it should be said, is a view of the relationship between French and Breton that can still be heard from local Breton-speakers. Hemon appropriated the relationship and made it internal to Breton: the 'patois' of popular 'Frenchified' Breton speech was to be replaced by a single, national, all-purpose Breton language (using the term *yez(h)*, a semantic neologism from the Welsh *iaith* ('language'), to describe this new status; see Hardie 1948:12; Hemon GIAB:3213; Morgan 1979:241). It was to be the one and only language of Brittany, since Brittany was a nation, and as such monolingual; bilingualism was for the regions. Hemon's statements on this have often been republished and quoted by modern militants:

> We can do without French. Now I will go further: as Bretons we must do without it . . . . Breton is our liberty, French our enslavement . . . .
> Breton must be, henceforth, a single language. Let us kill French, or French will kill us. (Hemon 1925, 1931, cf. 1939, and 1972a:119–37)

Unification into this 'single language' was to be achieved through a single orthography.

The notion of Brittany as a national unit with one language is a reflex of modern nationalisms and educated structures of definition. In earlier centuries, Breton was little used in writing, for which Latin and then French have always predominated. Breton entered the modern world of vernacular writing as a distinctly divided tongue, when missionary priests of the seventeenth century used Breton in their mission work with the local populace. It is from this time that modern scholars have dated an era of 'Modern Breton', littered with French and fraught with orthographic difficulties and irregularities. In order to explain away the modern, divided state of the language, modern scholars have had to look to an essentially imaginary past, pursuing a fully 'Breton-speaking' Brittany, with one Breton language (in a modern image of what a language is and does) back beyond annexation by France, into a theoretical world before modern differences and dialects emerged (an argument of which we have seen many aspects in Chapter six). Confirmation of such a world has been found in slender and fragmented textual evidence of earlier periods, in which some scholars have seen a single, if not wholly regular, literary code (see Guyonvarc'h 1973). We have, in fact, few means of knowing what literate men of earlier centuries thought of the Breton language as such, and no idea what the illiterate, popular world thought of it, if at all. We do know, however, that Breton marked a lowly, uneducated status from at least the sixteenth century onwards, within those areas that are now considered to be 'Breton-speaking' and united conceptually and politically thereby (see Croix 1981). Breton is unlikely to have implied politico-geographical or conceptual unity of the kind now demanded of it, and was probably, as it is today for the majority of its speakers, a medium in which internal social differences were expressed, in speech just as in dress, occupation, birthplace, and so on. There is an important popular conception in which there are 'dozens of Bretons' as opposed to 'the Breton language'; individual, family, hamlet, village, *commune* and parish, *département* and diocese, and more, could, and can, all manifest their status and idiosyncrasy by their use of these Bretons (often deemed by their speakers to be mutually incomprehensible).

The only linguistic border that Hemon and his colleagues wanted was that between Brittany and France. The most obvious internal Breton divisions were the boundaries of the dioceses and their dialects, seen as problems to be tackled on the way to unification. These dialects have been major stumbling blocks in the realization of Hemon's ordered, single Breton language. Part of the problem has been a common image of these dialects as descriptions of popular speech communities, or geographical areas of internal linguistic homogeneity with clear boundaries between them. We can, however, in order better to grasp their status, turn such an image on its head. Very briefly, the four old diocesan or cathedral towns are symbolically associated with four different dialects: Léonais,

Trégorrois, Cornouaillais, and Vannetais (see the map on p. 322). The diocese has its status as a linguistic entity largely because of the important place that the Church has had in education, with the power of the Church, in writing and speech, providing the educated register of Breton in each diocese. From the sixteenth century, with education officially organized on diocesan lines under the auspices of the cathedrals (Ogès 1934:81), linguistic differences which are now found in the established dialects, but which have existed from the earliest sources and at least since the twelfth century (Guyonvarc'h 1973:29), would have been caught up in a process of linguistic and diocesan self-definition, manifested in religious and educational texts. By the eighteenth century at the latest, there were separate catechisms for each of the dioceses, and official pleas to the clergy in the nineteenth century to unify these failed (see Chapter two).

In fact, the diocese of the Trégor, and even more so that of the Cornouaille, have been dominated by the power and prestige of the Léon. Only the diocese of Vannes had a distinct written form of Breton, evidenced in surviving texts from the seventeenth century onwards. Vannetais has never had the esteem of Léonais: the diocese had long had the reputation of relative poverty (M. Jones 1976:156), and, in the eighteenth century, Vannetais was felt, by a local lexicologist, to be itself poor and of limited intelligibility (see Tanguy 1977:216). However, we have seen (in Chapter three) that the Prefect of the Morbihan, in response to Montalivet's proposals of 1831 for bilingual schooling, spoke of the different literary form of the Vannetais, and the Quimper Committee felt that a considerable degree of mutual incomprehensibility was involved. It was true then, as it is now, that the more educated, particularly those in the movement, tend to minimize the problem of comprehensibility, while local Breton-speakers assert it, and sometimes with relish. For Breton-speakers from the western areas, the divide between Léonais and Vannetais (with Finistère/Morbihan or Finistère/Vannetais as congruent variants) is a line where comprehensibility definitively begins and ends.

The dialect of the Léon owes much of its prestige to the ecclesiastical influence of the area. The Léon had a large and well-educated clergy, who travelled widely in the diocese of the Cornouaille and Trégor, translated model Latin and French sermons into Breton, and developed a prized style of oratory. In the eighteenth century, Breton/French dictionaries were produced explicitly for the translation of these sermons. These factors combined to make the Léonais dialect the prestigious and educated Breton for the whole of the area that was to become Finistère. In the eighteenth century, it was stipulated, by the French monarch and by diocesan authorities, that locally appointed clergy should know Breton, and dictionaries became one means by which many external recruits to the western areas of Brittany learnt Breton; separate provisions were made for the diocese of Vannes, where recruits had to learn Vannetais (see

F. Roudaut 1975, 1:41–2). This consciousness of difference easily became, when the *départements* were set up, a difference between the Morbihan (Vannetais) and Finistère (with Léon Breton dominant). The learnedness of dictionaries and of the clergy was assimilated to the Breton of the Léon, which gained the reputation of being itself the most learned Breton. The prestige of Léonais should not be taken as meaning that the Breton actually spoken in the Léon, by the clergy or the lay populace, was inherently less 'French' than that of other areas; however, Léon Breton and un-Frenchness soon became the same thing for scholars keen to find a model Breton both literate and learned.

For nineteenth-century scholars, from the Celtic Academy to La Villemarqué and onwards, Léon Breton entered the stage as the purest surviving Celtic. The archaized and purified Breton these scholars themselves produced became, by definition, the Breton of the Léon, encouraged by a general image of the Léon peasantry as isolated in their farms, faithful to the religion, and far from French influence. Some idea of the prestige of Léon Breton was carried into popular thought by the priests, and by a missionary journal called *Feiz ha Breiz* ('Faith and Brittany'), launched in the Léon in the 1860s. Although this journal, and still more so the Léon catechism, had more 'French' than did La Villemarqué's pure Léon Breton, the idea of Léonais as a pure and educated form firmly entered popular consciousness – both in the Léon itself and in other areas. Many modern enthusiasts have seen Léonais as a purity surviving in the people from whom it was adopted by scholars. It would be truer to say that Léonais was given learned prestige by clerics and early scholars, that nineteenth-century scholars seized on this, emphasized it, and eradicated some of the French that was not meant, by definition, to be there, and that the language was then given back to the people of the Léon as an image of how their Breton ought to be.

In 1907, a tiny group of Celtic scholars established a unified orthography for the three dioceses of Quimper (the Cornouaille), St Pol-de-Léon (the Léon), and Tréguier (the Trégor). This orthography was called KLT (see Vallee 1935), taking the initial letters of the Breton names of the dioceses, *Kernev* (Cornouaille), *Leon* (the Léon), and *Treger* (Trégor). Léon forms dominated in the KLT. The Vannetais dialect is known in literary Breton as *Gwenedeg* (*Gwened* being Breton for Vannes), often shortened to 'G' in written orthographic debate. The KLT/G division has plagued orthographic debate in the movement, and attempts before the First World War to unify KLT and G failed (Olier 1960:8–9). The Vannetais area was only partly Breton-speaking geographically, and was closest to the French-speaking area of Brittany. The KLT/G (or, more specifically, the L/G) divide has often elided in argument with divides such as Celtic/non-Celtic, Celtic/corrupt Latin (or Gaulish), pure Breton/Frenchified Breton or simply Breton/French.[2] Hemon felt the problem could be solved by bringing in some Vannetais words, but he otherwise refused any compromise of the KLT orthography itself, arguing that a move towards Vannetais would 'deform and de-Celticize the language' (Hemon 1938:5).

A 'solution' came in 1941, during the Occupation. With Breton in the schools, unification seemed imperative and Hemon was urged – by Leo Weisgerber, a German philologist interested in Celtic – to 'make some semblance of bending a little before the Vannetais' (letter dated 26 January 1941, cited in Merser 1980:8; see also Fréville 1979). A compromise was duly reached, although KLT remained dominant (see Hewitt 1977; Jackson 1967:Appendix 1; Morgan 1979).

The 1941 unification, however, became, in later valuation, a source of division rather than unity. Much of the argument has revolved around the two perennially contentious letters *zh*, which were brought in by the 1941 orthography, now usually known itself as 'the ZH' (*le zédach*, Fr.; and *zedachek* or *ar zedacheg*, Br.). Words pronounced /z/ in KLT and /h/ (or /x/) in G, which formed one of the major differences, were written with a *zh*. The two letters were written as if Breton were a single system. Thus *Breiz* (Brittany) of KLT and *Breih* of G, became *Breizh*, a unified nation; *brezoneg* (Breton) of KLT and *brehoneg* of G became *brezhoneg*, a single language. Some feared that the /h/ of Vannetais was no more than an aberrant 'deformation', and disagreed with the *zh* sign, but a general sentiment of unity was found by viewing /z/ and /h/ as 'reflexes' of an older Breton /θ/, and Welsh and Cornish forms have been brought in to demonstrate the etymological authenticity of this /θ/ (see Morgan 1979:299). Even modern words that had never been part of a /z/-/h/ 'reflex' were given this new history: *Iwerzon*, for example, became *Iwerzhon*; and *Barzaz Breiz* became, for some, *Barzhaz Breizh* (see Hemon 1957).[3] It was later discovered, however, that other 'origins' could be found for certain instances of the *zh*, and much argument has resulted (see Merser 1980:7; Morgan 1979:297–302). The argument over orthography has never, at any time, been simply technical, but the 'unified Breton' (*brezhoneg peurunvan*) of the 'ZH' has been a particularly powerful source of upset and outrage.[4]

The unity which Hemon and his colleagues wrote into Breton in 1941, with German encouragement, dissolved into bitter internal strife after the war. In 1948, university authorities in Brittany urged that any official Breton teaching should not use the 'ZH', described as the orthography of the old 'collaborators' and anti-French 'autonomists' (see *Ar Falz* 1948, September:8). After the Deixonne legislation of 1951, therefore, the educational authorities urged Breton scholars to produce a new orthography for use in the schools, and, following meetings in 1953, a new orthography was worked out, and approved by the Ministry of Education in 1955 (see Falc'hun 1953, 1956; Merser 1980). This new orthography was called *L'Orthographe Universitaire* (Fr. 'University Orthography'; in

Breton, *Skolveurieg*), now commonly abbreviated as the 'OU'. In this, the *zh* sign was firmly excluded, as a 'nationalist' artefact, and the division of KLT and G (Vannetais) largely restored, with *z* in KLT and *h* in Vannetais. This flouted the cherished conventions of the 'ZH', which had, in the pursuit of Breton unity, littered Breton with *zh*s. Other differences, conventions in limited usage before the 1941 orthography, have not been as contentious as the *zh* sign, which conjures up Breton nationalism, collaboration, and the war, and is the *bête noire* of all OU proponents.

The OU became the chosen orthography of Brest University, while Rennes now adamantly teaches the 'ZH'. Both claim, in post-1968 populism, that they are fighting for the 'people': Rennes by giving them a standard language of national unity and dignity, and Brest by voicing their variety – a variety which the nationalist 'ZH' is argued totally to deny, in a typically 'French' centralist fashion. Both 'Rennes' and 'Brest' can and do accuse each other of being French (cf. Chapter six) – and also of collaboration. OU users taunt Rennes with the collaboration of the last war, and 'ZH' users retort with accusations of collaboration with the French authorities, under whose auspices the new orthography was worked out. Accusations and threats have flown between Brest and Rennes on this issue, strongly compounding the divide of the metaphorical Gauls and the metaphorical Welsh. The Second World War is still alive in the movement, and it is wise not to be caught in the cross-fire.

In the early 1970s, younger members of *Skol an Emsav* ('ZH') and *Ar Falz* (OU) began to organize summit meetings to end 'the orthographic war', as all these battles have often been described. Leading proponents, I have been told, often avoided being present at the same meetings, and the talks seem to have degenerated into slander and confusion. By 1975, relations had broken down. Apart from entrenchment of the 'ZH'/OU positions, the only result was a third orthography, generally known as the 'Interdialectal' orthography (or the 'Assimil' after the publication in which it first appeared: Morvannou 1975), which tried to claim a unity in diversity, without being 'supradialectal' in the manner of much of the 'ZH'. The *zh* sign had remained a major problem, along with Vannetais distinctiveness. The Interdialectal tried to find new compromises on such issues, and *Skol an Emsav*, *Ar Falz*, and the UDB all started using it, hoping that others would follow and peace be declared. It was not. *Al Liamm*, the most influential publishing organization, persisted with the 'ZH', and had produced the most comprehensive Breton/French dictionaries, compiled by Hemon. In a world of learnt Breton, dictionaries of this kind are essential and the Interdialectal had none. In 1979, *Skol an Emsav* officially reverted to the 'ZH'; many members had never stopped using it anyway. The war between Rennes and Brest continued, with Interdialectal proponents often suspect to both sides. It was a UDB member who first used the Interdialectal forms in print, and these are sometimes described, disparagingly, as 'UDB orthography'. The UDB uses French in its meetings, and is thus already condemned from a Rennes position. Since the UDB pioneer of the Interdialectal forms teaches at Brest, Brest is divided and weakened. Rennes, on the other hand, sits comfortably, as 'Breton' against 'French', and produces a linguistic journal which has been known to decorate its whole cover with triumphant *zh*s (see *Hor Yezh* ('Our Language'), especially 1974, no. 96, produced when the supposedly conciliatory talks were fast breaking down).

Different federations of groups in the movement have been created around the opposing poles of the 'ZH' and the OU, and have fought one another for shares in the money from the Cultural Charter. While some older members of the opposed camps have necessarily sat in the same room in formal meetings of the Cultural Council of Brittany, they have avoided speaking to one another. Younger militants, however, inevitably meet and discuss their views. The quarrels of the last war are not so alive for the young, and the 'Rennes' vision of Breton is, in any case, a *de facto* reality in militant gatherings, where Breton is the preferred medium of communication (even if the communicants cannot speak it, and independent of whether it be written *brezoneg* (OU, KLT), *brehoneg* (OU, G), or *brezhoneg* ('ZH'; interdialectal)). The old structures mainly come alive, I have found, in slander and insult, confided, aside, to the interested researcher. They still can come alive face to face, however, and when they do, sparks can fly. On one memorable occasion during my first year in Brittany, I saw a young 'Rennes' and a young 'Brest' take a swing at each other during a youthful summer festival. 'Rennes' declared that 'Brest' was 'destroying Breton', as a wounded 'Brest' stalked off shouting 'fascist' and 'collaborator', deliberately using French to add to the insult.

Commemoration: 'Lunfask'

The Second World War lives on, therefore, through orthographic wrangles and in the occasional drunken skirmish. It is also alive in an annual, and somewhat peripheral, gathering in which militants of the war period meet every Easter Monday in Lower Brittany to commemorate the Abbé Perrot, a Breton priest slain by the Communist Resistance in 1943. Perrot was, for many years, editor of a revived version of *Feiz ha Breiz*, but he also had links with *Breiz Atao*, of which church authorities did not approve. Local, oral history also has it that he willingly offered accommodation to German soldiers during the war. Perrot's parish was in the commune of Scrignac, which is of Communist leanings and where the Resistance was strong. It seems to have been a local Communist who shot him. I attended one Easter Monday ('Lunfask' in Breton) commemoration service for Perrot. This ceremony is not usually attended, I should stress, by young militants in the mainstream of modern Breton militancy; it has been, for the most part, a history they would rather forget. A vanload of police stood by, unashamedly taking photographs, and openly present also in case of trouble as they apparently are every year. Although some of the local population now laugh at the gathering, there are tales of fights and hostility in the past when militant attendance was higher.

The ceremony was held by Perrot's grave, in a neglected graveyard outside a chapel. There were some in attendance whom I recognized as the parental generation of prominent militant families. Posters of Hemon were on sale, as were *Al Liamm* publications. Some who spoke to me were persuaded that I must be Irish. One woman, whose brother is, I have been told, still in exile in Germany, eagerly told me tales, in French, of attempts to ship arms in the past 'from your country'. A well-known personality interrupted to explain, in Breton, the merits of the 'ZH' to me. Then the ceremony began, with speeches in French and songs in Breton. One speaker reminded us that Celts were 'not materialists': this common sentiment can mean, for the left in the movement, anti-capitalist; here it meant that ours was a 'spiritual fight' against the evils of the world, embodied in 'French' politics of right or left alike. We then sang the Breton 'national' anthem, the *Bro Goz* (now *Gozh*) *Va Zadoù* (a translation of the Welsh *Hen Wlad Fy Nhadau*, '(Old) Land of My Fathers').

After this, a small group of younger enthusiasts, whom I had not previously seen at any militant gathering, wanted to sing German songs. They had already been doing so, heartily, in a nearby café before the ceremony. 'Are you mocking us?' the arms-from-Ireland lady demanded of them, adding, 'I suppose you're going to accuse us of collaboration?' She indicated that she would accept the accusation without shame. The young group pleaded that they were perfectly serious and not singing in mockery. A few of the older men present were clearly unhappy, not wishing either Perrot or the war-time movement to be remembered as unambiguously pro-German. However, the younger militants explained that they genuinely preferred the older movement to the post-1968 enthusiasts, and one young man, who sported high leather boots and a conspicuously large leather belt, explained that such enthusiasts were all 'decadent'. One of his colleagues had a *Breiz Atao* emblem round her neck.

This young man had been a member of a Breton language organization until the early 1970s. He explained that he had left because the movement was involved in 'anything from anarchism to drugs'. Since 1968, indeed, 'Breton' had gathered every fashionable dissent, and for this young man and his friends, the only option between 'decadence' on the one hand and the 'French' world on the other was 'fascism', which they openly espoused, in their own private logic of oppositional alternatives. There was some suggestion also that 'royalism' might be an acceptable ambition, but a Breton royalism, evidently; one of their number was, I was told, connected with those who had blown up part of the palace at Versailles. Another member of the group was introduced to me as a 'Norman' – 'you know, the Normans, who came in and destroyed everything in the tenth century'. The 'Norman' looked suitably contrite and declared himself 'Breton now'. The Second World War and tenth-century invasions mixed with visions of a 'restoration', accompanied by the self-conscious click of leather-booted heels.

The First World War

Militant history tends to pass lightly or silently over the Second World War, but it will often highlight the First. There oppression is, at least statistically, easier to find. The First World War brought decisive changes to Brittany. Republicanism took hold in many areas in the years immediately after the war, and the Breton movement of the period met its greatest opposition from Breton-speakers, especially Breton-speaking soldiers (see Déniel 1976:69). The 1919 petition, which I mentioned earlier, would have had little support in Brittany in its political ambitions or in any attempt to establish Breton on a par with French. Two important points, however, which appeared in this petition would no doubt have had some echo in popular opinion: one was the sentiment that Breton soldiers had fought courageously for France, and the other was a plea for more language-teaching efficiency in the schools. More use of Breton might, it was felt, help pupils learn French (rather than using the old 'direct method': De L'Estourbeillon 1919). Similar sentiments, about Breton courage and the help that Breton could give to French, appeared on the forms of the 1934–8 *Ar Brezoneg er Skol* petition. When Louis Ogès had written on the Breton question in 1919 (see Chapter four, p. 67), it had been to try to end argument about whether or not Breton in the schools would weaken or strengthen France before Germany, and to stress Breton's role in helping the acquisition of French. The First World War increased awareness of the value of French in a wider world, and, in many ways, it paved the way for the 1934–8 votes for *Ar Brezoneg er Skol*.

Modern militants tend to view the First World War as an externally imposed destruction of the traditional Breton-speaking world; it was a disaster because Breton-speakers died and Breton-speaking declined. Militants now regularly observe that the proportion of Bretons (c. one in seventeen of the population) who died in the First World War was twice that for France overall (c. one in thirty-four) (for the source of the estimates, in *Breiz Atao*, see Déniel 1976:215, Le Sann and Férec 1973:13, and Morgan 1979:36; sometimes they are given as one in thirteen Bretons and one in twenty-eight for France; 240–250,000 Breton soldiers are said to have died in this war). The proportions involved have often been cited as evidence of a wilful slaughter of Bretons, rather than of a marked French patriotism. Some militants have explained that so many Bretons died because they could not understand orders in French (a view which leaves aside the great proportion of Bretons from Upper Brittany who would have known only French). Others have suggested that Bretons were deliberately and maliciously put in the front line by French officers. It is not acceptable that Bretons died for France. Mobilization in Brittany was intense and indeed, to militant chagrin, the proportion of Bretons who enlisted was double that of the French as a whole (see Gwegen 1975:45). A popular Breton singer of the time urged Bretons to enlist and die for France, as did the journal *Feiz ha Breiz*, which saw the fighting as a religious war (see Elegoët 1979:85; Stephens 1976:373). The young soldiers knew, many from school, that they were defending France, their country, and they were off, in *Union Sacrée*, to recapture Protestant Alsace-Lorraine for Church and Republic alike. Those who did not readily enlist were, unless absolved by family responsibilities, treated at home as irreligious or unpatriotic cowards. Every Breton commune has a proud monument to its dead of this war. In the area of the *pays bigouden*, in southern Finistère, which is one of the several areas reputed in French ethnography to be representative of Brittany, the much-studied commune of Plozévet has a striking memorial inscribed with the sentiment: 'We Died For Love of France. 1914–1918'. Some memorials are inscribed in Breton, suggesting both the transitional awareness of those times (or a newer self-consciousness, in coastal areas, from external interest and tourism), and the *Union Sacrée: Evit Doue hag ar Vro* ('For God and Country') is common in the Léon. Most common are those memorials inscribed simply: *Morts Pour La France*.

During my first year in Brittany, I travelled widely, wishing, among other things, to try out my newly learnt Breton on local speakers. The easiest people to approach often seemed to be groups of old men, standing on street corners or sitting in bars, talking Breton to one another. My self-conscious enquiries in Breton, asking the time or a direction, were often met with an immediate retort in French: 'I was in the '14–18 war, you know!'; 'I have seen the world.' The First World War was the first real encounter, for many, with the wider French world and beyond, and the soldiers brought home, along with French, tales of adventure and heroism. Those who still survive will tell such tales with pride, and they are told, elaborated, and commemorated in local meetings of the *anciens combattants*.

The First World War was one important high-point, throughout France, in the popular apprehension of Frenchness (see especially Weber 1977), but it was also an important way in which Bretons learnt what it meant, in this wider world, to be Breton. One set of images which many learnt at this time was that of Bretons as backward, stubborn, and conservative, or recensions thereof (an imagery in which *chouans*, Armorican granite,

Celts, clerics and nobles, and common images of the peasantry, and more besides, could all combine). Negative and positive evaluations of such imagery are two sides of the same coin, and easily receive empirical confirmation. The uncivilized Breton peasant, resistant to progress, was also, in the same structures, steadfast, trustworthy, and tenaciously courageous, as he showed himself to be in the Great War. Such imagery entered popular tales of the war itself. On various occasions since, in demonstrations against national agricultural policy, for example, or as a striking industrial work-force, Bretons have been able to appropriate a 'legendary stubbornness' as part of their self-image and effective sloganry (see Lovecy 1982). Such a self-image, however, is capable of a willing and self-conscious synonymy with the spirit of deepest, true-grit France, in a way that the new material of an oppositional Breton identity, as acquired and constructed in the educated circles of the movement, is not.

Chapter eight

Debates, demos, and dance

So far, we have seen that the writing of Breton histories and the speaking of Breton are key enterprizes in the movement. We have also seen that the movement is anxious that the 'Breton people' should live their identity and culture fully. In this chapter, I consider some other activities of the mainstream of the movement – including discussions, demonstrations (or *'manifs'*, Br. and Fr.), language festivals, folk-music concerts, and dancing – during which militants are being quite self-consciously 'Breton'.

Debates

The Breton movement often organizes 'debates', where militants can get together to air their Breton, and the 'problems of Breton culture' can be discussed. Such debates often become media events, with press releases, and journalists in attendance. All the events described in this chapter, with the exception of the last debate in this first section, were given some coverage in the press.

The UDB is particularly skilled at putting militants round a table, refreshments at hand, to talk about Breton (in French), and then publishing these 'debates' in its journals for both internal and public consumption. *Skol en Emsav* is also adept at organizing debates, although these are always in Breton. Together with *Ar Falz, Skol an Emsav* has also organized an important gathering of the movement called *Gouel ar Brezhoneg*[1] ('Breton-language Festival', modelled on modern Welsh-language festivals). First launched in 1974, this has been held annually in May or June, in a different site in Lower Brittany, usually in a large bourg or town. In June 1979, for example, it was held in La Roche-Derrien (or *Ar Roc'h*) in the Côtes-du-Nord. For the *Gouel*, militant *brezhonegerien* (Breton-speakers) usually take over rooms or a hall, or set up a marquee, and occupy a field in which some camp. They talk, dance, drink a good deal, listen to music, and perform or watch plays, all in Breton, and they buy and sell Breton literature and militant insignia, including posters, badges, and T-shirts with printed slogans. They also have debates, in Breton, about Breton.

Debates usually involve the citation of past oppression. The 'French' authorities, conjured up as the opposition, are rarely present, and so the debates are inevitably one-sided. In 1979, the main debate was about Breton in the schools, always a favourite topic, but especially so at that time. The major teaching unions (including the SNI) had been invited but did not turn up. The militants sat in a large room in the town hall, debating the issue with themselves. The 'debate' turned into outrage over the second language option (see Chapter four, p. 62). Militants who had initially congratulated themselves on this option now declared its granting to have been a deliberate 'trap'.

After this debate at the *Gouel* we watched a film, recorded by militants, of some people from the vicinity speaking their 'local Breton'. On the screen we saw and heard three old people, two men and a woman, talking and joking in Breton, over glasses of wine and cider, in their humble farmhouse kitchen. Their Breton, which seemed very abbreviated in relation to the fullness of standard literary forms, was not easy to understand, and the audience, largely Breton-speaking through assiduous use of standard texts, had some difficulty in following. There was a general air of awe and commitment in the room nevertheless. Some took notes, others helped one another to understand by supplying standard alternatives, and a few hardy enthusiasts laughed loudly at some of the jokes, indicating that they, at least, were following. Meanwhile, near the back of the room, were three much older people, two men and a woman, who had come in rather nervously after the film had begun. They were smartly dressed, unlike the young militants, who were mostly in old sweaters and jeans. Since they seemed to be understanding what was actually said in the film, I asked the woman, in Breton, if she lived locally. She replied, in French, that she did, and laughed: these were, in fact, the three people in the film. They occasionally spoke to each other, and to me, in French; on the film, they were speaking Breton, wholly and heartily. They were the only people in the room speaking French, and yet they were captured on film as 'Breton-speakers', for the contemplation of, and in the image of, committed *brezhonegerien*.

During the earlier debate, one militant, who was apparently close to despair, had said that the poor status of Breton was 'the fault of the Breton people' who had not fought for their language and had 'bourgeois' aspirations towards French. Others had quickly shifted the blame to the 'system', and sighed over the 'alienation' of the people. The succeeding film was not, therefore, without its ironies. The local people at the film were all dressed up, and talking nicely, in French, in deference to the educated company in which they found themselves. The educated company, on the other hand, made the locals' humble, unschooled chatter a privileged event in a peculiarly 'Breton' world. For the militants, it is 'bourgeois' to speak French, and they therefore spoke Breton, aspiring to the unbourgeois naturalness of the 'people'. The people, however, were speaking French, aspiring to 'bourgeois' nicety, leaving the 'Breton' world of educated enthusiasms to chase its own ever-disappearing tail. This is an important point, to which, in other forms, we will return in later chapters.

After the film another debate was threatened, as militants obeyed a compulsion to draw up chairs and talk about Breton; this time, however, most wanted to get away. They had already been indoors for over two hours, 'debating' for much of the time, and were now keen to get to the well-stocked open-air bars of the *Gouel*, to talk in Breton over wine and cider. Many also go to local bars and cafés, and generally talk among themselves. Although their custom is welcome, it is not clear that the local population always knows, or cares, that a *Gouel* is taking place, in spite of keen publicity. When I asked directions to the *Gouel* from locals in La Roche-Derrien, for example, there was some bewilderment and shrugging of shoulders, until one lady in a shop decided that I must want '*le truc breton*' (Fr. 'the Breton thing'), and duly directed me. This kind of reply was common, I found, whenever I was seeking a militant gathering. The movement has created a 'Breton' world and, by its keen publicity, largely usurps the Breton definition; as a result, 'Breton' things and 'Breton' culture are often associated with the movement, or with specific events of the kind that they create and participate in, 'folklore' included. For the lady in the shop the adjective '*breton*' did not designate her own world, but rather something special going on in the town, in which she was not involved. The three locals who were directly involved, through the video film, were there as spectators of themselves, morally transformed through a world not their own.

The movement always has a problem in trying to involve the 'people' in its debates. At one level, this is a definitional problem, for if the 'people' were sufficiently educated and intellectually confident to participate in the movement, then they would no longer be the 'people'. At another level, however, it is known that attendance at militant debates consists of recognizable regulars rather than any wider 'public'. As part of its campaign to 'conscientize the Breton people', the *Front Culturel* (described in Chapter five) organized an explicitly 'public' debate in Morlaix town hall, on 14 March 1980. In spite of ample publicity, little over eighty people attended, all known sympathizers of the movement, with some hardy militants having come from as far away as Rennes (almost 120 miles) for a couple of hours' discussion.

At the beginning of this 'public debate', *Talbenn* members (Chapter five, p. 90) outlined the Front's history and aims, in speeches delivered from a stage, using microphones and well-prepared notes. Bretons were urged, in strong terms, to fight for their culture and language. It was sad, as a

militant next to me whispered, that all the preparations and grandilo-
quence should have been wasted in 'preaching to the converted'. The
speeches were made in Breton, and then translated into French by an
interpreter, himself a member of both the UDB and *Skol an Emsav*. This
was the only time I saw an interpreter used in this way, and it did not last
long. The interpreter developed a blushing self-consciousness, sometimes
laughing at his predicament: the process was wearyingly long, and at a
practical level unnecessary, for all present spoke French. Speakers made
great efforts to give grand speeches in a studiously learnt and learned
Breton, and the interpreter struggled to put all this into French, while the
speakers listened and sometimes corrected him, for they could have
expressed themselves better in French in the first place. The interpreter's
role was of moral and political importance; although the aim was to allow
everyone to use the language of their choice, practicality and impatience
soon made this French.

The translation issue raised, however, an important question from the
floor. Was 'Breton culture' just a translation of 'French culture' into
Breton? The emphatic answer was, of course, no. 'Breton culture' was the
world of the people, and 'bourgeois' dominance and ideas were to be
discarded. Breton was a different language, it was said, and a language was
a culture, and a culture was a different way of life. This is a common
argument in the movement, and it is an argument in which a one-to-one
equation of language and culture (a common idea in many educated
circles) is taken through contemporary structures of difference supplied by
the majority world. Thus, for example, one noted *Skol an Emsav* militant
once told me that he had thought of going to India, in the early 1970s, to
seek an alternative life-style, but realized that Breton offered such
possibilities at home.

The 'Breton' world can, in opposition to 'French', fill all the map of
Brittany, and the existence of the French language in Brittany is something
that militant logic can deal with. More problematic, however, is the
existence, in Upper Brittany, of another 'minority'. Here we come to
the question of 'Gallo', and to our last debate in this section. The formal
debate in question took place in the Celtic Department of Rennes
University and was summoned by two young members of an organization
called *Les Amis du Parler Gallo* ('Friends of Gallo'). The debate was
advertised by a poster which read *'Les Gallos sont-ils Bretons?'* ('Are
Gallos Bretons?') Since they live in Brittany, the answer might seem to be
an obvious 'yes'. The issue is not so simple, however.

Gallo figures in orthodox linguistics as a 'dialect of French', and as part
of the *langue d'oïl* of northern France. It is not, in established categorizations, 'Celtic', and it occupies not only Upper Brittany but also areas
outside, including parts of Normandy. Gallo cannot easily claim a Breton
specificity in the Breton movement's terms, and there is no space for it on

the 'Breton' map. Educated investment in the popular Breton world, from the *Barzaz Breiz* onwards, has tended to concentrate on the Breton-speaking area to the extent that Breton stands, in minority enthusiasms, for all of Brittany. Gallo interests are, in many ways, a late back-formation, a copy of the Breton movement and its world. A *parler gallo* and a 'Gallo culture' were only drawn up with conviction in the mid-1970s, with enthusiasts looking back through a century or more of Breton folklore studies for every hint of a 'Gallo tradition'. *Les Amis du Parler Gallo* (claiming 300 members by 1980) was established in 1976, and is mainly composed of older folklorists, along with some young members who try at times to talk of a 'Gallo movement', in imitation of the fashionable political commitments of the 'Breton movement'. The first main publication of the association, launched by the young president ('an *agrégé d'histoire*'), is called in Gallo *Le Lian*. This is a direct terminological copy of *Al Liamm*, but the 'link' in question here is that between Breton and Gallo. Gallo enthusiasts assert that 'Gallo is a Breton language', and often point out, somewhat ingratiatingly, that 'Gallo has Breton words in it'.

Les Amis du Parler Gallo has been represented in the Cultural Council of Brittany, and also in the Front, but the movement only barely tolerates it, with token gestures of support. In rhetoric in which Breton rides the morality of 'pluralism' and 'diversity', and of linguistic and cultural tolerance and equality, Gallo cannot be dismissed. Nevertheless, some committed *brezhonegerien* do not hide their disapproval, for Gallo, to them, is merely 'getting in the way of Breton'. I have heard Gallo enthusiasts quietly but sternly warned by Breton militants to 'keep out of our way'. It was with some courage, therefore, that two young Gallos demanded an open discussion in Rennes University which, although in Upper Brittany, is a hot-bed of Breton language militancy.

In the Rennes debate there were, for once, two sides, although the Gallos were greatly outnumbered. 'Celtic' students, accompanied by a hefty contingent of militants from outside the department, lounged back confidently in their chairs and accused the two Gallos of 'folklore' and of defending a *'patois'* that was really only 'a kind of French'. The Gallos retorted angrily that they were 'fed up with being treated as second-class Bretons', that Upper Brittany was not a *'tabula rasa* to be re-Celticized', and that notions of 'language', 'dialect', and *'patois'* were in any case all relative and the product of French linguistic and political centralism. The Gallos stressed that they had common cause with the Breton movement against French centralism, but the Breton militants were clearly not going to share that cause in Brittany. Gallo could not be a 'proper language', they said, since it had no unity and no orthography other than French. The Gallos replied that one of their main aims was to give dignity to the many schoolchildren in Upper Brittany who came to school speaking what is usually seen as 'bad French'. Gallos feel that such children should be recognized as 'bilingual', and it is felt to be some credit to Gallo efforts that the Cultural Charter recognized the existence of Gallo, and that teachers are now encouraged to study Gallo forms, and to help children distinguish Gallo and French. 'Bretons', however, in the Rennes debate, dismissed Gallo ambitions as paltry. Gallo merely encouraged Bretons to speak French, when what was needed was to encourage them to speak Breton, which was at least 'a language'.

The Breton movement self-consciously usurps the entire 'Breton' definition, and will not happily tolerate another 'minority' competing for the same moral, philological, and sociological space. Students in the Rennes Celtic Department pin up maps that mark the whole of Brittany as *Breizh*, with all the towns, in Upper and Lower Brittany alike, given their Breton names. Furtive Gallos have been known to sneak in and cross out such Breton names as *Roazhon* (Rennes), *Sant Brieg* (Saint Brieuc), and *Naoned* (Nantes), and scribble in *Rënn, San Berieu,* and *Naont,* their Gallo names. Breton militants know, however, that their minority cause has stronger resources of self-definition and a more secure appeal. Some of those in the Breton movement are from what might be termed 'Gallo' homes, and in many ways 'Breton' has not only created but also pre-empted the Gallo cause, attracting many of its potential adherents; some younger Gallos within *Les Amis du Parler Gallo* are now learning Breton. Gallo, nevertheless, can quietly assert its own minority propriety. Some Gallos take their own definition against the Breton movement, smearing it with every accusation that the movement uses against French, and characterizing it as a bunch of 'raving reactionaries', or 'linguistic imperialists' or 'Jacobin nationalists'. As the competing minorities accuse one another of majority links and faults, the 'majority' world itself seems to be empty as a category of self-ascription – no one wants to be the 'majority' and no one is 'French'.

This does not prevent the 'majority' category from achieving a tragic realization of its own hollowness. A young teacher friend in Rennes, who teaches literary aspects of 'Breton culture', in French, at a secondary school, would dearly love to be more truly a part of a 'minority' world: 'But I cannot speak Breton or Gallo', she explained, in French, at a dinner party with compulsive Gallo and Breton enthusiasts present, 'so I have no language and no culture.'

Festivities

Any account of festivities in Brittany must begin with the *fest-noz* (pl. *festoù-noz),* which punctuates and ends militant gatherings. *Fest-noz* translates literally into English as 'night festival', and into French as *fête de nuit.* A summer visitor to Brittany will often find posters or signs to a *fest-noz*, for the event is now common and extends outside the militant world. In tourist literature and posters, the term is accommodated as '*un fest-noz*', with details of time and location in French, and it is often pronounced /ˈfɛsˈnɔs/, as if it were a French word. Militants and connoisseurs are careful, however, to pronounce it /ˈfɛsˈnoːz/.

The *fest-noz* is now commonly regarded as an ancient and peculiarly Breton and Celtic folk-custom. The term is relatively new to much of Lower Brittany. It seems to have originated in a small area of central Finistère, between Carhaix and Poullaouen, where it described a special celebration, with food, drink, and dance, that followed collective agricultural work, principally the potato and beet harvests in September. With the mechanization of agriculture in the 1950s and 1960s, the *fest-noz* virtually died out. Scholars and enthusiasts of 'Breton culture' revived (or, more accurately, re-created) it, and, by the early 1970s, it was part of a vogue for folk-music and country dance all over Brittany. The *fest-noz* became a paying affair, often subsidizing militant groups or activities, in which scruffy dress, heavy drinking, pot, and left-wing politics have mingled easily with often struggling conversations in a hastily learnt Breton. Large circles of sweating youths perform simple dance steps, shuffling round and round in newly bought clogs, in rustic celebration of a harvest they have not brought home.

Through the *fest-noz*, the 'Breton' world makes a clear claim to peasant authenticity. There has long been a romantic association of the peasant, the soil, and Breton, and the peasantry and the rural world are commonly seen as strongholds of the Breton language. It might seem obviously appropriate, therefore, that militants should don clogs and dance country dances, preferably in fields, speaking Breton at the same time. Two points should be made, however, about this implication of the peasant in the 'alternative' and 'minority' militancy of the modern, urban intellectual. First, a growing interest, in the 1960s, in peasant movements in the Third World made the peasant a respectable vehicle for 'revolution'. Second, it was not until the post-war period that the French peasant began quite obviously to disappear, and to assume, therefore, the glamour of a disappearing world, ripe for revaluation. '1968' brought together revolution and alternative life-styles, and it was after 1968 that the *fest-noz* began to take off, and that militants began to learn Breton in earnest, and to dance round and round in fields in peasant clogs. A good deal of my fieldwork with the Breton movement was spent thus dancing the night hours away, in rhythmic solidarity.

The dances of the *fest-noz* are usually simple forms taken from the repertory of 'traditional' Breton dancing, as established by the 'Celtic circles'. The first 'Celtic circle' seems to have been created by a Breton enthusiast in Paris during the First World War, but these circles only began to flourish in Brittany in the 1950s. The movement was still tentatively recovering from the Second World War, and in dancing, music and costume 'Breton culture' found an acceptable face. Dances and costumes, old-fashioned and disappearing at the popular level, were appropriated and recreated in stylized form by the 'Celtic circles', who studied them and paraded or performed them for public or tourist consumption. The movement now speaks disparagingly of such activities, as we have seen (in Chapter five, p. 91), and few militants would now ever wear Breton costume, but they nevertheless owe much of their dance repertoire to the Celtic circles. It is interesting to note that some of the dances have a distant origin in rural imitations of high and courtly society. The rural world danced its image of sophistication, and centuries later, educated militants borrowed back this one-time sophistication as an image of the rustic and pastoral. The costumes worn by Celtic circles have also passed, in the same way, from peasant imitations of high society to higher society's imitation of the peasant (see Creston 1978; Guilcher 1976, 1979).

'Celt' and 'peasant' now share a common status of natural simplicity and politico-economic minority. The music in the *festoù-noz* manifests, accordingly, the full range of such values, from ethnic acoustics, through protest songs, to the more aggressive rhythms of folk-rock. A Breton form of unaccompanied rondel-duet, known as *kan-ha-diskan*, which can serve as a dancing accompaniment for an impromptu *fest-noz*, is now used for protest songs; the Breton pipes, the *biniou* and the *bombarde*, have come to take pride of place as 'Celtic' and traditional instruments, in imitation of the Scottish bagpipes, which are also often played. At larger Celtic festivals, acoustic music often gives way, to the chagrin of the ethnic purists, to the greater amplification of folk-rock or progressive folk, with electric guitars, basses, and fiddles. Alan Stivell was the main innovator in Breton folk-rock after his success at the Paris Olympia at the beginning of the 1970s. Stivell has said that he sings in the name of 'Celtic culture' which has been 'suffocated' but which has 'roots that seem to come to the surface at every revolt against order' and against 'Germanico-Latin rationality and materialism' (see the record cover of '*Reflets*', Alan Stivell, Fontana label). Stivell sings sometimes in French, but prefers to sing in (learnt) Breton and on occasions in Irish, Scottish Gaelic, or Welsh. Even if few understand his Celtic, the political message is clear enough. Following Stivell, Breton musicians and singers of all kinds blossomed in Brittany, and some said, in the late 1970s, that they were 'born in 1968' (see *Autrement*, 1979, no. 19). Most will make a stirring speech about oppression during their performance, and will sing about 'revolt'. Many militants now in the Breton movement were persuaded to join by the success of Stivell and by the Breton folk-image that he made 'pop'. From Paris, in the aftermath of 1968, Stivell created a 'Breton' world, *à la Villemarqué*, but in modern dress.

'Celtic' groups from all over Brittany, and Britain and Ireland, now come to Brittany to play their 'Celtic folk music'. Much of this is obviously derivative of the American and English music scenes (Dylan, Baez, Steeleye Span, Fairport Convention, and so on), but it becomes definitionally 'Celtic'. Tin whistles, fiddles, bagpipes, and all manner of olde-worlde woodwind are accompanied by guitars, banjos, mandolins, hurdy-gurdies, bouzoukis, zithers, and sitars. One visiting group, half Irish and half Scottish, told me that they admired the simple Breton pipes, and the 'funky peasant dancing' of the *festoù-noz*. After one concert they gave, however, they were given brown rice and asked to sleep on straw, and by the end of a summer tour in Brittany, they were 'fed up with all this ethnic, Celtic stuff', and longing to get home 'for a bathroom, clean clothes, a good sleep, and some unadulterated rock'.

The *fest-noz* is a regular event in the programme of the *Gouel ar Brezhoneg* (the annual Breton-language Festival mentioned earlier, p. 138). If locals turn up at the *Gouel*, they are usually youngsters, who come along for the bars and dancing of the *fest-noz*, and have a merry drunken time, in French, while the militants, with their better education and higher social standing, gather in their own groups and get equally drunk in Breton. A 'Breton' event such as a *fest-noz* creates a requirement for a high level of inebriation: on several occasions, militants have told me that they drink so heavily at such events because 'that's what we Celts do, isn't it?' To confirm this, visiting Welsh enthusiasts, coming both as jolly Celts and hardy rugby players, set a heavy drinking standard that the Breton militants strive to follow. Many Welsh are present at such events, and it is not always a happy thing to be 'English', as I indicated in Chapter six. The Welsh themselves, however, are not immune to re-definition and exclusion. One drunken Breton militant who, 'just for a laugh', was trying out his school-English, found himself sharply rebuked by two Welsh visitors. He was not going to have his fun spoilt by two Welshmen, who at once became, for him, 'foreigners'.

At the *Gouel*, besides the *festoù-noz*, there are sometimes afternoon performances of music, often by 'Celtic' musicians, and in the first *Gouel* I attended some older locals came along to one of these. They particularly appreciated a Welsh group who performed an intricate clog-and-broom dance. While the older locals applauded loudly, a *Skol an Emsav* personality dismissed the performance with disgust, as 'folklore'. A Welsh girl present excited further disgust among hard-core militants by taking down the French *tricolore* from the local *mairie* or town hall. She was evidently used to such actions at home, in a very different political world, and was doing this for the Bretons. The militants knew, however, how much this 'activism' could antagonize the local people. A small huddle of militants stood in awful common dread, for a while, of the weight of popular historical association that might now pour down on them, and then went quietly to try to put the flag back. While some decided that the girl in question was really 'English', which apparently explained how she could have been so daft, others took the event as confirmation of whispered suspicion that 'the Welsh movement' was politically immature. Militants happily appropriate the Welsh image in the interests of being un-French, but they are not entirely happy with the Welsh, who do not seem to them to manifest all the desirable political commitments of a 'minority' group *(Plaid Cymru*, for example, the Welsh party that is best known in Brittany, is far from being politically radical in their terms). Visiting Welsh enthusiasts are uneasily aware of this, and, gathered in a local café at the *Gouel* in La-Roche-Derrien, a few discussed wistfully how they wished that Welsh were linked 'to ecology and politics and all that'. Wales, meanwhile, remains something like a Celtic paradise to Breton militants, for the official status that the Welsh language enjoys there.

For many Breton militants, it is Ireland, and, especially, Northern Ireland, that has eclipsed Wales as a favourite political identification. The militants are on the side of the 'Irish', which means 'Catholic' and, of course, 'Celtic'; the Protestants are usually talked of as 'English'. Debate and discussion on Northern Ireland is common during festivities, and the issue often resolved by recommending that the 'English' get out of Ireland. This usually implies shipping out all the Protestants, who are always treated as part of an intrusive English majority, and never as an indigenous minority. Militants who have spent a fortnight with members of *Sinn Fein*, or their associates, are deemed authorities on the question. Money is collected, through the sale of literature at gatherings and festivals, for despatch to related groups. It has caused some disquiet in the 'Celtic' world, therefore, when certain Welsh and Scottish representatives, in youthful 'Interceltic Congresses', have refused to vote for motions for immediate British withdrawal from Northern Ireland. The Bretons can both maintain their own views and keep their kinship with the Welsh and the Scottish structurally intact by declaring that such ideas show that even the most devoted Celt can be, unwittingly, 'English' or 'Anglicized'. We have already seen how the militants' world-view is self-confirming in this way: those who do not agree with them are variously 'alienated', 'French', 'Frenchified', 'English', 'Anglicized', and so on. There is much about Northern Ireland particularly (including aspects of its history, and such initially shocking discoveries as the presence of Welsh and Scottish troops in the province) which has swiftly been passed through this re-definitional system.

In some respects, the Breton movement's perceptions of Northern Ireland are born of more general mismatches between the political and economic contexts of Britain and France, mismatches which can come forcefully into play in matters that are sensitive to either side. For example, delegations from the Breton movement who have visited Northern Ireland have regularly returned with extremely lurid accounts of the conditions and sufferings there, and it has only become apparent to those Bretons who have also seen certain English urban areas that at least some of what, in the militant press, is categorically attributed to 'English' oppression is very much a part of an ageing, urban, industrial landscape more generally; such a landscape is unknown in much of France, and especially so in areas such as Brittany. There is also, in France, a strong and general conviction that the Northern Ireland situation mimics that of Algeria; such a comparison, potent and readily assimilable in France, dissolves under scholarly scrutiny from elsewhere (see, for example, Roberts 1986), but it has made a 'Catholic' position more easily appropriable as a cause by a traditionally anti-clerical French left, and also fits well with the enduring French image of Britain as an incorrigible imperial power (an image often revivified in EEC debate, in which butter from New Zealand and British troops in Northern Ireland can easily become the same problem). Another understanding of Northern Ireland with some staying power on the French left has been that of class warfare: working-class Catholics against a Protestant bourgeoisie, although the discovery, by some, of working-class Protestants and a substantial Catholic middle class has muddled this a little. These modes of understanding Northern Ireland and some aspects of the Breton movement's position on the question are common in France generally, and, in a variety of ways (some of them quite direct), such representations have defined and fed the conflict itself. Some educated opinion in Europe has begun to suggest that the Northern Ireland situation is perhaps more complicated than so far perceived, but such views do not meet with applause. The European Parliament's special report for example (see Haagerup 1984), launched to great anti-imperial and anti-British fanfare, fell into media oblivion with its conclusions that the picture was complicated and the solutions not simple. It is all the more understandable, therefore, that any attempts within the Breton movement to suggest that a rethink on some points might be helpful have immediately been countered and muted with the kind of explanatory schemes and re-definitional logic I have already outlined.

We have seen that the movement appropriates the causes and problems of others, in a manner not always very fastidious, to proclaim its own oppression. We saw, in Chapter five, how militants have taken for themselves the image of Algeria for example, and also Lorraine. The Irish analogy is particularly favoured, however. Many militants compare the 'Irish/English' question (for such it is to them) with their own Breton/French struggles, and are unashamedly envious of the 'Irish' who are, it seems, unambiguously oppressed, with guns turned on them.

An influential figure in the movement suggested to me, during my first year in Brittany, that if the French authorities ever moved in the army, with guns trained on the Bretons, then the movement's vision would be realized, and its work done for it. In February and March of 1980 it almost seemed that this ambition was to be realized, when the government was holding a public enquiry into a planned nuclear power station at Plogoff, in south-west Finistère. Most local people were opposed to the development, as was the movement; since the object of the enquiry was to judge public acceptance of the site, it became manifestly unnecessary, for the enquiry turned into an open fight against well-armed and tear-gas happy riot troops who went in to ensure that the enquiry proceeded according to the letter of the law. In their fight against power station and riot troops alike, one important metaphor for the older local people was that of the Second World War: some donned their medals for the struggle against the 'occupants', others made stirring speeches in the style of De Gaulle, and the local mayor wore the *tricolore* of his office throughout. This eruption of Frenchness was not what militants, who flocked to the area, expected or wanted. However, a 'Breton' dimension did become important locally, under this same external pressure, and it came alive principally in boasts of the obdurate tenacity of the Bretons (an image mentioned at the end of Chapter seven). The mayor of Plogoff himself used this image to the press, and it became the more pronounced as reporters from Paris and the national media sought, not the villagers of Plogoff, but 'Bretons' – and found them, in their well-known, if now anti-nuclear, resistance and stubbornness. They also found them in a new 'alternative' dress, and media publicity made no distinction between Breton movement and villagers: they were all Bretons. While Plogoff fought as the stubborn corner of true Republican, democratic France, militants wheeled in the opposition of 'Bretons' against 'French'. The imagery which this opposition brought with it was also imported, in other forms, by an educated, disaffected youth more generally, and Plogoff found itself dressed against the outside world and, in the eyes of that world, in the full modern clothes of the *Gemeinschaft/Gesellschaft* opposition, as the ecological, anti-centralist, anti-militarist, small-scale, simple, 'face-to-face' (etc.) community. The moral strength, support, and publicity that all this gave to the local cause meant that a windmill and a *maison autonome* project (both designed and imported by Breton militants living in the area I describe in Part four) and an 'alternative' sheep farm and a specially written Breton song (composed by a *Diwan* teacher, and recorded by a militant living, again, in the area described in Part four) were all temporarily tolerated or taken on board, for the duration of the enquiry, by the people of Plogoff. Any Breton/ French political gloss was quite strongly resisted and resented, but militants nevertheless grew very excited about the affair, organizing giant rallies and music festivals at Plogoff, with Stivell leading the dance at the largest of these (for further ethnographic comment on local sentiment, and a full account of the events at Plogoff, see Kuter 1981, especially pp. 245ff. and Appendix xviii; also Le Giouron *et al.* 1980; Pichavant 1980).

The issue of Plogoff was a regular feature of militant discussion, activity, and festivity in the first half of 1980, as plans were made, rotas of presence drawn up, and some militant arrests, trials, and releases celebrated. While Plogoff invigorated the movement, it was not the only focus by any means, and there was much toing and froing. The 'public debate' which the Front organized in Morlaix (see p. 140) was felt to be important. It was held during the six-week enquiry at Plogoff, and the organizers felt that more militants would otherwise have turned up to fill the hall. 'Militancy', the 'public' was told, with an air of satisfaction, 'is in great demand.'

Rounding off the Morlaix debate, the Front organized a demonstration through the streets of Morlaix, shouting, in Breton, 'Enough of French, time for Breton' (*Trawalc'h gant ar galleg, poent eo gaout ar brezhoneg*). During the march, much to the surprise of local shoppers and bystanders, some militants stopped to dance dances of the *fest-noz*, and others played bagpipes. We then pinned a notice on a local administrative building, warning the authorities that they were 'assassins' and that the Breton language, culture, and people were 'dying'. A similar notice was also read out, with some pomp and ceremony, as a 'public speech' to a lonely and somewhat diminished straggle of shivering militants. The demonstration ended in local bars, with a *fest-noz* in the evening. The demonstration had been organized to demand Breton in education and public life, and present were many members of the UDB, as well as some members of the *Diwan* organization which I discuss in Part three (some of these also being from the area I discuss in Part four). Leading the dance in the streets was the President of the *Diwan* organization, who was there, strictly speaking, as a member of the UDB.

The UDB is generally keen to organize *fêtes* and festivities to 'con-scientize' the 'Breton people'. At the 'national' level of Brittany, the party organizes a grand '*Fête du Peuple Breton*', sometimes called, in Breton, *Gouel Pobl Vreizh*. This annual event, originally held in Morlaix, has moved to Brest in pursuit of a wider audience. Over a full weekend, concerts, stalls, food, and drink attract a large gathering, which refills the party coffers and presents the UDB to a very mixed audience of militants, wandering tourists, young enthusiasts there for the drink and the music, and a few who are simply curious. The concerts are interspersed with political, 'conscientizing' speeches, in French, although the concert hall noticeably empties and the bars fill up when these are going on. The music in the concerts has changed over the years, from a purely 'folk' and 'Celtic' programme, towards the inclusion of singers and musicians well-known nationally in France, some from Paris (these guests are usually carefully selected, however, and deemed to be of 'radical' sympathies). For the UDB, this has been a deliberate attempt to attract a wider public, and also a recognition that 'folk' music was a fashion already beginning, in the late 1970s and early 1980s, to lose its appeal to the young public outside the movement.

This *Fête* has offered a wide array of alternative and minority enthusiasms, which can make it feel 'Breton' at a variety of levels. Militants from groups other than the UDB are always present, and set up stalls presenting their Breton-language literature. Musicians, artisanal goods, and literature from the other French 'minorities' and the North African former colonies of France also appear. There is a wide variety of stalls selling their wares of Breton dissent: these include home-made and wholemeal food, all manner of artisanal trinkets, pottery and weaving, folk-music records, old postcards, sepia photos of 'traditional Brittany' complete with peasants dancing in clogs, posters and stickers, Breton-learning manuals, books on yoga, on 'organic' farming and bakery, on Celtic linguistics, on alternative psychologies and sociologies, on Breton history and culture, and the inevitable party literature. Ecological and self-subsistence groups jostle for space in a large hall with societies for 'gay liberation', immigrants' rights, prisoners' rights, women's liberation, anti-army campaigners, anti-nuclear protesters, and an organization for the 'revaluation of the child as an autonomous being'. The *Diwan* schools always have a stall, too. The first *Fête* I attended also had a small stand run by two young Cornish nationalists, he with an ear-ring and she in a long ethnic skirt, selling postcards of Cornwall and their own literature; they explained that the UDB and its *Fête* gave them a chance to make their cause known, even if they did have to pay their own ferry fare home. In this grand celebration, the Cornish and the Kabyls, the Celts and the Third World, La Villemarqué and Zeuss and Marx and Fanon, and anti-imperialism and wholemeal bread, are drawn together, through 'Breton', in the struggle of the 'Breton people' for their language and their culture.

All the imagery we have seen has an easy oppositional congruence, and all these causes and enthusiasms can seem like one. The appeal of the Breton language derives its strength and colour from a variety of images, which give the Breton/French opposition a variety of persuasive realizations and considerable allure to Breton. The militant world holds a persuasive array of inducements to draw an educated youth into learning a language which, it is commonly said, is not easy, but fun.

Chapter nine

Teaching and learning Breton

Breton is taught in the schools and universities. It is also taught in correspondence courses and evening, weekend, and holiday courses, organized by militant groups, largely for militants and enthusiasts of post-school age. This chapter concentrates on the content and teaching styles of courses and lessons, showing how the 'Breton' world is expressed in teaching and learning. I observed several classes at all levels in the schools and also attended classes in Rennes University Celtic Department. We begin here with this official Breton teaching, and then move on to courses outside the schools.

Schools and universities

For the movement, as might now be clear, the Breton language is the real bearer of 'Breton culture'. Official texts make provision, however, not only for the teaching of Breton, but also for the teaching of 'Breton culture' in French (see Chapter four, p. 63). Here we will look first at how Breton and this 'Breton culture' are presented at school level.

In nursery and primary schools, public and private, 'Breton culture' commonly takes the form of dances, or of poems, stories, fairy tales, and legends, in French, from Breton folklore. Some feel that since such things are the very stuff of 'Breton culture', and also suitable for small children, then there is no need to introduce the Breton language at this stage of schooling, but simply to give a 'first introduction to the Breton soul' (see Hélias 1971:2). Also, many parents are more likely to accept dance and folklore, it seems, than they are to agree to the teaching of the Breton language. Indeed, in one primary school in southern Finistère, a special 'open day' had to be held to convince parents that some simple, local toponymical studies encouraged by one teacher did not amount to a teaching of the Breton language. They were calmed by explanations of the educational value of understanding the 'local environment'.

The Breton language is not wholly absent, however, from the nursery and primary levels. Apart from sporadic attempts at elementary conversation, the language, where it appears, is often introduced at this level in the form of songs, rhymes, or short stories. My observation of school classes was concentrated in the period 1978–81, and at that time, in certain private establishments in Finistère, a systematic 'five minutes a day' of oral Breton was already being attempted, mostly at the primary level. In a few state establishments, self-consciously progressive or experimental and where teachers had militant connections or sympathies, regular Breton language teaching also occurred. Otherwise there was, as yet, little systematic teaching of the Breton language at this level, although it was likely to increase, due, in part, to the efforts of the educational advisers created through the Cultural Charter. Problems are still presented here, however, by a lack of competence among those teachers who are willing. There are four *Ecoles Normales* in the Breton region, one for each *département*, but in 1979–80, for example, only two of these, Quimper (Finistère) and St Brieuc (Côtes-du-Nord), had student-teachers taking regular courses in Breton that counted towards the teaching certificate. Many student-teachers are total beginners at the language or have learnt only a little at school, even when they are from 'Breton-speaking' homes. The teacher at Quimper, himself a militant, recognizes that many of his students are beginners, and regrets that few will leave able both to speak and to teach the language with confidence.

In the secondary schools, some teachers explicitly bring 'Breton culture' into their history, geography, or literature lessons. The work of Chateaubriand and Renan, important figures in the French literature programme, can be used in teaching about the unworldly or anti-materialist Celt. This Celt takes on insular and oppressed minority dress in the French-language history books produced for the schools by *Ar Falz* (the texts called 'The History of Brittany and the Celtic Countries' (see *Skol Vreiz(h)*, 1974, 1975, 1976, 1978, 1980), referred to in Chapter six), and these are used by some militant teachers in their history lessons. Otherwise songs, dances, and toponymy are the main aspects of 'Breton culture' that teachers choose to teach at this level.

The minority insular Celt regularly appears in Breton-language classes at the secondary level, both in etymology and in general demonstration. One of the first Breton classes I observed was in a large *Lycée* in Rennes, during which the young militant teacher was teaching directions in Breton. He drew a map on the board showing only Brittany and Wales, with Cardiff (*Caerdydd*) and Rennes (*Roazhon*) marked, and spatial relations were taught back and forth between Brittany and Wales. Pupils were left in no doubt that there was a privileged relationship between *Breizh* and *Bro Gembre*, and the second half of the class consisted of a special talk, in French, on the Celtic minorities. The history of each of the 'Celtic countries' was presented as a common struggle for their languages and cultures, and Brittany was likened to a 'garden in which someone else plants their lettuces'. The horticultural invasion in question here was French, of course, not Welsh. The pupils followed attentively, apparently enjoying a political spice lacking in their routine timetable.

In contrast, in a Breton lesson in a nearby College, which I observed a few days later, the majority Gaul appeared. The teacher drew up Indo-European and Gaulish etymologies for his Breton vocabulary. The black-board was filled with majority 'Celtic origins' and also with the OU orthography; most teachers at the secondary level are 'ZH' or Interdialectal enthusiasts. This teacher explained to me that he had been in the movement during the war, and had little respect for Hemon and his followers. As a result, Gaulish asterisks and the OU filled his blackboard. His young pupils, however, found little in this to excite their attention. During most of the class, they had been reading French cartoons, fighting over pieces of chewing gum, or in one case engraving 'Melanie, I love you' in English on a desk-top. The teacher finally captured their attention by playing a record of a modern militant song entitled *Distro ar Gelted* ('The Return of the Celts'), the Celts in question here being minority insular Celts. The Gaul for the pupils is a figure of the past and part of the routine of French history; the insular Celt is a struggling minority with a much more immediate and contemporary appeal.

'Breton' has an appeal different from that of the normal timetable, and this is manifest as much in teaching style as in course content. The use of song to recapture the pupils' attention is significant here. It is not uncommon for Breton teachers in secondary schools to say that they are not teaching 'grammar and all that', preferring 'conversation and song'. French is strongly associated with grammar, *la grammaire*, and French teaching with lessons and exercises in its logic and theory. Many scholars in France now doubt the value of this tradition, some regarding it as oppressive (see, for example, Chervel 1977); by the time French pupils leave school, *la grammaire* is something of a nightmare for many. Not surprisingly, therefore, *la grammaire* tends to be absent from Breton, and a casual informality in 'conversation and song' is often contrived instead, with no *grammaire* conjuring up a world of no rules, no structures, and resulting in some self-conscious merriment. Even teachers who are trained language teachers, and who try to structure their lessons and to maintain order both in their pupils and in their presentation, will burst into song in their Breton classes in a way that they would not think of doing in their English or German lessons. In all the in-service courses for Breton teachers that I have attended, militants have stressed that Breton lessons must involve songs. A teacher once threw doubt on the pedagogical value of this, since the idiom of song is often very different from that of ordinary speech, but Breton teachers, for the most part, keep on singing. Appropriately, they sometimes sing the poesy of the *Barzaz Breiz*.

To an extent, the absence of a full degree and further teaching qualifications in Breton has meant that some Breton teachers have little knowledge of language-teaching methods. The pursuit of jollification and informality does not, however, stem from 'ignorance' on the part of the teachers, but is a consequence of a range of structures through which Breton is defined. Per Denez, the main Breton-language lecturer in Rennes University, offered regular courses in language-teaching methodology under the 'Permanent Education' scheme, and he took pains to stress the importance of well-structured and well-prepared classes, but often found himself battling against those who wanted Breton classes to be games and song. Breton must be shown, he stressed, to be 'fun' and 'alive', but lessons should 'not be fun and games for their own sake' (*n'eo ket c'hoari evit c'hoari*). Some tried to take his advice, but others who attended his course (both schoolteachers and militants teaching Breton outside the schools) continued to conduct haphazard and self-consciously carefree lessons. One teacher in a Rennes secondary school did little but sing and organize camping trips to the Breton countryside with his pupils. Parents and headmistress felt that the lessons were a waste of time, and Breton was discontinued in the establishment.

The *Rectorat* offers in-service courses for secondary-school Breton teachers, who can choose between courses in dance, music, or the language. There are also courses dealing with Gallo. I attended their main Breton language course. It was organized by the 'Technical Adviser' and conducted by militant teachers in Breton. The course took place in a schoolroom in Brest, and guest speakers came to give talks on Breton language, literature, song, and history. A lecturer from Rennes made an exceptional appearance in Brest to talk on language-teaching methodology, and was careful to use the Breton of his current home-base in South-Western Finistère, rather than the standard forms he would employ in Rennes (e.g., using *fi*, 'you' (pl.), rather than standard *c'hwi*, with *fi* being an easily recognized form commonly noted down by learners and researchers avid to prove grass-roots contact); forms which normally have their place in other, local systems of identity and distinction here became, within Brest/Rennes relations, a clear statement of authenticity against accusations to the contrary. However, the course was carefully arranged so that Brest and Rennes scholars were kept well apart. (Even so, the principal lecturer invited from the Brest Celtic Department had, it was said, refused to come at all.) To launch another session, a teacher of English and Breton in Finistère (and a UDB member) gave a model language lesson, using his own Breton text. The subject of his text was the *symbole*. He also gave an outline of how to conduct a Breton oral examination at the *baccalauréat* level. It was important, he observed, to get pupils to express themselves in Breton, and, to this end, an examiner could ask pupils what they thought of the *symbole*. Clearly, where teachers once used the *symbole* to elicit French, it now appears, in a different political and moral dress, to elicit Breton. The same teacher remarked wistfully that one candidate he had examined had spontaneously sung a song in Breton that he had composed himself. Such a high standard was said to be rare, however, and although few pupils fail, some were said to present themselves without giving any evidence of having worked at Breton at all. Breton is 'fun' (cf. Chapter four, p. 66).

The course at Brest highlighted a significant difference between militant ambitions and native Breton-speaking socio-linguistic reality. It was said, in the course, that some pupils had a headstart in Breton because they had heard Breton spoken by parents or grandparents at home. It was suggested, therefore, that examiners should be told of this, so that they could mark according to expectation. A young teacher explained, with a chuckle, that he always knew who came from 'Breton-speaking' homes in his own class: in Breton question-and-answer sequences, he said 'they reply in French'.

We now move on to consideration of Breton at university level. Both Rennes and Brest have Celtic departments, Rennes since 1897 and Brest since the early 1960s. Falc'hun, the main force behind the OU orthography, held the Chair of Celtic Studies in Rennes from 1951 until the new department was created in Brest, to which he then moved, taking the OU with him. The 'ZH' was definitively brought to Rennes by Per Denez, who joined the department officially as 'assistant lecturer' after 1968. Squabbles over posts have been part of the tension between Rennes and Brest. Brest has three permanent members of staff, and six temporary teachers. Rennes has only two permanent members of staff, and three teachers taken on temporarily year by year. Rennes has more students, however. In 1969, a local newspaper reported that:

> The students of Celtic at Rennes could be counted on the fingers of the hand a few years ago. There are more than 200 of them now. And they speak Breton amongst themselves in the corridors. (cited from *Le Télégramme*, in Fichou 1981:15)

By 1971–2, 559 students were enrolled in one or other of the Rennes courses (most taking 'cultural' courses or learning beginners' Breton). This number fell to 325 in 1972–3, but had risen again to 612 by 1978–9. Brest had 247 students enrolled in 1978–9, and a hundred more the following year. Both departments were still showing increases in the 1980s but, although it is Brest that is in Lower Brittany, it is Rennes that is the larger, the more 'Breton', and the more self-consciously militant department.

In the Rennes department, Breton is considered the normal language of communication, and in Brest French predominates. 'Brest speaks French' and 'Rennes speaks Breton' is a common image in the movement, and it is often invoked in condemnation of 'Brest'. Technically, each department is a 'Celtic Section' *(Section de Celtique)* within a larger unit of modern languages, but Rennes has given itself a Breton name: *Kevrenn Keltiek* (word-for-word, 'Section Celtic'; on *'kevrenn'*, see Hemon GIAB:1670). A core of a dozen or so students in Rennes spent a good deal of their time sitting on the tables in their department's library, talking in Breton about Breton. The library, doubling thus as militant common-room, was strewn with militant literature and tracts, and scholarly tomes were kept hidden in cupboards or had uncut pages. In Brest the library is larger, tidier, and has a research centre attached. An enquiry in French in the Brest library would hardly ever raise an eyebrow; in the Rennes library, enquiries or conversation in French were regularly met with the sniggers of young militants present. French-Breton dictionaries are well thumbed.

Both Rennes and Brest offer a 'Diploma in Celtic Studies' and a 'Higher Diploma in Celtic Studies'. Many teachers of Breton in the secondary schools possess these diplomas, over and above their other qualifications. No *baccalauréat* certificate (or equivalent) is required for entrance to these diplomas, rendering them exceptional in the university curriculum. Breton language and literature and some historical linguistics are their main content. For the Higher Diploma, another Celtic language is required, and both Brest and Rennes offer Welsh. Rennes also teaches some Irish Gaelic. All the Breton courses are also offered as options towards other degrees, and most students were studying Breton in this way, often as part of an English degree (which some openly resented). In the Rennes department, most courses are taught wholly in Breton, although a few classes (e.g., on the 'History of Celtic Languages'), which are taken by students who are not necessarily learning Breton, are taught in French. A Welsh language class, which was taught by a Welsh girl who had learnt some Breton, was conducted both in Welsh and Breton. The teacher had problems with French, and explanations were given in a slow and heavily-accented Breton, which students, all militants, at times found difficult to follow. English had been explicitly forbidden in the class, by both teacher and students. It looked for a while as if the minority worlds were heading for self-destruction for lack of communication, but dictionaries and some simple and well-prepared conversational exercises in Welsh saved the day.

Per Denez takes charge of all the Breton-language courses in the Rennes department, teaching some of them himself. He is also a member of the Economic and Social Committee of Brittany, of the Cultural Council, and of two militant federations. When he is not teaching, or in meetings, he also produces Breton poems, articles, and novels, some of which are studied in the Breton literature courses. The students have great admiration for Per Denez, who sets the militant tone of the department. In an introductory meeting for students in my own first year in Brittany, he warned us that Breton was a 'minority' language and that learning Breton involved a 'commitment to the people'. He also gave talks in which Gaulish origins (as promoted in Brest) were emphatically dismissed and in which historical figures from Grégoire to Ferry and on to the modern educational authorities were condemned. Students would duly write up historical citations of 'oppression' on the large posters regularly pinned up on the walls of their department (cf. Chapter six, p. 119). Per Denez also reminded us that we were engaged in a 'socio-linguistic battle', demanding constant vigilance and a self-conscious determination to use Breton.

The relationship between the self-consciously 'Breton' students and other students in Rennes university is ambivalent. Many express resentment of the 'élite little group' of Celtic students, who gather in the university restaurant at their self-allotted table, speaking Breton among themselves, with what is felt to be an exclusive exhibitionism. The 'Breton' students know, however, that theirs is an appealing minority cause, attractive to other students. At one stage, some students from the Celtic Department attended a general assembly of other language students in the university, called to discuss the problems of each language department. Although each department claimed its own problems, all acknowledged that the Celtic Department was a special case, in its struggle to get a degree in Breton. All the other students seemed willing to help, and were keen to organize a mass demonstration to publicize all their complaints together. The Celtic Department might, it was suggested, supply music and songs for the demonstration, for 'you are good at that sort of thing'. The Celtic students talked among themselves about what they could produce, pausing only to explain, in French, that 'we Celts are not good at organization, you know'. This comment elicited more exasperation than mirth or indulgence, however, and little came of the meeting, at which the Celtic students adamantly spoke Breton to each other, much to the resentment of their potential but fast dwindling supporters.

In the meantime, half a dozen of the students in the Celtic Department decided that they should set up their own 'Committee for a Breton Degree' (*Komite evit an aotreegezh vrezhonek*). Brest students were invited by letter to join, but they did not reply, which was taken in Rennes as 'typical'. The Rennes *Komite* took a few months of squabbling and argument to establish itself and to start collecting money and producing tracts and articles for Breton journals, a customary procedure in the movement.

Much of the quarrelling was about the very idea of setting up a committee. The students immediately involved summoned a general meeting to discuss the idea, and held it, with the teacher's permission, in the middle of a Breton language class for beginners. The meeting, conducted in French, lasted well over an hour, with a good deal of rowdy argument. Many of the students feared that a 'committee' implied 'falling back into the system'. Everyone present seemed to agree that the Celtic Department was '*pas comme les autres*'. '*Pas comme les Français*', cried others. All this was written up on a blackboard. A sociology student, wearing clogs (common in the Rennes department) and a tartan scarf, puffed contemplatively on a pipe and explained that he was there because he wanted to start a music or theatre group, and the Celtic Department seemed the right place to do it. Others joined in to say that the university was a 'sad' and 'academic' place, but that the Celtic Department should be 'joyful'. A *Skol an Emsav* member interrupted to stress the need for 'serious political commitment', but at every mention of a 'committee' came counter-cries of 'what about the Breton mentality' and 'Celtic joy' and 'Celtic expression'? The 'Celtic joy' camp argued that the department should live its 'difference' in its own 'Celtic community', like the 'real Breton mentality in the countryside'. 'We should have flutes, fiddles, Irish music, the Celtic milieu, and all that', it was said, and students should meet in the evenings for a sing-song and to '. . . like, talk a bit of Breton' (*causer un peu breton quoi*). The meeting ended when one student angrily pointed out that he had a job as well as study to do, and wanted his qualification; as a 'worker', he asked the 'typical students' to leave.

The main proponent of the 'Celtic joy' camp was a girl who (as is not uncommon in the movement) had been brought up in Paris. She has, she feels, come closer to the 'people' than most students in the department because she has learnt, and always speaks, the Vannetais Breton. The standardized forms of unified, literary Breton are taught in the department, and students can get away with the extra-curricular 'local colour' of Vannetais only if they also show competence in standard Breton. The Vannetais dialect is sometimes called, in the movement, the '*tch-tch*' dialect because of a chuinting of certain consonants, especially /k/, making it a palatalized fricative, pronounced as /tʃ/, or like '*tch*' (or like English 'ch'). (Thus, for example, the negative particle *ket* ('not') would be pronounced as if written (t)*chet*; the noun *kig* ('meat') as if written (t)*chee(t)ch*, (t)*che(t)ch*, or (t)*cheu(t)ch*, and so on: for such details of Vannetais, see Herrieu 1974, 1981 and Merser 1981.) The '*tch-tch*' is rarely heard in the Rennes Department, and the girl mentioned above was nicknamed '*tch-tch*'. She began to see herself as the true minority voice and was always the most ardent critic of the *Komite*. She organized some evenings of song, drink, and Breton, 'like the real peasants', but these were little helped by an official ban on alcoholic drink in the library and a dearth of music, for few could play, and were soon abandoned. The '*tch-tch*' girl was rarely seen thereafter, declaring the department 'too intellectual'.

The self-appointed Rennes *Komite*, having established itself, decided that part of its task should be to make all official signs in the university bilingual. The university authorities were asked, but hesitated (ostensibly on financial grounds), so the students decided to paint up translations themselves. This proved tricky, however, for although cans of paint were ready in the department for this kind of enterprise, translations were not easily found for the administrative and departmental terms required: *Scolarité, Remboursement, Psychologie*, and the like. For the last of these, the students hesitated between *Psikoloji* or *Psikologiezh* and *Eneoniezh*, a learned neologism. *Eneoniezh* sounded suitably un-French, but it was feared that few, even in the Celtic Department, would understand it. In the end, they decided simply to black out some of the French signs, and to daub '*Brezhoneg!*' ('Breton!') in large letters on the walls.

Such activities, discussions, and quarrels as I describe took up a good deal of the time of the students in the department, both outside and inside class hours. They are part of learning Breton, with all its Celtic and minority values. When I once remarked on all the quarrels and disagreement, I was told again by a smiling student that 'We Celts are like that'. A 'characteristic lack of organization among the Celts' was often pointed to by teachers in the department in their classes. It was variously invoked to help explain why 'Common Celtic' had 'disappeared', why the Celts had been conquered by the Romans, and why some of the classes themselves did not start on time.

The Celts learn their philology and origins in the 'History of Celtic Languages' class, in which it was stressed that students would be learning things not heard in the schools. The teacher, an eminent Celtic scholar who also lectured in Paris, did not neglect Gaulish, but the students were interested only in British or Welsh origins. Moreover, when the teacher suggested that some Britons had come to Brittany in the fourth century as a Roman army, there was stunned and angry reaction. The Celts came in a single influx in the fifth century, and had nothing to do with the Romans, said the students, or with 'Latin culture'. In 'Breton Civilization' classes, also promised to contain things unknown in 'French schools', the students heard about 'oral tradition'. A bibliography of this 'oral tradition' included 'the *Barzaz Breiz*, of course'. The nature of the authenticity of the *Barzaz Breiz* was not discussed; nor was the categorical status of 'oral tradition', the idea of which is in many ways a literate creation of those well educated in 'French schools'. In other classes, modern Breton literature is taught, in Breton, and the students are free to compose their own poems and stories for the 'Breton literature' examination: this is formally described as 'Celtic expression'.

The politics and values of Breton are manifest in the language classes. In one examination in French-Breton translation at the time of the Plogoff controversy (see Chapter eight, p. 149), students had to translate a piece arguing against nuclear power. In oral teaching, other appropriate sentiments appeared. In an exercise on the conditional tense, for example, one student volunteered, for translation, the sentence: 'If I were Duke of Brittany, I would make everyone speak Breton.' To help us to understand the habitual tense, we were offered the sentence: '*An Aotrou Barre a zo fentus*' ('Monsieur Barre is funny'; that is, 'laughable'). Monsieur Barre was then Prime Minister of France. It was explained that since he was always funny, then we had a 'moral and political obligation' to use the habitual tense. The sentence then became '*An Aotrou Barre a vez fentus*' ('Monsieur Barre is (always) funny'). In similar exercises in another class, students substituted 'Giscard' and then 'Brest University' for 'Monsieur Barre'.

A strong moral position was taken in language classes over the 'interference' of French syntax in Breton. We were particularly warned about the question of word order, which is often boasted as a distinctly Celtic and un-French aspect of the language. Some explanation is needed to understand this question. For example, in French, the sentence *je vais à l'école* ('I go to (the) school') begins with *je*, as does the English with 'I'. In Breton, however, there are several possibilities of word order. The most 'neutral' statement, which would usually translate the French *je vais à l'école*, would begin with a verbal noun or infinitive, followed by a form of the verb 'to do', giving *mont a ran d'ar skol* (word-for-word, 'going I do to the school'). A translation following the French word order, giving *me a ya d'ar skol* (word-for-word, 'me, I go to the school'), would usually draw attention to the subject, as in the French *moi, je vais à l'école*. If 'to the school' is put first, followed by a conjugated verb, this usually emphasizes where one is going, as in, for example, *d'ar skol ez an* (word-for-word, 'to the school I go'). These three possibilities, with their different emphases, might answer, respectively, the questions: 'What are you doing?', 'Who is going to (the) school?', and 'Where are you going?' Students in Rennes were frequently warned against always putting the subject first, in imitation of French word order. We were warned, indeed, against any tendency towards 'contamination' of Breton by French, syntactical or lexical.

The word-order pattern in Breton is usually explained as 'putting the most important idea first', and the whole 'Breton' world was commonly read into this, especially by younger teachers and by students. It was said in one class that Breton-speakers spoke like this because they were 'direct', 'frank', 'spontaneous', and thought 'concretely'. 'Celts' had a 'well-known hatred of abstraction'. Having to think again about putting the subject first opened up a different world in which *je*, for example, did not come first because Bretons were less concerned with the 'self' than with the 'community'. Such views about the word order of Breton are very common among enthusiasts, whether expressed orally or in print. When translated literally, word-for-word, the word order of Breton can make it sound very curious and often poetic, in French as in English. For example, a poet might say *beau est ce livre* ('beautiful is this book') in French, although this word order in Breton, as *brav eo al levr-man*, is a prosaic statement. None the less, many enthusiasts have, by literal translation, willingly seen poetry, metaphor, allegory, and even hints of philosophical and political subversion and revolution in the word order of Breton, along with revelations of a truly Celtic and minority world (for some of these ideas in print, see Brekilien 1976:96–105; CNB 1981a:9; Ozouf-Sohier 1970:7; Servat 1979:85). When read through the structures of French in this way, Breton can easily be made to confirm a wonderful world of different relations, in which the syntactical becomes the social, and in which poet and dissenter alike see hope and liberation. However, the French language and a French world are here the basis of the structural attraction of Breton, and of the values read into it (cf. the question of 'mismatch' or 'lack of fit' discussed in the Introduction, pp. 20–1). The interest that 'Breton' has lies in its 'difference', at whatever level this is sought, perceived, described, or lived. Breton has, in this sense, no autonomy.

Outside the schools

Many beginners learn Breton in correspondence courses organized by different sections of the movement. These courses began in the 1930s, on the initiative of Hemon and his colleagues. Per Denez himself first learnt Breton in this way. The oldest and best-known such course is run by a group known as *Skol Ober* ('Action School'); texts by Hemon and the 'ZH' are used. Students do graded exercises and translations at home, and send them to members of *Skol Ober*, who correct the work and return it, all on a voluntary basis. The texts employed show the commitment that Breton demands, as in the final text of the beginners' course, which students are asked to translate from Breton into French; in English the text would run as follows:

> Breton is our language. Without Breton there is no Brittany. It is our duty to learn our language, to make our language known, to spread our language everywhere. To learn our language, we have to study it, in order to be able to speak it, read it and write it. Let us speak Breton as often as we can. Let us read Breton every day, let us write a little Breton every day . . . . Breton has many friends but also many enemies. Its enemies are often people who are blind, who hate Breton, because they do not really know what it is . . . . Let us fight like others have fought before us. Let us leave behind those who lack courage, leave them to sigh and to find a thousand excuses for their laziness . . . . Long live Brittany: long live Breton. (Translated from Hemon 1975a:139–40)

The Hemon manual used by *Skol Ober* was mainly compiled in the 1930s, and has changed little through several new editions. One text (Hemon 1975a:109–10), dealing with God-given racial differences, has been dropped by the modern *Skol Ober* but the text immediately following is given prominence. This deals with the naming, in Breton, of all parts of Brittany and Great Britain (and its Celtic countries) (Hemon 1975a:112–13). Students are required to draw a map accordingly. A more modern correspondence course run by *Ar Falz* uses texts from a manual in Interdialectical orthography. In this, Celtic countries are not simply named or drawn, but visited: a typical Breton learner is described hitch-hiking his way to Wales on holiday. The texts offer letters home in Breton, from this student, praising *Bro Gembre* (Wales) and its people, described as 'happy and nice like the Bretons' (Morvannou 1975:596). The student also finds some similarities in the Welsh and Breton languages. The *Ar Falz* texts, unlike those of *Skol Ober*, offer Vannetais variants, too, and students are told to remember that 'the Vannetais is also Breton, and that it is at least as necessary to know it to say that one is a good Breton-speaker, as it is to undertake the study of Welsh . . .' (Morvannou 1975:189).

All Breton-learning manuals, especially those used in correspondence courses, emphasize that the oral language is all-important, and students are exhorted to practise reading Breton aloud and to converse in Breton as far as possible. The *Ar Falz* text urges learners to 'establish relations with the peasants' of Lower Brittany, for it is they who, along with fishermen, 'possess the true, living, abundant, varied and rich Breton' which makes 'the treasure of spoken Breton' (Morvannou 1975:616). Acquiring popular spoken Breton is a cherished aim but Breton is not, in spite of militant ambition, a language that can be easily learnt by going straight to the 'people', and it is not surprising that learners should find themselves enunciating their Breton in the solitude of their homes or in the self-consciously Breton-speaking militant milieu.

Apart from the correspondence courses, many Breton learners begin by attending 'crash courses' offered in the summer holiday at Rennes University. These courses were referred to in Chapter six (p. 107) in connection with a sketch on the Breton and the Gaul. They are, all in all, a great success, and draw enthusiasts from far and wide. Some students are regulars, enjoying their annual 'Breton' week. *Festou-noz* and 'debates' are laid on. I first learnt Breton at one of these courses in July 1978, and was lucky enough to be taught by two experienced teachers, one of them a son of Per Denez, who presented fast-moving and well-prepared classes. Other students were not so lucky. There were complaints of 'too much singing and drinking' and of constant interruptions from students waxing lyrical about Celtic and Breton poesy. In my own beginners' class, the main interruptions were in the form 'aren't the Celts clever to remember all that?!' or, less flatteringly, 'You've deliberately made up all these mutations to stop us learning Breton.' The 'mutations' of Breton are difficult for learners, and also for teachers (for 'mutations' see Hemon 1975b:5–16). They necessitate hard work, and modern Breton learning treads an uneasy path here. Teachers often find it difficult to stop fun and lyricism taking over in the classroom without appearing to demand 'work' or the prosaic rigour of majority schooling.

Skol an Emsav offers regular evening, weekend, and holiday courses in

Breton, run by militant volunteers. The evening classes I attended in Rennes were not for total beginners, and were explicitly political, with a vocabulary to match. Much of the time was spent discussing *ar gapitalouriezh hag an impaelouriezh* ('capitalism and imperialism'), and *an Dispac'h* ('the (French) Revolution') and its evil effects on Breton. Breton, it was stressed many times, involved a struggle that was not only *sevenadurel* ('cultural') but also *politikel* ('political'). At one weekend course, enthusiasts who had originally enrolled 'because my grandmother spoke Breton' or 'because I like Celtic music' or 'because I want to make friends in Rennes' found themselves presented with French political tracts to translate into Breton. The texts were often from anarchist or 'anti-repression' groups outside mainstream politics. Translation into Breton was sometimes heavy going and studious neologistic effort was required. When the going got too tough, the teacher quickly banished images of a school classroom by serving beer and reminding us that it was all much better than 'Racine or Balzac'.

Breton was also taught in these classes through the translation of phrases necessary for general conversation. In one evening class, phrases offered by the students for translation into Breton included: 'Things are getting worse daily'; 'Only we can get things moving'; 'Only others speak French'; 'I have little confidence in the future of French in Brittany'. Some enthusiasts gave rambling reports of visits to Wales, and one teacher reported to us on the 1979 General Assembly of *Skol an Emsav*. Everybody had had a good time, he explained: 'We talked of nuclear power and all that, and had a piss-up (*riboulat*) afterwards.' *Skol an Emsav* classes regularly ended in singing, drinking, and dancing, and this was especially true of the weekend courses, held in a youth hostel in Rennes. A complaint from one student that such classes were poorly organized drew an immediate response in an internal bulletin of *Skol an Emsav*, where we were told that such courses were simply 'a pretext for learning things through conversation, laughs, singing, dancing, eating and, of course, drinking' (*Tamm-ha-Tamm* ('Little-by-Little'), 1978–9, 4).

Skol an Emsav also offers holiday-courses of two to three weeks' duration every summer. At the very beginning of my field-work, I attended one of these in a small bourg in Lower Brittany, in a private school closed for the holidays. Where young Breton pupils had spoken French there in term-time, on serious business, we now spoke Breton in the holidays (a symbolically apt reversal shared with Celtic classes in Britain; cf. Chapman 1978:217). The atmosphere was definitely one of a holiday, and the use of Breton encouraged the conviction that normal rules no longer applied. At meal-times, some delighted in throwing bread; on one occasion an enthusiast put his feet up on the dinner table. Through 'Breton' came a flurry of releases that ranged from a scorn of 'structure' and 'grammar' in the classes to a flouting of conventional manners. On one occasion, when food was thrown and snatched at meal-time, it was explained to me that 'peasants do not say "thank you"', you see'. In the class, we were told that 'Breton does not have a word for *merci*', because politeness was all part of a 'bourgeois, French world'.

The question of *merci* (or 'thank you') and its related politenesses is an interesting one, and merits a slight detour in our discussion here. As we have just seen, the militants sometimes live their image of the popular peasant world by flouting normal manners. Food is not usually thrown or snatched by peasants in their own daily world, however, and such behaviour would be considered rude. The popular Breton-speaking world has, on the contrary, its own often strict politenesses (see Hélias 1975, 1977). My own experience with Breton-speaking peasantry suggests, however, how this misinterpretation by the militants might arise other than through metaphorical convenience. Social eating in the peasant world, beyond the immediate family, is commonly part of a system of giving and repaying, with its own obligations and courtesies. It is usually only when something is given (food or otherwise) that is not part of the local system of reciprocation, that 'thank you' is said, as *merci*. There is often reluctance to say *merci*, because it can imply acceptance of a debt to the giver, which the receiver has neither the means nor the intention of repaying appropriately: *merci* would, in this sense, close reciprocation. *Merci* is also used in the same routine sense that it has in the French-speaking world; as such, however, it is more commonly used by the women at village level, and also on special occasions, or with outsiders who are ambiguously placed in the local system of reciprocation.

The *merci* of local Breton-speakers is, therefore, rarer than the *merci* of the wider French world. The non-linguistic courtesies and obligations of peasant reciprocation do not find linguistic expression, and cannot be translated either linguistically or socially into the militant world, where no comparable system of reciprocation exists. The impression is readily formed, therefore, that 'peasants do not say "thank you"', and that, on this evidence, they live in a world of healthy rudeness and naturality. This exploitation of mismatch by the militants brings feet on to the table, bread flying through the air, and makes a playful holiday world seem like peasant authenticity.

Merci is, of course, a French term, and as such is classed by many as a 'contamination', an aspect of 'alienation', and is therefore defined out of 'Breton'. Breton-learning manuals operate with a translational model of two distinct languages, Breton and French, with each able, in some way, to offer full and competitive registers at the linguistic level. The live Frenchness of *merci* usually inhibits its inclusion in the Breton-language text, whether conversational or literary, but, if Breton is to be a full language, then it must have, in scholarly opinion, a term to match the French. *Trugarez* is the term that regularly appears here. In the commonly used manual of Per Denez (1972), for example, *trugarez* is used as an equivalent of the French *merci*. *Trugarez* is understood by some local Breton-speakers, but I have found that they view it as an olde-worlde expression that 'priests used to say'. It has connotations of religiosity, of forgiveness and humble gratitude, and of prayers for God's mercy on one's soul. It does not mean the same as the modern French *merci*, and usually appears now only in hymns sung in church. There are no priests or hymns in Per Denez's manual, but *trugarez* nevertheless occurs in everyday, secular conversation; family and friends happily say *trugarez* to each other in the book, and the glossary translates this as *merci*.

It is known in Rennes that *trugarez* is not in routine popular use to mean *merci*, although the manual claims that it presents 'everyday life' in 'everyday language, taking care, none the less, to avoid both *passéisme* and artificiality' (Denez 1972:13). 'Artificiality' is denied, at this level, partly because *trugarez* is sometimes recognized by local Breton-speakers (albeit with different signification), and largely because it is seen to have links with the modern Welsh *trugaredd*; a Welsh version of Denez's manual notes *trugarez* with 'cf. *trugaredd*' (see R. Williams 1981:15). The modern Welsh *trugaredd*, however, means 'mercy', not *merci*. *Trugarez* is prized for its Welshness, although it is translated into Welsh as *diolch* ('thanks'). In Rennes, where formal linguistics generates significant social fact, the modern *trugarez* has its etymology, its natural 'roots', in Welsh; as such, it is, in this learned Celtic world, authentically and autonomously Breton. This *trugarez*, however, has its semantic etymology in French. As a routine translation of the modern French *merci*, it is a semantic neologism. The characters of Per Denez's book are not saying 'mercy' (the Welsh *trugaredd*) when they say *trugarez*, nor are they intoning religious devotion; they are saying *merci*. The modern *trugarez* is derived from French, in this sense, and owes its existence to the semantic space of *merci* in French.

We can see that *trugarez* can seem naturally 'Breton', at one level, because seen to be derived from Welsh. However, as might be suspected, the introduction of the value of the modern French *merci* into Breton is not acceptable at all, and the militant 'Breton' world can generate its own internal divisions on the issue, according to the very structures of its constitution. *Trugarez* is often rejected as 'intellectual' or 'artificial', and as inappropriate to the uninhibited, 'natural' Breton world which militants pursue. Some of the teachers and the self-consciously advanced learners on the *Skol an Emsav* holiday course I attended were keen to display their knowledge of 'popular' Breton, and *trugarez*, seen as a giveaway of book-learning, was used, they said, only by those who had little contact with the 'people'. Few in the movement wish to be accused of this, and so *trugarez* is widely avoided. When 'thank you' and manners are not wholly eschewed, some shorten *trugarez* to *trug*, which causes amusement by its deliberate play on the colloquial French *truc* ('thing', 'thingummy'). Significantly, *merci* (rendered into Breton orthography as *mersi*) is becoming more common in parts of the movement, through an aspiration to truly 'popular Breton', a horror of 'artificiality', and a commitment to informality. At the same time, the use of *merci* is becoming increasingly common at the popular level, but there carries a social value of formality or urbane politeness.

This detour through *merci* has served, I hope, to show some of the complexity of the relationship between the militant world of Breton-learning and the popular world in which it invests its commitment and by which it measures its progress. In the *Skol an Emsav* holiday course in 1978, I was a total beginner, and learning Breton at this course was not easy, for a popular naturality was cultivated in the classes. Learners were taken out for walks in the Breton countryside, and we were expected to step out into the fresh country air, to stare at toiling peasants, fields and hedgerows, and to let Breton somehow spring to our lips. We sat over innumerable glasses of cider, in local cafés or out in the sun, listening as the well-advanced prepared articles for Celtic journals. We sat in the class-room, with desks arranged in a self-consciously informal circle, around a teacher who perched cross-legged on a desk-top. We learnt songs and sang them with gusto. We also often gave up trying to speak Breton, and instead had discussions with the teacher, in French, about ecology, setting up a small farm, or growing one's own vegetables. When we could not speak Breton, this seemed the next best thing.

Officially, the rule of the course, both in and out of classes, was 'Breton only'. This could have been useful, but it carried its own moral tyrannies. One girl, in her twenties, had come to improve the Breton she had learnt from her grandmother; on her second day, she was in tears, having been curtly and publicly reprimanded by a militant teacher of her own age, for having dared to speak *galleg* ('French') during a break. This was apparently the opposite of any reaction she had heard in her own 'Breton-speaking' home, and she soon left the course. Some form of reprimand was not exceptional, and beginners were sometimes reduced to a safe, if quivering, silence at general gatherings; our use of French in the privacy of our own small class, therefore, held something of defiance. One young mother, a teacher of English, had brought her small children to the course. They were all trying to learn Breton, but the mother was upset to find that she was speaking in English occasionally to her uncomprehending children, rather than be heard to speak French. Her anger increased when it became obvious that the 'Breton only' rule was not matched by teaching that provided the means to comply. On the final day of the course there was open hostility in general discussion, as this mother, on behalf of other students, criticized the teachers and the course for shoddy classes, bad manners, and 'Breton-speaking élitism'. *Skol an Emsav* members decided that it had been a mistake to accept beginners on the course. Other discontented learners decided that it was, in spite of a manifest political commitment, little more than an 'élitist holiday camp'. One told me of his resolve to learn Breton with 'real peasants' in future.

The last Breton course that I am going to discuss here involved learning Breton with the 'real peasants'. This course, in the late summer of 1979, was organized by a militant group in the Trégor area. It involved staying with farming families near a town on the coast; some local families had been persuaded to take individual students for a week in return for the student's help on the farm. Such a course is now considered, in militant circles, to be the height and cream of Breton-learning. About twenty students, myself included, gathered in the local town to be allotted to our respective families. We were told that the peasants had been asked to speak only Breton to us, and that we should insist on this, using only Breton ourselves: 'It will do you good, do the families good, and we will all benefit.' The organizers profited from my being English, and told the family I was to stay with, quite untruthfully if with good intention, that I spoke no French. To my embarrassment, an English girl who spoke Breton and no French made front-page headlines in a local newspaper (*Le Trégor Magazine* 8 September 1979, 36:1). The family I stayed with showed great patience and kindness and gently told me several times that I would do much better to forget about Breton and learn French. One aspect of my no-French status pleased them, however, for I spoke in English to the two teenage daughters, who were keen to learn. Neither spoke Breton, although they could understand a good deal. Both parents spoke French to their daughters, and Breton was offered in the local *Lycée*, but the daughters were not learning it.

In mid-week on this course, the students had a meeting in the town, to discuss progress and hear talks on local Trégor Breton by militants. The Trégor area boasts a group of militants who are enthusiasts of the Interdialectical orthography, many of whom are in the UDB. They often speak out against the 'ZH' for its Léon bias and its failure to take account of the Trégor dialect. Many words written with a final *z* in the 'ZH' are pronounced /z/ in the Léon, we were told, but are /–/ (or 'unpronounced') elsewhere. Words such as *menez* (mountain) or *nevez* (new), for example, come into this category; others, such as *noz* (night), *kleuz* (hedge), and many more, have the *z* pronounced in all areas. Other terms, we learnt, that are written with a *zh* in the 'ZH', and are /z/ in the Léon, are either /–/ or /h/ in the Trégor (for fuller details, see Hewitt 1977:23; Morgan 1979:301; the former work results from a strong commitment to local Trégor Breton, and to the Interdialectical orthography). All this was taught to us to steer us away from literary, standard Breton, and from Rennes and the 'ZH'.

In Rennes University, and in courses related to it, Breton is usually taught in its fullest possible forms; outside Rennes, the more sophisticated

Breton-learner usually avoids this kind of pronunciation, seen as another giveaway sign of book-learning, and learns, instead, to clip his or her Breton in imitation of popular speech. This is not necessarily done with a mastery of any single local system, but with a consciousness of missing out letters from the printed word, and of shedding intellectuality for popular authenticity. Dropping *z*s and *zh*s was felt, on this course, to be an important step, and students eagerly exchanged examples they had heard and noted. There was special delight in saying such things as /a'ne^e/ ('them'); in its fullest form, this would be written, and pronounced, *anezho*, and it therefore not only 'drops' its *zh*, but also 'changes' the final *-o* to *'-e* (/e/). We also exchanged notes on such local forms as *plazokoz* (or *prazokoz* on some students' notepads), apparently meaning 'why?'; in its full written form, this would be *petra zo kaoz?* (literally 'what is the cause?'); the more common term for 'why' is *perak*. Similarly, most had noted down *debara* (or something like it), also meaning 'why'. In its full written form this would be *'abalamour da betra?'* (literally, 'on account of what?'). Most students were less concerned with any difference between *'pl/razokoz'* ('why', but usually meaning 'what's the matter?') and *'dabara'* ('why', and usually meaning 'for what reason?'), than they were with their differences from the written, standard forms or textbook pronunciation. It was all very exciting, and many such localisms had been noted down. The learners eagerly exchanged and copied them, and some boasted collections resulting from months or years of such a pastime.

Besides collecting 'abbreviated' forms, we also took note of local vocabulary, especially relating to agriculture. Some students who were teachers sought to enlarge their vocabulary for teaching purposes. Otherwise, it was not clear what students were going to do with their lists, although the activity had its own compulsion. I sometimes found it difficult to obtain vocabulary that did not pertain directly to agriculture, because when I asked my hosts how they said such-and-such, they would regularly turn my question round: 'I don't know. What do you say? What does it say in the books?' We had been explicitly asked by the organizers of the course to avoid discussion of the movement or of politics that might cause discomfort or argument and spoil possibilities for future learners. In the family I stayed with, however, the subject was spontaneously raised by the father, an elected municipal councillor representing his own area in the larger municipality of the nearby town. From his remarks, it was clear that he had come across militants of a certain Breton party. They annoyed and embarrassed him, he said, by 'wanting to speak Breton all the time', and they wanted, he suspected, 'to raise the Breton flag on the town hall'. (Brittany has a flag – of black and white stripes, representing the old dioceses; it was created by the early movement, and is now largely folkloric and touristic. Occasionally it flies on the town hall, alongside the national French *tricolore*, but a Breton flag hoisted here by the party in question would have obvious political implications.) The family tactfully made it clear to me that I was not necessarily mixing in locally acceptable circles by learning Breton.

I spent most of my time on the farm helping the mother, especially with the milking, which is women's work, and with chores in the house. She had obvious difficulty in speaking Breton to me at times, and would regularly check herself in mid-French, laugh, say how odd it all was, and continue with self-conscious effort. She readily and unself-consciously spoke Breton to her husband, and to other local peasants, some of whom would come to look at me, test out my Breton, and then laugh uproariously when I understood and replied. An enjoyable time was had by all, and their laughter was less at my Breton, I was assured, than at the fact that I spoke Breton at all. They did not speak Breton to any young people locally, and never to outsiders; I was clearly muddling their social world. In their view, I was young, educated, an outsider, and ladylike; any one of these categorizations would normally create a French-speaking context or relationship in their local life. A combination of all of them made the use of Breton to me, and by me, wholly abnormal. It was not considered at all abnormal that the two daughters on the farm spoke French, or that they were unenthusiastic about helping out on the farm, which they had ambitions to leave. There was I, however, eagerly mucking in, in overalls, and talking Breton like an old peasant chum. It was hardly surprising that laughter broke out. One old peasant, who said he had never seen anything like it before, laughed until he cried. Even a couple of the local police called in to have a look at the phenomenon, and the dignity of their uniforms and their office was all, it seemed, that stood between them and open mirth; they spoke Breton to me (and French to the family), but it was a Breton punctuated by chuckles, politely restrained, and by a general shaking of heads. It was all very good humoured, and everyone knew that the exhibit would only last a week. It was just as well, for there was some concern in the family that their supply of cups and glasses would run out, and there were frequent rounds of washing-up; the mother said she had never had so many visitors in such a short space of time.

At the end of the course, the students met once more, with even longer lists and a greater sense of progress. All had taken great delight in the farm work and we exchanged, with competitive eagerness, tales of hard or dirty work. Many had bought clogs and wore them proudly in the town. Everyone felt that they had learnt a great deal of Breton on the course, and we all boasted some competence in the ellipses and abbreviations of a 'popular' Breton. In the students' terms, this was 'real Breton'. We bade each other farewell and went off with our lists of 'real' Breton packed, with our overalls, in rucksacks; one boy left, clogs and all, to return to Paris. All regretted that they were now to return to speaking French. Hours before, I had said farewell to the family I had stayed with. The parents told me that they had enjoyed having me, but that they would now be happy to 'relax' again, and 'speak French and Breton as we normally do'. Speaking only Breton, they said, had been 'very tiring'.

Part three

Diwan: Breton schools

Chapter ten

Growth, finance, and structure

'Germination' and growth

Diwan (usually pronounced /'diːwãn/) is a Breton term meaning 'seed' or
'germination'. It is also the name of a militant organization founded in
1977 with the aim of providing Breton-medium education. *Diwan* has
opened independent Breton-medium schools in many parts of Brittany,
and militants have looked to these as the 'last chance for the survival of
Breton'. Membership of *Diwan* overlaps considerably with that of other
militant groups, but *Diwan* members see themselves as the movement's
daring and practical pioneers. Through *Diwan*, they say, the 'Breton
people' are taking the future of Breton into their own hands, and are at last
offered the education they want, in 'their own language'.

A novel venture

There had been two earlier but very short-lived attempts to establish
Breton-medium schooling, one during the Occupation and the other in the
1950s.[1] Although militants sometimes cite these earlier schools to construct
a continuity of 'popular' aspirations to Breton education, *Diwan* members
also stress important points of novelty and difference about their own
enterprise. First, they do not wish to be associated with the wartime
movement, which founded the first school, or with the clericalism which
founded the second. Second, *Diwan* is not fee-paying – as these two earlier
schools had been – and is keen to offer a 'public service' to the 'local
Breton-speaking population'. Third, whereas the other schools were
bilingual, *Diwan*'s education is, ideally, only in Breton. And last, the
previous schools were primary level only, but *Diwan* has begun at nursery
level, intending to work upwards from there. Nursery education (2–6
years) is not compulsory in France, which means an easier choice for
parents interested in Breton, but unsure of their commitment.

Diwan also belongs to the post-'68 period, benefiting from the unprecedented following that the new Breton of the 'alternative society' has

attracted since that time, and recruiting much larger numbers than earlier schools. In 1977, there was one *Diwan* nursery school, with six pupils from six families; in 1977–8, there were four schools (thirty-eight children from twenty-nine families); in 1978–9, twelve schools (114 children from ninety-three families); at the end of 1979–80, thirteen schools (140 children from 113 families); and in 1980–1, sixteen nursery schools, involving about 150 children, were joined by *Diwan*'s first primary school.

The numbers involved

By the end of its third full school year (1979–80), the 'official members' of *Diwan* comprised the parents of the 113 families involved (parents who had left in the previous year were also still technically members, but were rarely seen), the thirteen teachers, and two office staff. In its second year, *Diwan* had already begun to need an administrative office, and one office worker was taken on, working in a small room in a municipal 'Cultural Centre' in Brest. He had been *Diwan*'s first teacher, and worked part-time in the office at first, also pursuing his other 'Breton' activities (mainly singing and acting). When *Diwan* began a monthly internal bulletin ('*Kannadig*'; 'Bulletin') in late 1978, his job became full-time. A second full-time post, created in October 1979, was filled by a UDB member. A history of militantism was generally a feature of the office staff and of most of the teachers. These two categories are the only salaried members of *Diwan*.

As *Diwan* grew, militants regularly commented: '*Diwan 'zo a tiwanañ*' ('*Diwan* (the seed) is germinating'). *Diwan*'s germination and growth have not, however, been untroubled.

Not every child enrolled in *Diwan* attended regularly, and some names on the school lists were wishful fictions. Non-compulsory nursery education frequently entails irregular attendance, and the non-compulsory aspect is congruent with Breton's appeal as an 'extra' (cf. Chapter four). New parents were often happy to see their commitment to Breton as irregular and non-compulsory, and some sent their children occasionally to French-language nursery schools, too – to be 'on the safe side'. This usually went unnoticed, since attendance was irregular anyway. When such cases were reported in meetings of *Diwan*, however, they were strongly condemned by the majority, who feared that *Diwan*, in pursuit of growth, had taken on parents who were not sufficiently militant. Told to choose between *Diwan* or a 'French school', a few families quietly withdrew. Despite such internal problems, *Diwan* has been skilful and bold in external self-publicity, making itself a media event and public fact. *Diwan* members who also belong to the UDB have been particularly adept at creating a media image of self-confident growth. Press, radio, and television statements had their own momentum: at one stage, when the schools held a maximum of 140 children, a spokesman announced that there were 'over 200 pupils' in *Diwan*; another enthusiast soon raised this to '250'. For internal consumption, however, with stress on the need for recruitment, effort, and finance, much lower figures were given.

In relative terms, *Diwan* is small. By 1980–1, for example, *Diwan* children still comprised only 0.1 per cent of the Breton regional nursery school population. Three pupils attended the primary school in its first year, and five in its second. Four pupils was the agreed minimum requirement for opening a school, but this was waived for the primary school. *Diwan* has wished to boast its size and rapid growth, but has also made a virtue of small class size, and these two publicity ambitions sometimes conflict. '250' pupils were talked of, for example, at a time when *Diwan* had thirteen one-class schools, and fifteen pupils was the stated maximum per class.

The virtue of small class size makes sense in the wider context of nursery education in Brittany, remembering that *Diwan* was created in self-conscious differentiation from the mainstream system. Nursery education is not new in Brittany, and had already begun to spread from the towns to the rural areas in the nineteenth century (see Anon. 1895; Ogès 1934). In the 1880s, official attention was paid to the nursery level, and establishments whose role had previously been custodial or child-minding were integrated into the education system in a general drive to reduce social disparities. Rural facilities and commitment lagged behind those of the towns, however, partly because the idea that very small children were educable was of urban and educated origin, but also because, in home-based agriculture, child-minding was much simpler (and not necessarily the mother's task anyway) than for the urban working mother. The demographic and economic changes of the 1950s and 1960s, changes in settlement, life-style, and ambition, increased enrolment in rural areas, but national funding arrangements favoured larger classes, and thus urban areas and larger rural communes. By the 1970s, new concern about the relative disadvantage which rural children suffered prompted the government to promote the nursery level in all areas, emphasizing its educational advantages and offering more staff and transport funds (see Daucé and Roze 1975; Halls 1976:78).

By the mid-1970s, virtually all children in Brittany (as in France generally) were receiving some form of nursery education, although enrolment was higher among children nearer school age, where the preparatory advantages had long been more obvious. Nursery schools became educationally better equipped and teachers received more in-service courses. Most are trained in the *Ecoles Normales* or equivalent. Rural facilities have largely caught up with those in the towns, and in rural areas nursery education is now popularly considered an important part of a child's schooling.

The upkeep and housing of public nursery establishments is largely the responsibility of local municipalities, but the State pays the salaries and lays down the legislative framework and guidelines for viability (in the private sector, which has just over one-third of the total school population at this level in Brittany, salaries are paid by the State only when the school is under contract; cf. Chapter four, note 20). Most nursery education in Brittany takes place in full *écoles maternelles* ('nursery schools', literally, 'maternal schools') or in nursery classes within a primary school. Budget cuts have led to more larger classes, and (particularly in rural communes) there are fears of school closure or loss of classes or staff. Overcrowding has become a significant problem, especially in towns. *Diwan*'s upper limit of fifteen pupils per class applies to all its schools, urban or rural. Within the public system, a class of this size would risk being closed, for economic reasons.

A few rural classes of under fifteen pupils do exist in the mainstream schools, but fifty pupils is the official maximum and twenty-five the minimum for state-run nursery classes. Official guidelines issued in the mid-1970s suggested thirty-five to forty-five pupils as an optimum aim, but teaching unions were arguing for a figure nearer twenty-five, and 'progressive' medical and educational opinion was suggesting an even lower ideal figure, nearer fifteen pupils (see Daucé and Roze 1975:66). Educational and economic requirements, if set in opposition, readily gather their own symbolic allies, and *Diwan* has opted, ideally, for educational priorities (with 'pedagogy' an important catchword in *Diwan*'s self-image and advertisement). Moral privilege over the state system is similarly assumed through a common representation of mainstream schools as 'inhuman' or 'impersonal' in scale – an image drawn principally from the situation at the higher level, in the Colleges and *Lycées* through which *Diwan* parents have passed and in which many teach.

Rural pupils over 15 years of age generally go, for their *Lycée* education, to the nearest large town; a combination of local aspirations and official, economic rationalization has meant that rural pupils often commute at the College level, too. These state Colleges and *Lycées* are frequently housed in imposing structures of concrete and glass, built in the 1960s and enlarged by amalgamations in the 1970s, when single institutions of mixed in-take were created, in 'comprehensive' style. Their scale encouraged *Diwan* to set an upper limit in its own establishments. The majority of *Diwan*'s schools have been sited in rural areas, perceived to be both 'Breton-speaking' and needing 're-animation' for an otherwise 'dying culture' and a dwindling population. Economic rationality, with large-scale schooling, is deemed to be a wholly contrary aspiration, and also to menace the individual child and education generally. There is a strong conviction in *Diwan* that 'French schools', at all levels, are 'factories' turning out 'passive consumers' and 'mechanically' schooling children into 'mass uniformity': 'Breton' and 'Celtic' ideals, with an appropriate concern for children and pedagogy, are easily invoked in opposition to the 'economism' and 'materialism' thus attributed to the mainstream system.

If 'Breton' education appealed more widely, a maximum of fifteen pupils per class would be difficult to maintain. Between 1977 and 1980, few of the *Diwan* schools ever attained this maximum. Where they did reach it, or exceed it (as happened in a couple of instances), neither enrolment nor attendance was sustained. In most schools, the problem was, rather, one of low recruitment, and there were sometimes fewer than the minimum number of four pupils in regular attendance. Thus, while it was possible to make a public virtue out of a maximum class size, this maximum was an unrealized ambition in most of the schools. Where recruitment *was* high enough pedagogically to justify two classes and teachers, expansion was nevertheless judged unwise on economic grounds, much to the angry disappointment of the schools involved, for whom the 'system' and its economic priorities thus reappeared in the *Diwan* administration itself.

The founding members

From *Diwan*'s absolute and relative growth, we return now to its creation and 'germination'. The project of independent, Breton-medium education was already being discussed within *Skol an Emsav* by the end of 1975. In 1976, certain members of the UDB were also contemplating such an undertaking. The principal *Skol an Emsav* enthusiasts were based mainly in Quimper (*Kemper* in Breton), and were joined there by other militants with children of the appropriate age. Among these was a well-known Breton musician called Gweltaz ar Fur, who had started learning (and singing in) Breton in the early 1970s. The Quimper group met and talked with the UDB members, who were led by Reun an Ostis (or, in French, René L'Hostis). Ostis (as he was often known, and will be called here) had started learning Breton, by correspondence, some months before. Other militant acquaintances who were centred, with Ostis, in the area around Lampaul-Ploudalmézeau (referred to as 'Lampaul' in French, and *Lambaol* in Breton) included Jean-Christophe Bozec, a teacher who had learnt Breton in Paris, where he had attended university, and who is well known for his contributions to Celtic journals. Gweltaz ar Fur, Ostis, and Bozec were important figures in the creation of *Diwan*, along with members of a militant family of long standing, the Louarns, who had also been largely responsible for the creation of *Skol an Emsav*.

The interested parties took their inspiration from two modern situations of 'minority' or 'Celtic' interest – the well-established system of Welsh-language education and the independent 'minority' system established by Basque militants. In early 1977, a militant sympathizer produced a slide-show of achievements in the French Basque country. A Basque group had established their first independent (but partly fee-paying) Basque-medium nursery school in 1969; by 1976–7, when discussions in Brittany were under way, they had seventeen nursery schools and two primary schools. (By 1981, they were to have forty schools, including their first secondary school: see *Ikastolak*, 1976, 2; *Kannadig*, 1981, 31:7.) This persuaded the Breton militants that their project was viable in France, and *Diwan* was officially declared an *'association'* in April 1977. The race was then on to open the first school.

After a scramble to find premises and a teacher, Lampaul opened the first school on 23 May 1977. The local municipality had agreed to give them an abandoned rural school, at a symbolic rent. One of the future parents was on the municipal council. The Quimper militants were less fortunate: the municipality refused them premises, and they ended up temporarily renting a tourist holiday-home, but were unable to open in these premises until the beginning of the school year 1977–8. Other schools then followed, in the order indicated on the map (p. 324). The 'seed' had been sown and was 'germinating' primarily in established militant circles. *Skol an Emsav* and the UDB have been especially active, and it has been rare for a school to open without the initiative of militants from one or both of these organizations.

Finance and structure

The financial needs and problems of *Diwan* have grown with the number of schools. It was always hoped that opening more schools, with more parents, would mean growing enthusiasm and increased income from fund-raising activities. New schools have brought new enthusiasm, but many parents in the older schools have tired, and their schools have become deeply in debt. The original idea was one of self-financing schools sending any surplus to a central fund, but older schools and rural schools have had to draw heavily on this fund to meet their own deficit. *Diwan*'s overall income has often depended on its urban schools, such as Rennes and Lorient, which have had greater help and a wider audience for fund-raising. Payment for the office and office staff soon ate into the central fund, and by 1979, *Diwan* was often running with barely six weeks' money to its credit.

Public subsidies

Public subsidies and local fund-raising activities have been two major sources of income. *Diwan*'s first important public funding came from the Cultural Charter (amid some concern about reliance on central government funding). Many potential sources of local funding, however, have been public bodies which included Breton Deputies or councillors who have disliked *Diwan*'s image. Certain Deputies of the right and centre have openly opposed the funding of an organization seen to be 'spending its time criticizing the State and teaching nursery schoolchildren that they are under colonialist domination'. Also, political parties and teaching unions have regularly accused *Diwan* of running 'private' schools, which has likewise inhibited the flow of public funds. *Diwan* has been caught up in the long-standing *laïque/libre* dispute, and this despite public avowals of political 'neutrality' designed to secure the widest possible range of recruitment and funding. Internally, *Diwan* members countenance only a left-wing stance. Their opposition to the mainstream 'French' system, however, has disturbed both left and right. Local Communist parties have usually been opposed (if only because wary of a 'bourgeois' cause) and local Socialists have been ambivalent (in several cases refusing *Diwan* funding or local premises). No political party, apart from the UDB, has been a reliable friend of *Diwan* in its search for funding and facilities.

In spite of these problems, however, and through careful political effort, *Diwan* has achieved significant funding from public sources. Apart from Charter money, separate departmental awards have included a large grant from the General Council of Finistère and money from official employment schemes (which, by 1980, already paid the salaries of trainee-teachers and of one of the office staff).[2] Apart from regional and departmental money, individual schools have tried to acquire local municipal awards, but often without success. Some schools have been loath to request such funds, fearing to jeopardize already delicate local relations or knowing from experience that they would be refused (by 1981, for example, only five schools had been allowed to use local, municipal premises). During the school year 1979–80, municipal grants supplied merely 0.05 per cent of the income needed by all the schools together. Most of this money came from Rennes, and the rest was made up of small, often token amounts, in six of the areas in which *Diwan* schools were established. In spite of repeated requests, another six localities, in Breton-speaking and rural areas, produced no income at all that year.

Since the beginning of the 1980s, there has been a concerted effort to gain more departmental and municipal funding. At the municipal level prospects have remained brightest in Rennes, with a UDB presence in the municipal council and *Skol an Emsav* interests in the local Cultural Affairs Office. Also at the beginning of 1980–1, *Diwan* launched a 'standing orders' campaign, urging each school to contact local people or relatives and acquaintances, and build up a regular income through a bank. The campaign met with some success. By March 1981, over 40 per cent of the necessary income of the schools was already coming from this source. This new income temporarily saved the entire organization from a menacing deficit, and a fear of school closures. The Le Relecq School in Plounéour-Ménez, the area I discuss in Part four, had been regularly in debt but, by

March 1981, over 100 standing orders were bringing in about half of its monthly requirements. This money came largely from members of militant groups, notably the UDB and *Ar Falz*, whose membership lists had been consulted in their offices in Morlaix, the nearest town.

Fund-raising events

For the first few years of *Diwan*'s existence, the organization had been heavily dependent on the second principal source of income that I mentioned, that of local, fund-raising events. These events were mainly *festoù-noz* and Celtic music concerts. By 1980, however, it had become clear that the vogue for such things was passing, and many schools organizing such events began to discover that they were achieving little more from them than a regular deficit.

The Secretary of the organization (then Bozec) had already posed the problem at a meeting in early 1979: 'We come from an idealist, Celtic society but can we live in a realist world on idealist means?' While some responded cheerily that it was inevitable and no bad thing that 'Celts' and the 'capitalist system' were incompatible, a few spoke out, as 'realists', arguing that 'like it or no, we are in the system, and have to live from it'. 'We cannot', they said, 'live on Breton culture any longer. It's sad, but true.' *Diwan* would have to be more businesslike if it was to survive. The organization had already launched a 'bazaar' stock, and this was stepped up. This 'bazaar' stock included decorated T-shirts and 'Celtic art', plus Breton-language calendars, *Diwan*-lettered stationery, and publicity stickers for cars. These were sold at militant *fêtes, festoù-noz*, concerts, Breton-language courses, or 'debates'. Some parents produced home-made or organic food-stuffs, and various arts and crafts, to sell in aid of *Diwan*. Such artisanal activities, all deemed appropriately 'Breton', brought in a steady, if small, income. In April 1979, however, a new school opened which brought a new dynamism into this gentle world of 'Breton culture'; this school was Tariec.

Tariec had a strong contingent of UDB members among the parents and on a lively 'Support Committee'. It brought a relatively aggressive campaigning and commercial-mindedness, which was feared or resented by many other *Diwan* members but which nevertheless made Tariec a model, self-supporting (and profit-making) school for many months. The school produced a series of stickers which have sold well in militant circles: they show a child with a clog slung round his neck. The *symbole* has brought in a steady income; business astuteness and 'Breton culture' were happily combined, and *Diwan* has often boasted the *symbole* in its publicity. However, the Tariec members went further than this. They organized cycling races, football matches, discos, fancy dress competitions, games of dominoes, and other fund-gathering activities very popular in Brittany at the local level. To many militants, however, these are not 'truly Breton', and are signs of 'alienation'. Smart publicity brochures for Tariec's events were funded by advertisements from commercial enterprises. This smacked of 'capitalism' to many in *Diwan*. While other schools were foundering with their *festoù-noz* and self-consciously 'Breton culture', however, Tariec was apparently doing well off the 'system'. Other schools gradually, if reluctantly, followed suit and widened their activities. By spring 1980, there were a few rock concerts, more football matches, grand sales and lotteries (commercially subsidized), plus sailing regattas, and then *Diwan*'s first 'sponsored walk' (introduced and explained by a sympathizer as an 'Anglo-Saxon' activity).

By this time, ten schools had established 'Support Committees' in their area, although some existed sporadically and a few existed in name only. In some instances, among them Tariec, militant Support Committees had been set up before a school actually opened. In urban areas, and in a few rural schools, *Skol an Emsav* militants often stepped in as a Support Committee to help wearied parents; their own enthusiasm did not always last long, however. Many of the rural schools had no Support Committee (or no material help from one), despite attempts by the parents to set one up. Nevertheless, by October 1980, there were at least six Support Committees in areas where there was no school (including in Paris). The Paris Committee provided the largest and most regular contribution from fund-raising events; 'Breton culture' has continued to sell well in Paris, which was, in many ways, its birth-place. However, when the Paris Committee asked to open a school in the capital, *Diwan* refused them permission, explaining that Breton education should first 'root itself' securely in Brittany if it was ever to be 'taken seriously'. *Diwan* was also concerned that the young teacher lined up by the Paris Committee was still learning Breton, and would 'learn it with the children'.

The *'Diwan'* name was patented in January 1979, partly to control the opening of potentially unviable schools and partly to control unauthorized fund-raising. 'One franc for *Diwan*' was becoming a common addition to the entrance price of *festoù-noz* or concerts, but not all the money thus raised ever reached *Diwan*. *Diwan* has also been concerned that its name has been associated with groups of the movement which have, at the same time, gathered money for FLB members, for example, or for 'political prisoners'. This kind of association has provoked some internal argument. FLB members were neither formally excluded nor absent from Diwan's own membership. While *Diwan* is, in principle, open to all, there has been some fear of publicly jeopardizing its 'image' and its 'neutrality'. In January 1980, the leaders of the oganization called for a vote that would prohibit *Diwan*'s public association with any other causes – including, for example, any open statement against nuclear power stations. While nothing prevented *Diwan* members from participating individually in other causes, they argued, *Diwan* itself should not be seen to be involved. To their annoyance, the members voted against this. The discussion clearly showed the tensions inherent in the establishment of an ideally 'neutral' education system that was also a 'Breton' cause. The leaders of *Diwan* have frequently found themselves attacked for their concern with 'neutrality', 'bourgeois respectability', and an *'image de marque'* at the expense, it has been felt, of authentically 'Breton culture' and its struggles.

Structure: from 'chaos' to 'Congress'

Those in *Diwan* who have received the strongest criticism on this score have been members of the UDB party, and it is to the role of the UDB in *Diwan* that we now turn. Since its beginnings, *Diwan* has had an elected, executive board, composed of president, treasurer, and secretary. Gweltaz ar Fur was the first president and Bozec the first secretary. Ostis was, briefly, treasurer, but he gave this up to forge his own political career in the UDB; another UDB member took over as treasurer. In December 1978, the three-member board was enlarged to include an assistant secretary and an assistant treasurer. The latter was also a UDB member. In June 1979, with new elections, Ostis took over as president. By the end of 1979, all the key posts on the board were held by UDB members. This UDB dominance effected certain changes: a self-conscious 'realism', increased use of the press and media, and a conscious 'structuring' of *Diwan*, which brought about the 'federations' (outlined on the map of *Diwan* schools, p. 324).

Diwan meets regularly in a 'Steering Committee' (once a month until mid-1979 and once every six weeks thereafter). There have also been once or twice yearly 'General Assemblies'. Representatives of individual schools and of the staff vote in the Steering Committee, and all members can vote in the General Assembly. In December 1978, I attended *Diwan*'s first major General Assembly. It was chaotic, and was seen as such (*'le bordel'* was a frequent, angry comment). Little was achieved except a sense that *Diwan* needed 'structure'. Some members tried to shrug off the chaos, but after a tiring day of angry shouting, mixed-up meal bookings, scrambling for seats in a small meeting hall, and arguments over voting procedure, few still wanted to proclaim their Celticness in defiance of 'structure' or 'organization'. Ostis was present at this meeting, although he had been absent from *Diwan* meetings for some time before that. He was the most vociferous critic, began regularly attending *Diwan* meetings thereafter, and encouraged a vote of censure on the president and secretary, in a Steering Committee meeting from which they were, exceptionally, absent. The next General Assembly came in June 1979. Ostis stood for the presidency against Gweltaz, who sought re-election; Ostis was elected, by 75 votes to 45. Memories of the earlier chaos were still strong for most in the meeting, and Ostis had carefully prepared this

Assembly, which was already being publicized as a 'Congress'. Discussions took place in Commissions, which produced written reports, and then general meetings and voting followed in a spacious hall. Invited representatives of other 'minorities' gave speeches, the meals were well organized. There were drinks for local dignitaries and statements for an invited press. Voting propositions were written, and badges, voting cards, file paper, and all the other trappings of a full 'Congress' were given to all. Serious study was also begun of the possibility of a new structure of federations.

Federations

A few months later, the federations were devised (mostly appropriating old diocesan names), and they became effective from 1 January 1980. Technically, *Diwan* was now composed of a parent body called *Diwan Breizh* (literally, *'Diwan* Brittany') – which was, in reality, the board and a central treasury – and of federations which were, strictly speaking, enfranchised organizations. The main reason for the federations was financial – above all, it was felt that if a severe financial crisis developed in any school or locality, a federal structure would prevent the downfall of *Diwan* as a whole.[3]

The summer of 1980 saw poor weather and fewer tourists than usual. Fund-raising events ran to a greater deficit than ever before. Many parents, especially in the older schools, now openly resented exhortations from the board for new dynamism. Militantism was the more difficult to sustain the more it resembled a full-time obligation or 'work' (cf. Chapter four, p. 66). Moreover, there was no easy lightening of the 'burden', as it now seemed. One board member, a UDB militant, suggested that some rural schools should move to the nearest town to gain new recruitment and wider support, but this brought angry retorts about 'economism'. 'If we follow that rationality', it was said, 'we'll all end up in the towns and in Paris – which is just what we're fighting against.'

The Léon federation had the largest number of schools, but was also the poorest. Even its once dynamic Tariec Support Committee was tiring. Richer schools were keeping their money, while poorer federations could not even ensure the teachers' salaries on time. Parents and teachers felt 'sickened' to see 'competition' and a 'lack of solidary in *Diwan* – in *Diwan!*' They lamented a loss of 'community feeling' and of 'the Breton spirit'. One year before, seven schools had been in debt. These debts to the central fund were cancelled when the federations were set up but, within a month, the Léon (commonly *Bro Leon* in Breton, *Bro* meaning 'area' or 'country') needed advances from the new central treasury of *Diwan Breizh*. Informal debts to the old central fund were now formal advances or 'loans'. By April 1980, *Bro Leon, Bro Kerne* (the Cornouaille), and *Bro Dreger* (the Trégor) were all receiving advances; by the beginning of

1980–1, only the newer schools and Rennes had advance cash of their own – money which, in earlier days, would have been easily available to all.

Diwan Breizh

Attention in these circumstances focused on the central treasury, but this was itself in trouble. When the federations had been set up, no one had given any thought to the financing of the parent body – *Diwan Breizh* (p. 185). During 1980, various schemes were tried. Since the schools and federations were enfranchised, the board argued that, legally, they could be expected to contribute. A fixed sum was demanded from the proceeds of the 'sponsored walk' which each school was urged by the board to organize, as a Breton 'national' event – a political epithet which angered some parents (cf. Chapter five, pp. 92–3). Others simply refused this 'Anglo-Saxon' activity. Very little money reached *Diwan Breizh*. A 10 per cent levy on monthly income was then tried, but with little success: the measure was resented as a 'tax'.

Many felt that *Diwan Breizh* should be self-financing, and there were queries, from May 1980 onwards, about precisely what the central treasury had done with public funding already received. Some of the money had, in fact, been used in substantial down-payment on new office premises, at Tréglonou (see map, p. 324). To buy these, the board had, for the first time, requested a commercial bank-loan. They planned to convert an abandoned boarding school into a paying 'Breton Cultural Centre', and to secure some autonomy, and property capital, for *Diwan*, However, in spite of extra public awards for renovation work and a scheme of purchase by multiple lots among acquaintances, it was still *Diwan Breizh* that was shouldering the major burden of repayment of the loan, with interest. All this raised suspicions of 'commercialism' and 'materialism', and the project was further resented because *Diwan Breizh* could not afford more advances when times were especially hard for the federations.

The ambitious investment at Tréglonou became a constant source of argument in *Diwan*. The publicity given to *Diwan*'s acquisition of property was said to have discouraged potential supporters from givng money because the organization appeared rich. The public image of self-confident growth was now seen to jeopardize *Diwan*'s survival, disguising its real plight. The decision to buy the Tréglonou property had been taken in late April 1980, at an extraordinary meeting of the Steering Committee. This meeting was hastily summoned, and most members did not know of it, or heard of it too late. The project was mainly discussed in, and implemented by, the board. Accusations of 'centralism' grew. *Diwan Breizh*, often synonymous with the board, became known as *'Diwan Kreiz'* ('Central *Diwan*') and gathered a pejorative sense.

'Truly French style'

Both Gweltaz and Bozec, the first president and secretary, had felt they were 'Celts', and had been keen advocates of an alternative, 'Breton' world, which they hoped *Diwan* would realize. In June 1979, when Ostis took over as president (the only contested position), Bozec nominally stayed on as secretary, but never again appeared at meetings and withdrew his child from the Lampaul school. Ostis, unlike Gweltaz or Bozec, was an experienced businessman, politician, and trade-unionist (or *syndicaliste*, Fr.). Neither Gweltaz nor Bozec, moreover, were members of the UDB, and they had resented the growing UDB dominance in *Diwan*. In this they were not alone. In *Diwan*'s first Congress, in 1979, many who welcomed some obvious 'structure' in *Diwan* had nevertheless been uneasy that a congress, commissions, voting formalities, 'federations', and so on, seemed to be a direct copy of the structure of the UDB and of political parties in France generally. There were noticeable abstentions during voting at the Congress, and some spoilt papers when it came to casting votes for the presidency, especially from the teachers. At the time, and in retrospect, there were fears that the 1979 Congress was the beginning of the end of a truly 'Celtic' and 'Breton' *Diwan*. Immediately after the Congress, members were already pointing out the 'formalism, bureaucracy, and paperwork' introduced at the meeting, conducted, I was told, in 'truly French style'.

The UDB had long been ripe for this kind of attack within the movement more generally (cf. Chapter five). Its ranks had grown after 1968, but fell again sharply in the early 1970s, following an internal purge of *'gauchisme'*. The party advocated an increasingly strict organization of its own ranks, and some in *Diwan* had left the UDB at that time. The UDB has deplored what it calls 'spontaneity-ism' and a 'grass-roots participation' resembling 'mere sterile chatter' (see, for example, UDB 1972:114). Some UDB militants have called this 'Celtic anarchy', and one UDB member called the earlier *Diwan* meetings under Gweltaz and Bozec just that – 'spontaneous chatter, no structure, no policy, no realism'. The UDB advocates, in its own ranks, 'democratic centralism' – a notion which often raises the spectre, for other *Diwan* militants, of the majority world. In *Diwan*, non-UDB members were commonly reluctant to take on the work-load and responsibilities which the board posts demanded, and the UDB members already involved often pleaded angrily for other candidates to put themselves forward. Nevertheless, rumours of a deliberate UDB take-over of *Diwan* had developed. The UDB's lack of a clear line on the Breton language, other than as a tool for the 'raising of political consciousness' among the masses, did not help its image. Nor did its policy of accelerated industrialization for Brittany, seen by some in *Diwan* to be resonant rather of a majority economy and rationality. All this had often caused the party to be scorned as 'French' by the wider movement (cf. D. M. Jones 1971:25), and this was repeated in *Diwan*. In terms of finance and structure, it has been largely due to the efforts of the UDB militants in *Diwan* that the organization has survived; these militants have, however, often found themselves defined out of the 'Breton' world in the process.

Chapter eleven

Teachers and teaching

Schooling and work

Deschooling and naturality

Since 1968, ideas of deschooling, free schooling, and 'alternative' education have abounded in France. In the 1970s, many *écoles sauvages* (lit. 'wild schools') were established, often known as *écoles parallèles* (lit. 'parallel schools') or *collectifs d'enfants* (lit. 'children's collectives/co-operatives'), all inspired by 'alternative' philosophies of education. They were set up outside, and in opposition to, the traditional education system (see L. Bernard 1976). The works of Ivan Illich, A. S. Neill (of Summerhill fame), and Célestin Freinet inspired many, in theory and practice (see, for example, Freinet (1948; 1968) 1977; Girardin 1971; Illich 1974; Mendel 1974; Neill 1972; Rochefort 1976). Breton readily appealed as a fitting medium for such a vision, and teachers and parents in *Diwan* often cited such authors when explaining their ambitions.

Diwan members envisaged their undertaking as the 'seed' of a deschooled society. However, if 'Breton' appeals in opposition to 'schooling', *Diwan*'s attempt to set up schools in Breton must inevitably be fraught with definitional problems.

When I first began regular attendance at *Diwan* meetings, in the summer of 1978, I was firmly told that *Diwan*'s establishments were 'not *écoles*' but rather '*centres de petite enfance*' (lit. 'centres of infancy/early childhood'). In Breton, the establishments are usually called *skolioù mamm* – a linguistic calque on the French *écoles maternelles*; a distinction was frequently made, however, between 'schooling' (French) and 'education' (Breton). The teachers in *Diwan* were often unsure what to call themselves. In French, a teacher at this level is commonly an *instituteur* (or *institutrice*, f.) A usual Breton term in Breton-learning manuals is *mestr-skol* (*mestrez-skol*, f.) which would retranslate in French as *maître d'école* (schoolmaster). In Brittany, young children tend to address their teachers as '*maître*' or '*maîtresse*'. The implications of hierarchy here, and the political and moral semantics of 'institutionalization' in *instituteur*, have made many *Diwan* teachers avoid both *maître d'école* and *instituteur* in French and *mestr-skol* in Breton. In French, they have often called themselves *enseignants* (*enseignantes*, f.) or *éducateurs* (*éducatrices*, f.) and, in Breton, *skolaerien* (*skolaerezed*, f.). Standard Breton–French dictionaries translate *skolaerien* as *instituteurs* (e.g., Hemon 1973:733); in *Diwan*, however, these two categories were, ideally, from wholly incommensurate worlds.

Most of the *Diwan* teachers had followed some form of higher education. Before employment by *Diwan*, most had drawn social security benefits or done odd jobs, or had abandoned their courses at university or in the *Ecoles Normales*. The majority had no previous experience of working with small children, but could nevertheless cite 'alternative' educational theorists, particularly Freinet, even if they had not always read the texts concerned.

Célestin Freinet (1896–1966) was born in southern France, and had been a rural *instituteur*, although he was also a qualified French literature teacher at the secondary level. Inspired by thinkers such as Rousseau, he left the mainstream system in the late 1920s, and in 1935 officially opened his own school, which many have seen as another Summerhill. His main work was produced in the 1940s and 1950s, and after 1968, there was much talk of a *'Mouvement Freinet'*. Some experimental schools in France, including a few in Brittany, practise Freinet's ideas within the state system, but Freinet is generally considered highly controversial. In 1978, one *Diwan* teacher, who had attended an *Ecole Normale*, confirmed that Freinet was 'taboo in National Education', thereby rendering Freinet all the more attractive to *Diwan* teachers. Freinet opposed the *tabula rasa* approaches and rote-learning of his own time, emphasizing instead the children's background, curiosity, and creativity. Freinet's ideas (and interpretations of them) put far more stress on the 'autonomy' of the child than does mainstream educational theory (see, e.g., *Ministère de l'Education* 1977) and are easily conflated with a 'Breton' ideal.

In the structures of the positivist philosophy that developed in nineteenth-century France, the unschooled, folklore, the 'Celt', religiosity, the 'primitive', 'tradition', and so on, had shared a common metaphorical space, as all that the school and the dominant rationality were not (cf. Chapter six). With post-1968 dissents, 'Breton', the 'Celt', and 'childhood' have re-emerged, sharing a common space again, but in a radical and secular cause of the 'oppressed': schooling is seen to have 'colonized children' (see e.g., Mendel 1974), just as it 'colonized' and 'alienated' the Bretons. Freinet himself gave no explicit guidance on Breton or other minority-language situations, but a posthumous, post-1968 Freinet has been appropriated in *Diwan* and united with the 'Breton' cause. One commentator has summed up Freinet's texts in the following way:

From being virgin clay, a *tabula rasa*, a little asocial animal to be socialized by acculturation, the school-pupil becomes '*l'enfant-roi*': it is all germination, impulse, spring-time, and the aim of pedagogy is to make the child bloom. This kind of language blossoms forth on every page, in a plant-like, floral model . . . . Everything the child produces is a precious pearl to be preciously kept.

(*CP* 1977, 155:10)

Diwan teachers often spoke of their pedagogy in such terms and emphasized 'natural pedagogy', 'spontaneity', 'autonomy', and 'self-determination'. One teacher explained that *Diwan* was 'the school of nature, the school of life' *(skol an natur, skol ar vuhez)*. Another wanted to turn out children 'like the North American Indians'; little Indians were (according to an article she had read and distributed) free, happy, spontaneous, and non-competitive, educated in communitarian 'Survival Schools', without interference from adults or teachers (see Pelletier 1970). Many teachers, particularly in the early days of *Diwan*, seemed to expect Breton to come to the children's lips if they were left to play freely. In practice, this often meant that the teacher talked in Breton and the children in French. Children were sometimes allowed to run on the roads, to go without shoes in all weathers, and to run around naked. One teacher advocated rubbing soil into wounds if the children hurt themselves – 'it's what animals do – it's natural'. It became clear, however, that such pedagogical optimism was largely misplaced, and not best designed to gain local credibility either. Some parents rebelled, and disputes arose in at least six schools. In October 1978, one teacher was moved to another school, and one was sacked in 1979. Several parents withdrew their children, and *Diwan* was forced to reconsider its position.

A Pedagogical Commission

Several attempts were made thereafter to set up a 'Pedagogical Commission', in which all the teachers could meet with parents' representatives to discuss problems and teaching methods. In the mainstream system at this level, parents have little say in pedagogical matters, but *Diwan* was to be a true '*école des parents*'. Parental involvement, however, proved to be some-times unwelcome. In one school with acute problems in its teaching and with little local credibility, one parent sat in for hours taking detailed notes, and then criticized the teacher in *Diwan* meetings. The parent was, the teacher told me, 'a member of the UDB, of course'. When I began my field research in the summer of 1978, parents and teachers were already wary of one another. Some parents talked frankly of 'incompetent' teachers, while teachers complained of the intrusive nuisance of parents.

Tensions between teachers, parents, and the board increased. In February

1979, the board sent out a letter to each school requesting details of the teachers' backgrounds (for tax and insurance purposes). Teachers suspected that they were being 'put on file'. The board's letter also suggested that *Diwan* should have 'someone responsible for teachers' and for teaching methods and approach. The teachers interpreted this as an 'inspector', which was 'not what one expects from Breton – soon we'll have a *Rectorat* and a *Préfecture*!' In one school, the teacher and militant supporters stood up, saluted and sang a derisive *Marseillaise* in response to the board's suggestion. The question was hotly debated in seven subsequent *Diwan* meetings, and voted out as 'reactionary' in June 1979. It reappeared, diplomatically rephrased as 'pedagogical co-ordinator', 'helper', and even 'co-ordinator of ideas', without result. Over two years after the initial suggestion, *Diwan*'s annual Congress of May 1981 finally agreed that there should be a 'teacher who is detached from teaching to help with pedagogy in a continually renewable post'. None of the teachers, however, would take the job, and they had urged a vote against recourse to an outsider.

The site of general *Diwan* meetings often changed. Although most were held within Lower Brittany, all involved a good deal of travelling. The size of Brittany made the monthly meetings of the Pedagogical Commission and of the Steering Committee time-consuming. The June 1979 Congress decided that the Pedagogical Commission, involving all the teachers and at least one parent from each school, need meet only once a term. Local commissions should meet once a month, but these and other local meetings were generally dominated by fund-raising or disrupted by teacher/parent quarrels. The 1979 Congress sought, therefore, to put pedagogical discussion of teaching methods, as well as teacher/parent relations, on a new footing, but even within the Congress's own pioneering Pedagogical Commission, there was much disagreement.

Most of the parents in this Commission were, significantly, from schools known to have had problems. They argued that children needed 'limits', 'frontiers', and 'organized points of reference'. 'Yes, even work, imposition, and discipline', shouted one parent, 'don't be so afraid of those words.' In 'real life' there could be 'no liberty without constraint', and it was 'utopian nonsense' to think otherwise. The teachers and some parents replied that 'you might as well sit all the children behind desks' or 'teach them all to be robots or to work in factories'; the teachers refused to 'reproduce the capitalist system'; Breton, they insisted, was the language of 'liberty, countryside, sea and fresh air – not schooling, work, discipline, and all that'. The Commission sat for a whole afternoon and evening, closing with tears and temper not far away. Finally, the teachers agreed to participate in the Commission, and to provide it with a discussion document relating their problems.

They did not do so. Moreover, at the first termly meeting of the new

Pedagogical Commission, in October 1979, six teachers were absent. At its second meeting, in January 1980, five teachers were absent. This time the board decided that the absentees should each lose a day's pay, a decision which took *Diwan* to the verge of disintegration. Several teachers rejected the Commission, along with all 'structure' and 'system'. Docking pay was 'the kind of thing one expects from the French education system'. Some parents, and other militant groups in the movement, took the teachers' side. The docking of pay was voted in, voted out, and voted in again. Some suspected that the measure was upheld when 'UDB parents' were present. Attention was drawn to the teachers' contracts, wherein one day per month for 'educational co-ordination' was part of their work, but the teachers retorted that if they worked to the letter, in 'formalist' fashion, they would do far less than they did.

The same questions arose in a particularly stormy meeting in March 1980. One teacher was absent, justified this time by a curt letter of apology. For much of this meeting the President, Ostis, sat with his head in his hands. The teachers accused the board of behaving like the 'police'. 'Where are our Breton ideals now?' they asked angrily. 'Breton is not something to be marketed, and we are not in *Diwan* for power, structures, and fame.' Neither were they willing to be 'exploited' – to work full-time on low salaries, attend meetings, raise funds, and be Breton militants as well. All this was said in Breton, and tension rose when it became clear that not all the board and parents could understand. The teachers, secure in their 'Breton' authenticity, then branded the board and parents as 'French capitalists'.

One outcome of this meeting was that the fine of a day's pay was quashed, and money restored as necessary. However, while most of the teachers sat back thinking they had won, the board devised an even more elaborately structured Pedagogical Commission, run by a board member, and with other parents absolved from having to attend regularly. When this new Commission first met, in April 1980, some teachers were again absent, and those present complained they now had 'a systematic system'. The Commission was still not working a year later, and was again debated in a riotous Congress in May 1981, where yet new structures were devised.

Exploited workers

Even before the March 1980 outburst, the teachers were clearly tiring of the constant commitment their enthusiasms required. 'Breton, Breton, Breton', said one teacher, 'nothing but Breton.' There are obvious problems in creating a totality and full-time activity out of a world that appeals only by its definitionally optional and part-time, 'minority' status. For the teachers, 'Breton' had to become everyday routine and 'work', and lost much of its appeal. In *Diwan*'s early years, commitment was unregulated by contract or formality. However, by June 1979, after quarrels and the first sacking of a teacher, the teachers wanted greater security and more money. Contracts were formulated, but the money question was shelved. The teachers' cause was not helped by the fact that, while the Congress debated their pay, some of them were getting uproariously drunk in a neighbouring room, shouting and singing. 'Listen to them – they're playing at being exploited', said one parent, as the jolly Celts next door sang out their oppression and their dislike of the new *Diwan* leadership.

Six months later, the questions of contract and pay reappeared and effected a definitive change in relations. The board proposed, in a general meeting, that the summer holiday of the first office member (originally the first *Diwan* teacher) be cut from eight weeks to six. This member protested that he never took his full holiday anyway, but was told that that was his fault; overtime payments might be negotiated. For many this was going too far. 'Working in *Diwan* is not like working elsewhere', they said. 'We don't need to formalize relations.' '*Diwan* is a family, a community – not a company.' The board was not moved: '*Diwan* cannot afford to finance the revolution; we cannot afford the ideal society.' 'If we cannot afford a truly Breton society', asked one member in response, 'then why are we bothering?' The office member in question subsequently resigned, and teachers in *Diwan* began to revise their ideas. They were no longer 'militants', with the glamour of voluntary radical commitment, but 'exploited workers'.

It was not long before the teachers openly claimed the title of *instituteurs* for the first time, and insisted on the same pay as teachers in the mainstream system, instead of about 15 per cent less. *Diwan* could not accept this immediately, on 'economic' grounds. Most parents were upset at the teachers' attitude; few had expected a class struggle inside their 'Breton' world. For many of the teachers, however, *Diwan* no longer represented anything 'Breton' anyway. One teacher explained to me that they were having to fight the board and the parents on their own terms: 'the French world', he said, 'is the only one they understand.'

During these conflicts, some teachers considered joining a teachers' union. The bureau had originally wanted this, hoping the teachers might thereby see their commitment as 'serious work, a proper career', but they now felt that the teachers were out to make trouble. Similarly, the board's invitation to the teachers to see themselves as 'employees' had convinced the teachers that board members were planning employer/employee conflicts, aimed perhaps at getting rid of teachers who openly resented the UDB. In the structures of *Diwan*'s membership, the teachers, as members of *Diwan*, were effectively their own employers. However, they eschewed behaviour that might be construed as that of 'employers', and censured any of their colleagues who took organizational roles. While some UDB parents openly declared this to be proof that the teachers were 'lazy' and 'dregs', the teachers themselves were caught up in, both motivated and constrained by, the definitional demands of their 'Breton' ideals.

Training and recruitment

Similar problems were created in the domains of training and recruitment procedure. The teachers generally resisted any notion of formal 'training'. Following problems in several schools, however, *Diwan* began to require candidates for teaching posts to work as trainees for five months in an established *Diwan* school, followed by a four-month trial in a school of their own. Official employment schemes paid the trainees, but the question of final acceptance or rejection of candidates was only deferred. Recruitment simply through parents or friends had proved embarrassing when problems arose, and so an intermediary 'Recruitment Commission' had been set up in early 1979 (later formalized by the June 1979 Congress). This consisted of one board member, two parents, and two teachers. Teachers took part reluctantly, however, not wishing to 'set themselves up as judges'. The board also suggested that teachers should submit reports on trainees, but the teachers refused to be 'inspectors' or to perform 'bureaucratic paper work'. Undisputed decision about candidates was, therefore, difficult to achieve and, two years after the creation of the Recruitment Commission, the same arguments continued.

It was usually the parents, therefore, who had to make decisions in the Recruitment Commission, even though they were often unsure of their ability to judge a candidate's competence in Breton and educational matters. Increasingly, parents wanted teachers fully trained in the *Ecoles Normales*, or with some visible diploma or qualification. The teachers resisted this, arguing that 'French qualifications' did not prove a knowledge of 'Breton culture'. Although the majority of the teachers had abandoned their own higher education, at least four, in 1979, had a 'Diploma in Celtic Studies' from Rennes University. They did not want to make this a condition of acceptance, however. 'We want deschooling not schooling', they repeated. 'We do not want examinations in *Diwan*.' The main result of all this was a growing reliance, by parents, on the paper qualifications of the 'French' world that the teachers sought to avoid, and a growing determination not to employ teachers who resembled, in background or attitudes, the teachers already recruited.

Through developments such as these, *Diwan* became less and less 'Breton' in the eyes of the teachers, according to their own self-conscious un-Frenchness. The more a 'Breton' world was pursued, the more it disappeared. The very structures defining the 'Breton-speaking' ideal, and by which Breton gains its attraction, imposed limits on the teachers' credibility, effectiveness, and training. The teachers did organize some in-service courses for themselves, lasting one week every summer, with militant sympathizers invited along to talk on aspects useful to their own endeavours. At such courses there was much drinking, and some time spent recovering from hangovers. In September 1979, two teachers retired exhausted before the week was over. Others left because they felt that, apart from some useful talks on music at the nursery level, the time was being spent fruitlessly. Some, morover, wished to attend a 'Festival of Minorities' being held elsewhere in Brittany at the same time, and where, apparently, North American Indians were present to join in the fun.

In the schools

Language dominance

French, as I have indicated, tended to be the dominant language of the children in the schools. Each of the first four schools had had at least one child brought up in Breton at home, by one or both parents. By 1979–80, however, at least two schools had no such children, and in only 16 per cent of all the homes was Breton alone being used either by one parent or both. A further 35 per cent of the homes used some Breton regularly, but in limited contexts such as games, meal-times, or bed-time stories, and 49 per cent of the children's homes used occasional Breton phrases, or no Breton at all.[1] For many of the teachers, it was the relative absence of Breton at home that was the major cause of French-language dominance in the schools.

The teachers tried hard to introduce an appropriate atmosphere of 'Breton culture' in the schools. One urban school in Upper Brittany advertized for Breton-speaking 'artisans, musicians, poets, peasants' to come and help. There was no immediate response. Eventually, a sociology student who knew a little Breton came in, and, with the children, cheerfully splashed paint over one wall, with a record of Breton folk-music playing loudly in the background. Most of the schools displayed anti-nuclear posters and Welsh emblems, and 'organic' gardening was encouraged.

Whether or not the children spoke in Breton often depended on the oldest child, or the leader, or even the bully. In one school, a five-year-old bully decided that speaking Breton was 'cissy'. He could speak Breton, but consciously avoided doing so. One day, the children were elaborating in turn a familiar story in Breton. At his turn, he began in French. The teacher translated each phrase into Breton as he went along. After a while, he was anticipating the Breton, and then forgot and came out with the Breton himself. He blushed, and clasped his hand over his mouth, before recovering his dignity in French. The teacher diplomatically kept a straight face. The other children knew he could speak Breton, but when I asked a friend of his if 'X' could speak Breton, he replied: 'Oh no, not him – he's been in prison and he's got a real knife.' 'X' did not have a knife, but he evidently commanded great respect. Until he left, few of the other children (especially the boys) would willingly speak Breton. Running out of alternative stategies to elicit Breton, the teacher eventually started tempting the children with sweets. During Breton question-and-answer sequences, she would place a packet of sweets on her head ('where is it?' – 'on your head!') then behind her back, under her arm, on a table, under a table, and so on. After a few minutes of watching the sweets appearing and disappearing, and dutifully speaking Breton, one child or other would raise a plaintive voice, in French: 'can we have them now then?'

Diwan teachers who had visited Welsh schools and received Welsh teachers in Brittany were shocked and disappointed to discover that some Welsh teachers gave sweets to children to induce Welsh-speaking and sometimes ignored those who spoke in English. This was the kind of approach they were fighting against: Breton was to come 'naturally' (cf. *Kannadig* 1979 (January), 4:6). When it did not, however, they were reduced to similar devices. Their further dependence upon leaders among the children sometimes brought its own conflict of different 'Breton' commitments. In one school, the oldest boy, much admired by the other children, was from a militant Breton-speaking home; he always spoke Breton, and the other children tried to do likewise. However, there was some relief when he left, for he had often come to school with stories about the FLB, with which his father was involved. In another school, two little sisters, Breton-speakers from a militant family, exercised a virtual tyranny over the other children. 'Don't speak French', they would say sharply, 'it's not nice. Anyway, you have to speak Breton – that's what we're here for.' The teacher here disliked hard-line militantism, feeling more sympathy for parents in her school who advocated an 'alternative' approach, without any 'directiveness'. Most of these parents did not know Breton; for some of them, free play and no 'imposition' was 'Breton' enough. The two little girls in question soon left, physically removed by a very angry father. 'If that's what happens to you', shouted another parent after him, 'then I'm glad I don't speak Breton!'

Fun and games

Sometimes militantism at home brought French into the schools. In one school with a large number of UDB members among the parents, the children regularly painted UDB posters, or approximations of them, and chanted UDB slogans, in French. At one stage, a favourite game was *'réunions'* (meetings). They would sit round a table, pretend to smoke, and shout loudly, without a word of Breton, which did little to endear the UDB to the teacher.

'Structure' inevitably intruded, in more or less obvious ways, into the world of ideally unstructured play. Left to themselves, the games the children played occasionally brought an ironic presence of the 'system'. '*Ecole*' was a favourite game in one school, with each child vying for the position of '*le maître*' and with all the children sighing each time their teacher demanded that they stop in order to enjoy 'fun and play' *(da c'hoari*, Br.) instead. Other children liked to recite the 'A-B-C' in French and occasionally sang it to themselves as they played. Most had heard it from older brothers, sisters, friends, or from parents. *Diwan* teachers strongly objected to such an obvious spectre of 'schooling'. However, it was the 'A-B-C' that older children often chose to recite proudly into the tape-recorder I seemed to be expected to produce occasionally. Some would also count in French. Others, when they had finished speaking or singing in Breton for me, under the guidance of the teacher, or when they could not manage Breton alone, simply made noises that they felt approximated to Breton sounds. Indeed, in one school, the teacher was both amused and worried to find one enthusiastic new pupil regularly speaking incomprehensible gobbledygook, cheerfully convinced that that was 'Breton', and what the teacher required.

The children's Breton

The children learnt that using Breton gained the teacher's attention. On one occasion, a five-year-old boy, who normally spoke little or no Breton at school, wanted to show the teacher his painting. '*Regarde ce que j'ai fait!*' (Fr. 'Look at what I've done!'), he said several times, but the teacher was busy talking to me and ignored him. Finally, he said: '*Sell, me 'meus graet an dra-se!*' (Br. 'Look, I did that!'). The teacher duly looked. Such a switch from French to Breton was common, and has interest here not only as an attention-seeking ploy, but also in the differences of construction between the French and the Breton. The boy did not translate directly, and the *ce que* of the French did not appear in the Breton, although it can find direct translation. Instead, the main Breton construction began with *me*.

It was very common in *Diwan* to hear the children beginning with the 'subject' – something noticed and regretted by many *Diwan* members as 'French'. In general, the children could not grasp and reproduce the different possibilities of Breton word order (see Chapter nine, p. 161 for the main possibilities). Even those children brought up wholly in Breton at home still tended to begin with the subject (*me, te,* etc., especially). The 'subject-first' order was frequently the one elicited by the relations between teacher and children in the schools. The children generally spoke Breton in direct response to a teacher's questions, responding, for example, to '*Piv eo?*' or '*Piv 'zo aze?*' ('Who is it?' or 'Who is there?') and so on, in games, or '*Piv 'neus c'hoant ... ?*' ('Who wants ... ?') at meal-times or in the distribution of paints and toys, for example. The 'subject-first' construction was often, therefore, inherent in the structure of the child's Breton-speaking relationship with the teacher, and was by far the most common form elicited and given.

Several cherished 'Celtic' aspects of Breton did not appear in the children's speech, to the distress of many *Diwan* members.[2] Also, the children frequently placed Breton words in an otherwise French sentence. For example, *'Je veux aller da bourmen'* ('I want to go for a walk', where *da bourmen* is Breton) or *'On va ober krampouezh'* ('We are going to make pancakes', where *ober krampouezh* is Breton). The children did not necessarily feel that they were speaking Breton in these sentences; for some, it was more a question of that being what one did in *Diwan: se promener* and *faire des crêpes* at home, but *da bourmen* and *ober krampouezh* at school.

In general, the children did not translate between Breton and French, but accepted the two as different ways of speaking, by different people or in different contexts. In just a few cases, however, translation did regularly occur.[3] One example involved the five-year-old daughter of militant Breton-speaking parents: if she did not know a word in Breton, she would ask for it, and if she heard an obviously 'French' word in Breton or any dubious constructions from struggling learners keen to talk to her, she would say *'vez ket laret mod-se'* ('that's not how you say it'). Deliberate avoidance of calques is not unknown in bilingual children elsewhere (see, for example, Saunders 1980), but the militant commitments of this girl's parents and the whole rationale of her own presence in *Diwan* were clearly implicated in her desire for Breton/French difference. She would translate into Breton conversations heard in French when reporting them to the teacher or her parents (and, similarly, translate Breton conversations when speaking French). It was generally those few children brought up wholly in Breton at home who tended towards a translational model of this kind, a model inherent in the militant ambition of Breton as a full 'language'.

Usually, and especially in the first three years of *Diwan*'s existence, the teachers did not correct 'mistakes'. Some parents were worried by this and by the freely allowed 'mixing' and 'contamination' of Breton with French. The teachers shrank from suggesting to the children that their Breton was unacceptable, partly for fear that Breton might be abandoned altogether. Also, they prized the children's 'spontaneity'. The children commonly spoke Breton in occasional stories, games, rhymes, and songs, but when these were over, they usually reverted to French. This concerned some teachers: 'Breton is not a natural language for the children, is it? They are playing a role, it's all make-believe.'

Some children knew, and played on, the anxieties of the teachers. In one rural school, the children went for a walk and ended up running among crumbling ruins, perching precariously on the edge of a deep pond, and, finally, lying down in the middle of a road. After open qualms about adopting a 'directive' stance, the teacher eventually gathered the children and told them off. They smiled, and one responded, in French, 'You're not supposed to do this. You're supposed to let us do what we like.' When they then saw that the teacher was truly angry, however, one or two began to comment in Breton about the surrounding countryside. Teachers were disconcerted to find that the children would use Breton occasionally just to please them, especially after a telling-off.

The children in *Diwan* have been offered, through Breton, an extra means of self-definition and self-assurance. The children brought up in Breton at home by militant parents were clearly aware that their utterances involved 'speaking Breton', and that every word could attract attention. One girl from a well-known militant family was often required to 'perform' at militant gatherings, which she evidently enjoyed. Another pretty little girl, also from a militant Breton-speaking background, became something of a photographic star in *Diwan*'s publicity. However, self-confidence soon became defiance, and she began to speak French. 'She's a proper little *Madame*', the teacher explained, 'and she speaks French to annoy me.' About a third of the children had experienced some French-language nursery schooling, and movement between *Diwan* and mainstream schools was not always without problems. In general, however, the children seemed to enjoy *Diwan*, and some felt sorry for their friends who were obliged to go elsewhere. The 'Breton-speaking' context of the *Diwan* schools nevertheless caused a few disappointments. In one school, for example, the teacher did not allow a travelling player to perform because he could not speak Breton. 'He won't come back, will he?' said one child sadly. 'You don't like French, do you? Mummy says so.'

Only a few of the children's problems have been linked to the language question. Differential language choice and commitment has occasionally been implicated in a split of generations, siblings and parents. In one school in Upper Brittany, a little boy constantly put strings of French words into his Breton. In this school (which was very small) such a phenomenon was exceptional and Breton and French were normally distinct, as different sets of relations. The children were manifestly very fond of their teacher, to whom they willingly spoke in Breton, although they usually spoke French among themselves. The boy's father was a committed militant who spoke only Breton to the child, often in a rather stilted way, while his mother spoke only French, and the parents were about to separate. For the little boy, Breton seemed to have a double and contradictory value: he wanted to speak Breton to the teacher, but he was much closer to his mother than his father. As a result, he spoke a Breton strung out with French to the teacher, suggesting to concerned observers that he was torn in different directions: affection for the teacher (Breton) and affection for his mother (French).

Another problem, in a school in Lower Brittany, was related to a sudden switch from French to Breton by one child's parents. This involved a boy whose father had occasionally spoken Breton to him, but whose mother had always spoken in French. With the birth of a new baby, both parents decided to speak only Breton. The mother was still a learner, and her Breton not fluent. This, together with the new baby and the hesitations caused by such a switch of language in a close relationship, persuaded the boy that his mother did not want to talk to him any more, and occasionally he became unable to speak to anyone at all. He received some medical treatment, but with sensitive help from the teacher, the problem was resolved, with the firm establishment of a Breton-speaking relationship in the family.

Elsewhere another little boy refused to speak any French to the other children, although his parents used French with him at home. He also regularly did the opposite of what the other children did, taking off his coat when he went outside and putting it on when he came indoors, for example. Such an instance of contrary self-definition was not exceptional in *Diwan*. The teachers were not always happy to see Breton thus used to define the 'self', as one put it, against the 'community'.

'Proper little schoolmistress'

Gradually, some *Diwan* teachers began to see their task as more complicated than they had at first imagined, and free play began to give way to consciously 'structured' activity. The school in Nantes was ahead of almost all the others in this respect. There, the teacher, who was in his thirties and slightly older than most of the other teachers, had been an engineer before becoming an 'idealist', as he put it, and joining *Diwan*. He soon recognized that his ideals required some educational 'structure' for their realization. His wife was a speech therapist and together they developed carefully organized games for the children.[4] The Nantes school was unknown to most in *Diwan*, however, and few ever visited it. Much better known to the teachers, by reputation at least, was a school in the north of the Léon. There, the teacher had developed effective teaching methods, insisting on regular times for specific activities, including regular stories and conversation with her in Breton. In no other school were the children so fluent in Breton, and the teacher had easy conversations with them. Many teachers envied this, but at the same time condemned the means of its realization. The teacher in question was 'too strict', or a 'proper little schoolmistress'. Her activities were 'too structured' and 'artificial', and the children had 'lost their spontaneity'. Every *Diwan* success seemed also to be a blow to some 'Breton' ideal.

Although the other teachers liked to see their own approach as 'natural' and more authentically 'Breton', there were inevitably contradictions between the children's 'spontaneity', which was largely French, and the aim of producing Breton-speaking children. However subtly they glossed their approach or activities, all the *Diwan* teachers made it clear that Breton was prized over French. One teacher who strongly advocated 'natural pedagogy', 'autonomy', and 'spontaneity', was nevertheless led, in desperation, to pretend not to understand children who spoke French to her. In another school, children heard their teacher speaking French to a visitor. 'You're speaking French!' they cried accusingly, happy to have caught the teacher out. Children did this to one another as well. There was no need of the *symbole*. One small boy would have none of his teacher's claim to be unable to speak French. 'Yes, you can!' he shouted in French. Another child joined in: 'Why do you bother?' he asked. 'Why do you go to the trouble to speak Breton to us? We can all speak French!' 'What can I say?' the teacher said to me. 'Sometimes I don't know myself!' By the end of my stay in Brittany, the teachers were all agreed that their task was 'hard work', and they were none too sure how 'natural' or how 'Breton' it was.

Chapter twelve

Bretonization and integration

Breton-use in *Diwan*

Presidents and teachers

Since *Diwan* was intended to be a model 'Breton' society, this meant that it should itself be Breton-speaking. This posed increasing problems, however. Breton was little used in *Diwan*'s general meetings and the larger *Diwan* became, the more French-speaking parents there were. We have seen that the new 'structure' of *Diwan* was readily assimilated to 'Frenchness'. Now the Breton/French duality, always an apt organizing principle of internal argument, took a linguistic turn and came also to organize *Diwan*'s own history: some began to claim that *Diwan* had always spoken Breton and that it was only since that first Congress (in June 1979) that the French language had come to dominate in the organization.

Blame for this situation was inevitably attributed in part to the UDB. All three members of *Diwan*'s earlier board had been competent Breton-speakers (although they usually spoke French in meetings). The non-Breton-speakers in the new Bureau were UDB members. Ostis, the new president, earnestly espoused Breton and used as much of it in meetings as had his predecessor, Gweltaz ar Fur. However, Gweltaz's Breton was deemed better, with more obvious localisms, and, under the new presidency, he made conspicuous use of Breton in discussions which were otherwise in French. Ostis would try hard to match this, in competitive display, and he made increased efforts to speak Breton in *Diwan* meetings, if only in his opening address. The historical scheme I mentioned long remained resistant, however, to such linguistic labours – which, rather than gaining Ostis Breton authenticity, tended instead to be dismissed as a symbolic tokenism typical of the majority world.

Questions concerning who spoke the most Breton or the best Breton were always available as counters in moral, political, or organizational dispute – between old president and new or between president and teachers. The teachers were the most marked group of Breton-speakers in the organization, and were able and willing to use their fluency to claim an oppositional authenticity against others who did not understand (cf. p. 193). Ostis, though learning fast, could not keep up with them, and the teachers thoroughly enjoyed a quiet conspiracy to 'try to find the most difficult Breton words, so Ostis won't understand!'

Teachers and parents

Interjections in Breton during *Diwan* meetings sometimes supplied a morally compelling hiatus, being listened to with respect whatever their content. Parents who had been angrily attacking a teacher's 'incompetence' would fall silent while Breton was spoken, even when they did not understand it. They knew that admission of failure to understand Breton would, within *Diwan*, weaken whatever case they were trying to make. Trouble between Breton-speaking teachers and French-speaking parents often recurred, however, with the teachers regularly using Breton as a weapon against the parents. It is significant that when Gweltaz ar Fur had sought re-election in 1979, he did so on a 'Breton-speaking' platform, but parents who might in other circumstances have liked the idea, merely groaned at the prospect here, and the Breton-speaking ticket failed. Teacher-parent tensions had developed such that an emphasis on speaking Breton in a militant organization was thus guaranteed to lose votes.

Teachers used their Breton against the parents, but parents were also able to use Breton symbolically against the teachers. Once *Diwan* became known, students from all over Brittany and France began to bombard *Diwan* with questionnaires for their dissertations and projects, many of them copying one another and asking *Diwan* parents whether they saw *Diwan* as an 'alternative' education (an *école parallèle*) or as a school for 'the Breton language'. This divison of commitments, initially senseless or misleading to most parents, nevertheless helped to exacerbate existing tensions in several schools and to conjure up a real division in these terms in the wider organization. I watched more and more parents pointedly giving priority to Breton in the questionnaires, explaining to me that this was to make it clear that they disapproved of the teachers, and wanted no more 'drop-outs'. This commentary did not, of course, appear in the questionnaires or dissertations; nor could there, in such projects, be any moral or political space for, or any comprehension of, the teachers' conviction that parental concern for Breton was concern for 'bourgeois respectability'.

Teachers and teachers

Clearly, Breton could be used in some way by everybody in search of the more authentic commitment. Official *Diwan* policy was that 'local' and 'popular' Breton be used in the schools, and teachers competed among themselves over who spoke the most 'local' or 'popular' form. In Rennes, where Breton had never been spoken, there were no localisms to adopt, so the teacher spoke standard or textbook Breton. Other teachers tended to make fun of her and her *Roazhoneg* ('Rennish'). The Rennes teacher, for her part, did not care to follow the 'affectations' of the others: 'They know they're speaking with apostrophes.'

In many instances, the teachers' speech was, indeed, 'popular' or 'local' only by virtue of its self-conscious difference from standard, literary forms (cf. Chapter nine, p. 169). Several teachers regularly mixed Breton from different areas or mixed different registers (formal words like *komz*, for example, or learned neologisms such as *pellgomz* ('telephone', literally 'far-speak'[1]) were often used with clipped localisms such as *de'añ* (in full, *dezhañ*, 'to him')). Militants can perhaps more easily create and tolerate such forms because they do not share a native-speaker's sensibilities and competence. Similarly, they seem the more easily able to construct, accept, and use expressions that might otherwise seem curiously metaphorical. Over the years, many strange neologisms have resulted (cf. Chapter six, note 11; also Chapter fifteen).

One sunny day during one of *Diwan*'s first teachers' meetings, some teachers decided to sit outside and construct new words. Breton terms were sought for a variety of French words, including helicopter, kangaroo, and harmonica (Fr. *helicoptère, kangourou, harmonica*). For helicopter they devised *lost-houarn* (lit. 'iron-tail'), although *labous-houarn* ('iron-bird') was discussed. For kangaroo they chose *godell-lammer* ('jumping-pocket'), and for harmonica *rabot-beg* ('shave-mouth'). Later, more experienced scholars declared these suggestions 'daft', and then suggested that since 'kangaroo' and 'harmonica' were not Celtic animals or instruments anyway, they could stay as in French. They also suggested using Welsh terms. The teachers had wanted to do this, but no dictionaries were at hand, and they were understandably unsure of the Welsh for 'kangaroo'. When the Welsh *carngarw* was later discovered, they happily accepted what had previously seemed a 'French' word (for one list of the teachers' inventions, see *Kannadig* 1978, 3:4ff).

Teachers and the board

The teachers were always keen to define some members of the board out of the Breton world, morally and linguistically, and it is perhaps not surprising that, when the board fined the teachers a day's pay (see p. 193), the victims quickly found a 'French' formula in the language used. A board member had said '*kemeret hon eus un diviz*' ('we have made a decision'), and it was observed that the Breton used for 'make a decision' was a thinly veiled rendering of the French *prendre une décision*. Some research has argued that Breton, in militant circles, is often heavily calqued upon French syntax (see Hewitt 1977: ch. 4), and this could describe the Breton of the *Diwan* teachers. However, it was usually in the context of specific conflicts that syntactic calques of this kind were seized upon by one party to the dispute, with the syntactic made moral and political, and the opponent's Breton declared 'French'; otherwise, such calques generally passed unnoticed.

Significantly, *Diwan* has increasingly used 'Welsh' terms to describe its own structure. 'Committee', for example, is usually expressed in Breton as *komite*; in *Diwan*, however, *poellgor*, modelled on the Welsh *pwyllgor*, has become common. Similarly, *kengor* (cf. Welsh *cyngor*, council) has replaced *komision* (for 'commission'). Neologisms such as these appeared in *Diwan*'s internal bulletin, occasionally with more comprehensible terms or French translations in brackets after them (a technique Hemon tried in his own, comparatively fruitless, attempts at popularization; see *Kannadig* 1979, 9:9; 10:1–5; 12:8). Welsh-derived terms have not always managed, however, to distance unpalatable organizational realities. For instance, one bureau member coined the term *atebeg* (taking the Welsh *ateb* (answer), plus the Breton nominal suffix *-eg*), trying to translate, literally, *(un)responsable* or 'someone answerable' or 'responsible'; it was this term which nevertheless came alive in *Diwan* politics as a very French concept indeed – a school 'inspector' (see Chapter eleven, p. 192). More generally, the new terminology has been criticized as 'too intellectual', with some reluctant to see easily Bretonized French terms being replaced by learned neologisms. The same people, however, happily use neologisms from the inter-war years (e.g., *Iwerzhon*, Ireland, or *Kembre*, Wales). For Hemon and his colleagues, who coined such terms, much spoken Breton was a *patois* (see Chapter seven, p. 127), and they did not hesitate to supplement its inadequacies. For the post-1968 movement, however, the naturalness of 'popular' speech is highly prized. It has been one of *Diwan*'s major problems that its enterprise of education requires learning and sophistication, and at the same time a fidelity to the appealing unaffectedness of the unschooled.

The 'mother tongue' and Bretonization

Important among *Diwan*'s reasons for starting with nursery education, rather than at a higher level, was the conviction that small children acquired languages more easily. Militants had felt that 'Breton-speaking' parents were failing to exploit this – thus failing to produce the next generation of Breton-speakers. In the early 1970s, Bozec, who was to become the first secretary of *Diwan*, had estimated that about 15 per cent of the young people aged 15–24 in Lower Brittany used some Breton daily; of those aged 14 and under, however, this proportion was at most 4 per cent (figures cited by Gwegen 1975:56). These figures were based on very small samples, but for militants they were the factual confirmation of a problem: Breton as the 'mother tongue' was disappearing. This perception, more than any other, had spurred militants on to serious discussion of *skolioù mamm*.

The use of French to children at home had been noted in the late nineteenth century by a Celtic scholar, who felt the increasing number of *écoles maternelles* was to blame (see Anon 1895:5–6; the 'anonymous' author here was Fransez Vallée, later a colleague of Hemon). By the late 1920s, leading members of the movement noticed some Breton mothers effectively taking on, morally and linguistically, the role of the 'mother' in an urban, French world. They were speaking French to their children – an 'atrocity' (Gwegen 1975:68, 267–73). In 1974, *Skol an Emsav* decided that their older colleagues were too 'intellectual', producing complicated literature in Breton for themselves, while a new generation of Bretons was speaking French: they therefore ejected the 'intellectuals' and began to discuss setting a proper example to Breton mothers.

The notion of 'mother tongue' has many moral associations. From early philology to modern education, the 'mother tongue' has served as an image of primordial cultural attachment. In 1950, when the French socialist Deixonne was arguing for local languages in the schools, he used the 'mother tongue' image to win over opponents of his bill (see Chapter four, p. 53). In rural areas, grandparents often still had the moral and *de facto* responsibility which the 'mother tongue' seemed to accord the mother, but the metaphor was powerful. The Breton movement has, for over a hundred years, made the moral imperative of the 'mother tongue' part of its argument for Breton in the schools. In the late 1960s and early 1970s militants were arguing in these terms (e.g., SV 1967, 11:4,7; AEB 1973:51ff), although by then overtaken by socio-linguistic realities, which the background of *Diwan*'s teachers may help to illustrate. In 1979–80, the majority of the teachers were in their early or mid-twenties: eight of the thirteen had been brought up in French by Breton-speaking parents; two had been brought up largely in Breton by militant parents; two had heard no Breton at home (one was from outside Brittany), and one (the Nantes teacher, in his thirties) had been brought up mostly in Breton until school age, by his peasant parents and grandparents in southern Finistère. All the teachers who had heard Breton at home would sometimes boast a 'Breton-speaking' childhood, but in all cases their parents (especially their mothers) had spoken French to them.

Outside the movement, 'mother tongue' (*langue maternelle*) has no obvious translation into Breton, but a standard term has been coined – *yezh mamm* (cf. the Welsh *mamiaith*). If Breton is the 'natural' language of the Bretons, then it is, in the militant view, *yezh mamm ar vugale* ('the mother tongue of the children'). Since the mid-1960s, Brittany's mothers who speak Breton to their children have been predominantly militants who have learnt or re-learnt the language. Militants often say they are thus 'mending a chain', the 'chain' being linguistic continuity between the generations (cf. Chapter fourteen, note 4), 'broken' by 'imposition' from Paris.

Such imagery has made special demands of the mothers in *Diwan*. Of the 119 mothers involved in *Diwan* during 1979–80, under 23 per cent felt they could speak Breton fluently to their children. Only 7 per cent (eight mothers), along with their husbands, used (ostensibly) only Breton in the home. None of these eight had been brought up to speak Breton by their own mothers, and four were from outside Brittany (on these figures, see note 1 to Chapter eleven). Overall, almost twice as many fathers as mothers spoke some Breton to the children at home. In only one case was the mother (a teacher) alone using Breton. The children of these Breton-speaking mothers, moreovr, often spoke French in the *Diwan* schools. Militant families sometimes complained that, after all their efforts, their children learnt French at *Diwan*.

With some awareness of a problem, a special 'Bretonization' (*brez-honekadur*) Commission was created in 1980 to discuss how to get more *Diwan* parents to use Breton in family life. During these discussions (which were in French), mothers especially were urged to learn Breton and speak it to their children. One mother present had been trying to do so, and her small baby was a prospective *Diwan* pupil. She was finding it hard and 'unnatural', however – 'I don't even know how to say bottles (*biberons*) and nappies in Breton'. Such things were not prominent in standard Breton texts, but she was promised that suitable vocabulary lists would be drawn up. She also complained that she lacked 'baby talk' in Breton, and was sometimes reduced to constrained silence. She spoke French to her two older children, and did not want to change this. Life was getting complicated – 'I'm not sure how long I can hold out'. Some suggested she go to a Breton-language 'camp' (*kamp*), where militant families gather to share their Breton. Other *Diwan* members, however, had found in these camps that they had wasted time moving the tents to escape 'contamination' from French-speaking holidaymakers. Special evening classes for parents (which some schools had already started) were suggested, but the mother in question sighed. She had a full-time job as a teacher and did not relish the extra 'work' of Breton-learning. Other mothers objected that they, too, had jobs and it was 'chauvinist' to expect them to bear the load. If Breton meant a 'different society', why couldn't fathers learn Breton? Fathers should help, the Commission agreed, but the idea of *langue paternelle*, or 'father language', caused the chuckles and unease of anomaly. It could not easily, it seems, replace the 'mother tongue'.

Sometimes, invocation of the 'mother tongue' brought another kind of contradiction and a serious clash of reality and aspiration. This was apparent when one *Diwan* teacher took her pupils to visit a fair. Some of the children were badly frightened by a clown in ghastly make up; they were weeping, and one was in a serious panic. The teacher tried to comfort them using Breton, but only succeeded in calming them down when she switched to French. When she afterwards recounted this incident to some of the parents, a *Skol an Emsav* member insisted that she should have used only Breton. The teacher, unsympathetic to *Skol an Emsav* and its aims (see p. 197 for a previous clash), retorted that the children were 'more important than your Breton-speaking State', and that 'besides, the mother tongue of the children is French'. Her critic found this difficult to answer, aware that he risked seeming like a caricature of the world he opposed. 'I'm not a fascist', he said, forestalling the worst, 'but ...'. He gave up.

A primary school

'Too serious'

Discussion of a *Diwan* primary school began in earnest in November 1979. *Diwan*'s second Congress, in June 1980, voted for the idea 'in principle'. In September 1980, the first primary school opened, with three children from three UDB families. Among the parents were two members of the board, one of them the president, Ostis. The school opened in the new *Diwan* premises at Tréglonou.

Some *Diwan* members felt (as they had about the purchase of Tréglonou itself – see p. 186) that the primary school was presented to them as a *fait accompli*, which they first found out about by reading the newspapers. The project was always controversial, with some convinced that it was a complete mistake. However, it was argued that nursery schools alone were a 'dead end', and that moving beyond them had always been *Diwan*'s ambition. Indeed, the first Congress, in 1979, had explicitly incorporated into *Diwan*'s published aims the ambition of establishing Breton education 'from nursery through university level' (*Charte de Diwan*, art. 2).

At first, it was suggested that the primary school should have a different name, so as not to implicate *Diwan* if it were to fail.[2] After discussion, however, the name *Diwan* was retained. Viewing the *Diwan* venture as one of different levels was, in any case, to 'accept the structure of French education'. Many parents nevertheless wanted some distinction between the *skolioù mamm* and the *école primaire* (Fr.) or *skol kentañ derez* (Br.). Some even urged a 'whole new start'.

Almost every *Diwan* school had children reaching primary school age. As discussion progressed, however, more and more of the parents began to find arguments against a primary school, especially in their area. It was 'too soon', 'too expensive', 'too serious', or 'too risky'. Primary education was 'serious schooling'.

Reading and arithmetic

Meanwhile, two Commissions were set up to study basic problems and methods in reading (*lenn*) and arithmetic (*jedoniezh*), and to produce texts. The 'arithmetic' group progressed swiftly, researching earlier Breton schooling texts and French texts. *Skol an Emsav* produced lists of neologisms for addition, subtraction, multiplication, and so forth (with frequent reference to Welsh), and a nun with long experience as 'educational adviser' for Breton in church-run schools gave advice (although for political reasons, this was not publicized at the time).

The other Commission, for 'reading', inspired less confidence. With only a few months to go, neither reports nor reading texts were forthcoming. A version of a 'natural' or 'global' reading method was ultimately chosen, partly because it did not need prepared written texts, and partly because it was felt to be consistent with *Diwan*'s philosophy. This approach is generally seen to stand in opposition to the traditional syllabary and the 'A-B-C'. The mention of a 'natural' method, however, worried some parents, who had had enough of 'natural' education at nursery level.

Very few members of *Diwan* participated in these preparatory Commissions. Most parents adamantly resisted attempts to recruit their activity and interest. '*Diwan*', they said, 'does not want a primary school.'

The first school

By the June 1980 Congress, when discussion of the imminent primary school was fully launched, a few parents who had previously supported the project were fast abandoning the idea. *Diwan* parents who might previously have vaunted their children's Breton suddenly declared, when faced with a primary school, that their children were 'not really Breton-speaking'. Some parents who remained enthusiastic became, in contrast, even surer that their own children *were* 'Breton-speaking' – prompting suspicion that 'UDB parents are using their children for political ends'.

Eventually, there were parents in only three nursery schools seriously interested in opening a primary school: in Quimper, Lampaul, and Tariec. The 'Quimper' school had by this time moved to nearby Plomelin, and the 'Lampaul' school to nearby Portsall. Both had moved in search of premises, recruitment, and finance. These had been *Diwan*'s first two nursery schools, and rivalry was sustained and encouraged by the fact that Gweltaz ar Fur was in 'Quimper' (Plomelin) and Ostis in 'Lampaul' (Portsall). Quimper could, however, produce only two pupils, and the legislation (dating from 30 October 1886) under which *Diwan* was opening its primary school required at least three pupils from two different families. Lampaul and Tariec had three potential pupils between them (including Ostis's son), and were close enough to combine at Tréglonou. Quimper was too far away to join in (and boarding had been ruled out); Quimper was also in debt, while Tariec had its notable Support Committee (see p. 182) behind it. The first primary school opened at Tréglonou, therefore, with 'Lampaul' winning this second race also. The Quimper children went to a mainstream school.

'The orthography of the future'

Primary schooling raised the issue of orthography, on which *Diwan* had never taken a clear stand. Different orthographies regularly appeared in the organization's internal bulletin, on the same page and even in the same article.[3] *Diwan* members had claimed 'tolerance' on such matters, saying 'we do not want to repeat all the old quarrels of the *emsav*', or 'we are not taking sides'. In any case, in the nursery schools, the teachers resisted any preparatory role, being loath, as one put it, 'to start the children on writing and schooling' (a policy which worried many parents). A Breton primary school, however, put writing on the agenda, and dispute began in earnest over the choice of orthography.

'We cannot go on playing scrabble with orthography', it was said. The movement had been doing this 'for over a century'. A known Breton scholar among the parents insisted that it was Vannetais which had 'always brought *le bordel* (chaos) into the whole issue'. This same parent, a staunch upholder of the 'ZH' and of 'standard' Breton, was on the first formal Recruitment Commission for a Vannetais teacher. Vannetais teachers usually expected their minority authenticity to be admired, but in this case the 'ZH' parent demanded that the Vannetais candidate do a written test in Breton. This had never been asked of other candidates. The 'ZH' parent made no secret of his distaste for Vannetais, and the candidate (encouraged by other teachers in the Commission) became increasingly 'Vannetais' in his speech in response. He did the test, which the parent eagerly read. To his satisfaction, he found a 'mistake', and corrected it. However, amid smiling protests from the Vannetais candidate and supportive mirth from other teachers present, the 'mistake' was shown to be simply a different orthographical convention, derived from the Inter-dialectal orthography.[4] The 'ZH' parent threw up his arms in disgust.

Just as socio-linguistic relativism has become a common creed in the movement and all dialects deemed 'equal' (e.g., Morvannou 1975:630), so, too, all orthographies were considered ideally equal in *Diwan* – until the primary project seemed to make choice necessary. The OU orthography was the first to be dismissed, on the grounds that it 'divided the Breton language', was 'clerical', and 'smelt of French' (cf. Chapter seven, note 4; also Jackson 1967:830). Dismissals of the 'ZH' or of the Interdialectal systems were usually more discreet; some whispered of the *boche* (Jerry) at mention of the 'ZH', and others groaned about the UDB at mention of the

Interdialectal. The internal bulletin began to carry more openly angry argument (e.g., *Kannadig* 1980, 16 and 19).

On 9 March 1980 at two minutes to noon, a small 'Orthography Commission' chose an orthography, after a morning's debate wholly in Breton. A small group of *brezhonegerien* from *Diwan* discussed the relative merits of the Interdialectal and 'ZH' systems: a choice was to be made, on a vote, between the two. There was an air of awed expectancy in the room: *Diwan*'s decision would, it was felt, determine 'the orthography of the future'. The Commission consisted of seven parents and three teachers (including the Vannetais teacher mentioned above, p. 211). The parents included Ostis, a parent from the Vannetais, the 'ZH' parent mentioned above (p. 211), and a *Skol an Emsav* militant from the Quimper school. The meeting had been strategically sited in Lorient, in 'Vannetais' country, but 'ZH' enthusiasts had made the journey.

'We must go beyond passions', Ostis began, '. . . beyond old questions of Resistance and Nationalists . . . beyond politics.' 'Go beyond politics!' muttered one parent, eyeing Ostis's copy of *Pobl Vreizh*, the Breton-language UDB journal written in Interdialectal. The Vannetais teacher defended the Interdialectal in the name of the 'Vannetais dialect', but his old 'ZH' opponent interrupted to say that there could not be a 'biology and a mathematics and so on, for every dialect'. Breton had been one language in the past, and should be one now. 'Learn standard Breton first', he said, 'and play with the dialects afterwards.' Many old arguments were then rehearsed, between 'popular speech' and 'standard forms', 'local variety' and 'unification', and so on (cf. Chapter seven). The Vannetais teacher had some of his own oppositional moral discourse turned on him, and was reminded that the Vannetais which he himself spoke was a literary 'standardized' dialect which 'neglected' internal differences in Vannetais. 'No system', it was said, without irony, could incorporate 'all local differences'.

Ostis eventually called for a vote. The 'ZH' won, by seven votes to three. Ostis and the Vannetais parent voted for the Interdialectal. Two who voted for the 'ZH' were offspring of members of the wartime movement, who said it was an 'emotional' vote for them, for their parents. Besides, these teachers did not want to vote 'for the UDB'.

'All we know is what we are not'

Only one established *Diwan* teacher put herself forward for the primary school post, and was selected. She knew the 'ZH' well, having done Breton courses with *Skol Ober* (see Chapter nine, p. 162). It was this teacher who had earlier been labelled a 'schoolmistress', and accused of destroying 'spontaneity' (Chapter eleven, p. 201). During discussion of the primary project, within structures so often invoked in *Diwan*, she had to stress that 'of course' she would include song, music, and art, and would not use a 'strict programme' or a 'timetable'. 'What about the Breton mentality?' some had asked, and 'the spirit of *Diwan*?', all of which again seemed threatened by 'the school'.

In September 1980, days before the opening of the primary school, this concern re-emerged in strength among the teachers. '*Diwan* is beginning to sound like the Third Republic', said one, during a teachers' course. The schools were already *laïques* and *gratuites*, and 'soon they will be *obligatoires!*' These had been the slogans of Jules Ferry. 'What does Breton mean?' the teachers asked, and 'what is *Diwan*?' 'It must be different', they said, 'but how?' A board member had talked of a 'victory of Breton over French', but this victory did not seem to introduce the required 'difference'. One teacher, who had grown suspicious of language militantism, asserted that 'nothing is different just because we speak Breton'. Others continued to insist that Breton '*must* mean a different way of life' but felt that this had eluded them in *Diwan*. They had pursued their ambitions through 'Breton' and through *Diwan*, opposing these to 'French' and the 'system', and had dressed these oppositions with a host of congruent metaphors. The more success their project achieved, however, the more it seemed like failure; the closer *Diwan* now came to realizing its ambition of a full education in Breton, the more 'French' it appeared. 'All we know', reflected one teacher, 'is what we are not.' 'We are not French!' came the automatic, if now somewhat self-parodying, chorus. 'We are not the French education system', specified one teacher, 'that's our main point of reference.' '*Diwan* is a door', offered another, groping for positive definition, 'an opening . . . .' 'A door!' someone retorted. 'If it's a door, it's the door of an aeroplane. Open it, and you fall into the void!' The teachers agreed they were 'getting depressed'.

The children, meanwhile, untroubled by such definitional problems, enjoyed their first year of primary school. By the end of its first year, the children were eagerly reading and writing in Breton. One child proudly showed me her exercise book, in which an early sentence read: '*amañ e komzer brezhoneg*' (lit. 'here one speaks Breton'). The teacher here did not agree with 'Freinet and the other teachers'. 'If you want the children to speak Breton', she explained, 'then you must make them do it, and not just let them do as they like. This is a school.'

Local integration

Peasants and 'a real prolo'

Diwan has often called its enterprise one of 'popular education'. Local recruitment and acceptance have been less obvious problems in the relative anonymity of the large towns than in the rural areas, where most of the

213

schools are sited and where, typically, it has been incomers who have opened them. The four schools in major towns with industrial interests have, by virtue of their small and 'alternative' nature, recruited the overflow from local Freinet or Montessori schools. Industrial workers were, however, conspicuous by their absence from among the parents (and, in general, there were far more parents involved in art or music than in any form of mainstream industry). During 1979–80, 25 per cent of all parents in *Diwan* were students or 'housewives' (many with university education); over 50 per cent were in top white-collar and professional jobs (as against 15 per cent for Brittany overall, see INSEE 1980:81). Most were teachers, or involved in social and medical services.

The wider movement has sometimes criticized *Diwan* for being too 'intellectual'. One *Diwan* mother, during a language course in Rennes in 1979, met this by saying that there *were* 'peasants' in *Diwan*, and some in her own school (indeed, in 1979–80, about 7 per cent of *Diwan* parents were 'peasants'). A *Diwan* father qualified this claim, however. He had a degree in English, but had 'dropped out of the system' and gone to work with his hands, as a builder. The *Diwan* parents 'are peasants', he said, 'like I'm a builder'.

At one of *Diwan*'s older schools, established parents were delighted with a new recruit: 'his father is a plasterer', they said, 'a real plasterer – a real *prolo*'. They were pleased to have truly proletarian recruitment; the *prolo*, for his part, was impressed that teachers and a local doctor had their children there. He did not intend to send his child to the *Diwan* primary, however, and although a Breton-speaker himself, spoke French to his child. Like the great majority of Breton-speakers of rural origin, he had given his children 'French' names. His son, Jean-François, stood out on the *Diwan* register among the Yanns, Gwendals, Vefas, Mikaels, Kristens, and Erwans who made up his class-mates.

Local views of *Diwan* can vary (as we shall see in Part four), but certain images recur. *Diwan* is *Breiz Atao*, or is conflated with the FLB, and some have feared that bombing raids were being planned in their area. In rural areas, *Diwan* teachers rarely conform to the traditional image of a teacher. They drink and smoke, and I have heard it said that they are drugged all the time (see below, Chapter fourteen, p. 261). In some areas, *Diwan* has been accused of taking children away from already threatened rural schools (and some *Diwan* parents have, in response, enrolled their children on the lists of the local public schools, as phantom figures, to maintain official numbers). Alternatively, some people have been convinced that the poor *Diwan* children must be backward or handicapped, since they were having to be taught in Breton.

In the northern Léon, a few aged peasants apparently imagined *Diwan* to be a strongly Catholic organization for small children, and approved *Diwan*, however, has been contemptuous of such 'white', 'right-wing', an

Feiz ha Breiz (cf. p. 130) mentality. In general, any real or potential recruitment from local peasants has arisen because someone in a high-prestige occupation (especially nurse, doctor, or teacher) had his or her child in *Diwan*. At the same time, educated militants, such as those in *Diwan*, regret that they are themselves so 'intellectual' and 'Frenchified'. It is generally true, in the movement as a whole, that militants define out of their world the very features through which it might achieve popular acceptance. We shall see further twists to this in Part four.

'Local Breton'

Diwan's policy of 'local' or 'popular' Breton in its schools was aimed at local integration. This seemed especially important in the Vannetais. In keeping with other Vannetais militants, who have vigorously rejected the 'Léon bias' of standard Breton, the teacher in Lorient had made a great effort to learn and speak Vannetais. Breton-speakers where he lived, however, considered the 'Breton of Finistère' or the 'Breton of the Léon' much better than theirs.

In *Diwan*'s first Recruitment Commission for a teacher for a *pays bigouden* school in the Cornouaille, in southern Finistère (initially at Plounéour-Lanvern, later at Pont-l'Abbé (see p. 136 and map on p. 324)), the only candidate was from outside Brittany and had learnt standard Breton. It was felt that his Breton was not sufficiently clipped and 'local', which might prejudice the school's success. He started giving Breton classes at a cultural centre, and some enthusiasts who came along knew some local forms, having heard them at home. They came to learn standard forms from him, and to read and write, while he learnt localisms from them; everybody was happy to have their Breton thus 'improved', and *Diwan* gave him a job. This teacher also learnt, however, that 'local' Breton had no easy definition, that speakers deemed their 'Bretons' mutually incomprehensible over short distances, and that they claimed, again, that 'Léon Breton' was best.

Breton use, whether 'local' or not, is no easy route to local acceptance, either here or anywhere else. When I first visited the *Diwan* school in the *pays bigouden*, I naïvely asked directions in Breton from ladies wearing the tall white *coiffes* of the area, who were speaking Breton among themselves. In their postcard outfits, they seemed obviously 'local' and 'Breton'. They turned on me, however, and one snapped in French: 'We know French as well as you, you know!' *Diwan* parents explained to me that local Bretons, such as those *bigouden* women, 'still have the *symbole* round their necks' (cf. Chapter five). We shall see more clearly in Part four some important differences of socio-language involved here.

National integration

'Problems for the Government'

Diwan had officially voted, in a contentious vote in early 1978, to be integrated one day into a 'renovated public education system' – one, that is, which would take account of Breton and *Diwan*'s ideals. A persuasive factor in the vote had been the support for *Diwan* which even a theoretical plea for integration into mainstream education might win from the most important teaching union, the SNI. The SNI was influential in the refusal of some local municipalities to give funds or premises, and an alliance of the SNI and Socialist and Communist party members actually brought about the first closure of a *Diwan* school (at Callac, in the Côtes-du-Nord, near the Communist commune of Scrignac – see Chapter seven p. 133).

The vote for integration into the public education system was widely publicized and managed to convince one section of the SNI – in the Morbihan – that *Diwan* was not a 'private' school, opposing the mainstream system; this was the only SNI section which offered *Diwan* a formal statement of support. Public demands for integration were subsequently made by the union on *Diwan*'s behalf, however, and newer *Diwan* members were always horrified to discover that the oganization had ever voted for such a thing. By early 1980, nevertheless, the board was writing on *Diwan*'s own behalf to the educational authorities, demanding integration. Few imagined that this would ever become a reality, but they felt that the request would at least 'create problems for the government'.

'We wanted a different society'

By the time of *Diwan*'s third annual Congress, in May 1981, Mitterrand had beaten Giscard d'Estaing in the Presidential elections; the government was changing, and the Socialist Party had already formulated a bill of law which would give *Diwan* (and other regional language schools) official status within the public system. A special 'Integration Commission' was created at the Congress to discuss this bill: 'We must now take integration seriously'.[5]

In general discussion at this politically critical Congress, representatives of the Integration Commission tried to argue that the bill of law and Mitterrand's victory meant a new and financially secure future for *Diwan*. There were inevitably *Diwan* members who felt, however, that 'integration' was morally and politically irrelevant: '*Diwan* is just like the system already.' 'We want a different society', they shouted. Many old issues and conflicts reappeared at this Congress, and *Diwan* suffered a clear crisis of identity. There were whispers of possible schism, and of a new and more 'Breton' organization being established. 'We wanted a different society', came the repeated cry. 'We expected different relations in *Diwan*.'

In the midst of this came a report on the primary school's first year. This made it clear that it was not necessary, after all, for parents to know Breton for their children to learn Breton quickly at school. Indeed, poor Breton at home could hinder progress at school. Parents who had been struggling through in Breton, 'mistakes and all', felt cheated by this news. It was also noted that the good Breton-speakers at the nursery level had not necessarily heard any Breton at home, but rather had attended school regularly.

The primary school report confirmed a picture of French at home and Breton at school. This seemed like a simple inversion of the linguistic policy of the Third Republic. Whatever *Diwan* did, it seemed to be morally redolent of all that it opposed, and the shades of Ferry and Carré loomed large. 'Here we go', muttered one parent, 'the old direct method, and a language imposed at school . . . .'

Some parents, increasingly suspicious of 'Bretonization' – seeing in this, as in the policies of *Skol an Emsav*, the beginning of an enforced language policy in a 'Breton-speaking State' – had begun to resist the learning or use of Breton in their homes. Most *Diwan* parents, however, held strongly to 'alternative' educational ideals which emphasized continuity between home and school; they had 'Breton' enthusiasms, and wished Breton to be taught to their children; they were also faced, however, with the blunt fact that the spontaneous language of their homes was largely French. There seemed to be no way out of this definitional dilemma, no way of promoting Breton that was not, pedagogically and morally, evocative of a 'French' world. The primary school had served to emphasize the contradictions in which *Diwan* was caught.

Old internal sores, together with 'integration' on the horizon and the insecurity of 'Breton' definition in a France now moving politically from right to left, all helped to make the 1981 *Diwan* Congress very rowdy, with argument and dissent on almost every question that arose. One parent commented to me, 'this must be the worst you've ever seen!' He then went on, 'But just wait until we start talking about examinations, grammar, and *fautes d'orthographe* in our schools!' (The English expression 'spelling mistakes', often used to translate *fautes d'orthographe*, does not carry the same moral load as the French.) The strong French emphasis on *fautes d'orthographe* (merging with the horror of *grammaire*) has often been taken, within *Diwan* and among French intellectuals generally, as a metaphor for French centralization and 'linguistic and cultural imperialism' (see, e.g. Person 1973b:102). The standard Breton term *faziou*, however, had already come to occupy the semantic space of the French *fautes*.

Amid the general tumult of the 1981 Congress – and further adding to it – four of the *Diwan* teachers announced their resignations. They were fed up with 'bosses' and with seeing the world they sought regularly disappearing into all that it was not meant to be. These resignations meant that no teacher from *Diwan*'s most troubled early years now remained in the organization. One of the orginal teachers had already left, to visit the schools of the North American Indians. The primary school teacher also left, and now lives in Wales. She never received, at this Congress, the recognition and thanks which some felt she deserved for her work in setting the school on its way. Any applause for her was muted by the general noise of unrelenting argument.

Accusations of being 'French' ricocheted around the Congress hall, and Ostis, particularly, was caught in the cross-fire. 'I'm fed up with this', he said angrily. 'I've had enough of being told that I'm not Breton every time I make a decision or try to structure the organization and ensure its future.' The board, which was due for re-election, then refused to resign, for fear that others might take over who would nullify all their hard work. Ostis finally declared the Congress closed, and shouted, as argument raged around him: 'Just remember, we are all united in a struggle for Breton . . . .'

Part four

Plounéour-Ménez: peasants and Indians in Finistère

Chapter thirteen

Politics and education

In the mountains

Plounéour-Ménez is a rural, agricultural commune covering over 5,000 hectares (or 12,500 acres) of the northern flanks of the Arrée range. Plounéour (as it is commonly known, for short) is just inside the old Léon diocese, but has little of the relative fertility of the Léon plain, stretching away to the north-west. Until the 1950s, when the first tractor arrived, this was an important horse-rearing area, and otherwise one of extensive polyculture. Nowadays, cattle have replaced the horses, and milk is a major product, with barley, oats, beetroot, and maize grown as fodder crops. Potatoes are still grown, to be sold or eaten, or fed to the animals.

About one-tenth of the commune's surface area is woodland and over a third is *landes*, or heath and moors, patched with heather, gorse, and broom. Apart from the central village or 'bourg' (see p. 19), there are twenty-six inhabited villages in Plounéour and the visible remains of at least five others now wholly abandoned. Villages have long fluctuated in fortune and importance, but depopulation has been particularly marked in Finistère's mountain communes.

For the outsider, Celtic mists tend to swirl around the heath and heather of the Arrée region. Plounéour-Ménez's very name (*menez*, Br.: 'mountain') sets it in the educated topography of the isolated fastnesses of tradition: it is always in mountains and wildernesses, it seems, that Celtic languages and cultures have survived. For enthusiasts in the towns, the upland area of inland Brittany has long served as a metaphor of true, surviving Bretonness. When I left the regional capital of Rennes to live in this area of deepest Finistère, militant friends assured me that now I would find a popular culture of the kind to which they themselves aspired. It was with some excitement, therefore, that I first set out from Rennes for the mountains, on a three-hour drive along the small central road running through the interior of Brittany. Only much later did I reflect that a large dual carriageway around the edge of Brittany would have taken me there much faster. At the time, however, I did not want that brash connecting strip of continuous modernity to exist. The excitement lay in a symbolic boundary, marking off 'real anthropology' country, into which I was determined to cross (cf. McDonald 1985).

On the inland road, the land eventually rises, becomes wooded in patches, and the road itself increasingly winding and narrow. After a climb over the eastern tips of the Arrée range, a sign-post left shows the way to Le Relecq, the first hamlet on this road in the commune of Plounéour-Ménez. Scholars, mostly archaeologists and historians, have shown interest in the old Cistercian abbey of Le Relecq; indeed, it is the only well-documented thing about Plounéour (see J. Laurent 1972; Pérennès 1932). Its crumbling ruins suit a picture of isolated enchantment, and those who have consulted their modern 'Guide to Mysterious Brittany' (Le Scouëzec 1979:541ff) stop and stand enthralled before an abbey described as a source of traditional Breton legend and a centre of popular devotion.

The thirty or so inhabitants of Le Relecq are dispersed in half a dozen houses on one side of the road, after the abbey, and three on the other, and in dwellings lying just off the road around an overgrown square. Here, there is also a lake and an old water-mill, all hidden from the road. Beyond Le Relecq, up a sharp hill, and behind the lake and lanes of the abbey, is the village of Kerguz, where I rented an old farmhouse whose former peasant owners had moved to smarter accommodation in the bourg. Kerguz is strung out on its own circular track, surrounded by hedges, trees, and fields. One popular etymology of Kerguz is *Kerguzet* (Br.) meaning 'hidden village'. These villages are on the more obviously mountain side of the commune, with craggy heathland stretching away to the south. Breton enthusiasts once described the neighbourhood as a 'charming corner, unknown to the hurried tourist', inducing 'meditation, *rêverie* and senti-mental walks' (*Ar Falz* 1950, 21:5). More and more enthusiasts have since shown interest in the area, and there is no strong desire locally to deny the glamour that external interest might bring. However, as I got to know these villages, other images emerged.

I learnt that the last keeper of Le Relecq's old mill drowned in the lake and another man shot himself in the old square. Here, and in other villages, there were stories of locals having drowned themselves, or hanged themselves, or cut their throats. Such stories might be understood in a variety of ways (including identity problems for those without kin, land, or active, productive life on the land to offer) but people told them as gruesome elaboration of the hard local life they had known. This rural mountain world clearly lends itself to different interpretations. People in Plounéour have their own self-images, and their own problems. They also have their own sense of hard-won sophistication.

While enthusiasts in the towns have been imagining their 'Breton' world tucked away in the mountains, the people in the Arrée mountains have themselves been actively espousing, within their own structures of identity and aspiration, the ideas and politics of the French Republic. Early this century, a French political researcher, André Siegfried, looked at Brittany's voting patterns, principally under the Third Republic, and was surprised by the mountain communes of the Arrée region. He had expected to find 'reactionary' ideas in these 'solitary and wild mountains' but instead found people who seemed to have 'long since affirmed their independence of the priests' (Siegfried 1964:173).

Siegfried showed particular interest in the canton of Saint-Thégonnec, which is made up of Plounéour-Ménez and four other communes: Le Cloître to the east, Loc-Eguiner and Saint-Thégonnec to the north-west, and Pleyber-Christ to the north. These last three communes are in the more fertile Léon plain, and all but Le Cloître are in the old Léon diocese, that 'clerical fortress of Brittany' (Siegfried 1964:174). Siegfried noted a 'striking' contrast between the three communes in the plain, which were politically 'white', and the two in the mountains, Plounéour-Ménez and Le Cloître, which were strongly 'republican' and 'radical' (ibid:174, 177). The canton is now an electoral area for the election of councillors to the *Conseil Général* of the *département* of Finistère. Plounéour-Ménez and Le Cloître have regularly voted for republican and 'red' candidates, unlike the rest of the canton, and they have voted similarly in legislative elections and in their own municipal elections.

In the domain of politics, the 'mountains' stand, in local identity structures, as a metaphor of the 'red' and radical. This image has been important in Plounéour's self-definition and has carried its own auto-matisms at election time: 'We are red here. Plounéour votes for the left. That's how it is in the mountains.' Plounéour takes its definition here in opposition to the Léon plain and, although Plounéour is just inside the old administrative boundaries of the former Léon diocese (at a point where the old Léon, Trégor, and Cornouaille meet), it is the 'mountain' definition, rather than any diocesan title, which has political salience and which Plounéour assumes.

Nineteenth-century education

Plounéour embraced the principles of the 1789 Revolution, in its own understanding of them, and the commune's authorities denounced local priests in office, who were forced to flee, having refused to swear the civil oath of loyalty to the new Republic. Unlike many communes further into the Léon, Plounéour accepted priests who had sworn the oath, and in 1793 the mayor of Plounéour, a local notary, boasted that the commune had more *civisme* (or more of the public-spiritedness expected of the Republic's citizens) than had its neighbours in the Léon plain (see *BCD* 1917:171ff). This boast was directed principally against Pleyber-Christ with which Plounéour was briefly coupled at this time in a two-commune canton.

Pleyber was the principal commune, which the then much larger Plounéour resented. At least part of Plounéour's initial burst of republican fervour can be attributed to local competition of this kind.

Plounéour's sworn priests did not necessarily have an easy time. One such priest arrived from Saint-Thégonnec ostensibly seeking a site that promised easier acceptance of his status (see F. Quiniou 1929:126). All went well until, in 1794, a special 'French language teacher' also arrived in Plounéour, following the legislation of Barère and his colleagues (see Chapter one, p. 33). The District of Morlaix advised these teachers to take over the churches as schools, and Plounéour's 'French language teacher' duly went to the church in the bourg and began to read out the District's directives. The priest urged local parishioners to attack him. The mayor put the priest in gaol, and the 'French language teacher' went on to gain a full certificate of *civisme* from the municipality (Ogès 1941: 82–3; *BCD* 1917:276ff).[1]

When I recounted this story to local people in the town hall of modern Plounéour, it was greeted with some pride and amusement. Plounéour's authorities like to feel that they have long been more 'advanced' politically than the neighbouring communes of the Léon, even if Plounéour cannot match them in wealth and general social amenities. There was also mischievous delight at the thought of a public teacher setting up school in the church.

Plounéour complied as best it could with national legislation concerning education in the nineteenth century. In 1814 there was a lay schoolmaster in the bourg, but in 1820 Plounéour's teacher was denounced from Saint Thégonnec because he had no *brevet* (certificate) and his 'moral and religious conduct' did not befit a schoolmaster under the Restoration.[2] By 1830, he had been replaced by a qualified teacher, who received an indemnity from the commune, and almost one-quarter of whose pupils attended free.[3] The municipality undoubtedly had a commitment to schooling (even if sometimes only to compete with other municipalities) but formal education was not an obvious option for Plounéour's population, the majority of whom had other preoccupations, wringing subsistence from the land. Moreover, for those who could afford them, there were more prestigious boarding schools in the Léon neighbourhood and in Morlaix. Plounéour's mayors have always been literate in French, but in 1831 only eighty men and fifty women shared this ability. The neighbouring communes in the plain had a far higher percentage literacy (especially among the men) (see ADF:IN 192). However, in 1833, an inspector reporting for a national enquiry launched by Guizot, gave a good account of Plounéour's well-qualified lay teacher, who taught 'intelligently', used *colloques* (see p. 28), and had at least twenty-seven pupils (roughly estimated at the time to be about one-twentieth of the school-age population) in the winter months, over half of whom attended free.[4] This teacher ran the school until the 1850s, commanding a relatively high sum for his teaching from those who could pay, which suggests that he was well respected locally (see Ogès 1934:111–12).

By the 1850s, the school had almost 200 children, and was outgrowing its rented accommodation to the point that the authorities began to see it as a health hazard. Plounéour was advised to build its own school-house, and to finance this the municipal council began to sell off communal lands (lands which had mostly accrued to the commune from the old nobility and the clergy following the 1789 Revolution). The situation became urgent in the early 1860s when, amid new ideas about 'hygiene' in France, the higher authorities briefly closed Plounéour's school on health grounds.

Local efforts to build a school-house did not help relations with the clergy, and intermittent battles now gained new substance and momentum. The municipal council had refused the local priests money for repairs to the presbytery in the 1840s, and in the 1860s refused to make up their salary in full, arguing in both cases that all available funds were needed for a school-house (AM 7 January 1847; 27 September 1863). The priests suspected some municipal councillors of plotting against them. The sale of old church lands brought extra tension and the active dissent of one section of the commune which is now a separate commune in its own right: Loc-Eguiner.

Loc-Eguiner (1975 pop.:366) is Plounéour's immediate neighbour to the north-west, between Plounéour and Saint-Thégonnec (see map, p. 325). Loc-Eguiner, with its own church, had become part of Plounéour-Ménez after the 1789 Revolution. There were regular squabbles over Loc-Eguiner's church lands, which Plounéour claimed as its own and now wanted to sell to raise money. Loc-Eguiner gained parish status in the 1840s and finally won its independence as a commune in 1866, by which time Plounéour had built its school-house. The municipality was not wholly sorry to see Loc-Eguiner go, for its inhabitants were by this time demanding money to build their own school also (AM 3 December 1865; 8 July 1866). In any case, Plounéour's municipality had long regarded that section of the commune as too much under the influence of clergy and bishop (see, for example, AM 17 December 1843). Plounéour's attempts to portray Loc-Eguiner as backward, incompetent, or reactionary sometimes misfired, however, for in many areas the clergy indeed held sway. In 1852, for example, a Plounéour delegate in a departmental education committee had complained about a nun teaching in a private school in Loc-Eguiner: he wanted her removed because she had used Breton texts; the committee, however, which included a number of the clergy, allowed her to stay (see CAF 20 January 1852). Some members claimed that 'article 28' allowed such texts anyway, and that they were a proper means to learn good French.

The catechism, in Breton, held an important place in Plounéour's own school in the bourg, but the teachers' efforts to teach French were praised by both the municipality and the higher authorities. The school had several French grammars by the 1850s, and Plounéour was winning prizes for *écriture* in the *département* by the early 1870s. The municipality was so pleased with its school that, in 1867, it made a special gift of 100 francs (no mean sum at the time) to the headteacher as a sign of local 'gratitude' (AM 14 February 1867).

This school was officially for boys, and boys' education took precedence locally as it did nationally. Educational provision for girls was, at best, irregular. Local priests generally taught girls their catechism, but female lay teachers were few. This was partly due to a lack of teacher training for girls and to difficulties faced by female teachers in finding suitable spouses in rural areas. It was also a matter of politics, especially in the Léon. Just after the Revolution, for example, one Léon commune wanted an *institutrice* but could not persuade anyone to do the job: 'no woman yet dares to show herself as a republican' (year VI; cited in Ogès 1942:133). The male teacher in Plounéour's bourg taught a few girls in 1820, but mixing the sexes was not approved by all. Plounéour had a female lay teacher in the early 1830s, and again from 1844 to 1846 (see AM 15 February 1846). In 1846, another commune happily reported that a woman had begun educating local girls and that this was introducing a 'healthy morality' and 'the habit of using French', all of which had brought a 'certain polish which softens the savagery and natural roughness of the peasants' (cited in Ogès 1934:143). Adopting a similar view, Plounéour's municipal council rejoiced when, in the 1850s, a qualified local girl offered to be the *institutrice* in the bourg. The council paid for the renting of a separate girls' school (in accordance with the Falloux law) and urged higher authorities to give supplementary financial support to this teacher, 'the need for whom was strongly felt by everyone' (AM 7 October 1855). This girl resigned in 1858, however, anxious to get away from local poverty and to seek a new life elsewhere (ADF: T65/2, 1858).

Meanwhile, in 1855, a wealthy family in Morlaix had installed some nuns in the old abbey in Le Relecq (about two miles from the bourg). This abbey, with its monks expelled, its lands confiscated, and its buildings ransacked after the 1789 Revolution, still had provision for a convent, and had been kept up by this devoted family. The nuns began teaching some girls from Plounéour and neighbouring communes. In 1867 new legislation urged the establishment of a communal girls' school, at a time when Plounéour's bourg had no female teacher at all (AM 31 October 1867). However, the municipal council, after much debate, decided that the commune's financial resources were strained – aiding the poor, maintaining roads, and, importantly, building the new boys' school-house: 'for the moment', therefore, the nuns' school at Le Relecq, which cost the municipality nothing, would have to fulfil the commune's legal obligation (AM 3 July 1870).

Always multi-functional (nursing the sick and dying, for example), the nuns were generally welcome. The municipality was not wholly happy with their school, however, and, in keeping with the mood of the Third Republic, declared 'an urgent need to have a public *institutrice laïque* in the commune' (AM 10 November 1872). Within the year, the higher authorities posted another female lay teacher to the commune, and she received separate rented accommodation for a girls' school in the bourg. This teacher stayed longer than had her predecessors, and ended up marrying a local male teacher. By 1875, the nuns of Le Relecq had left, their pupils depleted in number. The commune then set about raising finance for a girls' school-house, and in 1880, frustrated by delays, one inhabitant wrote directly to Jules Ferry for help in this (see ADF:0–II 2–0 783). by 1882, there were enough girls in the school for the municipal council to request a second female teacher (there were already at least two male teachers). Local accommodation and finance were juggled, yet another boys' school was built, and the girls moved into the old boys' school by 1884. Plounéour now had two new communal school-houses in its bourg; both were overcrowded again before the 1880s were out.

The *Filles de la Croix* of Le Relecq had taught local girls to launder and sew, and to read and write French if they attended long enough, but otherwise the reading of devotional works in Breton was the most their pupils achieved. In the modern town hall of Plounéour, it is regretted that the commune should ever have tolerated this *école libre*, even if it lasted barely twenty years. Of even greater regret is the fact that another order of nuns, the *Filles du Saint-Esprit*, who had already opened schools in the neighbouring communes of the Léon, also opened an *école libre* in Plounéour's bourg, in 1892. This second *école libre* has managed to survive to the present day.

Church and state

The old convent building of the *Filles de la Croix* at Le Relecq was destroyed in two mysterious fires early this century, and memories of it have also been erased from the image of the locality. This side of the commune, and especially Le Relecq itself, is regarded as having been the major contributor to Plounéour's most radical republicanism and determined anti-clericalism. Two closely related factors are repeatedly cited as reasons for this by inhabitants of modern Plounéour: first, Le Relecq has had its own *école laïque*, and second, one of Plounéour's most radical mayors, Pouliquen, mayor in the 1920s and 1930s, came from the hamlet. Francis Pouliquen was already in the municipal council before the First World War, and his father before him was deputy mayor at the beginning of the century.

Le Relecq sought its own *école laïque* from the 1880s onwards. The modern hamlet, with its ruins, overgrown square, and close horizon of barren wasteland, is not an obvious site for a thriving school. However, in the 1880s, it still had its own markets and fairs, some better attended than those of the bourg. The narrow road through the hamlet, linking Plounéour with centres inland and to the east and also joining roads to Morlaix in the north and Quimper in the south, was classified as a major road on account of the hamlet's commercial importance (and also, in the 1890s, because the municipality felt that 'an eminently republican area' merited a major road: AM 22 November 1891; 12 March 1893). The principal Morlaix–Quimper road runs through the eastern tip of Plounéour's bourg. Both the bourg and Le Relecq, therefore, formed important crossroads in the commune, and there was some rivalry between them, and between Le Relecq and other villages. Several Le Relecq notaries had gone as mayors to the town hall in the bourg. The idea for a school in Le Relecq came initially from the Prefect and local Inspectorate who, in the 1880s, saw that the hamlet, although itself small, had several larger villages around it (including Kerguz, then with a population of about 200) and the children would no longer have to walk to Plounéour's bourg for their schooling. Local inhabitants eagerly took up the idea, and it was discussed in at least ten meetings of Plounéour's municipal council between 1887 and 1905. With the help of the educational authorities, Plounéour ultimately managed both to enlarge and embellish the public schools in the bourg – to stay competitive with the *libres* there – and to build this new school. The *école laïque* of Le Relecq, for both boys and girls, eventually opened in 1906, on land donated by Hervé Pouliquen, father of Francis.[5]

The nuns of the *école libre* in the bourg inhabited a new school-house donated by a wealthy local priest, but they did not have an easy time. They included women of some refinement, and attracted many local girls (and a few small boys) to their school. The manuscript *Annales* of the private school reveal that the sisters found Plounéour 'very dirty' in the 1890s, and that they encountered considerable hostility from teachers of the *école laïque* and the municipal council. Councillors feared that the *école libre* would cream off numbers from the public school and threaten free education for the local poor, who needed it most. The council, backed by the higher authorities, therefore did its best to make the public school more attractive. Increasingly, local inhabitants withdrew their daughters from the *école libre*, especially if the fathers wanted to stand for election to the municipal council, for which a coherent 'republican' stand was becoming necessary. The *Annales* recount how some pupils in the *école libre* began to play on local tensions, their behaviour becoming increasingly 'difficult'. The measure of Combes in 1901 (see Chapter two, p. 40) closed many schools of the same religious order in Finistère, and in 1903, as they had feared, the nuns were turned out of the school. Nine months later the school reopened, with the nuns employing Catholic lay teachers. These teachers were unqualified initially, and the school lost some credibility. Moreover, the *Annales* report that the reopening of the school was met with 'violent political pressures' from the municipal council. The schoolchildren of the *école laïque* were given more and more free books, medical help, and prizes. In 1908, the *Annales* record that there were definitely 'friends of Satan' in Plounéour. By this time, an important date in Plounéour's history of itself had passed: '1905', the separation of Church and State.

The manuscript *Registre Paroissial* (or Parish Register) of Plounéour, in which priests have confided their trials and worries, and their warnings to their successors, is equally plaintive. It opens, in the early years of this century, with tales of 'the fight of the municipality against the clergy', tales which continue virtually unabated thereafter. Following the separation of Church and State, the municipality confiscated more local church lands and sold them. One priest recorded that, in 1906, local people would come to Mass, then pointedly get up and leave when he began his sermon, making considerable noise and deliberately 'banging their clogs'.

The municipality dealt the priests an extra blow by confiscating their home and demanding a full rent: the presbytery was now declared the property of the commune rather than of the 'parish' or its representatives. After protracted negotiations, the priests offered a nominal rent, which the commune refused. In October 1908, at eight o'clock one morning, the priests were forcibly evicted under the supervision of the mayor, who had called in a number of police to help. According to the Parish Register, there were many local onlookers, but no protesters. In response, the deanery in Saint-Thégonnec deprived Plounéour of its priests and of Mass and sacraments; the church was closed, and the deanery and diocese declared Plounéour-Ménez 'the forbidden parish' – a status which lasted ten full months. This episode leant ample confirmation to Plounéour's moral and political image, both in the neighbouring Léon and in Plounéour itself. Some inhabitants in modern Plounéour now say that it merely taught local people that they could 'live without priests'. However, the priests returned. A few faithful and relatively wealthy parishioners, among the 'white' (or pro-clerical) minority of the population, clubbed together and bought the priests a new home, some distance from the church, which is still the local presbytery. The priests returned in 1909, and the church reopened. The grand old presbytery, one of the largest buildings in the commune, still stands near the church. It was cheekily used for a while as accommodation for the old girls' *école laïque*, to prevent the 'reactionaries' from repossessing it (see ADF: T65/2; 0–II 02–785). It is now the local post office. Every 14 July, on 'Bastille Day', the municipality places a large *tricolore* on its post office, next to the church; when only one good flag is available, it is there that it flies.

Some inhabitants in Le Relecq like to recall how people on that side of the commune used to march to the bourg in triumphal procession behind a *tricolore* during elections after '1905'. The priests' Parish Register often mentions Le Relecq, and especially the Pouliquen family of the hamlet, with concern. Francis Pouliquen was the first local mayor openly to take a party ticket, as a 'Radical Socialist'. The 'Radical Socialist' party was one of the first great national parties (established in 1901) and, locally and nationally, traced its descent from figures such as Ferry and Combes. It was patriotic, anti-clerical, and devoted to popular education. Francis Pouliquen came to power with two *tricolores* stamped on his election list. The Pouliquens of Le Relecq have been peasants, horse traders, and general *entrepreneurs*. Francis Pouliquen bought up some of the valuable lands confiscated from the clergy and refused to hand any back when implored to do so by local priests. He was excommunicated in the 1930s as a result, which ensured him a star-studded place in Plounéour's political history of itself.

While I was in Plounéour, the current mayor was also a 'Radical Socialist', with leanings to the modern *Radicaux de Gauche* party. He had been mayor since 1959, and on the municipal council since 1953. He was a partly retired peasant from the bourg who had received a secondary, technical education, and had briefly worked in Paris. The other members of the municipal council included seven Socialists and four Communists; a further 'Independent' member, who ran an electrical shop, usually took the mayor's line. The deputy mayor was a Communist. All four Communists had farms locally, as did four of the Socialists. The other three Socialists were a retired postman, an owner of a bar in the bourg, and a teacher of English.

Whatever their internal differences, these councillors were all 'red' in self-image, in opposition to 'white'. After the Radical Socialist declarations of the 1920s and 1930s, the reds of Plounéour regularly fought among themselves in municipal elections, claiming a variety of 'Radical', 'Socialist', and 'Republican' labels, each accusing the other of being more right-wing than themselves. It is a regular feature of the commune's political self-commentary, however, that 'Red and white have always been more important than divisions of left and right.' Plounéour has, in many ways, fought the battles of the Republic longer than the Republic itself. Immediately after the Second World War, the local reds were united in a single municipal election list, as a 'Republican and Anti-Fascist Union', under a Communist mayor. The Resistance was strong in Plounéour, I was told, especially 'on the mountain side' of the commune. Many in the villages nearer the mountain slopes claim a more robust republican and red definition, distinguishing themselves from 'the other side of the commune' (meaning Loc-Eguiner and its neighbourhood in the Léon plain). With this image come Resistance claims and modern party political distinctions. The most vivid Resistance stories came from a Communist in Le Relecq, and

Communists in general recall the years immediately after the last war as a high point in their Party's public support. Thereafter, Plounéour's reds were divided again at municipal elections, but united in 1971 when the minority 'white' section of the local population dared to stand as a list 'For a Little More Social Justice'. The reds immediately forgot their internal differences and, as a '*Union des Gauches*', swept home in triumph in the first round. After that, the elections were uncontested.

The plea 'For a Little More Social Justice' arose largely because of the municipality's attitude to the *école libre*, which had regularly been refused public aid or communal funds.[6] The municipality has insisted that 'public funds should not go to a private school'. It therefore came as a terrible shock when, in March 1981, the higher authorities tried to oblige the commune to accept a *contrat d'association* with the *école libre*, which meant giving the same funding (per pupil) to the *école libre* as to the *école laïque*. The private school had already, since 1960, a *contrat simple* directly with the State, by which the State paid the teachers' salaries; this contract (see Chapter four, note 20) did not involve the municipality or local public funds. Then, after the 1977 *Loi Guermeur*, the private school began to demand a *contrat d'association*, a new contract that would involve the municipality direct. The municipal council unanimously rejected this, but since the higher authorities had declared the private school fully in order, the municipality was formally required to comply. Plounéour defiantly held out, however, and in June 1981, when the legislative elections brought a Socialist government to power, there was special delight at the news that Guermeur, the Deputy of Southern Finistère behind the new contracts, had lost his seat. The majority in Plounéour wholeheartedly welcomed the results of those elections. Louis Pouliquen, son of Francis (and himself mayor of the commune in the 1950s), saw it all as a vindication of Plounéour's long stand against the clergy and the *libres*. 'There have been two real Revolutions in France', he announced, '1789 and now.' The *Marseillaise* and the *Internationale* were sung in local bars after the election results, and Plounéour's reds drew up a single, unbroken struggle from '1789' to 1981, passing through '1905'. 'That used to be the presbytery, you know,' explained one councillor proudly, gesticulating towards the post office.

In the town hall, in the secular world of the commune, '1789' and '1905' are matters of pride. They inevitably have a different value in the presbytery. The priest of Plounéour felt that 'the Revolution of 1789' had been a '*malheur*', which still had a 'bad influence' locally; and he talked of '1905' with evident irritation, for, in his view, a 'fiasco' had followed it in Plounéour. When I first visited the priest, he received me with great courtesy, pleased to meet someone interested in 'the other side'. During subsequent months, when I moved between *libres* and *laïques*, between parish and commune, and between presbytery and town hall, he was sometimes none too sure which 'side' I was on. During my stay in Plounéour, I was obliged to perform some acrobatics of diplomacy, and gradually local inhabitants, *libres* or *laïques*, in presbytery or town hall, generously came to allow me excuses such as, 'You have to get to know everybody, no doubt, for your work'. In this way, my transgression of local boundaries was incorporated without too much discomfort.

The municipality's attitude to the *école libre* is echoed in its attitude to the local church buildings. The abbey chapel in Le Relecq has been classified as an 'historical monument', and in 1976 responsibility for it passed from the diocese to the *département*. In 1980, the municipal council refused contributions requested for its upkeep. Until the 1950s, weekly Mass was said in the chapel, but depopulation helped to end these services, and by the 1950s Plounéour only had one priest. Mass is now said in the church in the bourg. Local people enjoy telling scandalous stories about the old monks of the abbey (although there have been no monks now for almost two hundred years) – how the monks, for example, forced girls to sleep with them before they married. It is commonplace for peasants in France to feel that monasteries and the higher clergy had excessive income from the land (Le Roy Ladurie 1974), and such stories about the monks, often told to illustrate the justice of '1789', are far from new.[7] The abbey chapel is now open only on special occasions. When I have attended services there, leaflets have been available rebutting scandals about the old monks. The obvious distress that such stories cause the clergy tends, however, to encourage their telling.

One occasion for which the abbey chapel is opened is the annual *pardon* (or penitential religious service and procession) of Le Relecq on 15 August. This *pardon*, one of many in Brittany, declined somewhat with the commercial wane of the hamlet and wider depopulation, but has always offered an occasion for social gathering beyond the level of the village or commune. Revelry and fights (often between mountains and plain, or countryside and bourg, or peasant and tradesman) have been common in the past. A small *fête foraine*, rather like a traditional British fairground, and run by travelling fair people, is installed in the old square of Le Relecq for the *pardon* every year, and two old bars in the hamlet do good business. Many regard this as time to catch up with gossip and meet old acquaintances. Only faithful parishioners participate in an open procession which follows the afternoon service, and which leads past the lake to an old spring where there once stood a holy statue of Saint Bernard (the supposed founder of the Cistercian abbey). The clergy once had to retrieve this statue from the lake, where it was thrown by a local inhabitant. It is not visible now – stolen, it is said. The *pardon* also includes an early morning Mass, which was itself the occasion of irreverence during my stay in Kerguz: the son of a local Socialist and strongly anti-clerical peasant marched with his friends into the chapel during this Mass, and stalked up the central aisle in rowdy parody, banging sticks on the floor. The priest and a few of the faithful threw them out, and barred the doors before continuing. The priest took it as a sad comment on the state of the parish that he should have to lock himself in to celebrate Holy Mass.

This priest, a man claiming some sophistication, had worked in other parishes of the Léon plain, and felt he had been in office in Plounéour for 'eight long years'. He recalled wryly that his 100–50-strong weekly congregation in the bourg increased significantly during poor weather or drought, when harvests were threatened. Attendance is also higher at the Feast of All Souls and All Saints in November, when families offer Mass for their dead and a procession leads from the church to the cemetery, on the edge of the bourg. The graves are scrupulously cleaned by relatives before the ceremony, and some are very grand. 'It's all for show', the priest explained: the fulfilment of family obligations and the 'prestigious' graves were merely a matter of 'social pride' for many of his recalcitrant flock. The priest is well aware that even some of his regular congregation vote 'red' at election time, and that his church does not have, and has not had, priority in the communal budget. The church in the bourg, once part of the abbey's domain, was built and embellished in the seventeenth and eighteenth centuries on the model of other churches in the Léon. It was classified as an 'historical monument' in 1914, but until the 1950s the municipality refused to contribute to its upkeep.[8] The municipality and the clergy agreed that each should pay half the bill for repairs in 1955, and again in 1969, by which time the church was in a precarious state. From the 1970s onwards, the municipality then renewed its refusals to pay.

I once commented in the town hall, rather tactlessly perhaps, that Plounéour-Ménez easily evoked images of the super-typical French commune described in the novel *Clochemerle* (Chevallier 1934), and added that at least Plounéour did not seem, as yet, to have contemplated building a public *pissoir*, as did the mayor of Clochemerle, in ribald triumph of Republic over clergy. The mayor of Plounéour good-humouredly interrupted me, and pointed towards the church where, sure enough, there was a public convenience, built by the municipality in the 1960s, within the old grounds of the church itself. Such small conveniences commonly exist next to churches in France, but Plounéour's mayor was happy to assimilate Plounéour's urinal to political triumph. 'And we built it without permission', he added, with a mischievous smile.

Modern schools in Plounéour

All Plounéour's schools are now within the bourg, and all are coeducational. The *école laïque* of Le Relecq, which had over 100 pupils in the 1940s, closed in 1972 due to depopulation, and the remaining nine pupils were transferred to the bourg (see AM 30 November 1972). On the eastern side of the bourg there is a primary school (the local *école laïque*) which has two primary classes and a nursery class (some nursery provision having been available since at least the 1930s). Next door to the primary school is a public College (11–15 years). These two schools form Plounéour's public *groupe scolaire*, and were established on the present site in the 1960s, with a new road leading to them. The municipality has proudly named this *'rue Jules Ferry'*. Pleyber-Christ had just given this name to its own school-road, and Plounéour was not to be outdone. The *rue Jules Ferry* lies about 70 metres behind the town hall, running parallel to the main square (see map, p. 326). On the opposite side of the bourg, about 200 metres away, and on the same side of the square as the church, cemetery, and former presbytery, is the small *école libre* (with a nursery section). Recruitment to the *école libre* is generally from this side of the commune, or from the plain. When I arrived in Plounéour, there were thirty-three children in the *école libre*, two-thirds of them girls; fifteen of this total were in the nursery section. In the same year, there were eighty-six children in the *école laïque* – thirty-three in the nursery class and fifty-three in the primary.

The very existence of a public secondary school or College in this small, rural commune is boasted as evidence of local commitment to schooling. No other commune in the canton has such a College. Plounéour's municipality first asked for schooling beyond the primary level in 1907, and repeated the request thereafter as more pupils sought higher qualifications but could not afford to travel to, or to board in, the public secondary schools of Morlaix, 17 kilometres away. The College first opened (as a *Cours Complémentaire*) in 1946. Its first teachers recall how they were met with insults from the *libres*, and mutual insult between *laïques* and *libres* has been common at all levels, between both staff and pupils. There are tales of stone-throwing, of the *laïques* spitting at private pupils, and mocking them as 'Holy Water frogs' (*les grenouilles de l'eau bénite*); the *laïques*, on the other hand, claim to have been shunned, labelled 'the devil's school' (*l'école du diable*), and despised as poor. One of the first College teachers (now in the municipal council) recalls with particular bitterness how, early in the College's existence, he was one day publicly insulted in such terms by a local priest in the centre of the bourg.

When, in the 1950s, the government sought cuts in educational expenditure that would have threatened Plounéour's hard-won College, the municipal council of Plounéour responded vigorously: such cuts ran counter to the 'primordial needs of the *pays*, among which National Education reigns supreme' and would not be 'in the interest of the Nation', merely encouraging the *libres* and threatening the national supply of 'qualified workers' (AM 14 May 1950). By the late 1950s, some pupils from the local *école libre* were going into the College, convenient and free, rather than to private secondary schools elsewhere, and primary level pupils from neighbouring communes were also coming in. The local pries increasingly feared that Plounéour's 'wicked' influence would spread.[9] Opposition from the clergy, depopulation, and finance posed constant problems, although the priest's opposition seems, if anything, to have strengthened local resolve.

The College is housed in prefabricated buildings loaned by the *département*. The municipal council has regularly requested permission and funding for proper concrete buildings, but falling numbers have threatened the school with closure.[10] The canton forms an educational catchment area at this level, and the other communes tend to find it unbecoming to have to send their children to this mountain commune for their secondary education. Saint-Thégonnec has been the slowest to offer public support for Plounéour to keep its College, and this has been no surprise to Plounéour. Saint-Thégonnec, the most notable local stronghold of 'white' politics, has both a primary *école libre* and its own private College. Its *école laïque* is small and barely thriving. In the smarter commune of Pleyber-Christ, north of Plounéour, and now the wealthiest and the least agricultural of all the communes of the canton, many would prefer to have the College in their own commune, or to send their children directly to Morlaix. Concern is often voiced about academic standards in rural Colleges generally, and Plounéour is openly described in Pleyber as socially 'hick' (often using the term *ploucs* (Fr.), meaning 'bumpkins' or, quite literally, those from a *plou*). Plounéour is uneasily aware of this and demands much, therefore, of its College. Despite a lack of certain facilities (such as gymnasium and laboratory), the College has a good record for sending pupils on to higher levels in Morlaix, at 15 years of age, and its teachers are all concerned to maintain high standards.

Do you teach Breton?

The College has had problems with the range of modern languages it can offer. English and Spanish are taught, and most pupils choose English as their first modern language, and Spanish (or, for some, extra English or remedial French) as their second modern language option. There is a teacher who could also teach German, but no paid hours for this have officially been granted. Many parents, including some from Plounéour, are said to use the 'excuse' of wanting German in order to by-pass the College and send their children directly to the more prestigious schools in Morlaix. Amid such problems, there has been little space for Breton. While the language teachers (and indeed the majority of the staff, including the headmistress) know Breton, no Breton has been taught. One former headmaster of the College looked somewhat askance when I enquired about Breton teaching: 'No one has ever asked for that', he said dismissively. The present headmistress explained that it was hard enough keeping the College going: 'Anyway, parents would not want it here.'

No Breton has been taught at primary level in the *école laïque* either. The headmistress of the primary school, a locally born woman, had taught in the commune since 1953, and only once, in the 1950s, had she encountered a child who came to school knowing virtually no French. Her response (and the initial responses of other teachers, too) suggested that she thought I was asking if Breton was taught because I imagined the children could not speak French. She explained that the school had occasionally had problems with children who spoke a 'peculiar French' and, although schools were 'more tolerant of Bretonisms now', parents were most concerned that their children should 'master French well'.

In the public nursery class, the children had learnt a few simple modern Breton songs from the young teacher, but this teacher emphasized that she was not teaching the children to speak Breton, and that they did not speak it at home. She was careful to correct the children's mistakes in French, and stressed the preparatory value of the nursery class, and the importance of a regular timetable of activities. Fearing that she might seem too strict, the nursery teacher explained that some 'discipline', 'routine', and 'structure' were essential. She did 'of course' like things to 'come from the children', and liked 'beginning with what they know'. At both primary and secondary levels, teachers liked to begin with some knowledge of the locality – 'the school, the commune, the *département*'. In the College, for example, history and geography lessons include the 'declining population', the climate, and agriculture of the commune, and some aspects of Finistère's history (with the 1789 Revolution prominent). Pupils also learn about the old abbey of Le Relecq, and hear about the old presbytery. Teachers described this as beginning with 'local culture' or the 'local environment'.

In the *école libre*, some Breton had been periodically taught in the past, and it is now one of Finistère's private schools which attempts 'five minutes a day' of oral Breton, largely in stories, rhymes, and songs. The school does not emphasize its teaching of Breton, however, and is more concerned to stress that its standards are wholly competitive with the *école laïque*, whose teachers often claimed that the modern *école libre* was not only reactionary but sub-standard. Nuns keenly showed me paintings, materials, and carefully kept exercise books that might combat this image.

Although Plounéour's teachers were generally aware of a new interest in Breton, my queries brought uneasiness and suspicion. In all the schools of Plounéour, it was my explicit enquiries that raised the issue of Breton. The teachers' own priorities were always elsewhere. It has not been easy to convert Breton into a fashionable asset in a commune where many parents are still worried about their French or about that of their children. In Plounéour, Breton can now appear both fashionable and backward. In the context of wider 'Breton' enthusiasms, the *école libre* could use its teaching of Breton to claim fashionable one-upmanship in relation to the *laïques*, but they know that such a claim could too easily be collapsed locally into images of rampant clericalism or social retardation. Moreover, there is another enterprise in Plounéour with which neither public nor private sectors wish to be associated: *Diwan*, in Le Relecq. 'It's not a school', the public nursery teacher explained. 'I don't know what they call it – but it's not a school.' Such comments were common: 'The teacher there is not even qualified.'

Diwan

Diwan opened in Le Relecq, in 1977, in the empty building of the old *école laïque*. It was opened by young outsiders, most of whom had appeared in the area in the early 1970s. They have become 'peasants', 'artisans', 'Celtic' artists, folk-singers, and country-dwellers, living in their own image of rural, 'Breton' naturality. By the year 1979–80, a total of sixteen couples were directly involved in the Le Relecq *Diwan*, five of them living in the commune of Plounéour itself, although none actually in the hamlet of Le Relecq.[11] All were part of a youthful and much wider 'back-to-the-land' and 'back-to-the-country' trend that had swept France after 1968 (see the special issue of the journal *Autrement* 1978, 14, entitled *'Avec nos sabots . . .'*, or 'With our clogs . . .', for details of this trend in France). I knew of at least twenty-five couples, and sundry individuals, living in and around the area of Plounéour-Ménez, in studied and rugged 'ecological' simplicity. It is from this milieu that Plounéour's *Diwan* came, and gained its recruitment.

During its first two years, the *Diwan* at Le Relecq got through at least four teachers. One stayed only a few weeks, one was moved to another *Diwan* school elsewhere, and another was sacked. This particularly swift turnover is a point to which we shall return in Chapter fourteen. None of the teachers came from Plounéour, although one originated from neighbouring Pleyber-Christ. *Diwan* parents had hoped that she might help local integration, but there was much about her that defined her, not as local, but as an outsider. In a multiple controversion of local aspirations, she had left her smart family home in the bourg of Pleyber-Christ to live, with her bearded boyfriend, in a tumble-down house further up in the mountains. She became, in local eyes, one of 'those people'.

Two of the teachers from Plounéour's College lived in Le Relecq, next door to *Diwan*, on the hamlet's main road. There were frequent quarrels between *Diwan* and the teachers next door. The College teachers regularly complained that *Diwan* children were badly behaved, noisy, and were spoiling their home. People in Plounéour, and in Le Relecq itself, commonly complained that *Diwan* children were 'dirty', 'wild', and 'they do just what they like'. What *Diwan* parents saw as healthy naturalness was, for many local people, simply 'dirt', naughtiness, and rudeness. Dirt and poverty are too close here to be revalued as the wonders of nature and ecology.

The abandoned classroom which *Diwan* took over was in a poor state of repair. The municipality offered no funds to help out, and *Diwan* parents did not dare to ask. The sentiment that *Diwan* was just not a proper 'school' was confirmed by the state of the buildings, and it was also confirmed in the *école laïque* in the bourg in September 1980 when, for the first time, two children from *Diwan* were among the new primary intake. According to their new teacher, the children could not sit still for long, did not always complete activities begun, and were slower to learn to read and write. One child had particular difficulty. He chose to 'roll on the floor' in the middle of one class, and then wandered off to pick flowers from the smart school garden. When told off, he replied to the teacher in Breton, evidently thinking this an appropriate response – more likely in automatic appeasement rather than defiance. The child was manifestly confused by the new school, and worried by the new and different expectations. He wet his trousers several times in the early weeks. Although concerned about the child, the primary schoolteacher found ample confirmation in this of *Diwan*'s image: 'Of course, they probably pee where and when they like there.'

Another *Diwan* child went into the primary school in neighbouring Pleyber-Christ at the same time, and the teacher there also reported finding the child slow to 'settle down'. These public schoolteachers referred to their ex-*Diwan* pupils as '*mes Diwans*' or '*mes Bretons*' and compared notes, exchanging complaints and mutually confirming their convictions. *Diwan* children would nevertheless survive the transition, they thought, for 'most of the parents are university educated, aren't they?' Significantly, the child said to have 'settled down' more easily in Plounéour's primary school was known to be the son of a psychologist. The other child was the son of 'alternative' peasants, and criticism flowed more freely here of 'drop-outs'. One College teacher in the bourg went further: the parents must be not only 'drop-outs' but 'mental defectives' to be involved in *Diwan* at all. 'They might just as well be sending their children to catechism.'

Catechism is taught locally in the presbytery and, on Wednesdays (a nation-wide school holiday, ostensibly for this purpose), in the *école libre*. A number of *laïques* do send their children to catechism, although they are very careful to explain that this is because 'the children seem to enjoy it'. The priest is concerned that catechism attendance in the parish is lower than it might be, and that some families refuse to send their children. A choice of catechism in French has been offered locally since at least the 1920s, and by the late 1930s few were still learning it in Breton. In early 1980, the priest told me that *Diwan* deserved praise as an 'opposition to the State' which had 'oppressed the Church' for so long. He found *Diwan* socially suspect, however, and, despite a willingness privately to applaud any opposition to the State, he did not share the politics of *Diwan* parents or their ideals of life-style, and he did not feel that educating children in Breton could publicly help his cause or theirs, or be of any use to the children.

Plounéour's municipality has sometimes preferred to ignore the existence of *Diwan*. In 1972, municipal records note that Le Relecq's *école laïque* had closed and, in 1979, the school was declared *désaffectée* (i.e., no longer a school building): the municipal council noted that it had, in any case, been 'unoccupied since 1972' (cf. AM 13 September 1979). *Diwan* had, in fact, been there for two years. *Diwan* parents sought a written lease but the municipality refused them any security. In 1981, the municipal council put the building up for sale without informing or consulting the *Diwan* parents. The College teachers next door wanted to buy it, to protect and extend their home. *Diwan* tried unsuccessfully to rent alternative accommodation in the commune, and was rescued by the authorities of a Natural Regional Park (*Parc Naturel Régional d'Armorique*) of which Plounéour has formed a part since 1969, along with twenty-eight other communes, almost all of them in the mountain area of Finistère. The *Parc* authorities, who have offices further up in the mountains, aim to conserve and develop the region's 'eco-cultural' life (see Chapter fourteen, p. 271ff.). They offered *Diwan* an old converted house on the square of Le Relecq, which had been used by a bearded young jeweller and sculptor from Alsace. The *Parc* has expressly tried to encourage young 'artisans' to live in the area, and had bought and renovated the house for that purpose. It was not ideal for a school with a display workshop and a high, unprotected staircase, but *Diwan* moved in, for want of anything else, and with some parents noting with deliberate irony that the area's 'eco-cultural' life was thus saved.

A vote for Breton in the schools

Plounéour-Ménez, in its own self-image, has not sought to have Breton in the schools. There is no record of the commune having voted for the 1930s *Ar Brezoneg er Skol* petition. However, the municipal records in the town hall suggest that the municipality voted a motion in 1961 which included a statement regretting the lack of Breton in all levels of schooling (AM 10 September 1961). This motion had been circulated to municipalities in Brittany by a little-known group supported by the MOB (or the *Mouvement pour l'Organisation de la Bretagne*, mentioned in Chapter five, p. 80; also Fouere 1977:86). The text contained only one sentence about Breton, being mainly concerned with economic development plans for Brittany put forward by the CELIB. Another separate motion promoting these plans, and which came directly from the CELIB, was voted by Plounéour's council in the same session. The CELIB text itself made no mention of Breton. Plounéour was one of the many Finistère municipalities which gave subscriptions to the CELIB in its early years. The mayor of Plounéour could recall the CELIB's 1961 motion, when he was already in office: 'It was for jobs and industry', he said, explaining that Plounéour itself had tried to attract small industries in recent years, but these had never lasted long. Plounéour's only industry is a small chicken slaughterhouse to the east of the bourg, near the main Morlaix-Quimper road. Opened in 1957, this employed 170 people by 1980, seventy of them from Plounéour itself. A large proportion of the commune's revenue comes from this enterprise, although the mayor gave it only passing acknowledgement. It is owned by a noted local supporter of the *école libre*, who headed the opposition in the 1971 municipal elections. The CELIB motion, in the mayor's view, was one which had rightly urged more industrial revenue for rural communes such as Plounéour; he did not recall the other motion voted alongside it, but said that it was 'probably the CELIB too, wasn't it?' I said not, and that it had included a sentence asking for Breton in the schools. The mayor was incredulous. But it was there, in black and white, I said, in the manuscript deliberations of the municipal council, in which the texts of the motions had been written out in full. The mayor looked horrified. 'Never', he said, 'never!' He eventually concluded that it had been an error or oversight; the town hall clerk of the time must simply have copied out the entire two texts together: 'but we did not vote for that; I don't remember that'. Other municipal councillors were emphatically of the same opinion: 'We have never voted for that here.'

The symbole

It was similarly made clear that *Diwan* was not 'local' initiative or history. For one Communist municipal councillor, *Diwan* was 'aberrant' and a 'school for aristocrats'. Another Communist, a former headmaster of the old *école laïque* of Le Relecq in the 1940s and 1950s, was especially upset at what his school had become. He let his wife (a locally born woman who had also taught in the old Le Relecq school) explain: 'Those people are all *Breiz Atao*.' 'No one was ever harmed by learning French at school,' her husband added. 'We barely remember learning French ourselves – we certainly did not suffer from it.' I asked about the *symbole*. 'We have read about that in books', he replied, 'but I cannot remember it from my own schooldays. Perhaps I had it – but we were punished for other things.' There was a 'certain publicity' given to the *symbole* now, he explained. 'Memories get confused, we start to imagine it, but it was not important.' Both teachers felt that they had never 'deliberately punished Breton' when they were teaching; it was hardly necessary, they claimed: 'the children learnt fast, and the parents wanted them to learn.'

Another local woman who taught in the Le Relecq school from 1945 to 1970, chose to recall that when she had herself been a pupil there in the 1920s, parents were already speaking French to their children, 'even bad

French'. As a teacher, she had used Breton sometimes, in the early years of her teaching, to younger children when they did not understand her – but 'most children managed without that'. In her own days, as pupil, there had been a 'piece of stone' – 'that's what you mean by the *symbole*, is it?' Sometimes it was passed around among older children who spoke Breton in class, but often it was 'given to anyone at the beginning of the day, and then left on one side in a cupboard'. Pupils had sometimes reported on each other if they heard Breton, 'just to please the teacher'. This, together with an occasional mocking laugh from others at a pupil who spoke in Breton, provided a self-sanctioning among the pupils which helped to keep the piece of stone redundant. Girls especially, it seems, had mocked others who spoke in Breton.

I met several former teachers of the old *école laïque* of Le Relecq, some of whom had also been pupils in the school. They feared that they might be unfairly represented in the ideas and histories of a 'certain milieu', and that I might be misled. The Communist former headmaster, however, was adamant that 'we do not have to justify ourselves'. He was the most confident of those I spoke to, with his confidence partly drawn from his Party allegiances. Another former headmaster of the school, who had been there in the 1930s, was at pains to point out that 'ideas were different then'. In recalling his days as teacher, he did not mention any punishments for Breton, but was concerned about changing attitudes to discipline and punishment in general, in the light of which he might seem old-fashioned and authoritarian. Indeed, in local memory, this teacher seems to have been feared by his pupils: tales of cuffs and blows from him are common among his former pupils in the area. One such former pupil recalls once hiding under a desk to try to avoid punishment because he had 'spoken in class'. This local peasant seemed bewildered when I asked if he had spoken in Breton or French; that was not the point: 'I don't know', he said, dismissing my question and continuing with his story, in which all other details were vivid.

Diwan's presence in Plounéour has inevitably given new significance to the question of Breton, but the contours of local history are not so easily redrawn. Former teachers of Le Relecq could easily recall problems they had faced: poverty, poorly fed children, lice, dirt, and frequent illness among some of their pupils. Former pupils regularly pointed to additional hardships – walking to school in winter, or having to find presentable clothes and shoes – but their tales of school punishments did not spontaneously include the *symbole*, or any such device. It required explicit questioning to raise memories of the piece of wood or stone that occasionally moved about the classroom. When schooldays were being recalled, and young militants were present, the latter would often try hard to inject the requisite contours of oppression into the stories told by local people, who seemed to be missing the point: 'But what about the *symbole*? You

were punished for Breton, weren't you?' Responses were disappointing.
'But we had to learn French!' was a common reply, or 'We hid it', 'we
threw it out of the window', or 'we just passed it on as soon as possible'.
Breton had offered scope for naughtiness, especially for the lads (see
Flatrès 1920 for some contemporary accounts, by a harassed teacher, in
neighbouring Le Cloître). Sometimes, the one with the piece of stone or
wood at the end of the day had to stay after class and help the teacher to
clean up or do extra homework or write lines. 'I can't remember if I ever
wrote them, though!' said one peasant, who liked to regard it all as a good
laugh. 'It was warmer in the classroom anyway,' and staying after class
sometimes meant avoiding farm-work at home. To the dismay of one
militant, a local peasant went on to say how parents often made great
'sacrifices' to find money so their children could have extra lessons of
French after school, to make sure they spoke well and succeeded. There
was no 'oppression' by the *symbole* here, but rather tales of mischief, and
the apparently inexorable thrust of local ambition.

The structures of recollection and self-representation here are obviously
not those of the militant world. The stories people tell sometimes take the
form and force they do as a mode of political opposition to the militants
themselves or as a way of excluding them and asserting a self-consciously
'local' authenticity. 'I knew no French when I went to school' can be heard
in these recollections, but it is not, in local terms, the prologue to militant
history or ambition, but part of a statement of hard-won sophistication.
Any suggestion (such as young militants might make) that life would have
been easier if schooling had been in Breton is taken as irrational or
nonsensical; on the contrary, it might have been easier if Breton had been
prohibited altogether: 'the more direct the better'. In keeping with aspects
of this same general thrust of ambition, there may well come a time when
certain features of the new educated *genre* of history, as told in the militant
world, take over. For the moment, however, history is told within
structures of self-definition in which sophistication has a different dress.
This was made particularly apparent in Kerguz, when one former pupil of
the old Le Relecq school showed me a cherished photograph of himself
taken at the school in the late 1940s: in the photograph, he stands in his
father's old army coat, converted into a smart school coat, with a French
textbook placed on a table in front of him, specially posed for the
photograph. This local peasant had gone to school knowing no French, and
he commented that he probably 'couldn't understand a word' of the book
placed before him for the photograph. He urged me to take the photograph, delighted that I might reproduce it (see p. 328). It was certainly not
given to illustrate any imposition or oppression, however. Rather, 'It looks
good, doesn't it?' he said proudly. The picture of a glum child suffering the
symbole, so common in militant texts, on posters, and on *Diwan* stickers, is
the construction of a different history.

Chapter fourteen

The peasant life

In this chapter, some differences between the newcomers' values and local aspirations are illustrated through details of local peasant life. We begin with the women and their views of life on the land, but we shall need first to have in mind again wider images of both women and Brittany, images which, in various ways, have long been implicated, the one in the other.

Femininity and feminism

Femininity: a political imagery

The political imagery of women and of regional languages and cultures, such as Breton, has often been associated at the national level, and it is of some significance here that women in France gained the vote only in 1945: it had always been feared that women were too closely linked with the Church and the forces of clerical reaction (cf. Chapter two, p. 42). However, images of Breton and of women have been associated not only by those who were active in constructing the French Republic, but also by those who, on the contrary, have conflated an image of women and of Breton language and culture in opposition to the majority French world. In various ways, ethnic identity and female identity have been drawn into mutual support, and this is true of their nineteenth-century romantic construction as well as of the modern desire for 'liberation' from these same constructs. In the nineteenth-century, Breton culture and femininity were drawn up out of a common oppositional symbolism; and then, in the twentieth century and particularly since the late 1960s, Breton culture has been aligned with the oppositional symbolism of feminism. In this section, I expand on certain aspects of these symbolic conflations and their ethnographic reality, beginning with femininity.

In France, modern femininity as an idealized image of woman, her essential nature and her place, became firmly established in the nineteenth century, and particularly during the reign of Louis-Philippe. Much of the structural imagery still involved in the modern feminine/masculine duality (with all its positively or negatively evaluated correlates of irrationality/ rationality, emotions/reason, domesticity/politics, and so on) was carried on from the élite salons of the eighteenth century. The fighting women of the Revolution were placed in parentheses, and all the dominant political groups of the nineteenth century sent their ideal woman back to the home, and to wifely and maternal duties, but not without a certain charm and glamour. By the 1830s, under Louis-Philippe, the *citoyenne* of the 1789 Revolution had already become, once again, *Madame*.

This was also a time of wider material and secular prosperity. The rationalism of this new age, under the 'bourgeois king', Louis-Philippe, was quite explicitly characterized in some educated circles as a 'masculine' force, and in contra-distinction to this, the moral and spiritual values of sentiment, intuition, and prudent tradition became equated with a 'femininity' that might counteract rationalism's excess (see Albistur and Armogathe 1977, 2: 364–8, 406–8). Woman as guardian of morality and tradition was not an entirely new notion, but the symbolic dualities involved now took on a coherence they had never had before, and femininity became one metaphor of traditionality in ethnographic description.[1] The metaphorical femininity with which Brittany was endowed in this romantic topography received confirmation from other sources, and entered the political domain. Those who saw themselves as the moral and spiritual defenders of a distinctly 'Breton' world used an available imagery of femininity in symbolic synonymy with a traditional, Celtic Brittany seen to be morally and politically threatened by, and opposed to, the rationality of the French Republic (see Chapter six, pp. 102–4). As some members of the Breton clergy and aristocracy conflated Breton, faith, and salvation into an even purer, isolated, rural simplicity that was, for them, Breton culture, so Church and State had become involved in a spiralling educational battle to win over the women (see Chapter two; also McDonald 1986b). The linguistic gloss in Church/State divides has progressively given way to other priorities in their expression, but any recombination of Breton and traditional Catholic values can sometimes, at the local level, forcefully evoke old battle lines. I gave some indication of this at the level of the schools in Chapter thirteen, and it can also happen at the level of church services.

During my first summer living in Plounéour, I went to a Breton-language Mass in the old abbey of Le Relecq. Apart from the occasional Breton hymns, Mass is usually everywhere celebrated in French. This once-a-year Breton Mass has been mounted by a section of the diminishing Léon clergy, partly out of Catholic nostalgia and partly with an eye to the possible attraction of newcomers and tourists. Any funding from collections at services is also very welcome. The bishop of the diocese came along for this Mass; he delivered an impassioned sermon in Breton, to a full congregation, mostly women, and many of them no longer practising

Catholics but there for this special occasion. The bishop complained that Brittany was no longer producing its traditionally high quota of boys and girls for Holy Orders. He blamed it on the mothers: they were not bringing up their children properly. Quiet smiles appeared on several faces, and I afterwards had coffee with a group of local women, who spent some time ridiculing the sermon, and doing so in French. Among these women was the wife of a former mayor of the commune, and the conversation involved some self-consciously republican family pride.

Related evidence of local sentiment and ambition was offered, in a more secular vein, when a new priest took up office in the parish in 1981. This new priest had just returned to Brittany after many years' mission abroad. Unlike his predecessor, he had, in an earlier era, been actively involved in the Breton movement. One of his first actions was now to increase the number of Breton hymns at weekly Mass. The local faithful quite liked this, noting at the same time that he had also re-introduced the old Latin *credo*. However, this priest then tried to deliver his weekly sermons in Breton, and was met with swift reaction. Notes were delivered to his presbytery, from local women parishioners, expressly asking him not to speak Breton. With sadness, he explained to me: 'It is almost as if Breton smells of cow-shit (*kaoc'h saout*, Br.) to them. They think they are ladies (*Mesdames*, Fr.).'

Femininity: from cow-shit to finery

During the course of the nineteenth century then, a recognizable meta-phoric of 'femininity' was established among the bourgeoisie in France, as well as among the clergy and the fading ranks of the aristocracy. This image of women was one that education brought, so aristocratic and bourgeois notions of ideal femininity had no obvious popular hold among the early nineteenth-century peasantry. In the 1830s, educated visitors to central Brittany, including to the Plounéour-Ménez area, reported that women there seemed to be less valued by the men than their animals, and were the 'submissive vassals' of the peasant men (see Ariès 1948:ch. 1; Brousmiche 1829–31, 2:205). The general lack of 'feminine' qualities and attraction which these travellers explicitly reported is a clear statement of the existence of such a femininity in their own world, and the mismatch of values between their own world and that which they reported served to confirm them in their view of uncivilized savages in the Breton mountains. We have to grant the peasant world its own unacknowledged metaphoric of male/female difference here, but we can certainly allow that life on the land was hard and very different from the life of a town lady. Peasant women would only barely have recognized the symbolism of femininity that was opposing them and their men to France.

For both men and women, living-in service on larger farms was often an important part of growing up. Marriage was late, and separate households, when achieved, still depended on supplementary income.[2] The men might be periodically away, in slate mines or on larger farms, but the women were not 'housewives' putting leisure time to profit. Young girls and older women took on spinning and weaving; other women sought dressmaking; and others had no option but to beg (see ADF:6M, Plounéour-Ménez). The selling-off of communal land (see p. 229) or the formal distribution of it between villagers, which occurred from the mid-nineteenth century to the 1920s, offered new possibilities of land ownership and more security, but otherwise mobility had been common, with some families moving from one farm to another in the commune each September, in search of fairer rents or better land.

By 1900, the production of crude home-spun, home-woven cloth, for the linen trade or local use, had declined, partly in the face of more elegant fabrics and fashions, which women in Brittany began to make part of their own world. In 1929, a visitor to Saint-Pol-de-Léon, near the north coast, reported that young women there had abandoned the long, dark costume of their mothers, with its apron and discreet white *coiffe*, and were 'all flaunting themselves in lavish city attire; their legs, pinkened by flesh-coloured stockings, are perched on high-heeled shoes' (cited in Ariès 1948:59). This would have been especially shocking to anyone expecting Léon sobriety, but the association of fashionableness and towns round the coast was already being made.

Since the eighteenth century especially, government finance had helped to create relative wealth and security near sections of the Breton coast, in maritime and administrative interests. Popular scorn of the land was progressively manifest in the nineteenth century, and migrations away from the land became permanent emigrations in the second half of the century. The towns, the coast, security, finery, and French were increasingly framed as a single powerful pole of all that the peasant condition was not. Pleyber-Christ, Plounéour's neighbouring commune to the north, had acquired a railway station by the beginning of the 1870s, and this gave Plounéour's horse-dealers a faster outlet to markets in other parts of France, but also encouraged a steady movement of population. In the 1920s and 1930s, local depopulation was becoming more marked. Paid holidays introduced by the Popular Front in 1936 gave the life of wage-earners extra attraction and also brought more of the departed home on holiday with tales of their enviable situation.

The flight of both men and women from the land, well under way in the 1930s, was overtaken by a predominantly female exodus from agriculture after the Second World War. Since the end of the nineteenth century peasant women had had growing aspirations to become housewives, or town ladies, or anything but a peasant's wife (cf. Weber 1977:174). This trend was now accentuated, particularly as the length of girls' schooling was beginning to catch up with that of boys. From the mid-1950s to the mid-1970s, the rate of female emigration from the land rose steadily, surpassing the figure for men for Brittany overall and for Finistère alone (see Trégouët 1978). Plounéour is still an agricultural commune, in land use and in external image and self-image, and agriculture is still by far the largest single occupational sector. By the mid-1970s, however, only 18 per cent of the total population, or 46 per cent of the active population, was actually working farms, whereas a little over a decade before these proportions had been 37.5 per cent and 72.3 per cent respectively. Over the same period, there was an overall drop of almost 18.6 per cent in the population of the commune, and yet significant increases in nearby and less agricultural communes all the way up to the nearest town of Morlaix, near the north coast. Of the young, aged 15–24 years, in Plounéour-Ménez in 1962, one and a half times as many of the girls as the boys had left by 1968. The economic area of the *pays de Morlaix*, which includes Plounéour, shows an increase, over the same period, of almost 11 per cent in women working in the tertiary sector (and 1.7 per cent in men; SEMENF 1976:49). In the village of Kerguz itself, villagers can conjure up a time in living memory when over 100 people were still living off small plots of land; there are now only three farms, and two active peasants' wives. Each has sisters who have moved away and married salaried men. Another woman recently persuaded her husband to give up their farm and take a job in Morlaix. She is now a proud housewife, working part-time in a shop, and has elegant clothes and a new house with the modern furniture, amenities, and general organization of space that peasant homes lack. She would frequently show off her new home to visitors, and point out, in careful French, the welcome difference between her new life-style and the 'hard, dirty' life she had previously known on a farm, and which she so hated.

Femininity and French have arrived, and together they can speak a sophistication that is other than peasant work. The comment of the new priest that 'they think they are ladies' (p. 245) is suggestive of the reality of these values in local life, but such values do not necessarily manifest themselves in overt action such as taking plaintive or hostile notes to the presbytery. Rather, they present themselves through the unreflecting proprieties of daily behaviour.

Women can define their femininity, and men their masculinity, through the language they use, and language use has its correlates in social space. The fields and certain bars (to which we shall return) tend to be male domains and, in all-male company of a certain age, Breton is the usual language of communication. Sanctions against the use of French here include a fear of being thought 'stuck up' (*fier*, Br.). Contrasting with this world of rough-and-ready masculinity are certain obviously female domains such as the special *salon* or parlour set aside in many farmhouses for guests. Sanctions against the use of Breton here are tacit but still forceful; Breton is not used at polite tea-parties.

Village women in Kerguz commonly speak Breton to their husbands and other men, and both Breton and French when helping the men in the fields. One locally born woman has returned to the village with her husband after a working life as a domestic in Paris; her husband, from a nearby village, worked on the railways there. Anna speaks Breton to her husband, but likes to speak French as the voice of sophistication in the village, including when helping out in the fields. Whatever her life was like in Paris, Anna is glamour in the village. She soon installed a bathroom, toilet, and central heating in her house – none of which the other local women had. When the men are out drinking rough red wine, playing *boules*, or working with the machines, women like to visit each other for coffee and sweet cakes in the afternoon. This has long been a rather special, and now distinctly feminine, thing to do. Anna prefers tea to coffee, and often declines the cakes, as she is slimming. She prefers dainty savouries anyway. The other women admire her sense of refinement, and allow her to conjure up, in French, a world of fashion and ladylike good taste that the female Breton world has ample space for.

Such afternoon conversations over tea and coffee move between Breton and French, arbitrating on matters of social nicety. The women enjoy a part of the social world here from which men are symbolically and actually excluded, and which these ladies readily assume. As guardians of social propriety, they eagerly exchange selected information and stories about local people and life, and need to do so. A line between proper 'women's talk' and improper gossip (or the *commérage* of wicked tongues) has itself to be drawn, however, and this is often done through a switch from Breton to French. (Certain summary details of someone else's hurtful talk may be recounted by the injured party in Breton, for example, and then some statement such as *'mais c'est de la jalousie, tout ça'* ('but it's jealousy, all that') will launch the conversation off into a chorus of condemnation of the gossip, in French.) On other occasions, when the company is mixed, real men will mark themselves off from any women's talk in progress through silence (thereby easily confirming images of the 'taciturn' peasant – cf. above, p. 49) or through rugged men's talk (if only of the weather) indifferent to the nonsense of women. When the men are present at evening gatherings of the whole village, such as occurs at New Year, the women sit together at one end of a long table with their sweet cakes and sweet drinks and speak predominantly French, and the men pack together at the other end in a haze of cigarette smoke, eating cheap *pâté*, drinking hard liquor, playing dominoes or cards, and speaking predominantly Breton. While Anna at one end speaks French to the women, her husband at the other end speaks Breton to the men.

A sense of finery and fashion as the prerogative of the woman is well established. Peasant women still often buy all the clothes for their husbands and unmarried sons, including their 'best Sunday shoes'. Peasant men take some pride in saying that they 'couldn't care less' about what they wear, not because they do not dress up when appropriate, but once again because men can, symbolically and actually, leave such things to women. Such a male/female distinction extends also to what is, in local self-perception at least, the relatively novel notion of romantic love: 'The women like that sort of thing', they say. In order to halt the exodus of women from the rural areas in the 1950s and 1960s, Catholic groups worked hard in Brittany, as elsewhere in France, to try to publicize the idea that love and romance could exist in a peasant setting (see, for example, JAC-MRJC 1979:72–3; here one sees somewhat unlikely pictures, produced in the 1950s and 1960s, of peasant men giving bouquets to their women). Marriage, traditionally an alliance between families, and arranged by parents or a go-between with a keen sense of social status and an eye on access to land, had become, especially for the women, a matter of individual choice that could operate with rather different criteria. French terms had already come in: for example, an *akord* (/akɔrd/ cf. French *accord*) was an initial agreement after which a couple became *fianset* (/fiːaⁿsɛd/ cf. French *fiancé(e)*), or 'engaged'. A girlfriend or boyfriend, a relatively new status, is a *bon ami* (/bɔn amiː/ cf. French *bon(ne) ami(e)*). There is a more live and obvious Frenchness in this area, too. I was talking one day, in Breton, with a rather drunken group of ageing bachelor peasants that I know; suddenly, one took hold of my hand, much to the amusement of his mates, and kissed it, and said '*Enchanté, Mademoiselle*'. Everyone laughed. 'Be quiet', he said, back in Breton now, 'just shut up – you're jealous. *Je fais la cour.*' It was generally agreed that he was 'a one for the girls'.

Liberation

In the meantime, feminism has appeared with some force in French educated circles. Simone de Beauvoir's work (*Le Deuxième Sexe*), published in 1949, has produced its own industry of dissenters, but it was one of the pioneering works of modern feminism and was keenly taken up after the wide protests and upheavals of May 1968. Femininity was denaturalized, declared to be arbitrary, and a myth for the definition and pleasure of men, whereby woman had become man's own incorporated 'half' (Beauvoir 1949, I:205–38, 313). Well-known feminist writers in France have since explicitly elided their 'struggle' with that of the 'oppressed' and 'ethnic minorities' everywhere, including that of the Bretons in France (for example, Groult 1975; Halimi 1973). Similarly, the modern Breton movement has brought together feminism, the peasantry, and Breton in pursuit of a new 'alternative' society. We have seen that women's liberation and the cause of 'Breton culture' can share an oppositional platform. For female militants, learning and speaking Breton can sit in synonymy with liberation from a bourgeois, French, and male-dominated, urban world. Similarly, young female enthusiasts who have moved back to the country-side have often taken up 'peasant' and 'artisanal' activities as a liberated existence.

One young couple in Kerguz, keen on wholemeal food and home-weaving, work a tiny vegetable plot, live in a tumble-down house, and have set up a windmill to generate electricity. Kerguz has had mains electricity since 1955. Anna, their nearest neighbour, complains that the windmill is noisy and unnecessary, and regards all their bits of metal and old crocks as 'mess' that mars the view of the smart, renovated frontage and garden of her 'modern' home. What Anna regards as mess, the young couple regard as 'recycling'.

Another back-to-the-country, militant couple in Kerguz command a little more respect, partly because they (unlike other newcomers) are married, and the husband is a psychologist commuting daily to a clinic in Morlaix; the wife is a teacher-turned-artisan, having taken a course in carpentry. Next door to them live a lively local widow, called Thérèse, in her late sixties, and her 42-year-old unmarried son, Iffig. Thérèse and Iffig still have some livestock and wood-holdings, but rent out most of their farmland since Thérèse's husband died, and Iffig now commutes daily to a job as a railway-workman further north. Thérèse has often shown me her hands: 'Look at them, all red, swollen and ugly', she would say. Years of farmwork and helping her husband and then their son on the wood-holdings have taken their toll. Many of the local women, including Thérèse, would often admire my hands: 'so white and delicate', they would say, 'like the hands of a town lady.' At first, I was sceptical of such comments, which might easily be made in mockery; such scepticism, however, while not wholly inappropriate, was born of another world. When helping out in the fields or in the woods, I was seriously urged to put on gloves: 'Don't spoil those hands', I was warned. Meanwhile, Thérèse's educated neighbour was gaining splinters, blisters, and callouses from her carpentry – and yet she could, in her own Breton world, display her hands with a certain pride.

One day when I was with Thérèse, she broke wind. She bit her lip and blushed. I told her not to worry. 'They do it', she said, gesticulating to her neighbours' house and going on to explain that the psychologist's wife had done it in front of her and had said that it was quite 'natural' and all right. Thérèse paused. 'Does she do it in front of you?' she asked. I said she did, and Thérèse seemed reassured. A few days later, another peasant woman, from another village, was having coffee with Thérèse, and, after she had left, Thérèse broke wind again. 'I had to do it', she said to me, somewhat less embarrassed this time. She explained that she had been wanting to all the time that 'Madame' (her friend) had been there. I asked her why she had not simply gone ahead. 'Women don't do that sort of thing here', she said, 'it's not nice.' One is left to admire Thérèse's social competence: she had been moved, by her esteem for town and educated ladies, to adopt ladylike or 'feminine' good manners, and she can also contextually accommodate a new and sophisticated 'naturality', which is her own humble condition revalued, as spontaneity unconstrained, by that same world to which she looks for a sense of propriety.

Newcomers to the area live in a world where a function such as breaking wind is definitionally an aspect of a truly 'natural' and 'Breton' life-style (cf. the question of manners and *merci*, discussed in Chapter nine). Often it has been a self-conscious part of the Breton-learning process for them, and something I have myself experienced in Breton-language courses in the movement. Thérèse, meanwhile, has a space in her world for her educated neighbours' sense of what is fitting and 'natural', and she can act, and gloss her actions, accordingly in their or my presence; however, she knows when breaking wind is acceptably sophisticated ('natural') and when it is 'not nice': the two are not the same. If the two contexts or interpretations have any common structural feature, this is not through an unstructured naturalness which the peasant woman lives daily and the militant finds, but rather through a propriety the peasant woman seeks and which the educated sophisticate is seen to embody.

The world of the peasant women and that of the educated sophisticates are, in some ways, in mutual pursuit, each chasing the virtue seen to inhere in the other. Where cultural mismatches once served to confirm the educated traveller in his view of a brutish and sadly unfeminine world in the Breton mountains (see p. 245), now a lack of cultural fit at any level can serve to confirm educated newcomers in their image of a world unfettered by the femininity which modern feminism rejects. The fact that local women in the rural world have usually continued to be known by their maiden name after marriage has been seen as evidence of the already feminist, liberated nature of the native-speaking, female Breton population. However, the use of the maiden name does not conflict with or contest the civil use of the husband's name, and it is usually by the title of *Madame*, plus the married name, that village women like to be publicly presented, particularly to strangers. Outside the contexts of kinship and locality, the use of the maiden name easily feels, to these women themselves, misplaced or intrusive, or parochial and old-fashioned.

Such different evaluation, in the militant world and in the local world, of what might appear to be the 'same' objects, titles, acts, or gestures clearly has linguistic correlates, and very different evaluations of Breton and French, and of the Breton/French language difference, are involved. The popular world values French and education highly, and the women are particularly implicated here. Maternal responsibilities now demand a special sensitivity to education, and a childless woman risks low esteem on a number of counts. When a woman is childless, her womanhood is suspect, and when, on top of this, she is herself uneducated, social respect can be hard to attain. Local evaluations that village women have of one another fully suggest this complex of values. Thérèse herself, for instance, is well regarded among other women. She has a hard-working son and, for her age group, is relatively educated by local standards: she stayed on at school until thirteen years of age, and continues to read a lot now and to take a wide interest in current affairs. One of the other women in the village is regarded as particularly stupid, however. This woman had relatively few years of schooling. It is said of her, with some amusement, that when told of Kennedy's assassination, she simply asked: 'Kennedy? Is he from Plounéour?' This same woman is childless, will readily speak Breton to me, and has problems with French. She is rarely invited to coffee by the other women (only once a year, it seems, at Christmas time); indeed, the other women said they found her fat and uncouth, and, on one occasion, my attention was drawn to the fact that she has a moustache. One of her redeeming features, however, as far as the other village women are concerned, is that she keeps a pretty flower garden. She would often invite me to see this and proudly give me bouquets (*bokedoù*, Br.) to take home. Where there are women on the farms, they milk the cows, tend to the poultry yard, and keep house, increasingly in the manner of a housewife, leaving the fields an ideally male domain now; gardening of this kind is, by contrast, very feminine. All the women set aside a patch for flowers, and like to plant more than the common chrysanthemums which they, as guardians of kinship and status, place annually on family tombs at the All Souls and All Saints holiday. Much to militant regret, the popular Breton terms for garden and flowers – *jardin* (/ʒaːrdin/) and *fleur* (/flør/) – are, as in so many areas of ornateness and finery, taken from French. Militant 'standard' Breton prefers *liorzh* and *bleunioù*, which, to the women of Kerguz, signify untended or overgrown land and wild blossom, respectively.

Just when the militants are aspiring to a certain ruggedness and naturality, to the countryside, Breton, and grass-roots authenticity, local women are looking to femininity, the towns, and French. It is another facet of the striking contrast between France and Britain that an apparent overlap of this kind should be possible, telescoping changes into the space of a few decades, and rendering a revaluation of the local women, their lives, and their language possible within their own life-times. We have already seen other aspects of this apparent overlap, and we shall see more, but we might first draw out a few points bearing directly on the opposi-tional nature of the 'Breton' world, and the symbolic alignments of Breton/women/French. The symbolism of 'femininity' was used, we remember, by the early Breton movement to cast Brittany in opposition to France, and to declare it distinctly un-French. The modern discourse of feminism might, revealingly, see this as the definition of Breton culture into a self-limiting and self-denigrating 'half' of an overall French world (cf. Chapman 1978, where the Scottish Gaels are described as having been defined into a metaphorically feminine 'half-world' in this way). The Breton militants prefer to see the phenomenon as part of the general 'colonization' of Brittany, and in Breton-language courses it was often said that Breton women had been 'twice colonized', by France and by men. For members of the movement, we recall, the minority identity is assumed to have been historically overlain with external accretions that bring false consciousness. Whether local women use French (=oppressed, colonized, false consciousness) or Breton (=liberated, true identity, etc.) can easily appear to the militants to be confirmation and justification of their cause, and all women in Brittany will, within this framework, achieve liberation once accretions such as femininity, finery, and French are absent or taken away. The imagery of femininity, once used to cast the 'Breton' world in studious opposition to all things French, has, once, translated into the popular, peasant world, been a powerful motor of Frenchness. Further, women's double 'colonization', in the militants' terms, by both France and men, has given them now a greater competence in, and access to, a world of refinement. Pursuit of this refinement has virtually emptied the countryside of young women, and, in their own terms, this was a form of liberation. For local women, liberation has not been measured against some male-dominated, bourgeois life, but against the rigours and insecurities of the peasant life – that 'hard, dirty' life.

The mother tongue

All this has left a high toll of unmarried men in the rural areas, especially in the central, mountainous area of Finistère; male celibacy is particularly high among men with smaller, unmodernized farms and who have been brought up in Breton.[3] It is perhaps significant that a very common New Year greeting in the mountain area is '*Bloavezh mat hag ur bougeoise a-raok fin ar bloaz*', which might translate as: 'I wish you a Happy New Year and a ladywife before it's out'. Sometimes, the only apparently available women are back-to-the-land enthusiasts, who would like to speak Breton to their children. However, the local ageing bachelors tend to be in awe of these women's education, and it is a common sentiment among them that they would, in any case, be strongly opposed to any wife of theirs speaking Breton to their children.

In contrast with this, we have already seen, in Chapter twelve (pp. 206–9), the importance for the movement of Breton as the mother tongue, even if this can, contextually, bring its own internal contradictions in the militants' 'Breton' world (see also McDonald 1986b: 185–6). Breton-speaking mothers speaking French to their children are not the 'Breton-speaking mothers' of the militants' discourse or political vision, and the generational gymnastics that can now seem to be involved here, within any one family at the local level, usually have a wholly unreflecting symbolic rectitude of their own. In order to give the reader a very general idea of the familial socio-linguistic relations in which the local Breton-speaking mother might now commonly live, I have given an ideal-type schematic summary in a note.[4] It is, I would stress, a note with little contextual grain apart from the rather crude strokes of generational difference. Some of the finer grain of the wider socio-linguistic picture is embedded in other, and not always obviously linguistic, illustration.

In a curious and interesting way, the structural values of femininity, feminism, the peasant, and French and Breton have met and crossed. Such a crossing, or apparent contradiction, of values need not, however, cause conflict at the local level. In a relatively undramatic way, and without great upheaval, women in Brittany have been able first to take on French, and now the new image of Breton, and to incorporate issues which elsewhere have been a matter of great political debate. The pressure of new ideas is inevitably felt most keenly by the women, but local women can incorporate new enthusiasms, including enthusiasm for speaking Breton, without this assimilation of new values being, for them, the political stand or the 'liberation' that militant politics and epistemology require it to be, and would present it as. This point seems important to stress, and will become clearer through further illustration in this chapter and the next. While enthusiasm for speaking Breton is commonly, within the militant world, a political enthusiasm, response to this enthusiasm by local people which involves them actually complying and speaking Breton rather than French, as the educated outsiders now require, is not, in their own terms, a political act. Nor is it an act congruent with the other moral enthusiasms of the militant world. It is a compliance which, in their own world, follows other channels, other structures of identity and evaluation. As we have seen (including in the example of breaking wind), different values may simply be incorporated into existing structures, and gather their own contextual properties. Breaking wind and the mother tongue are no different in this respect.

Jeanne is in her forties, and a hard-working, Breton-speaking peasant's wife on the largest, most modern farm in Kerguz. She keeps her home spotlessly clean, visits a hairdresser nearer the coast when she can, tries hard to slim, and has held great ambitions for her five sons, aged from seven to twenty. Paul, her eldest son, failed his studies, did his military service, and then 'dropped out' – doing odd jobs elsewhere. In Plounéour, however, he met a very wealthy newcomer named Katrin, who had dropped out of her own higher education to come and live in Brittany, where she joined up with the Breton militants. Katrin feels she is a liberated woman. One afternoon, Jeanne, well-groomed and in a smart dress, came to my door. She spontaneously spoke some Breton to me for the first time, and invited me to coffee: Paul, her son, and Katrin, his girlfriend, were there. I went to coffee, still somewhat puzzled as to why Jeanne had suddenly spoken some Breton to me like that. Katrin talked, over coffee, of glamorous trips to America, and how she would show Paul the world. There were some hints of marriage. Jeanne looked proud at this prospect for her son. Katrin had a Breton-learning manual with her: 'Tell her how you learnt Breton', said Jeanne to me excitedly. 'She wants to learn it too.' As if by way of explanation, Katrin then talked inspiredly of Atlantis, the Incas, the Indians, of strange mysteries, of Woman, of Babylon, the Celts, and the Beginning of the World. She smiled at her boyfriend and said what wonderful, natural people these were, and there were suggestions that her parents might buy him a farm. Katrin was ready to be a peasant's wife. Paul, the 'peasant' now of his girlfriend's world, then tried to stammer out a few Breton words. 'I never learnt it', he said, 'my mother never spoke it to me.' Jeanne looked embarrassed, self-consciously tidied her hair, and busied herself with the coffee and cakes. 'I can help you learn some now', she volunteered finally, as the dutiful mother who had always tried to do the best for her son. Katrin tossed her long, untidy locks aside, rolled a cigarette, and wiped her hands on her kaftan and fashionable dungarees. 'You must speak some Breton to Paul,' she said to Jeanne, 'so he can teach me.' Jeanne obligingly uttered a few Breton phrases, and then changed into old trousers and overalls, and went off to milk her cows. Outside in the gathering dark, her hair-do was wrecked in the wind and rain, and I later heard her shouting a few words at the cows in Breton, as she usually did, when taking them back to the fields – in a totally different Breton world.

This is a world where a good mother, by definition, speaks nicely to children, but this can involve a structure of values so strong that in a peasant family nearer the coast, where I stayed for a week during my research, the mother spoke French to her own two teenage daughters – and then Breton to cows, but French to calves, and Breton to hens, but French to their chicks, and Breton to pigs and sows, but French to piglets. My stay with this family had been arranged for me by a militant group who like to send Breton learners to 'Breton-speaking' peasant families where Breton can be learnt in exchange for helping on the farms (see Chapter nine). However, all the families, it seems, have great difficulty speaking Breton to unknown 'outsiders', and particularly the mothers, and especially so when the outsider is younger and female. The mother on the farm just mentioned explained that she had been asked to try to speak Breton like this by a nice, young local teacher; it seemed the young and educated were doing this sort of thing now. Towards the end of the course, however, she and other peasant women were shocked and upset to find that, at a special dinner given by the militant organizers, they were expected to stand for a Breton national anthem (see p. 134). Militant press cameras clicked furiously. This is just one obvious example of the general point of earlier paragraphs – that local women are summoned, metaphorically and actually, in the militant world into a role which, in their own terms, they are not performing at all. Putting it more extremely, we might say that local women can, and do, find themselves standing as radical feminists and Breton nationalists when, in their own terms, they might have imagined they were behaving in a way more evocative of sophisticated French ladies.

Peasants and Indians

Modernization

Newcomers to the area who have chosen to be 'peasants', *Diwan* parents among them, have not found quite the rural simplicity they expected. The peasant, in Breton, generally remains *ar paysan* (/pei:zān/) in Plounéour; in French, however, there is a lively semantics of progress and sophistication. Local peasants, while retaining contextually, for the French urban world, the corporate *paysans*, internally differentiate on an axis of increasing youth and modernity, sometimes using the term *cultivateurs* or the even more recent and more advanced *agriculteurs*. The number of confidently self-defining '*agriculteurs*' increases as one moves from the mountains to the plain.

Plounéour emerged into the years after the Second World War with many small farms, often with divided and dispersed fields. Any larger farms had generally been sold or rented piecemeal, or broken up through shared inheritances. However, the remaining peasants had often bought up or rented the land of their departing co-heirs or neighbours, and some carefully negotiated mutual exchanges have, since the 1960s, enabled the regrouping of land into larger, workable units. Modernization is uneven within Plounéour, and has been tempered by several related and self-fulfilling perceptions, including a lack of wives and self-definition in relation to the smarter communes of the plain. In the local self-commentary in which the more one goes up geographically, the more one goes down socially, Plounéour has accrued wealth and virtue to itself in its own terms, turning the mountains/plain imagery to assert its own moral privilege. Debt is eschewed, bills paid promptly, and a conspicuous flaunting of money is something that other communes do. Plounéour is hard work and substance, while other areas are flashy, and a common Breton saying quoted to this effect runs, in translation, 'There are airs and graces in Pleyber, but there's money in Plounéour.' One result is that many in Plounéour still perceive 'debt' where others perceive 'investment', leaving agricultural credit quotas relatively unused in the mountains, and the farms relatively unmodernized. Modernity tends also to be generationally located, however, and a younger generation, sometimes armed with basic agricultural diplomas, will commonly talk now of investment and 'management' while an older generation, close to retirement, will talk of a necessary thriftiness and saving, and of the peasant know-how and self-sufficiency into which they were born, as a way of life. From the 1950s to 1970, the number of farms halved in Plounéour, and was down to a total of ninety-eight farms by 1979; at the same time, the average farm size more than doubled, reaching thirty hectares by 1980.[5] Most farms are, at least in part, owner-occupied, but the larger farms incorporate sections of the upper slopes, the heath or *landes*. Much of the land in the commune is low category, but the *landes* are the most difficult and evoke the 'old days' when people worked unviable plots, when they had no tractors or modern implements, and when 'poor people' went up the slopes to cut grass and gorse with sickle and scythe for their meagre livestock.

The authorities of the Natural Regional Park (the *Parc Naturel Régional d'Armorique*, see p. 239) have tried to persuade the local peasants to use the upper slopes for sheep, but no one wants to step 'backwards' so soon into the 'old days', or into dispersed, extensive farming. Moreover, there are often several owners of each tiny section of heath, which might make the necessary negotiations in themselves inhibitive. A few people in neighbouring Pleyber now keep a few sheep, for meat, in a fenced-off section of their gardens. Sheep are a modern luxury 'extra' for those who no longer have a farm, or they are a reminder of days gone by. No self-respecting peasant in modern Plounéour would turn over his time and land to sheep. Several of the newcomers, however, have made sheep the major element in their 'alternative' farming, and some also have goats, or goats to the complete exclusion of other livestock. In local eyes, goats ('the poor man's cow') are even more shocking than sheep. Newcomers are also working the poorest (and cheapest) soil, often abandoned ground they have cleared up in the *landes*. In local agricultural geography, the plain and warmer coast are the only viable areas for vegetables, apart from potatoes, but the newcomers also grow vegetables, using organic methods, and sell them themselves in a special 'bio' market in Brest. They commonly deplore local 'commercialism', 'modernism', and the use of chemical fertilizers, and those newcomers who keep cows have not adopted the modern dairy breeds but have tried to revive a hardy mountain race abandoned locally because of its low milk productivity. The newcomers also prefer to use their milk for home-made yoghurt, cheeses, and butter, rather than sell it to the commercial milk co-operatives that collect from other farms. In general, the home-production of butter is a task that local women are thankful to be rid of.

Several of the newcomers now working individual farms had orginally tried, in the first flush of post-'68 enthusiasm, to set up a collective *communauté* (or 'commune') working land further up in the mountains, but this venture was torn apart by structural conflicts of a kind we have already seen in other domains of the militant world. Machines had been scorned in favour of horses, and all were keen to work the soil with their hands in communion with each other and nature. When some began to advocate 'realism' and a more 'rational' approach, others left for India, or spiritual sects and ashrams elsewhere in France. All had wanted to live together in a 'community', and like a 'large family' (on an 'extended family' model, with the generalizable kinship structures salient in local life interpreted, not as a way of talking about land and inheritance, for example, but as the 'extension' of sentiments, of nuclear familial affectivity; this, in other forms, is an interpretation which has been common in anthropology – see Needham 1962, for a neat critique). By contrast, cohabitation with in-laws (with the choice of husband's or wife's depending on the more promising farm-site and inheritance arrangements for house and land) had helped to drive many in Plounéour away from the peasant life. State subsidies facilitating individual households for young married couples in rural areas came too late to halt the exodus.

Newcomers have not inhabited the necessary categories and networks for easy access to local reciprocation in agricultural tasks. Militants without farms generally like to help out anyhow, viewing as something of a holiday pursuit what locals accept as routine work and necessity. The newcomers' hay-making, potatoes, and beetroot have generally demanded extra help. Local farms are cutting down on potatoes due to declining profits, and beetroot is coming to be considered old-fashioned and replaced by maize, which the poorer soil worked by the newcomers cannot easily sustain. The newcomers often maintain their own potato and vegetable fields, therefore, in their own system of reciprocity, their own 'community' and 'Breton' world, with some who do not have farms keeping plots on the land of those who have.

Local reciprocation in the fields has commonly been guided by an ideal of self-sufficiency, whereby no one helps anyone unlikely to be able to offer equal help in return. For access to both land and reciprocation, village and kinship relations have been important, as well as comparability of farm size, the contiguity or proximity of fields, and, importantly, political compatibility. Newcomers have gained a foothold through proximity of fields, and the more easily the lower down the slopes they have been able to move. In Plounéour, one politically 'white' family, with a relatively large and prosperous farm, regarded it as a charitable act to offer help to a struggling young militant couple with three small children, and they did not expect equal help in return. However, they urged the father to take up a 'proper salaried job', for which he was qualified, and to move out of or 'modernize' the crumbling stone farmhouse in which he lived. The father had his own 'modernization' plans, however: an ambitious energy scheme based upon a large pile of steaming compost and manure.

The struggle towards 'modern' farming, as locally perceived, has no been easy in the mountains, but agriculture could seem a rational option for young people now, with a large, mechanized farm, nice house, and the necessary capital. However, the kind of farming that young 'alternative' enthusiasts have taken up has appeared more like an irrational self-repression than a liberation of any kind, and such is the overlap between the new 'alternative' enthusiasms and the still uneasily 'backward' agriculture of the mountains that the educated newcomers have often seemed to be uncomfortable caricatures of the local peasant life-style. 'Those people are mocking us,' I was told, with some peasants expressing similar sentiments about the newcomers' Breton.

'Those people'

Confrontation

The 'peasants' among the newcomers have sometimes received criticism to their faces (and in French) for their enthusiasms, but it is only local characters known for their bravado who have dared to criticize the non-peasants, apparently a more formidable opposition. Moreover, other local people present, especially any women, have usually felt bound to try to change the subject should such a confrontation seem threatened, in order to avoid impoliteness in educated company. Direct and open confrontation, therefore, has been relatively rare. 'Those people, working their arses off for Breton . . .' has been a common prelude to critical comments behind the militants' backs, but if this is turned, to their faces, into 'you people', then militants have to accept criticism with good grace, coming as it does from 'real peasants' in whose favour their 'Breton' world is morally loaded. The bottom line in any arguments is often phrased as political difference. 'We don't agree with your politics' is a politely dismissive full-stop that locals will draw, with a sharp 'you know full well' volunteered to any militant innocently pressing for elaboration of just what kind of politics is meant. Only on a couple of occasions has it been known for each side to lock into a spiral of mutual confirmation of the other's more denigratory perceptions and re-definitions, so that the authentic Breton rustic becomes, instead, the truly 'Frenchified' opposition and the educated sophisticate a true reactionary or a parasitic 'drop-out', to the point that violence has seemed a very real possibility.

The UDB

Sometimes the UDB, to which many of the Le Relecq *Diwan* parents belonged, has been an explicit target of attack. People in Plounéour who knew of the UDB were unsure which 'side' it was on; it seemed neither clearly 'red' nor 'white', although each side could choose to place it in the opposing camp for convenient dismissal. Not unexpectedly it was also joined in derision with *Breiz Atao* or the FLB, or with 'SAV' (meaning the nationalist *Strollad ar Vro*, see Chapter five). Communists especially liked to condemn it as right-wing, 'reactionary', or simply 'fascist', and *'la souche est de droite'* was a milder comment from Socialists and Communists alike. The UDB and *Diwan* are inevitably associated, although there are UDB militants living in Plounéour who, while they support *Diwan*, have pursued other priorities. These few UDB members commute to good salaried jobs, and their deliberate public emphasis on *laïcité* and economic development has given a locally perceived common ground of commitment – although the very articulacy of these newcomers, and the fact that they now lead the cause of Plounéour's College, has also raised fears, especially in the municipal council, that Plounéour might be overrun by 'those people' and local politics taken out of local hands. There was considerable suspicion, moreover, about 'separatism' and 'autonomism', and those who could say what the 'UDB' title meant in full were wary of the last word (*Bretonne*) in the arena of party politics.

Towards a serious Breton politics

The business of the agricultural unions, like that of the municipal council, is carried out in French, and the unions' organization has not traditionally followed regional boundaries. However, as the CELIB (see Chapter five, p. 80) had shown, significant possibilities of a regional economic self-consciousness existed, which the UDB sought to kindle into a full-blown 'Breton' politics. UDB members realized, however, that the CELIB succeeded through appeal to local rationality and respectability, and those Le Relecq *Diwan* parents who were UDB members came to feel their 'serious' Breton politics to be gravely prejudiced by the symbolic demands of an 'alternative' world that inhered in the allure of Breton. Increasingly, when *Diwan* required any business done with the town hall, they would send along well-dressed parents in locally respected professions, and they would speak in French. UDB members here came to see that, if there was to be an acceptably 'Breton' dimension in politics, then it would be through popular esteem of much of what the wider movement claimed to oppose or reject.

This is an important point. Some of the problems of the Breton movement and *Diwan* generally can be more easily understood in the light of the local problems which the Le Relecq *Diwan* faced. The Le Relecq school, one of *Diwan*'s oldest and most rural schools, situated in a relatively isolated, peasant, and Breton-speaking area, had been singled out to me early on in my research with the movement as the best-placed school, one on which militant hopes were pinned. However, it was also a school which provoked many of the arguments outlined in Part three. When I first arrived in Plounéour, teachers and parents of the *Diwan* at Le Relecq were already exhausted by their own internal quarrels and divisions. Parents who were both UDB members and 'peasants' had been the first and toughest critics of a teacher in this school, and then of his successors. The parents' chosen way of life jeopardized their own credibility locally and that of their party. They were soon joined in their criticism by other UDB members who were not 'peasants', and most of whom privately wished that they had no 'peasants' in their number at all, let alone teachers who seemed blithely insensitive to popular opinion. There was scarcely disguised pleasure when a few of the more overtly 'alternative' parents, and those most uncomfortably divided between UDB ambitions and their own 'peasant' life-style, left to set up a new *Diwan* in Huelgoat, on the other side of the mountains (where local acceptance proved no easier, and the school eventually closed). A marked rift had developed between UDB and non-UDB members, and this caused continuing quarrels and withdrawals to the point that, by the end of my first year in Plounéour, there were only two 'peasant' (and non-UDB) couples with their children still in the Le Relecq *Diwan*; others had left and were not missed by the UDB (and non-'peasant') parents.

The more the parents of the Le Relecq *Diwan* came to see where their chances of local acceptance might lie, and acted accordingly, the more their actions were denigrated within the wider movement. At one point the Le Relecq school, cherished as an ideal, nevertheless came to be castigated, conversely, as the 'French school'. The increasingly strict attitudes of the parents there were otherwise incomprehensible, not only to other *Diwan* teachers, but to many *Diwan* parents – especially those involved in urban *Diwan* schools, who had not been so readily disabused of their images of the rural, peasant, and truly 'Breton' world. In the meantime, at the level of the Le Relecq school itself, these same UDB parents asserted their own authenticity through the attribution to others of attitudes and activities detrimental to the serious 'Breton' politics which they themselves sought. It was their non-UDB colleagues, they insisted, who had brought upon them the locally pejorative images of 'drug addicts', or 'sculptors, people with goats and sheep, and all that', or *les blev hir* (meaning 'long-haired'), or *les barbus*. All of these were common elaborations of 'those people' (*ces gens-là* (Fr.) or *ar re-se* (Br.)) in local parlance. Such images were, in part, the consequence of the militants' own activities, pursued within a range of structures through which an appealingly 'Breton' world was defined, and in distinction from which a 'serious' Breton world could now find its own definition. But such images were also a matter of local perceptions in Plounéour of the militants' enthusiasms, and the mismatch of values could be such that a militant seen smoking a cigarette might be enough in local eyes to confirm a whole world of drug addicts, or one change of partners enough to conjure up images of orgies and harems. Such an apprehension, by local people, of moral disorder and uncertainty, deriving from the 'lack of fit' (cf. p. 21) between their own values and those of the newcomers, found ready expression and conviction here in the well-known self-image of landed, moral security on the part of the peasantry, taking its definition in symbolic opposition to a non-peasant population who, as every peasant has long known, can be a feckless, morally dangerous, and shifting lot. Centre/periphery relations, whatever their scale, tend to be drawn in similar colours, but landless mobility can lend easy confirmation to the images of naturality in which the periphery is commonly dressed (see, for example, Okely 1983 on a sedentary population's view of traveller-gypsies). In other circumstances, these might be the images held of Brittany by Paris, or of the peasantry by urban sophisticates, and so on. From *within* the peasant world, however, the images are here reversed. It is the newcomers who are peripheral to the peasant society as it draws its own boundaries, and the more so as these newcomers have boasted and enacted their own moral opposition, as 'alternative' or *marginaux*, to the majority French world.

UDB members in the Le Relecq school dealt with the problems which their own local marginality presented not only by its displacement, in the present, on to others, but also through the construction of an irrational 'alternativeness' as part of their history – a past from which a responsible and rational world in the present could draw its definition. From these militants, I heard increasingly frequent and harrowing tales of how many young people, including themselves, had flocked to the mountain area after 1968, and had lived through wild parties, drink, and drugs, many abortive attempts to live from Celtic music and art, weaving, pottery, sculpting, and all manner of dissent, until most had worn themselves out mentally and physically. Some 'Celtic' artists and artisans had virtually starved rather than go 'commercial', and there had been a trail of bankrupt 'alternative' farms and broken relationships. The mountains had buzzed with 'alternative' life, much of which was fizzling out when *Diwan* actually opened in Le Relecq. The young teachers taken on in this school could not carry on this vogue with impunity. Parents began to see their own 'errors' repeated and magnified. When arguments began between parents and one teacher, and continued with others, the parents found themselves presented with counter-arguments from all the *Diwan* teachers, *en masse*, which included the determination to make *Diwan* like the schools of the North American Indians (see Chapter eleven, p. 191). 'Can you imagine how that would have gone down with local people round here?' said one parent to me, during these tales of the past, with some incredulity that such ideas should ever have been given a serious hearing. This rural, mountain 'Breton' world produced *Diwan*'s first transferral of a teacher (to a coastal school, many miles away) and its first sacking of a teacher, as well as resignations from both teachers and parents. At the same time, this school externally so ideal and promising to the movement more generally, could itself summon for the movement, when the occasion demanded it, a special authenticity – by boasting that it had 'peasants' among its parents (see Chapter twelve, p. 214). Behind this public boast, which came from a UDB and non-'peasant' parent of the Le Relecq school, lay a torment of private ambivalence, internal argument, local rejection, and autobiographical fatigue.

Going native

In spite of some continuing internal squabbles, *Diwan* in Le Relecq was, by 1981, moving towards a respectability which the whole venture had, in some ways, been mounted against. The remaining 'peasants' among the parents were beginning, after almost ten years, to settle into an ambiguous but more promising local acceptance (partly helped by new modes of agricultural reciprocation – the formal CUMAs, with their subsidies and advantages (see Saizieu 1984) – and also by the dawn of EEC collective production quotas). The more extrovert artists and 'artisans' had withdrawn their children, new accommodation for the school had been found (see p. 239), yet another teacher recruited, and survival seemed possible, especially with national 'integration' promised. The parents breathed collective sighs of relief. However, this relief was interrupted by reports in the early summer of strange goings-on way up in the mountains, somewhere in the *landes* beyond Le Relecq.

A local peasant, who had tried planting saplings on a small section of the *landes*, discovered that some of his saplings had been eaten. He found two goats, the evident culprits, and he was spoiling for a fight with 'those people'. However, all 'those people' who had any goats denied that the goats in question were theirs. There then came reports of sitings of tepees up in the *landes*; North American Indians had, it was said, arrived in the mountains. At first it seemed that a popular Celtic imagination was excelling itself. Local people were insistent, however: 'Indians – just like the Westerns on the telly!' I decided to investigate this Breton Far West late one afternoon, but found myself in danger of getting lost in the *landes*, with darkness approaching, and ultimately retreated to the relative security of a main track that runs from Le Relecq over the mountains. When descending this track in the dark, and still about a mile from Le Relecq, I heard the sound of a horse's hooves, and a frightening vision emerged out of the night: a youth on horseback, an Indian headband across his forehead, dark hair trailing over his shoulders and behind him in the wind, a crude hide waistcoat baring his chest – and a long knife, glinting in the moonlight, tucked into a leather thong. The vision passed and went off the track, disappearing into the *landes*.

Local curiosity was mounting. In the town hall, however, the mayor seemed remarkably phlegmatic. After everything else that had gone on in these mountains over the last decade, tepees and Indians apparently came as no real surprise to him. However, the town hall clerk (a man from

Le Relecq) and two other local people keenly took me on a trek into the *landes* in daylight to investigate more closely. We ultimately came across the remains of a camp-fire and the imprint of at least one large tepee which had been removed. The town hall clerk decided that the Indians had moved further on still into the *landes*, and, in spite of an overt calm in the town hall, there was nevertheless some relief that, wherever they were, the Indians did not seem, for the moment, to be encamped within the boundary of the commune. There would not be the awkward problem of collecting any dues from them, therefore, or any problems of eviction; they were not, it was conveniently decided, Plounéour's responsibility.

While the municipality, and local people generally, treated the phenomenon with some amusement, it was not so appealing to *Diwan* parents. Some had not only seen the tepees but had also received visits from their occupants, who turned out to be a new version of 'alternative' peasants, a new vogue of 'community' living. They were young people, from elsewhere in Brittany (and from other parts of France, including Paris), who had decided to live together, with horses and no machines, and to live off goats and goat's milk, chickens, a few vegetables, and the hunting of wild game (albeit rabbits and birds, rather than buffalo); they sought to live, as near as was possible, the life-style of North American Indians. They had formed an association called 'The Native West' (*L'Ouest Indigène*) with tepees, the mountains, Celtic dolmens and menhirs, and nature's elements as its emblems. The Arrée mountains had seemed the most obvious site to make their true, native homeland. Just how many of them there were was never clear, although there were at least six adults camped in the mountains at one stage, some with their small children. When I managed to speak to one of them, he told me: 'Our movement is just beginning. It's a new movement, a movement of regeneration.' What worried *Diwan* parents especially was that these 'Indians' were not only keen to learn and speak Breton, to go really 'native', but they also wanted to send their children to the Le Relecq *Diwan*. After a quick panic, the Le Relecq *Diwan*, previously struggling for recruitment, was suddenly declared full. *Diwan* boasted, in principle, that it was open to everyone. 'But how could we accept *those people*?' said one (UDB) parent of the Le Relecq *Diwan* to me, in exasperation. Even the 'peasants' among the *Diwan* parents said that 'those people' had no real understanding of the land anyway: 'They have chosen a poor spot, exposed and unworkable.' No 'real Indians' (and no 'real peasants') would, it seems, have selected such a site.

As the new school year began, the 'Indians' organized a giant 'Free Festival' in the mountains, with several days and nights of entrancing dance and song, and some individuals in the nude under an ideally full moon. Some local peasants could not resist such a spectacle (and the issue of the goats and saplings was forgotten) but *Diwan* parents remained self-consciously aloof. The following spring, I learnt that the 'Indians' had gone; the winter had been cold. The renewed sense of relief among *Diwan* parents was obvious: all had returned to 'normal', I was told.

Festivities and tradition

Traditional drinkers

Bretons have long been thought of in France as heavy drinkers. This image, definitively established through the reports of educated travellers in the nineteenth century, conformed with the more general picture of an uncivilized and problematic Brittany, and was encouraged and confirmed by local modes of drinking and drunken behaviour which differed from those of the observers' world (see McDonald 1986c). We have already seen in Chapter eight (p. 146) how the 'Celts' of the movement appropriate the image as part of their oppositional jollification, thereby lending it further reality. It readily gains statistical and observational reality at the local level now for drinking is an important feature of social intercourse among men, especially peasant men here, and militants and visitors to this mountain area can imagine themselves to be participating in a common, unbroken tradition when they drink certain drinks or enter certain bars. In this section, I pick out a few summary points about local drinking culture which seem to be of particular relevance to the meeting of the different aspirations at hand and the process of revaluation involved. I would stress that, conceptually, we do not leave the question of Breton language and culture behind here, and the virtual homology of the themes of these sections demands that they be treated in the same pages and paragraphs.

The drinks

There could be said to be a limited structural continuity in some of the occasions and relationships of drinking which now exist and those which existed several generations ago, but there is little continuity of content (by which the 'traditional' is commonly measured). This is especially obvious in the domain of what is actually drunk: while cider is now the preferred drink of outsiders in pursuit of the traditional, it seems to have spread to these parts of western Brittany only at the end of the nineteenth century, and was already being replaced by red wine after the First World War. The Occupation helped to institutionalize the idea of manual workers needing a ration of red wine, and it is red wine that is now drunk in the homes and in the fields, by the men, at any time of collective agricultural labour. Beer, however, is often the preferred drink of the young, or the non-agricultural. In this range of increasing sophistication, from cider to wine to beer, newcomers, visitors, and militants generally prefer cider, which a very few households still produce locally, and who thus find their produce, and the ageing equipment used to make it, suddenly promoted in social and economic value. It is generally cider, albeit of an industrial kind, that is served in tourist cafés and restaurants in Brittany – along with *crêpes* (or *krampouez*, Br.), a food which has similarly emerged from the peasant hearth to be given new social and economic form and dress (often involving, quite literally, anything from jam to sardines). The situation is such that a few peasants who, on lean days, may still 'make do' with simple home fare of the pancake-and-cider kind will now, as a special outing, go to eat their simple fare, morally and economically transformed, as the pancakes and cider of new sophistication, served in a *crêperie* recently opened for tourists further up in the mountains.

The bars

The bars in the mountain area (and there are many of them) can be very broadly divided into three types. First, there are the very simple, single-room bars equipped with bottle and glass, where strong red wine is the principal drink. Rolling and chewing tobacco are on sale, along with *Gitanes Maïs*, the workman's cigarette that sticks to the lips. There may be sawdust on the floor, men are commonly dressed in working overalls, and Breton is the usual language of communication. The second type of bar, more sophisticated, will contain different areas or spaces for different ages and interests (e.g., dominoes for older people in the back, a juke box for the young in the front). A wide range of drinks is stocked, wines, spirits, and beers – both home and imported – and a corresponding range of cigarettes. Both French and Breton will be heard, and some women may occasionally be seen drinking in these bars, although usually away from the bar, seated at tables, and never alone. The third type of bar is the *boîte*, or night-club/disco. These bars, the most sophisticated, are far fewer in number, and always expensive and situated a long way from centres of habitation. The distance and their cost are important. A car is essential (and cycling to them wholly incongruous). Both sexes are present, and the clientele young. No wine is on sale, only beers, spirits, and cocktails, all at high prices (sometimes at least ten times the price paid elsewhere). French, often with a high *franglais* content, is the language of communication. The dads of those present in these *boîtes* may well be in the first type of bar I mentioned, and they themselves, on other occasions, in the second type. These different ways of going out for a drink bear some similarities, in their extremes, to the English sawdust pub at one end and the English wine bar at the other, but with greater degrees of humility and extravagance in their expression. The coexistence of such extremes, and their common exploitation within one family, or by the 'same people', is another indication of the telescoping of changes which, to British eyes, France presents. The next stage of sophistication, after the *boîtes*, is already available: to go into the old, single-room sawdust bars, and speak Breton. This is, of course, precisely what many educated visitors and newcomers do. The effect of their presence, however, is radically to transform, morally and politically, the context of those bars. If the visitors and newcomers persist, some compromise may be reached involving, where possible, spatial or temporal discrimination (with self-conscious 'locals' choosing their own times to come), but otherwise the bar may simply be re-defined, and the locals go elsewhere.

Gender and generations

With the exception of the *boîtes*, the bars are generally run by women: women serve the drink, and men drink it. This is also true in the homes, where drink (usually red wine) is always offered to all male visitors. The femininity/masculinity duality is important in the local culture of drinking, and various versions of it are commonly offered in explanations of why men drink and women don't. (Women commonly express the view that they don't drink because they are more socially sensitive and moral, whereas men are the unsophisticated victims of natural urges; a common male view may concur with this, or, alternatively, give it a negative hue: women are sober spoil-sports, and men spontaneously fun-loving, etc.). These familiar expressions of gender difference share some features with other male-centred constructions of the men's world and their women, wherein women are ambiguously placed in the 'wild', and are generally the point of entry of social disorder (see E. Ardener 1972b, 1975b). Elements of a discourse which commonly makes sense of centre/periphery relations can here distribute qualities between the sexes (and the congruence and conflation of these two discourses were pointed to, in rather different terms, in Chapter six and in the opening 'femininity and feminism' section of this chapter). Within these same constructs, however, men can also claim their own 'wild', for which the women have no equivalent, and it is this domain of masculinity which is asserted in Plounéour in bar-crawls (*pistes*), fighting and football, in hunting (cf. p. 277), soil, dirt, and drinking. It often becomes, within these same structures of difference, the task of the women to stop the men drinking, and of the men at least to affect to avoid being stopped by the women, with each party congratulating itself (this is most obvious during mixed gatherings in the homes, such as mentioned on p. 248). It is perhaps no surprise that those who drink most are the ageing, unmarried peasants, who have no woman to stop them, and who cannot conjure up the sometimes equally effective picture of a worrying, disapproving woman awaiting them at home.

I have already pointed out how the symbolism of fuss and finery, caring, and the niceties of sophistication and social discrimination are the symbolic lot of the women (see p. 248; also McDonald 1986b), and women trying to stop their men drinking is one more aspect of this same responsibility for social propriety. Another is that men have, in the bars, options of drinking and smoking available to them that are not available to women.

The men can, for example, drink both wine and beer or imported spirits, depending on who they are with or how they wish, socially or generationally, to place themselves, and they can smoke ordinary French *brunes* (the dark-tobacco cigarettes) as one of the lads, in contrast to the girls, or the foreign *blondes* (or light-tobacco) cigarettes, which place a distance between themselves and their parental generation. The young, feminine woman, if she smokes at all, will smoke the *blondes*. There was a time when women both smoked and drank in Brittany (which added to the moral exclamations of nineteenth-century travellers). After the First World War, such matters became increasingly assimilated to statements of masculinity, and femininity as it came to these areas found expression in not smoking and not drinking – or only on special occasions, and then usually a very sweet white wine or liqueur (cf. p. 248). Women born after the Second World War, however, have been able to show their sophistication by taking up smoking and drinking within a new evaluation of what smoking and drinking involve. They can now, in the more sophisticated bars, take light beers and exotic cocktails and smoke imported cigarettes, in statements of cosmopolitan and Anglo-American chic. Only outsiders, however, or women cast as such, would take to the *brunes* or the roll-your-own cigarettes, the property of the male, and generally of the older male peasant. While the educated outsider, male and female (see e.g., p. 255), might find an advance in sophistication in this, the local girl would simply be uncouth. However, as the roll-your-own, cider and red-wine drinking outsiders bring sophistication to these items, then their appropriation (or re-appropriation) by local young women, and the young men, in pursuit of refinement, may become fully possible – in another moral transformation of the material substances, which relocates them and their consumers in the new, sophisticated world of the traditional and the authentic.

Traditional dances

In despair, a parent from the Le Relecq *Diwan* once commented that a fund-raising event sure of success in Plounéour would demand 'wine, pinball machines, topless girls, and the Rolling Stones!' The one thing that marred the 'Indian' festival (p. 264) for local peasants was that there was no wine. There were, however, reports of topless girls.

One order of local event which *Diwan* has daringly entered is that of the *kermesse* (Fr.), or school fête, putting on its very first one in 1980. It was held, not in school premises, as is usual for the local schools, but in the bourg of Plounéour, in an open space that bridges the moral and historical chasm between the church and the post office. The space was not wholly neutral, however, and a few *anciens combattants* found it inappropriate and upsetting for 'those people' to be setting up their militant wares just a few metres from Plounéour's large and well-kept war memorial, a monument first built by Francis Pouliquen in the 1920s, and inscribed with over one hundred and sixty names (at least one hundred and thirty of them from the First World War), all *Morts pour la France*. Moreover, the history therein commemorated seemed, in the new context that *Diwan*'s presence created, to be old-fashioned – and a distraction from a more authentic tradition which the militants were now properly restoring.

Diwan has been more at home with *festoù-noz*, putting on several a year. These have not always been well attended, and municipal premises have not been made readily available in poor weather. However, an annual *fest-noz* which the *Diwan* parents mounted on New Year's Eve *did* gain municipal shelter, and was a great success. New Year's Eve is an important time of public celebration in France generally, and *Diwan*'s *fest-noz* offered, for a while, the only organized public event in Plounéour on this date. The *laïques* in public office did not attend, but at least one nun from the private school danced with everyone else round the beaten earth-floor of the communal *salle des fêtes*. Some in Plounéour told me they had never seen or heard of a *fest-noz* until *Diwan* mounted one in the commune. (Catholic groups and the *école libre* had, in fact, tried to introduce *festoù-noz* in the mountain area in the early days of their revival, but majority political memory in Plounéour does not record these.) Many young people in Plounéour, in their teens and twenties, have now been to *festoù-noz* elsewhere in Brittany, and the young gymnastics teacher in Plounéour's College is contemplating teaching *fest-noz* dances in the school. Smarter Pleyber was already offering evening classes, in a 'Celtic circle', although these generally involved the fancier dances of the coast rather than the simpler *gavottes* of the mountain area, which the more secular post-1968 enthusiasts have preferred. Older peasants in Plounéour sometimes recognize the steps of *Diwan*'s dances from special occasions of their youth (when, however, the accordion was the main musical instrument), but there is now a wide middle band of people in the commune, aged particularly in their thirties, forties, and fifties, who have to learn the rural, mountain dances from the newcomers, the militants, and the occasional tourist at these *festoù-noz*. These local learners include peasants who, every New Year's Eve, thus learn how to be properly festive peasants, in the image created and expected of them.

Local dancing has shifted, very broadly, from country dancing of the kind now evoked in the *festoù-noz*, to varieties of ballroom dancing and rock and disco. These last types of dancing are commonly seen at the ordinary Saturday night dances or the *bals populaires*. Militants and tourists shun such events, or have been known to leave in open disappointment and go instead in pursuit of a *fest-noz*, more common now in the ever more sophisticated communes of the plain. The 'Breton culture' of militant enthusiasm and the 'traditional' Brittany of tourist expectation collude here in very similar structures (cf. McDonald 1984). The wealthier, more modern communes of the plain and coast can also show their sophistication in being more self-consciously 'traditional' now for the outsider's gaze. Saint-Thégonnec, for example, in the Léon plain, has put on *battage à l'ancienne* displays in the summer and parades of the old peasant life – with local people dressed up in clogs and costumes, perched on floats of straw, and surrounded with sickles and scythes, and replicas of stables. Plounéour is not yet able confidently to dress up as a glamorous image of itself in this way. There is still too much of an uncomfortable overlap. The old-world peasant or hayseed who, through the perceptions of the tourist, is morally transformed into the quaintness of the postcard is still enough of an everyday reality in Plounéour to be more readily assimilable to parodic self-presentation. For Plounéour to put itself through the hoop of revaluation, it will have to be confident that the backward bumpkin is comfortably disappearing or gone from its own visible everyday midst.

The country dances of the *festoù-noz*, one-time rural imitations of higher society which were then borrowed back by the sophisticated, after the 1960s, as an image of the rustic (Chapter eight, p. 145), have now become part of the urban image of the rural world which the rural world is re-appropriating to itself. At the beginning of the 1980s, Plounéour's calendar of public events already listed five planned *festoú-noz* of its own, and *Diwan*'s New Year event made six. Public events are organized by local fund-raising groups, generally with obviously intra-communal partisan interests (notably *libres* or *laïques*), but there is a municipally funded *Comité des Fetes*, drawn largely from people in the bourg (tradesmen, shopkeepers, and café/bar owners), which includes both reds and whites and aims principally at attracting visitors to Plounéour and business to its tradesmen. The *Comité* has been keen to promote *festoù-noz*: that, it is now recognized, is what visitors want. It is perhaps to be expected that those with a modern eye on financial gain, and those from the bourg rather than the surrounding *campagne*, will more readily appropriate an urban image of the rustic and unchanging without the discomfort of assimilation to their own everyday backwardness; however, any relative sophistication of the bourg in relation to the *campagne* is an internal discrimination which is muted when Plounéour turns its communal public face to the external world, and is transmuted into a deference to the *Comité* of the bourg to know what that public face should be. The *Comité*, in turn, is meta-phorically deferring elsewhere, to the structures of 'minority' enthusiasm and tourist good taste.

'*Le Parc*' and tourism

Apart from the *grands voyages* of the nineteenth century, the shee banality of the rustic contributed to a very much slower development c rural tourism in Brittany (as in France generally) than in a country such as Britain. The mass tourism of the twentieth century has been largely concentrated on the coast, but, with the modern decline of the peasantry, rural tourism has re-emerged as an altogether more high-class affair. The inland areas in Brittany now attract a generation of discerning and 'intelligent tourists' (Duigou 1979), who often take their definition in opposition to the seaside *hoi-polloi*. The Natural Regional Park mentioned earlier (p. 239), which covers this upland area, has become an increasingly important site for this new tourism; it is managed by a specialist in open-air activities and an ethnologist. Such parks have been created in part to give town-dwellers access to rural roots and an ethnological heritage, and the Park has, since its inception, invested its regional, departmental, and municipal funding in such ventures as centres for artists and artisans (cf. p. 239), and aid and advice for the conservation and restoration of old buildings. Other activities include walks and horse-riding. Such activities again turn what locals have associated with labour and drudgery into leisure and respite, but there is no necessary conflict: where land has been cleared for walkers and horses, for example, local peasants have been pleased to pass with their new cars or tractors.

The still largely agricultural villages covered by the Park have great potential appeal to a sophisticated visitor disaffected with urban progress. However, the local populace does not always seem to know that it is meant to be an unspoilt rural world, invested with all that urban modernity is not. The Park is working well at the level of attracting visitors, but local reaction has been mixed and changing. Much of the Park is a 'classified site', and scholars have begun to pay great attention to its 'traditional' and 'vernacular' architecture (see e.g., Meirion-Jones 1978, 1980). However, one major, if unintended, initial influence of *Le Parc* was to encourage local people radically to change their old houses and to install kitchens and even bathrooms, copying the smart facilities of the Park's own offices. Building is a boom industry in Brittany, and building a new house (even if you do not actually live in it) has, since the late 1960s, become an important public facet of modernity and success. In keeping with this, one local family has built proudly and prominently at the entrance to Plounéour's bourg, a new, light, airy home, contrasting strongly with the old stone farmhouses, and it is finished off with a bright blue plastic verandah. Newcomers and conservationists almost weep at the sight of it. Increasingly, however, 'traditional' houses are coming to be revalued and restored in the mountain area, and sold for large sums to the incomers or rented to tourists. A few of these are in the *Gîtes Ruraux de France* scheme and some local peasants in Plounéour have been pleased to muse that it might be possible to earn more, in rent, from being a 'farm' for the delight of summer tourists than from actually working a viable farm all year round. Running the *gîtes*, moreover, is attractive to women (on this, see R. Simon

1974). For the moment, however, the agricultural market, and the silage plants, milk hangars, hen-batteries, and industrial pigsties, are easily winning out over the tourist market for the peasant life, and, where *gîtes* exist, the different aspirations are commonly enshrined in the *gîtes'* noticeable difference from the (sometimes spanking new) homes in which the owners themselves prefer to live. Typically, the tourist will be left to enjoy a large open fireplace, for instance, while the owners on the farm next door will themselves have ripped out the fireplace, if ever there was one, and installed central heating. It is not uncommon for the newer generation, on inheriting the house, to re-install the fireplace that their parents rejected, thus fully incorporating, at some expense, an urban image of what a rural house should really be like.

A similar process is evident in an artisanal centre set up by the Park in the mountains for artists and artisans (many of them *Diwan* parents and friends) to sell their goods. The goods on sale are expensive, putting them deliberately up-market from seaside trinkets and souvenirs, and they include larger items such as pieces of furniture. These items are sometimes deliberately crafted and stained to make them look rustic and old. Many local homes had been only too keen to replace such old 'rubbish' with clean formica. Grandfather clocks, wooden dressers, long farmhouse tables and benches, enclosed wooden beds, fire-irons, bed-pans, horse-leathers, and more have passed through a whole range of evaluations, in turn as modern, functional, old-fashioned, dirty, and rubbish, before acquiring the scarcity value of disappearing tradition. Some local people have started to buy small items at the artisanal centre in the mountains and there may come a day when they will actually be buying back versions of their old goods and furniture, expensively fashioned into Breton and rural traditionality by urban, 'alternative' craftsmen.

'Eco-museums', another and important venture of the Park, are generally old houses or whole villages, bought up and conserved by the Park, in the style in which they were lived in and abandoned. Local reactions in each case have, initially, involved some anger, disgust, and hostility – with complaints (especially from women) that it was a disgrace to show the public how dirtily and poorly people lived, sometimes with little visible separation between animal and human habitat, in an all too recent past. Gradually, however, as urban visitors have poured in with their note-books and cameras, their sophistication and their shrieks of delight, a few local people have been known to come along and boast, to an admiring audience, how they themselves lived like that in their youth. Some of them still live like that now, but in such cases few are confident enough of the revaluation process at work actually to say so.

As might now be evident, the Park, its ventures, its aspirations, and its effects are part of a very much more general process. Many activities have been conjured into existence, or maintained, by external interest, giving a traditionality that might otherwise not exist or that might have been forgotten. These activities take on a new temporal and social existence, and find a place in a new economic structure in which the educated sophisticate, militant, researcher, or tourist, plays a definitive role. This is the case whether we are talking about 'folkloric' and costume parades, say, such as are common on the south coast, or the many demonstrations of *battage à l'ancienne*, or the *festoù-noz*, now put on inland for tourists every summer (or, indeed, Breton language courses). There may be varying degrees of temporal and social discontinuity between such dress or activities as they were once worn or performed (if ever) and the way in which they now appear before the external enthusiast, but it is through external evaluation that such features of local life are made traditional and authentic, although they may, in many ways, be new. The situation becomes difficult to disentangle, and there is a growing resistance to any notion of novelty, when, as is now happening in this part of rural Brittany, various 'alternative' potters, carpenters, sculptors, weavers, and artists have claimed the rural world as their own, carrying on in imagined continuity from artisans of a very different ilk, and have then supplemented their own livelihood by offering summer courses to cultivated holiday-makers keen to learn the 'traditional' arts and crafts which they, as 'local' craftsmen, ply. Some of the 'alternative' peasants are similarly offering to teach Breton, in exchange for help on the farm.

Near the end of my stay in Plounéour, a young woman from a tourist centre appeared in the town hall and asked what attractions the commune could offer; she was keen to organize some tours of the area. After some hesitation she was told: 'Well ... we do have potters, weavers, and sculptors'. As the list expanded, it began to include much of what I have described, largely stemming from, and congruent with, the enthusiasms of 'those people'. Scratching his head, the town hall spokesman finally extended the list to include 'monuments': the abbey and church. A rural commune, divided internally and uneasily backward, was thus united for the modern, external gaze; any visitor – militant, tourist, or, no doubt, an anthropologist – could see in it an uncomplicated, unchanging, rural simplicity, untouched by conflict, external events, modernity, and progress.

Chapter fifteen

Breton language and culture

We have now seen two worlds meeting and have glimpsed the way in which the militants' enthusiasms are incorporated locally. It only remains to examine more critically the conceptual space between 'the Breton language' or 'Breton culture' of the militants and the customs, codes, and proprieties, linguistic or non-linguistic, of everyday life in Plounéour. I want to stress at the outset that I shall, for important reasons that will become clear, be paying particular attention in this chapter to a couple of people in Kerguz whom I mentioned in Chapter fourteen: the peasant widow Thérèse and her bachelor son Iffig (see, e.g., p. 250). They have militants living right next door to them in the village and have been in close contact with new values and ideas.

Animals, savages, and culture

Thérèse and Iffig befriended me from an early stage in my research, and through Thérèse I gained easy access to other areas of life in Plounéour. Thérèse's neighbours, the psychologist and his wife (whom I had met in militant gatherings and especially *Diwan* meetings), had been my first introduction to Thérèse herself. Always keen to keep up with new ideas, she was pleased to meet her educated neighbours' friend, and through her, my own enthusiasms and association with 'those people' then became contextually laundered as necessary. On several counts, Thérèse seemed the right person to be associated with: she owned land to which others in Plounéour aspired, and managed her life without debt or obligation, and could, I was told by other villagers, 'recite La Fontaine'. Indeed, verses of La Fontaine and Racine, learnt on school benches in the 1920s, were duly recited to me on our very first meeting.

I often ate with Thérèse and her son in their home, and after special efforts to provide appropriate food – especially cakes – we eventually settled into a routine of simple meatless fare, in which Thérèse and Iffig would apologize for, and I would delight in, their 'peasant food' (cf. the discussion of pancakes-and-cider on p. 266). Iffig still works some of his own land in Kerguz, but in his other capacity, as a railway workman in the heart of the Léon plain, he has become uncomfortably aware of different foods and styles of eating. The differences do not elide neatly with occupational difference (knives and forks, for example, rather than the spoon and all-purpose peasant knife have long been common in wealthier agricultural families, or the *Julots* of the plain (Chapter fourteen, note 2), whose food content could also differ markedly from that of their poorer neighbours: see Flatrès 1920); there is also a symbolism of locality involved. 'We eat like pigs here', Iffig would say, frequently apologizing for his manners also. I was soon reassured, however, that things could be worse. Very early on, Iffig related how another bachelor peasant had, for a dare, recently eaten a boiled toad, 'eyes and all'. His reward was a bottle of hard liquor, but he could have died for 'toads are poisonous'. Thérèse thought little of this proof of raw celibate manhood, and regained some cultured standing for the area by pointing out that those involved in such oddities were, of course, from further up the mountain slopes; however, she later added that another peasant had similarly eaten a mouse once, and yet another was known to have regularly eaten snails, sometimes raw. 'There are some real savages (*sauvages*, Fr.) here', she warned.

Snails are also known to be eaten in posh French restaurants. Indeed, one of the newcomers to the area had once tried to set up a small snail-farm. When a journalist from Paris one day arrived in the hamlet, seeking to write an article about one of the exciting projects going on in the Arreé mountains, she was disappointed to learn that the snail-farm had collapsed and that another venture – attempting to rear wild pigs – had also failed. She decided instead to write an article about *Diwan*. Clearly, any one of these projects would do. Within the space of a few minutes, she was directed from mountain snails to wild pigs to *Diwan*, by her own Parisian sense of the exotic and refined and by local capacities to lump all these things together, to incorporate external good taste, and to move them accordingly from the realms of the bizarre, rude, or backward into those of the fashionable and sophisticated.

Thérèse and Iffig were curious to know what we ate in England, and were surprised when I manifested disgust at the idea of eating horse-meat. Horse-meat is known to satisfy sophisticated palates (and some of Plounéour's own horses had ended up on smart dinner tables elsewhere). I was also asked if we ate cats. In a foreign world, all things were possible, and if horses, animals of the working farm household, could be food to other people, then so could cats. Thérèse and Iffig knew I liked salads, including beetroot, and that salads are common in restaurants. They did not eat beetroot themselves, however, for this was something only fed to animals, and Iffig was still shocked that restaurants should serve it. In our conversation, we got on to the subject of wholemeal bread (something that they knew I liked also); unrefined flour had been used for baking bread in times gone by, but bran, ideally, was something only fed to horses. I was not able to buy wholemeal bread in Plounéour. In the bakery in the bourg, which is stocked with white loaves in a variety of shapes, I was given the knowledgeable advice that I would have to go 'en ville' ('to town') for it. Wholemeal bread, like so much else in Plounéour, has passed from evocations of poverty to sophistication. The rough old *pain noir* of hard times has become *le pain complet* of fine living (although remaining in Breton *bara du*: lit. 'black bread').

One food for which several villagers expressed a clear distaste was mushrooms. Indeed, Iffig had 'accidentally' eaten mushrooms once in a restaurant, where they had been 'disguised' in a sauce. Mushrooms are not animal food, or poor food, and the reason for wariness did not lie here. 'I thought I might be poisoned', and he was surprised that he had not been ill afterwards. It was, in fact, a discussion of mushrooms which had led directly to the story of the peasant who had eaten a toad (p. 275). We had been talking in French, and passing from talk of *champignons* ('mushrooms') to talk of a *crapaud* ('toad') could seem a *non-sequitur*. In Breton, however, the one is easily evocative of the other. A 'mushroom' in Breton is *skabell-touseg* (lit. 'toad's stool'), with much the same image as toadstool in English, and these native Breton-speakers are, through the semantics of Breton, wary of all *champignons*. I often found that here French conversation would pass, unwittingly, through the semantics of Breton in this way, just as in the militant world, by contrast, Breton terms and conversation often passed, unwittingly, through the semantics of French.

In Rennes University, a lecturer in the Celtic Department had once advised students that if ever they wanted to show any peasants in Lower Brittany that they knew Breton, then a tactful strategy might be to be heard to speak Breton to a dog, or another animal, on a farm as one approached. I certainly found that local people *did* use Breton to animals but not *all* animals are addressed in Breton. In Chapter fourteen, in connection with the 'mother tongue', I outlined one especially striking example of differential language use to different animals, on a generational axis (see p. 255). On the same farm, but on a rather different axis of animal classification, the mother also spoke Breton to the dog, but French to the cat. When I pointed this out, she laughed and explained that the cat was a pet, while the dog was a 'farm dog'. I will conclude this section now with a brief elaboration of this differential evaluation of animals, which ties in with different language use, and with the way in which militant enthusiasms can be, and are, incorporated and transformed within the context and framework of local identities and aspirations.

Apart from one small vegetable farm set up by newcomers, the hamlet of Le Relecq, next to Kerguz, no longer has any working farms of its own. The population is generally ageing, but some are relatively wealthy; a number have been to the towns and returned on retirement and others made their money in the heyday of the horse trade. Many of the ladies in Le Relecq have pets, dogs and cats, or both. An especially hardy hunting man (a *chasseur*, Fr.) in Plounéour is contemptuous of Le Relecq, with its 'useless' pets, as he sees them, and what he sees, too, as 'hoity-toity' pretension. One fine spring morning, two of the precious pet dogs were found poisoned (by fox poison). I tried to help by taking one of the dogs to a veterinary surgeon in Pleyber-Christ.

When Thérèse and Iffig, back in Kerguz, heard about this, Iffig was openly surprised that 'so much fuss' had been made about a dog. Thérèse was also surprised but nevertheless reproached her son, telling him, as she often did, that he was ignorant. In her view, it was no wonder he had never found a wife. Iffig, in turn, would reproach his mother for having brought him up in Breton, and Thérèse would say, apologetically, that there she realized she had done the wrong thing. Thérèse does know, however, about pets. Indeed, her nice neighbours (the psychologist and his wife) have a pet dog and cat; the cat, however, has spent all the time in her house, where it is put to good use to catch large rats. We were talking in French, and the subject came up of my stay on that farm where I had learnt some Breton and had heard the mother speak different languages to different animals, including French to the pet cat. Thérèse has become used to the idea of young people wanting to learn and speak Breton (her neighbours do, for instance), and she was intrigued that the mother on that farm had dutifully spoken Breton to me. Her interest focused on the family: from my description, they were obviously well-to-do peasants, she concluded, with nicely educated daughters, and, moreover, they lived near a town on the coast. 'Those people are so sophisticated up there', she said, 'unlike we savages here in the mountains.' She sighed, and then picked up the cat. A straggly, rat-catching cat then found itself being gently stroked and petted on her lap, and spoken to in French. Previously, I had heard Thérèse speak only Breton to that cat, but when I enquired, she paused and then was quite insistent: 'I always speak French to my cat', she said to me finally, and she said this in a pointedly careful Breton, tailored to satisfy the enthusiasms of any town lady aspiring to 'Breton culture'.

The Breton language

Different languages

As suggested by the above example of Thérèse and various examples elsewhere – in Chapter nine (p. 170) and Chapter fourteen (especially in the 'femininity and feminism' section, pp. 243–56), for instance – there are quite obviously contexts in which local people, faced with new enthusiasms and ideas, will speak in Breton as these enthusiasms require. Many more examples could be cited. The Breton which local people may thus summon – in many ways, through esteem for the very world against which militants have defined most clearly their own cause and authenticity – has no simple continuity with the Breton these native-speakers might normally use to each other, unselfconsciously, in their everyday world. The one does not have the same social value as the other.

The contextual proprieties of Breton and French in Plounéour are composed of many extra-linguistic factors already mentioned, investing language difference with values different from those operative in the Breton movement. It might seem that a picture of local socio-linguistic properties could have been summarized by listing, in a single sentence, a series of apparently congruent dualities (e.g., public/private, socially distant/familiar, French/Breton). However, lining up dichotomies in this way, while economic and elegant, readily colludes in the misleading positivism still common in many areas of socio-linguistics (on which, see Wardhaugh 1986). Such an exercise leads to key misunderstandings – of a kind which the militants exploit – of the popular socio-language, and we shall return to these at the end of this chapter. Language difference, change or choice, or who speaks what and how to whom and when, depends on very many factors, including such obvious elements as topic of conversation, place of conversation, age, gender, occasion, occupation, and the relative statuses, familiarity or distance, of the speakers; however, all such axes of identity or elements of 'context', rather than being externally constraining 'givens', gain their effectiveness only through the perceptions of the speakers involved. There would be little point in saying, for example, that French is a 'public' language and that it is also 'feminine', only to be surprised by women talking Breton together out in the street when shopping (and then perhaps talking French when back at home: see Chapter fourteen, p. 248). In order to grasp the nuances of differential language use in local talk, it is not the linguist's or the sociologist's perception of context which is required, nor the economy and cosmic objectivity of lists of apparently fixed and neutral pairs, but rather the perceptions, classifications or definitions, and the self-definitions of the language-users themselves. Perhaps I can summarize a certain tautology involved in the self-evocative symbolism making up the speakers' own perception of context, by saying that the use of Breton or of French, or of varieties of these, defines the context (spatially, relationally, topically, and so on) and the context defines the language spoken, or the way of talking. We know in our own world that, whether our different ways of talking have names or not (as particular accents, dialects or languages, for example), we are able to change our way of speaking according to our own social proprieties, our own perception of the context, and to define ourselves and others, or the relationship or occasion, and so on, thereby. We do no necessarily change our way of speaking with any self-consciousness. Whe local people speak in Breton to me or to any of the militants, however, they often know they are doing it; they know they are 'speaking Breton'.

All Breton-learning manuals – from whatever faction of the movement they may come, and whatever kind of Breton, linguistically, they may use – fail to offer the learner a grasp of popular socio-linguistic values. A use of Breton and only Breton, for all purposes, by popular characters in the pages of these manuals, describes the militant world and its aspirations rather than native-speaker realities. In the movement, I did not learn popular manners, aspirations and proprieties, only popular default. If a manual were ever to try to present the 'language' of native Breton-speakers, then considerable literary skill, social sensitivity, and numerous textual notes and qualifications would be necessary; at the very least, the manual would show a toing and froing between Breton and French. Putting it perhaps over simply, we can say that the militant world and the popular world have different 'Bretons'. They are not talking the 'same' Breton; they are not talking about the same thing in commentary upon Breton; they do not have the same social value of Breton; they do not share the same level of education or the same linguistic and social sensibilities and competences. They are not, we might say, speaking the same 'language'.

No ordinary Breton-speaker

In moving between the militants and the local people in Plounéour, I was clearly moving between different socio-linguistic worlds. My ambitions to learn and speak Breton, carried over from the militant world, inevitably brought some of the internal transgressional hilarity and testing that I have described earlier (Chapter nine, p. 170). Once the party-piece was over, however, French was once again normal. The fact that I did know Breton nevertheless meant that villagers in Kerguz, and in Plounéour more widely, gradually came to speak Breton unselfconsciously to each other in front of me, without my very presence defining a French-speaking context. If I then joined in in Breton myself, however, the context often changed, and their own Breton was launched into self-consciousness to the point that it stopped. This was especially so among the women. Sustained conversation in Breton with men was often easier, although I had to tread carefully, particularly in a world in which mixed gender encounters are still often perceived as sexual encounters, and my use of Breton with the lads could easily launch a conversation of little more than sexual jokes. My association with Thérèse was of particular use in such circumstances, and a tolerance of my enthusiasms developed. It is important to stress, however, that – no matter what one's gender – one does not, by virtue of having learnt some Breton and being permitted to speak it, become accepted as any other ordinary Breton-speaker. One's status as a *speaker* is especially strange. There are very many young people in Plounéour whose understanding of spoken Breton is very much greater than one's own, but who would not be willing to converse in Breton, for socio-linguistic reasons alone. Outside the peculiar socio-linguistic framework one creates, largely composed of older people and in which a researcher speaking Breton gradually becomes tolerated and possible, one would be like other people of one's own age, speaking Breton very little if ever at all.

Masculine chic

One thing I had to learn in Plounéour was that use of Breton, by Breton-speakers among Breton-speakers, was sometimes positively laughed at. After working in the militant milieu, this was difficult to take at first, and could easily seem fascist and immoral. However, I did not feel it was my task to argue with native-speaker sentiment. There was a variety of circumstances in which this ridiculing sanction was operative, but it was most strikingly common in gatherings of young men. If Breton appeared among them at all, it was generally as a joke. Sexual jokes were common, as were jokes about older ideas of 'work' in the agricultural milieu. These last jokes were made by a younger generation engaged in a 'modern' agriculture or in other occupations (typically, if there was a complaint made about any manual task at hand, then a chorus would respond, in Breton, and in deliberate parody of the older peasantry: 'Once upon a time we worked and worked, and we never complained'). If a young man then seemed to be launching conversation in Breton, continuing in Breton after the joke, he would find the full force of parody coming down in various forms upon himself and he would very clearly be defined into an older generation, or as a bumpkin, and certainly not as one of the in-crowd of drinking young men in Plounéour's bars. (One young man, in his late twenties and from a particularly struggling, tenant farm household, would regularly find himself the object of ridicule in this way, and was mocked for his misplaced Breton by the older generation also: he was, in local eyes, 'backward'.) Youths from the *campagne* rather than the bourg, or from the agricultural rather than the commercial milieu, might seem to be the most vulnerable to such parody, but they are also its most able and witty perpetrators. Their French is consonant with their imported cigarettes and beer (see p. 266). These young men are not copying their mothers in speaking French, but are finding their identity in a masculine chic which their fathers did not know, and which young women admire and require.

Socio-linguistic confusion

Since I kept close contact with both militant and local worlds, it was perhaps inevitable that, in the sheer fatigue of the different conformities required (including the sometimes very different social hours involved), I should at some stage confuse the two socio-languages. This happened one day when, after a visit to a *Diwan* school elsewhere in Brittany, I returned to Kerguz, tired and with an unthinking Breton-to-children reflex. The seven-year-old, youngest son of a peasant family in the village came to visit me, as children often did. I unthinkingly spoke to him in Breton. He looked surprised and replied in French. His parents (typical of virtually all parents in their mid-forties or over – cf. Chapter fourteen, note 4) often spoke Breton to each other; their young son could understand a good deal, but was not accustomed to being spoken to in that way, and was certainly not expected to speak that way himself. However, he was undoubtedly flattered that I had, on that one occasion, spoken to him in the way I usually spoke to the posh children of *Diwan*. The posh children, on the other hand, to whom I usually spoke in Breton, urged me to speak French to them in the village, apparently wanting me to treat them like their local friends.

I was not the only one who risked becoming muddled by the different demands: the *Diwan* teacher in Le Relecq soon felt she had consciously to stop herself from automatically speaking Breton to all children – partly for fear of parents' reactions. In the automatisms of the two different worlds, it required conscious effort on both sides for the one to accommodate the other. There were a few local people who, out of curiosity, visited *Diwan* in Le Relecq. Typical of these visitors, one woman from the hamlet, in her seventies, spoke French to the children but sometimes hesitated because she knew that *Diwan* expected Breton. 'We speak French to children here', she one day explained, after much confusion, and blushing at her own apparent ineptness.[1] Another woman in Le Relecq, in her late forties, clearly enjoyed mixing with some of the professional parents who came to collect their children from *Diwan*, and agreed to help the teacher with some simple Breton vocabulary. Her standing with the parents depended on her being a local repository of 'Breton culture'. 'Don't tell your parents I speak French to you!' she once told a psychologist's child, whom she had been asked to look after for an hour one evening.

Explicit socio-linguistic self-consciousness is not, of course, an everyday affair. The linguistic gymnastics of some peasant families can be perplexing to the observer who does not possess the same unthinking automatisms. For instance, there is a family in Kerguz where one son, born in the 1940s, was brought up by his maternal grandparents, in Breton. Two younger children, a son and a daughter, were brought up by their parents, in French. When the children, now all married and salaried elsewhere, come to visit the parents, the latter often switch between Breton and French, according to which child is being addressed. The parents speak Breton and French to each other, and two of the children can change the way they speak also. The children all speak French to each other, but the younger of the two sons, although brought up in French, will often, like his brother, speak in Breton with other peasants when helping out in the fields; the daughter speaks, and is spoken to, in French. When we add to this the fact that changing topics, tone, and jokes can involve swift moves between Breton and French all around, the picture can become quite complicated, to the point that the naïve observer can begin to wonder how all these people understand what is going on and know what to speak next. When I sometimes expressed surprise in Kerguz at all the changes between Breton and French, villagers tended to express their own surprise in response, laughing at the very fact that I should notice such things. 'We don't think about it', was a common comment.

It is worth reminding ourselves at this stage that the parents on a farm near the north coast, where I had pursued a Breton-language course, had found it 'very tiring' to speak only Breton (see Chapter nine, p. 171). What can appear to the observer as demanding and complex socio-linguistic gymnastics can, to the speakers themselves, be quite unreflecting (cf. p. 281), and so, too, what might appear to the external enthusiast to be a straightforward use of one 'language' can be very complicated, confusing and wearing for local speakers. It is perhaps forgiveable to imagine that if, by some means, the supreme militant ideal of a fully Breton-speaking Brittany were realized, then local speakers themselves might be flat out on the ground, in a daze of socio-linguistic confusion and fatigue. It would be expecting too much, either among militants or among locals, to ask that every verbal enunciation be charged with reflection or commitment. Even in the militant world, commitment to speaking Breton is not, and cannot be, a full-time activity, and we have seen in earlier chapters how the movement's vision of a truly 'Breton' world has been incapable of full and autonomous realization, not just because of all manner of popular default or political obstacle, but because it has been structurally so, requiring things 'French' for its definition and appeal.

A teacher of 'real Breton'

Obviously, Breton could not be learnt in Plounéour simply by going around speaking it. Particular circumstances were required, and it was largely through Thérèse in Kerguz that I managed to learn and speak Breton in Plounéour. Learning a language is no innocently technical matter (as we saw in Chapter nine), and the commentary in which the language is embedded, the models and morality invoked, are very much a part of the language-learning process. The paragraphs of this section briefly describe some aspects of this process in Plounéour – a process, I would stress, which was not without its effects for those involved. In particular, the transformation of Breton required, from a medium of communication into an object of contemplation, contributed to an important transformation of Thérèse herself – and we shall come to this a the end of the chapter. It was a transformation in which we find crystallized many of the issues and problems which the whole question of Breton language and culture entails.

Professeur de breton

In Kerguz, Thérèse had sometimes been drawn in to help with informal Breton language classes which militants once held in the house of her neighbours. This had given her new status and glamour, and a way of coping with militant enthusiasms. She had been *professeur de breton* (Fr.), she half-jokingly explained, and after learning that sophisticated people near the coast had spoken to me in Breton (p. 277), she came to take on the status of *professeur* with me at times. This categorization allowed us to have conversations in Breton, about Breton, and to override, much of the time, reflexes to turn to French.

It is a frequent complaint from those Breton-learners of the movement who have managed to speak Breton to the 'people' that the slightest hesitation or quirk in their Breton brings a precious Breton conversation to an end. 'It's not the same Breton' has become a standing joke in the militant world, mimicking a common brushing-off from local Breton-speakers faced with attempts at Breton conversation with them by militants. 'It's not the same Breton' and 'I don't understand them' were, in Plounéour, ways of reasserting local proprieties. There were certainly many instances when militants' Breton (or my Breton) could sound like a foreign language to local speakers, but they could also choose not to understand when they wished. The confusion of local values provoked by a young, educated person speaking Breton meant, in any case, that people sometimes did not understand simply because they were expecting to hear French. Militants can claim that there is a single 'Breton language', and that all forms of Breton are really mutually comprehensible, because they do not, as learners, expect to understand every single word that is said to them, even among themselves. For local Breton-speakers, accustomed to understanding what is said to them, the picture is quite different, and a few words out of place or a different vocabulary from their own can be enough to confirm the conviction of mutual incomprehensibility (and of 'dozens of Bretons', cf. p. 128).

When talking of 'Breton' in Breton, some people in Plounéour used a Bretonized form of the French term, *breton*, but Thérèse would sometimes use the term *(ar) brezh(/z/)oneg*, although this did not imply the singularity of a 'Breton language' as it is perceived in the militant world. When talking of 'French' in Breton, the term *(ar) français* was usual, although a few of those who, like Thérèse, had had their catechism in Breton, would sometimes come out with *(ar) galleg* – the term that militants use, and which, like *brezh(/z/)oneg*, had also been heard from priests. Iffig, Thérèse's son, is of a generation for whom catechism was wholly in French, and he is very shy and has not had the same contact with the militants as his mother. It was, in any case, more fitting for a woman to be involved in the new-fangled discussions I seemed to be pursuing. In conversation about Breton in his home, Iffig would regularly refer me to his mother, although he became used to my interest and queries, and inevitably became involved. He began to speak Breton with me too, but would often blush and correct himself, changing *français* to *galleg*, for instance, and cursing at his inability to get it right first time.

Anyone who, through Thérèse, helped me with Breton was very concerned that I should maintain and learn more of *le bon breton* (Fr. 'good Breton') or *le vrai breton* (Fr. 'real' or 'true Breton'). In a positive sense this seemed to mean using a register of which the terms *brez(h)oneg* and *galleg*, for instance, were a part (but in which other elements were shifting and unclear, for it was not a single register actually used). In a negative and stronger sense, the admonition to use 'good, true Breton' also meant I should use a Breton that was relatively empty of local and, often, individual esoterics, and in which the implications of mimicry would be less pointed. It was bizarre enough that I should want to learn and speak Breton at all, let alone going around trying to do what could seem like skilful impressions. On one occasion, Thérèse felt the need to intervene and explain to other people (some of whom I did not know so well): 'No, but she wants to learn some Breton for her work'. '*Elle fait une thèse*' and '*elle écrit un livre*' became important glosses.

'People would think I'd fallen on my head'

Although there was an ambivalent admiration in Plounéour for some of the Breton vocabulary employed by the militants, the militants' Breton also very clearly supplied the possibilities of a local authenticity for the villagers. Thérèse herself got some amusing mileage out of being *professeur*. A favourite story she recounted to other people in Kerguz was how she had once heard *ar re-se* ('those people') discussing 'testicles' (*ke(/ɛ/)llloù*), when they thought they were having an earnest discussion about 'news' (*ke(/e/)loù*). This story was always heartily received. More mirth was generated by the fact that I (like militants in the movement generally) used the term *kaotigell* for 'jam' – a neologism intended to replace the more common term *konfitur* (Br., cf. *confiture*, Fr.). When I once asked for *kaotigell* on my bread in Thérèse's house at afternoon tea-time (or coffee-time, as it is locally), she and her son nearly choked. Thérèse, her eyes still streaming with tears of merriment, finally advised me to go out in the farm-yard. In Plounéour, *kaotigell* means 'muck' (and things undesirable on bread). No doubt, that one will have passed into the local stock of jokes in which boundaries between insiders and outsiders can be drawn.

There are some clear and amusing mismatches – of which *kaotigell* is but one example – between the semantics of standard Breton and those of local native-speakers. In earlier chapters, I pointed to instances where standard Breton, in its desire for un-Frenchness, is at odds with local semantic values (e.g., *liorzh* and *jardin* in Chapter fourteen, p. 252). There are many more examples of this kind,[2] and of the metaphorical strain placed on Breton by neologistic activity (cf. Chapter twelve, p. 205). In all such instances, the apparently 'French' term (e.g., *jardin*) cannot easily be replaced, as simple synonym or semantic equivalent, by the more obviously Breton term (*liorzh*): they do not mean the same thing. Inevitably, some of the militants' own arguments have been turned back on them in worries within the movement that the *emsav* is actually destroying an idiom it seeks to conserve, that it is impoverishing Breton, or effecting a loss of semantic richness, by excluding even the most obviously 'French' terms (for one published example of militant worries along these lines, see Gourmelon 1976).

The semantic shifts that *emsaverien* expect may be more than the Breton of native-speakers will be able to tolerate, and the aliveness of the metaphors of standard Breton, translated into local semantics (see note 2), can be, and is, used by local speakers to underline that there are different Bretons involved. Thérèse and Iffig in Kerguz, who became most aware of the Breton of militants (either directly, or through me), present cases of native-speakers who could potentially take on the new Breton vocabulary themselves. Some of the oddest Breton that I or militants used could easily be classified as 'good Breton', since it came from well-educated people. Moreover they live, we should remember, in a world of the *Académie Française* (see p. 5), of regulated standard language. In many domains, however, they held a clear division between what they and others would (and could) normally say among themselves and what I and 'those people' might say or require. When Iffig was one day trying to be gravely professorial about it all, he told me that some of the terms the militants used, particularly technical and scientific terms (some of which were not known, or not in local use, in French either), and even words like *c'harr-nij* (meaning, in standard language, 'aeroplane', but in literal translation 'flying-cart' cf. note 2), all had a very 'strange' ring in Breton – but some, he said, also sounded 'fine' or 'posh'. 'Those words are all right for those people', both Thérèse and Iffig explained, but they could not use them themselves. As Iffig then put it: 'People here would think I'd fallen on my head.'

'We don't speak properly here'

There was, among these native-speakers, a growing awareness that their Breton was 'mixed' with French, a fact which 'those people' often discussed. Their daily Breton was not really 'good Breton', Iffig explained, because '*deformet eo toud*' ('it's all deformed'). Even as he said this he realized that both *deformet* and *toud* were like French, and quickly corrected himself: *'mesket eo kentoc'h'* ('it's mixed, rather'). He and other local people, he went on, were always *'transformiñ'* ('transforming') French words into Breton. I could not help smiling at this, and his mother soon saw what I was smiling at. Iffig was perplexed. *'Transformiñ* is French, too!' his mother said. 'What should I say then?' he asked, embarrassed. Thérèse reflected. 'I don't know ... *chenj* perhaps.' 'Okay – *chenj*', he said. Luckily, *chenj* did not immediately raise the spectre of *changer*: 'soon we'll have nothing left to say!'

The use of French terms in Breton has, in Plounéour, its own rules, and these vary contextually, and within different villages and families. However, there were certain areas of Breton vocabulary shared by all in which newly inserted French terms were readily picked out as such (no one speaking Breton, for example, would insert the modern French terms for 'cow' or 'horse', however Bretonized, unless for deliberate effect). Otherwise, differences of convention were noticed particularly in encounters with *Kernev* (p. 292) where, by definition, the people obeyed no rules in their speech, mixing French and Breton freely, and in ignorance.

For some people in Plounéour, the idea of not mixing Breton and French was understood not as avoiding French in Breton, but as a renewed and rational condemnation of Bretonisms or 'bad French'. It was noticeable that some people would move, virtually in the same breath, between heavy 'Bretonisms' (or a common local form of French most obvious among, although not peculiar to, native-speakers of Breton) and a formal, literary French usually picked up at school or from the media (and often used in casual conversation); they sometimes did not, and could not, manage the different registers of French in the way the educated militants could (the latter would move in and out of Bretonisms as they chose). Now there was also the problem for these speakers that they could not quite match the Breton of the militants, and could not always hear (with the ear of a linguist or militant) when their Breton was Breton and when it was French. 'But it's true', Thérèse went on, 'we do mix the two. But that's how we speak. What can you expect? We are not *diplômés* like those people'. Her son agreed: *'Meskiñ a reomp ar brezhoneg hag ar français, quoi ... ar galleg kentoc'h. Gast. On ne parle pas bien ici'.* ('We mix Breton and *français*, like ... *galleg*, rather. Damn (Br.). We don't speak properly here (Fr.)'.)

Translation

The presence of the newcomers might leave some people in Plounéour not only with worries about their Breton, but also with a heightened awareness of their poor French. There are some older peasants in Plounéour who quite clearly had difficulties with French, and who sometimes seemed to be translating from Breton. Those who have obvious problems with French are not in the thick of local social life (cf. Chapter fourteen, p. 252), and readily become the substance of private jokes, one oft-cited case being that of an ageing peasant couple who boasted of having *étoiles* (Fr. 'stars') on their roof: they meant *tuiles* (Fr. 'tiles'). Local authenticity could be constructed on such matters, however: 'those people', I was told, were – quite pointlessly – struggling to put their thoughts into Breton, while 'local people' (*les gens du coin*, Fr.) sometimes had to struggle to put their thoughts into French.

In particular contexts or for particular purposes, some notion of conscious translation from Breton into French can be invoked. The next step now, however, has become a reverse process involving actually translating this French into Breton: a new process created by new enthusiasms. Towards the end of my stay in Kerguz, Thérèse told me she had noticed that she had begun to translate from French into Breton sometimes, particularly to me and some of the militants, since it was clearly Breton that we wanted. Even conversations heard in French which are usually reported in French, were sometimes reported to me in Breton (cf. Chapter eleven, p. 199).

External interest in Breton, and the numerous queries and the commentaries that went with it, had the effect of summoning other instances of translation between Breton and French and of underlining, for local speakers, a 'lack of fit' (cf. Introduction, p. 20) between the two languages. Certain differences between Breton and French which are well known, cherished, and frequently drawn on by militants, raised for local speakers a novelty of translation with very different interpretations of the significance of the mismatches involved. If pressed for explanation or translation, local people will sometimes grammaticalize Breton in the direction of French, and while militants like to exploit any linguistic differences between Breton and French in moral terms favourable to Breton, local people will often do the opposite. A well-known mismatch of colour categories between Breton and French was given different interpretations in this way,[3] and the question of word order offered a similar example of lack of fit which, if brought to local speakers' attention, elicited a very different moral commentary. Whereas, in the militant world, the Breton word order, relative to French, underlined the wonders of Celtic frankness, spontaneity, and naturality (cf. p. 161), for local speakers it conjured up a sense of gruff impoliteness.

'Grammaire'

Through listening to Breton in Plounéour, I learnt several syntactical forms different from those constructed in standard Breton-learning manuals.[4] Learned militants have quarrelled about the errors and artefacts of their respective manuals, and worried about their departure from spoken Breton, but a common conclusion in Plounéour if I explicitly noted these differences between the Breton I had learnt and that which villagers spoke was that 'we make mistakes in Breton'. 'We do not know *la grammaire* for Breton', Thérèse explained. There was some surprise from other people to learn that there was, or could be, a *grammaire* for Breton but Thérèse could attest to its existence in books '*chez ces gens-là*'.

Trying to get people in Plounéour to translate between their own Breton and the full standard forms would often become embarrassing and pointless. For most, the literate register, or the means of matching their own speech to it, were simply not available. Unlike most other local people (including her son), Thérèse could read Breton. Writing Breton was a separate issue,[5] but the fact that Thérèse could read Breton, largely from the catechism, meant that she was able to give me some full realizations of certain local terms and expressions. I often slipped into the kinds of ellipses prized in the militant world, but 'our Breton is *emberret*' (Br. 'shortened'), I was told here, and not the model to copy. 'We make *fautes d'orthographe* when we speak Breton'.

In the Léon

Modern grammars aside, there was an established *pays* or unit of local identity available wherein a model of Breton linguistic propriety could be found. Contrary to all expectations (see Chapter nine, p. 168), I noticed that people in Plounéour did not pronounce the final -*z* in terms such as *menez*. The exception was when they sometimes said the name of their own commune, in full – but in French. (More usually, Plounéour-Ménez, simply *Plounéour* in French, was similarly just *Plounaour* or /plu'nɔ:r/ in Breton.) I, too, began to pronounce *menez* as /'me:ne/, without the final -*z* or /z/. However, I learnt that although this was what was actually said, it 'should really be *menez* ('men:nɛz/). We are in the Léon here, so we should say *menez*'.

The Léon, one element in a taxonomy of *pays* which draws on old diocesan boundaries, also supplies, as we have seen in other chapters, customary boundaries of 'good Breton'. The *Kernev*, by contrast, was a common categorical dustbin for odd Breton. When a militant friend from Rennes once visited me in Kerguz, and villagers heard his Breton (which was a mixture of standard pronunciation and many localisms from here and there), it was concluded that his must be '*Kernev* Breton'. For the militant this was an exciting compliment from the 'people', although it was scarcely intended as such. Plounéour is ambiguously placed, in the mountains and in the Léon, and in limited matters of propriety 'the Léon' as *self*-ascription comes alive.

For Thérèse, self-insertion into the Léon category befitted a *professeur de breton*, and a claim to the Léon could, in her case, be fed by other modes of identification. Although she had grandparents who had originated from Kerguz, she had herself been born in the Léon plain, and had married into the village again. (Women increasingly aspired to marry in the opposite direction, but marrying back into an area in this way had been one common strategy in the consolidation of land.) She could, through this autobiography, claim a non-parochial vision and network beyond the village and beyond Plounéour, and yet also claim to be 'local', as the occasion demanded (for an interesting comment on English village women in this connection, see Strathern 1984). The notion of being 'local' can take its definition, we have seen, in conceptual distinction from 'those people'. There are many other, shifting systems of identification in which the 'local' exists, one of them being the symbolism of kinship and associated village nomenclature.[6] One important aspect of this idiom has been its capacity to situate people according to family and land. ('Dallas' is eagerly watched by many in Plounéour and loved for the muddling of kinship-and-land identities it evokes.) Although linguistic differences may be calqued on kin-and-land boundaries, they are often given expression now in the idiom of diocesan difference which tends to dominate language commentary of this kind. In the linguistic domain, Thérèse entered the diocesan taxonomy and explicitly situated herself 'in the Léon'. Others could contextually choose to do likewise. The categories of this language commentary are not simplistically geographical, but symbolically arbitrary (cf. the 'Celt' and 'English' classifications, Chapter six).

Léon, Kernev, Trégor: moral identity and dialects

The images of linguistic difference in this taxonomy are informed by, and subordinate to, the non-linguistic identities involved and their salience and evocations in everyday life. We have seen how, in matters political and moral, the plain/mountains (often simply '*là-bas*'/'*ici*') divide is important. In those domains in which the diocesan titles are operative, it is the Léon/ *Kernev* duality which is the most common. The French term for the Cornouaille, *La Cornouaille*, often designating an area well on the other side of the Arrée range and running down to the south coast, is less common here than is the Breton term *Kernev*, which is used in both French and Breton conversation and, like the 'mountains', takes its social and moral shape in contra-distinction to the Léon. While Plounéour may take on the 'mountain' definition, it has not traditionally assumed the *Kernev* title for itself; from the Léon and the plain, however it is often placed in the *Kernev*, derogatively and in synonymy with the 'mountains'.

Parish officers of the surrounding dioceses had long talked of a rather arrogant Léon, an image achieved through its clergy, petty nobility, and the wealthier *Julots* (p. 352 n. 2), but a systematic ethnological imagery distinguishing the three diocese of the Léon, Trégor, and Cornouaille (or *Kernev*) seems to have taken on a definitive coherence in the later eighteenth and nineteenth centuries when the Léon and the Cornouaille, in particular, shared out the symbolic halves of certain dualities which themselves came to be systematized into those that commonly deck out, in various forms, the differences and priorities of positivism and romanticism: the rational, serious, dignified Léon of sobriety, sophistication, and thriftiness, for example, and the carefree, festive, warm-hearted Cornouaille of profound emotion, naturalness, and generosity (see, for example, Cambry 1801: 229ff.; Souvestre 1971, 1: 3, 8–10, 20, 34, 44–6, 58, 68). And so on. The systematization and propagation of this common discourse of difference to describe the Léon and Cournouaille have been effected not only through romantic authors and travellers, but also through the press and school textbooks, and these are now common metaphors of expression and interpretation in local plain/ mountains or Léon/mountains or Léon/ *Kernev* ethnology.

We have already seen other versions of this imagery – of order/disorder – in earlier chapters, with each half of the pair representing, in virtue and vice, what the other is not. In social science and social policy in France and in Britain, there has been a general tendency to move from the nation down to the level of the region, minority, or ethnic group, or down to the *pays*, community, or locality, and so on, imagining that, at every stage, one is moving towards a more authentic and natural order of identity and 'roots'. It is important to bear in mind then that the taxonomy of identities available and their boundaries, content, associations, and imagery are symbolically arbitrary, cultural achievements. They are all creations, from nation to small-scale *pays*, and with the increase of literacy, education, and mass communications, they are creations which tend to partake of a common discourse of difference and self-assertion.

Partly encouraged by a modern pursuit of the *pays*, within Brittany as in other parts of France, various systems of *pays* now exist, of which the former diocesan categories are only one set or one taxonomy. Others have been created out of the *bricolage* of different elements at different times, a particular dance defining one *pays*, a particular style of *coiffe* or lace bonnet defining another (see Kuter 1981). In each case, the role of the observer and outside interest has been definitive, and artefacts of this interest and investigation have readily become self-defining groups of people with their own traditions and boundaries. Within any one set, the mode and celebration of one *pays* may well encourage others to step into the same semantic geography, on the same scale (as the *coiffe* of the *pays bigouden*, for example, has encouraged other *coiffe*-conscious *pays* to emerge), but no one set or system is exhaustive of the entire geographical space, and there will always be, when viewed from within any one system, areas of conceptual silence. The Breton language, important in the modern construction of Brittany itself, has given the diocesan taxonomy of *pays* special salience within Brittany. While the Léon generally dominates in matters of language, in others, and within the same imagery of difference the Cournouaille has triumphed. It is the Cornouaille which is the busiest area of costume-consciousness, for example, containing within it many known *pays* defined by their *coiffes*, those bonnets so familiar on post-cards. The story of the *coiffes* (which is generally all that remains of local costumes), of their proliferation in the Cornouaille and their disappearance in the Léon, is one which underlines how external interest and the intervention of mass communications have the capacity to conjure certain identities into existence and lend them confirmation (see McDonald 1984). The lazy, hazy, fun-loving image of the Cornouaille receives regular confirmation from a strong tourist interest and presence, and women in their *coiffes* can buy postcards of themselves. The variously hard-working, tenacious, or clerical Léon, on the other hand, is seen to be confirmed in its stronger tradition of agricultural syndicates (see Berger 1972, 1975). Some of the most violent peasant demonstrations in France, from the 1950s onwards, have occurred in the North of Finistère, in the northernmost strip of the Léon. While such events might serve, within a taxonomy of nations, to confirm a British view of France as a nation of the backward or volatile, in another taxonomy, within France, they serve to confirm an image of archaic resistance to change in the Breton region, and within Brittany, in another taxonomy again, some of these demonstrations have served to confirm those in the Cornouaille and the mountains in their view of the Léon as a bunch of reactionaries, out for money, power, and themselves.

I have already indicated how Plounéour can, within the imagery of mountains/Léon, accrue political and moral virtue to itself (e.g., p. 224, in the domain of politics, and p. 256 in agriculture). Other versions of this commonly heard in Plounéour's self-commentary include: 'We may be poor but we're happy'; 'we know how to have fun – but they're cold and miserable'; and so on. The same symbolic structures attract many from the Léon to drink in Plounéour, and there is much about these encounters which can confirm the image, positive or negative, which each may hold of the other (McDonald 1986c). Plounéour does not play football against the smarter communes of the Léon, since it is ranked in a lower division, but these communes have met in communal games (resembling the televized *Jeux sans Frontières*). At the first such event in Plounéour, a visiting team walked out in anger at poor facilities and organizational incompetence – all typical, in their view, of these '*ploucs du Kernev*' ('*Kernev* bumpkins') or '*ploucs du méné*' ('*méné*' being a deliberate use of the local Breton form for 'mountains'). Plounéour had little doubt that these miserable, proud *Léonards* had really left because they were losing.

In the contexts of such rivalry, or commentary upon them, Breton linguistic differences between the mountains and the Léon may be drawn upon, especially by older peasants in Plounéour, to Plounéour's moral advantage. In the Léon, some words are longer because 'they are as careful and mean with their words as they are with laughter!' Or they are said to use *c'hwi* (Br. cf. French *'vous'*) all the time in the Léon, as opposed to the *te* form common in Plounéour, because the *Léonards* are cold and unfriendly. More commonly, and especially in mixed company or among the women, Breton linguistic differences, when invoked or commented upon at all, are discussed in a framework which places Plounéour in moral *dis*advantage to the Léon ('we *should* use *c'hwi* more here, but they have always been more polite') – or which places Plounéour actually *in* the Léon (cf. p. 288, above), leaving the mountains and *Kernev* alike to recede up the slopes.

Different conventions of Breton/French 'mixing' could be offered as modern illustration of the *Kernev* backwardness of those further up in the mountains (p. 286 above) but a Breton linguistic difference more commonly referred to involved a difference of mutations (see p. 163 on 'mutations'). Putting the commentary in a linguistic's terms, we might say that the *Kernev* was seen to be characterized by mutations of lenition in some instances where, ideally, spirantization prevailed in the Léon. In the terms of the local commentary itself, the *Kernev* was definitely retarded because the people there spoke a Breton that 'children used to speak' (on this, cf. Chapter eleven, note 2). It was also remarked to me that in the *Kernev* they used one word when they meant another (e.g., sometimes using *ober* – meaning only 'to do' in the Léon – when they meant *reiñ*, the Léon and more common word for 'to give'); such an exploitation of linguistic mismatch is familiar enough, and in this instance the *Kernev* was clearly deemed, not wonderfully poetic, but mentally deficient.

An important point to note here is that there were generally extra-linguistic factors (including the sometimes obvious presence of an interested researcher) involved in the elicitation of examples of Breton linguistic difference, and such differences were cited in confirmation of boundaries and differences which were also drawn in other ways. Sometimes it was deemed inappropriate to conjure up, or remark on, any Breton differences at all, since this could imply unintended social divisions or exclusion. In any local evaluations of Léon, Trégor, and *Kernev* Breton, it was generally in that order that their relative merit was ranked. This is also the ranking order of relative advances in agriculture, and sometimes this elision, or explicit cross-reference, was made (any peasant known still to use horses, for instance, was said to be *Kernev* and definitely spoke 'bad Breton'). Linguistic atlases (e.g., Le Roux 1924) do not tell us the social context, proprieties, or implications of the similarities and differences they attempt to plot.

The Léon, Trégor, and *Kernev*, like other *pays*, whether linguistically drawn or not, have their local existence largely in the newspapers and in the conversation and anecdote, often scurrilous and insulting, of daily life (The 'Vannetais' required prompting and explanation, and then became a metaphor of the definitively odd). The use and knowledge of these categories in this area should not be taken to mean knowledge of the large-scale dialect units which, in the world of linguistics, they are commonly assumed to denote. An apparent ability to assess dialectal origin has usually been pre-empted or prejudged, since people would know where a stranger was from before, if ever, speaking Breton to him. The use of the diocesan nomenclature might then appear to be a knowledge of the linguist's dialects. However, these categories are one local idiom for the distribution of moral qualities, in which linguistic illustration may, or may not, figure. There were, in Plounéour, many who had little sympathy, political or moral, for the Léon. When faced with a new, secular interest in Breton, however, they were willing to summon and appropriate the Léon, and place themselves on the side of sophistication and order – against which poor manners, poor speech, and poor morals might, further up in the mountains, be found.

Access and Angleterre

The material I have presented was gained only gradually and over a long period. It could not have been obtained by simply walking into Plounéour and asking questions. Many people were most curious to know what I could possibly find of interest to write about in their commune, and there was some relief when it became apparent that I was not going to focus on the lost grandeur of church buildings. Acceptance was eased when I was seen to take an interest in the schools, in the archives in the town hall, in the commune's political triumphs, and also in the progress of local agriculture.

Talking about agriculture, or helping out with an occasional harvest, is one thing, however – but it was another matter to get into the fields on a regular basis. Acceptance in a rural milieu is not quite the untrammelled celebration that much anthropology might lead one to believe. Acceptance in an urban shop, bar, or factory is easier than acceptance on a farm in Finistère. One cannot simply tug the udders of someone's prize cow, or fall on one's knees and weed the beetroot with the rest of them. Who are you? What are you doing here? Why do you want to help? How can we repay you? Sorry, it's all too embarrassing. Are you sure you're not from so-and-so's farm, snooping to see what we're growing here? Or checking up on our milk maybe? If you're so keen to work on a farm, why don't you go to one of the bigger farms in Pleyber? And so on. Eventually, I found a way in. The key was to accompany someone else, as part of their package in the system of reciprocity, thereby being repaid through them, through the help they received in return. I often accompanied Thérèse, and then, through her, some of her friends who also found in me a novel resource for getting work done and repaid, and, at the same time, a source of entertainment. No one quite knew what I was going to do next. One minute I was cleaning out cow-shit, earnestly talking about so-and-so's cousin's new tractor and how he was sure to ruin himself with such debt, and the next minute I was sporting high heels and a briefcase and was off to an official appointment in Rennes or Quimper, or packing to give a research paper in 'Denmark, did she say?' It was already widely known that I went all the way to Morlaix to buy wholemeal bread. Rumours abounded, until by the end of my stay, I was going to Russia and America for the weekend and could speak ten languages. Thérèse herself thoroughly enjoyed being the closest source of knowledge about *l'Anglaise*, and watching such stories grow.

My knowledge of English was always useful, gaining me increasing hospitality during my stay, and many requests to help out with English teaching. Several people suggested that I should teach English in *Diwan*, which would have made the project more attractive and rational in local eyes, although it would scarcely have helped my standing with *Diwan* teachers and parents, or my position in the movement more widely.

There were certainly aspects of an 'English' identity which helped my acceptance in Plounéour, but it was not without its ambiguities. Very often, my being 'English' would evoke tales of the First or Second World War and admiration of Churchill (especially if there was any whisky available – a drink often called 'Churchill' since the Allies apparently left quantities of it behind them). My presence seemed to go down especially well at meetings or ceremonial gatherings of former Resistants and the *anciens combattants*. Certain topics or contexts could bring forth, however, in a single breath, Mers-el-Kebir and Joan of Arc. One such sore topic was the EEC, and Britain's role in it. The EEC is one area in which several mismatches, political, economic, and demographic, between Britain and France become obvious. 'Agriculture' is not '*agriculture*', although many in Brussels imagine themselves to be talking about the same thing, and when the British think they are talking about the price of milk, the French might perceive the end of France as they know it. To many in Plounéour, the position was clear: the 'English' were responsible for EEC problems and in the wrong from the lamb war to the turkey war to milk quotas. The 'English' were all rich and yet wanted to take everything and give nothing; it was always France that had to make concessions; it was always the 'English' who reaped the benefit. Why should the French support Britain's old Empire? (For they felt that they were subsidizing New Zealand lamb and butter.) Why should they help the reactionary '*farmer*' (Fr.) to get even richer? And so on. When the British wonder why, under the guise of an agricultural policy, they are having to pay for a French social policy or subsidize an inefficient peasantry, the entire metaphoric of an alternative ecological future is being stacked on France's side.

The construction of Great Britain or the United Kingdom in terms o

heir component and related countries posed, in this milieu, similar
roblems of cross-Channel translation. The picture became even more
omplicated if ever I tried to use Breton terms learnt in the militant milieu.
n discussion in Kerguz, and in Plounéour more widely, the terms *Kembre/
Bro Gembre* (Br. 'Wales') and *Iwerzhon/Bro Iwerzhon* (Br. 'Ireland')
vere not understood. Thérèse thought she had heard *Iwerzhon* from the
nilitants: '*Where is it?*' she asked. A more common reaction from others
o such terms was to ask *what* they were ('*Pet'a eo?*' (Br.) and '*Qu'est-ce-
ue c'est que ça alors?*' (Fr.) were typical). *Irlande* (Fr.) many could place,
ut *Pays de Galles* (Fr. 'Wales') was more problematic. The *Prince de
Galles* (Fr. 'Prince of Wales') was one evocation that helped, but villagers
ould not easily tell me what they said for *Pays de Galles* in Breton: 'We
on't talk about it' was the simplest answer. When I explained where the
Pays de Galles was, the reaction was no more promising of a minority,
Celtic identity: '*Mais tout ça c'est l'Angleterre!*' (*Fr. 'But all that is
England!'*) or, in Breton, '*Angleterre eo*' ('It's England'). Thérèse could
ntervene with the more learned *Bro Saoz* (Br. 'England') but even she
vould become impatient with this apparently pointless carving up of
Angleterre into its constituent parts: '*Anglichen toud!*' she once said, with a
ismissive wave of her hand (Br. 'They're all English!'). This was, of
ourse, very much how these people felt about the relationship between
Brittany and France: Brittany was a *pays* within France, and Bretons they
night be, but they were all French. Brittany and France were not of the
ame taxonomy, and they simply matched up the French geo-political
ontext with that of 'England': *la France* and *l'Angleterre* were, there-
ore, similar inclusive categories.

It has been common in France to refer to the whole of Great Britain as
Angleterre; *Grande Bretagne* (Fr. 'Great Britain'), which offers greater
ossibilities of perceiving a link with *Bretagne* (Fr. 'Brittany') has not had
he same currency. It did crop up a few times in Plounéour, partly
rovoked by the 'GB' plates on my car, and often in jokes about pairing up
a *Grande Bretonne* (which was me) with *un petit Breton*. Cross-Channel
nks are perceived, of course, and it was common to hear boasts that 'the
French' had peopled the islands across the water. We progressed on one
occasion to 'the Gauls' having performed this migration, and ultimately to
he Bretons' – thereby satisfying an etymological link between *Bretagne*
nd *la Grande Bretagne*. 'Gauls' and 'Bretons' were interchangeable here,
nd there was one chorus from old school-texts that often emerged from
ocal people, whether in a simple display of erudition, or if pressed by me
or the 'origins' of Brittany: '*Autrefois, la France s'appelait la Gaule, et les
abitants les Gaulois ...*' 'Once upon a time, France was called Gaul, and
he inhabitants Gauls ...').

Plounéour is no isolated community cut off from progress and new ideas,
nd one expression of this came from a man in the bourg (who had been,

professionally, in the armed services) who liked to tell me and others that he had heard or read somewhere that 'there are people who speak Breton in *Angleterre*'. A few conversations on this topic took place with people in the bourg or Le Relecq, most of whom had long since left the land or who had erudition above average in Plounéour, and who could claim educational qualifications of some kind, if only from night-school or home-study ('I'm an *autodidacte*', one such person, a retired electrician, told me, with his very knowledge of this term intended to demonstrate his learning). A special relationship with *Angleterre* (or one of its *pays*) was attractive to many, and these people became increasingly interested in the link between Brittany and Wales, knowledge of which is likely to become a new mark of learning, even if the intervention of other issues (EEC included)[7] may prevent the model taking on the political shape and force it has in the Breton movement.

Breton culture

I found it frustrating at first that people in Plounéour were often far more interested in the curious traditions of England than they were in telling me about themselves and Breton. I had to educate myself out of an impatience I sometimes felt to get to the point or to move on to people who might perform as required. My car was regularly a source of interest, exotically constructed as it was for driving on the left. There was also great interest, if only for the scandal, in the Royal family, and great curiosity about our strange weights and measures (some of which used to exist in Brittany and in other parts of France, but which they have 'lost'); and very much more. I brought some presents from England, and there is little doubt that a number of people invited me to their homes because they knew they would get some exotic 'English' gift in return. Christmas puddings, tea, and whisky were an important part of the process by which 'Breton culture' became available to me in Plounéour, with one identity and exoticism summoning up another, in a mutual exchange which fitted well with the strict local system of reciprocity. I often had cause to reflect that it was perhaps no coincidence that the standard anthropological text on gift exchange had been written by a Frenchman (Mauss 1966).

During my first year in Kerguz, I gave Thérèse a birthday present – some English toiletries of olde-worlde lavender. She had never had a birthday present before, let alone this. The gift sent her scurrying into cupboards to find something to give me immediately in return. She could find nothing *merci*, she said blushing. I was searching for a way to apologize when Thérèse had second thoughts. An old cardboard shoe-box was pulled out of a cupboard, and in it was a small pile of papers. 'Somewhere in here I've got Breton *proverbes*', she said, visibly cheered. 'They are called *trioù-lavar* in Breton, I think, but I'm not sure.' A young student (

militant) who was doing a *maîtrise* thesis had asked her for some Breton proverbs and sayings (he was studying 'oral tradition'). She had hounded her relatives for old copies of *Feiz ha Breiz* (see p. 130) and was planning to learn some off by heart. The exchange was rounded off with a Breton saying that was later to go in her shoe-box; everyone, she said, must have '*un dorn da reiñ hag un all da gomeret*' (Br. 'one hand to give and another to receive').

It was important in Kerguz to visit all *les gens du village* (Fr. a category which excluded 'those people'), and I did so with a spiralling, reciprocal regularity in many cases. In the exchange scheme which thus constructed itself around *l'Anglaise*, I was only permitted to leave out those whom no one else visited much either (these sometimes being, of course, precisely those few people who might unwittingly transgress the boundaries of good manners and come straight out with Breton to me; cf. p. 252). As time wore on, more and more villagers, in Kerguz and elsewhere, were keen to help me with Breton. At one stage, even a special 'Breton-speaking' party was held. One of the peasants' wives invited me to coffee, with other villagers present, mostly women. I could bring my tape-recorder, and they would help me with whatever I wanted to know. All the women tried deliberately to speak only Breton, and Thérèse was there to help out, trying to bring the conversation back into Breton whenever she remembered herself that it was for Breton that we were all assembled. There was some relief when the tape-recorder was turned off, but satisfaction all round that they had all been able to teach me something, and perform as the new sophistication required.

Iffig, Thérèse's son, was more diffident than his mother before a tape-recorder. He had never done as well as his mother at school, he muttered – but he could sing. Thérèse could not ('we had to sing at school, in choirs and by ourselves sometimes, I hated it'). Persuaded to sing one day for the tape, Iffig sang a few French songs, and verses of a Breton song. His mother then helped out from her shoe-box, where she also had some songs from *Feiz ha Breiz* (which she was going to recite for the student, along with the proverbs; he also wanted songs, much to Thérèse's horror). With his mother's prompting, Iffig then sang about a young girl who left the countryside and fell into immoral ways. 'But it's not modern', he said. 'Those people' knew modern Breton songs. A few weeks later, he bought himself a record player and set it up, among the grain and potatoes, in his attic bedroom. He went to a supermarket in Morlaix, bought some records of modern Breton songs, and then played them in his attic, trying to learn them. It was very difficult: he found he could hardly understand them.

It might seem a telling comment on the 'Breton culture' of militants that native Breton-speaking peasant in the mountains of Finistère should have to spend hard-earned money, and shut himself in his attic, in order to try to acquire the culture lived and defended in his name. A good deal was demanded of these people in order to live up to the image expected of them, and they were never quite sure if they were getting it right. Iffig did not even speak French to the cat (and had been startled when his mother had told me that she did: 'You speak French to the cat?!' he had exclaimed, '. . . in God's name!' His mother told him to be quiet). If Iffig could not be properly 'Breton', it was, in his view, because he had not been brought up properly. He had not been educated to know how to do it. 'The best thing', he told me, late on in my stay, 'would be to be brought up in French like those people and then learn Breton.' The culture required of these people did indeed demand an understanding of the world through which it was constructed.

There are people in Plounéour who have struggled to achieve their own liberation, who have worked hard to be educated and qualified (and *autodidacte*) and who cannot now, without great difficulty, recall the Breton of their childhood. They cannot, even if they wanted to, easily summon up Breton to be part of the new sophistication. They would have to learn it all over again, from standard texts. The sophistication of such people has had, and does have, minority glamour and appeal in the local, rural world, but they do not have such glamour in the different context of very well educated 'minority' enthusiasms, and cannot be summoned into the space which these enthusiasms create. No one comes to record their utterances, and their culture is not 'Breton' as it ought to be, It is only because so many people in Brittany have abandoned Breton that the young and the radical have been able to assume 'minority' virtues as they have. At the other end of the scale in Plounéour (and elsewhere in Brittany) there are those who live in poor homes, have poor French, little schooling, and little local appeal, and who simply do not know, and probably never will, that they are now very modern, or anti-modern, or super-modern according to taste. At two extremes, there are those who have abandoned their Breton altogether or those who will be dead before they realize its new value, and the main moral beneficiaries are the militants themselves.

Here, in the uneasily backward parts of Finistère, are some people who stand somewhere in between: who have local esteem and who *could* also act in the new scenario of 'minority' glamour. Those who could do it well, however, and do it with the trappings of peasant simplicity still around them in their homes are few indeed. Thérèse is one person who could do this, and if I have paid her a good deal of attention, it is not simply on the grounds of a proper ethnographic concern with details of daily access and the status of one's data. Following the combined attentions of 'those people' and *l'Anglaise*, she became, for Plounéour, a self-selected typicality and exemplar of the world that external enthusiasms required. Through careful thriftiness, she had never modernized her home, and still has a good deal of the old wooden furniture and also a large open fireplace of a kind now eagerly sought after. In the very simplicity of her surroundings, Thérèse has been suddenly launched into super-modernity, through an urban and educated world. The recommendation that she knew Racine or La Fontaine (p. 274) was gradually displaced; instead, she was said to know Breton well, and to know many Breton proverbs, songs, and stories. Increasing numbers of young Breton enthusiasts were directed to her, gathering material for essays, theses, articles; then journalists from within the movement sought her out when they found themselves employed in the media, with increased hours of Breton on radio and television (due partly to the efforts of the 'Front' (Chapter five) and also to the changes in government after 1981); amateurs' tape-recorders were replaced by professional sound-recording systems, and then by the bright lights of regional television. By the time I took up field-work again in Kerguz, after a few months' break, in 1982, Thérèse had been launched on to a national stage as a television star. She had, within the space of the three years I had known her, followed the evocative path of much of the simplicity of her surroundings, and was now able to contemplate herself, materially unchanged but morally transformed, in an image thrown back on the television screen. The appearance on national television summoned her into a role which, both within the film itself and in commentary upon it, she never fully understood. It was a film which required her to speak Breton, and which relocated her both in the period of the First World War and in a modern world of militant fantasy. For the very first time, a film in and about Breton was shown on national French television (with French subtitles). Thérèse was terrified. She had even been persuaded to sing. The press interviewed her repeatedly, and she was flattered. But she was launched into a discourse over which she had no control. Why did they keep writing that she had never been further from home than a few kilometres in her whole life? Did they not know that she had travelled to Léon markets regularly? And why did a television journalist cut her off when she insisted her father had known good French? What was the film about anyway?

Her appearance in this film (and then in other regional television films) duly won Thérèse some open acclaim in Plounéour ('Here comes our television star!') and numerous invitations to coffee (including at the presbytery). Indeed, many people in Plounéour subsequently began to suggest that they, too, could tell stories and sing, and different traditions of song, from choirs to competitive display to party-pieces and the sing-us-another-one variety, became relocated, as one single tradition of popular song, ready to perform for any willing microphone or camera. But the media attention carried its ambiguities, and muted those who had little comprehension of, or insufficient confidence in, the revaluation process at work (cf. above, Chapter fourteen, pp. 272 ff). Thérèse sensed she was colluding in a media construction of herself which might, in local terms, suggest the very negation of her aspirations. Shifting from showing off her clogs and her Breton into the more obvious dress of her Sunday best made no difference to journalists. '*On dirait une sauvage*', she commented, reading reports of herself. At the same time, she received congratulatory notes from *emsaverien* – people writing in Breton, whom she had never met. She was being summoned into a role which in her own terms she was not performing at all. Thérèse sensed some ripples of tension and incomprehension among other local people, and sensed that she did not have a full grasp on the world in which she and her culture were constructed. '*Je sais parler français quand même!*' she one day cried in embarrassed indignation at the image created of her and which she was powerless to contest.

We have seen, in earlier chapters, how the Breton movement's interest in Breton language and culture has its own momentum and persuasiveness. The movement's focus on the language, and the values within which that language and culture are defined, do not include, other than as aberrations or default, the manners, proprieties, and aspirations of the people whose world the Breton movement would seem to be claiming to defend. We recall that if people do not speak Breton in all contexts this is, in the militant view, because they are oppressed, suffer from alienation, mental blocks, and complexes, and are ashamed of their language. This view is constructed in discursive independence of the world it purports to defend but, at the same time, can find ample confirmation of the alienation, complexes, and shame (etc.) which it sets forth. Since educated people such as those involved in the movement can create around themselves a French-speaking context, this alone might seem to confirm both the disappearance of Breton and the 'shame' attached to Breton by its native-speakers. It is assumed that, were the native-speakers *not* ashamed or complexed in some way, then they would simply carry on in Breton. There is no space in this model for respect of the customary boundaries of which it is demanding transgression, or for the complex system of social proprieties into which are woven, at the popular level, the use of Breton and French. Breton can easily, within this system of proprieties, appear less formal, less posh, less polite, less prestigious, or less sophisticated. It might seem that shame must, therefore, be attached. However, there is a more complicated distribution of moral pluses and minuses here, and if Breton can seem less formal, and so on, then it can also be more friendly and intimate. Such an image of Breton, although the mere obverse of apparent 'shame', is not, we know, difficult for militants to accept. In certain bars, in the fields, and among the men at some mixed gatherings, for example, there might, as I have indicated at various points in these chapters, be contexts in which French is inappropriate. Popular sanctions, tacit or ribald, against the use of French (if only surprise, or a sense that someone was angry, or the expectation of a joke, and so on, which an unexpected use of French might create) might be taken within the militan world to be simple confirmation of the right and natural way for Bretons to behave. When Bretons do *not* speak Breton, they are ashamed (and so on) and when they *do* speak Breton, they are still confirming the militants' views. If it is accepted however, that there may be popular sanctions against French, it has to be accepted that there are also strong contextual sanctions against Breton. The contextual proprieties involved in each case cannot be understood independently; together they form a coherent system of values. The 'shame' which the Breton-learner may personally encounter among Breton-speakers is not quite what it seems. It is not shame of Breton, but shame of Breton in specific social contexts, part of which may be the educated learner himself. When the learner or militant is not there, Breton may again be in lively use and will be without shame. The militant view of Breton identity is one that demands, we have seen, the identification of a people with a particular language and culture. Militants focus on the language. Bretons not only have their language, however, they also have their manners.

To accept the militants' views as a proper description of the popular world would demand that much of what has happened in Plounéour over the last 200 years or more become a distortion of the proper course of history. A point for which ample illustration can be found within these chapters is that the meeting of the values of militants pursuing Breton and of the popular world pursuing French could give the concept of 'shame', in association with Breton, a new whole new career (the case of Jeanne in Kerguz, Chapter fourteen, p. 255, is but one obvious example of this). This would be particularly so for those who have 'forgotten' their Breton, or in some related way been 'negligent' of it (such moral language being common in militant argument). There is already a reality of such 'shame' among some people at the local level when faced with educated Breton enthusiasts. If there is continuity between the aspirations of people in Plounéour and the 'Breton culture' of the well-educated world, it is not in a sudden liberation of a popular 'Breton culture' long hidden beneath layers of historical, ideological accretion, but in an esteem of educated people and ideas, and through aspirations to be educated, not to appear behind the times, not to be backward. That, it could be argued, is what Plounéour has been doing for at least the last 200 years. Part of these aspirations is a capacity to incorporate new ideas from the towns, always held in more or less grudging respect – ideas which are now right next door, and within one's own home, on the radio and television. Inevitably, since the new ideas take no account of local proprieties or the identity structures of everyday life, then they are going to be charged with ambiguities and have the appearance of a certain capriciousness. It is possible for these people in the mountains of Finistère to be part of an educated world, and suddenly bathed in attention, only while the educated enthusiasms and spotlight remain directed their way. When the educated world directs its enthusiasms elsewhere, the peasants will be one step behind yet again. The Breton-speaking peasant can find glamour in a structure of values in which the educated sophisticate plays a definitive role. Shift the focus elsewhere, however, and the space of glamour collapses: the Breton-speaking peasants who cannot speak French well and grasp the loop of enthusiasms in which they are revalued fall back into the wild. The ambiguous position in which the native Breton-speaking peasant of wit is placed accounts for some of the ambivalence with which that position is held. Thérèse echoes, in various ways, the sentiments of a world in which the power and centre of definition have always been elsewhere.

Conclusion

Much of this book has been written in such a way that the points are contained within the material presented, and the chapters can largely be left to bear their own conclusions. These last pages, therefore, offer only a brief recapitulation, and a few valedictory comments. These include an ethnographic update concerning the reactions, within Brittany, to the research on which this book is based.

What has become of Breton in the schools?

We began, in Part one, with a history of Breton in the schools. One of the highlights of the modern end of this story was the 'second modern language option', a status first introduced in 1979. This measure brought confusion, disappointments, quarrels, and much debate in its wake. In this story I did not cover, except by passing reference, the period of Socialist rule after 1981, or renewed right-wing rule after 1986, or the left-right *Ouverture* of 1988. In fact, the only major innovations since the 1979 'second modern language option' were effected under the Socialist government of 1981–6. When in opposition, the Socialists had formulated a bill of law concerning 'the languages and cultures of the peoples of France' (see Chapter twelve, note 5); when the Socialists became the government, this bill became a circular more cautiously entitled 'The teaching of regional languages and cultures' (no. 82–261, June 1982; this document received confirmation and additions in subsequent circulars: especially no. 83–547 of 30 December 1983, and no. 84–047 of 3 December 1984). Through this circular, it became possible to take Breton in a category apart from the 'second modern language option', as a special 'regional language and culture' option (paragraph II,A,2). This move was intended to take away the problem of competition with other modern languages. Breton can now be taken as a 'third modern language option', replacing other options, or it can stay in the 'second modern language' option slot. By 1987, figures established for the regional Academy of Rennes suggested that the overall number of those studying Breton in the schools had increased, and that the 'third modern language' slot had become more popular than that of 'second modern language'. However, the old 'facultative' or 'extra' regime remains by far the most popular still (accounting for about two-thirds of all students studying Breton at the secondary level; see *Académie de Rennes, Rectorat Dossier 3, Langues et Cultures Régionales*, Table II). Posts of full-time Breton teacher have been created, and Rennes University gained, with effect from 1981–2, a full degree in Breton (with 'Celtic' options). Brest University soon followed suit. By 1986, a postgraduate teaching certificate (a certificate known as the 'CAPES' or *Certificat d'Aptitude au Professoriat de l'Enseignement du Second Degré*) had also been granted.

These measures of the 1981–6 Socialist government shared the ambition of a report commissioned early on in the government's term, which talked of making 'historical reparation' to the regions (Giordan 1982). The government circulars which I have mentioned tread carefully, however, on the question of history. We learn that the teaching of a regional language is undoubtedly the teaching of 'regional identity' and the 'consciousness of a culture' in the region, and that going along with this must be some awareness of the 'regional past'. In this regional history, 'the *rattachement* to France will always represent a complex, sensitive but essential period'. Teachers are urged to approach it in a way that will give pupils an awareness of what it means to build a State – 'with the enthusiasms, pain, partisan interests and passions which go along with this process' (circ. no. 83–547, 30 December 83, par. 1). While works of 'regionalist inspiration' may have their place, the teaching of 'regional languages and culture' should emphasize their contribution to 'the richness of the national cultural heritage' (ibid.: par.2). Tensions of this kind beset the Socialists throughout their term in office.

What has happened to the Breton movement?

In Part two of this book, we turned from those in sympathy with the French Republic to those who have sought a distinct Breton identity. The politics of this identity were described, from nineteenth-century Catholic legitimism to twentieth-century left-wing and leftist radicalism. The modern Breton movement has owed much of its self-definition to the protests of 1968 and opposition to a predominantly right-wing Republic. 1981, therefore, with Socialism triumphant within the very bosom of the Fifth Republic, might well have been expected to bring about a sea-change within the heart of the Breton movement. This may yet prove to be one legacy of that decisive Socialist victory (revived by the second victory of 1988). Certainly, without the clarity of opposition that the right-wing Fifth Republic offered, the Breton movement was, to a great extent, left floundering in search of itself. The *Front Culturel* or *Talbenn* (Chapter five) came to a halt, and the fight for Breton in the schools was led, for a while, by heirs to the old right-wing and Catholic movement, invigorated by Socialist opposition. The FLB (Chapter five, p. 79) declared an amnesty, and kept to it for at least three years. One bombing escapade destroyed the war memorial in the commune of Scrignac (once the home of the Abbé Perrot, and the site of *Lunfask* – Chapter seven, p. 133). This bombing, which was said to be in retaliation for local defacement of a memorial to Perrot, generated serious fears within sections of the movement that Breton identity, under a Socialist government, might once more become the property of a right-wing nationalism whose ghosts they thought they had laid. Among the other groups of the movement, *Skol an Emsav* has continued, but stronger break-away groups have periodically threatened to eclipse it. The *gouel ar brezhoneg* celebration (Chapter eight), through want of an audience, ceased for a while, but re-emerged after 1986 with the epithet *broadel* (national) defiantly attached. A dwindling audience has been the more lasting fate of the UDB's grand *Fête* (pp. 150–1). The UDB party survives but has experienced internal divisions putting its continued existence in question. A politically changing France and Brittany's future in Europe, as region or as nation, furnished the main contexts and issues of disagreement. There has been a concerted effort by some UDB members to keep the party left-wing but to distinguish it from the Socialists by claiming a more authentic left-wing politics for the UDB. Others, however, have sought to divorce the left and the Breton cause, and, openly Breton nationalist, have attempted to set up on their own. By the time of the 1986 regional elections – the first direct elections to the Breton Regional Council, when the UDB might have been expected to come out in force – a hastily assembled, compromise group entitled 'Breton convergence' emerged to claim the 'Breton' ticket. No seats were won by any of its candidates.

In many of its enthusiasms and problems, the modern Breton movement has been both creation and casualty of the heady 1960s and 1970s. There is now, among observers of France and within France itself, a certain nostalgia for those times. The student protests of 1986, it was often noted, were very different from 1968. 'Radical politics so pure and so innocent', it has been said, 'can never be revived' (*THES*, 9 January 87: 28). This comment, from a British editorial, summed up a common sentiment on both sides of the Channel, including among members of the Breton movement – for some of whom the events described in the chapters of this book have already become the innocence of their youth.

Since the beginning of the 1980s, many great intellectual figures in France, some of whom gave inspiration and support to minority causes, have died (including, for example, Jean-Paul Sartre, Raymond Aron, Michel Foucault, Roland Barthes, Fernand Braudel, and Jacques Lacan); or they have withdrawn from active life or virtually retired (e.g., Louis Althusser, Claude Lévi-Strauss). The obituary of the French intellectual left has been written and re-written, and a sense of void and lack of direction constructed and examined by, among others, Jean-François Lyotard in his *The Postmodern Condition* (Lyotard 1986). The Breton movement has not escaped the problems of an intellectual world which has lost old securities. The more general demise of the left in France has been part of this disillusionment, with 1960s optimism become 1980s recession and *realpolitik*.

We have seen how an antipathy between regional causes and the political left gave way to confusion in the years immediately after the Second World War, and how, through left-wing opposition, the position was clarified from the late 1950s until 1981. Thereafter, optimism gave way to confusion again, in which no clear alignments have been available. For a while, demands for a degree in Breton and then the CAPES seemed to give occasional oppositional unity and force to the movement in the years after the Socialist takeover. Under the Socialists' right-wing successors (1986–8) and under the Socialists' new government (from 1988), the movement continues to make demands for greater security for Breton in the schools, and for an *aggrégation* for Breton teachers. (This national diploma for top teachers means shorter working hours and more prestige than for those who have only the CAPES.) The demands for these diplomas and continuing demands (partially met, if only in the interests of tourism) for official recognition of Breton generally have not been enough to rekindle, under either a right-wing government or the Socialists' *ouverture* to the right in 1988, a left-wing unity of opposition – uniting both the movement and the left – such as existed previously. It is in such a reunion, however, that some commentators have seen the future of both the political left in France and of regional autonomism (e.g., Keating 1985; Ross and Jenson 1985).

What has happened to *Diwan*?

One cause which has managed, more than any other, to gather and maintain support has been that of *Diwan*. We looked at this venture in Part three. By 1987, *Diwan* claimed to have more than 400 pupils, over a quarter of them at the primary level, in a total of seventeen schools (with two classes), and a secondary school was imminent. However, the continuing existence of the schools had again become precarious. Some funding came from the 1981–6 Socialist government, but the promise of full integration became lost in legal and constitutional discussion, and in ignorance and confusion.[1] The government of Chirac then seemed to reject any idea of integration. The new right-wing government felt that their Socialist predecessors had been 'playing electoral politics' with the regional minorities, and saw no reason why they should foot the bill of Socialist electioneering. Within Brittany, the Breton movement, flagging in every other venture, was re-invigorated by the issue and began careful campaigning. Politicians at several levels, from departmental councils to the regional council to the European Parliament, were lobbied for support, and some was forthcoming. Children's futures were at stake. It was also noted that, in 1984, the Ministry of Education had vetted and approved *Diwan*'s schools. There was apparently no excuse. *Diwan* had by now constructed for itself a 'serious' image, an image which had sent so many militants running in the past, but which now gave the organization a credibility that the earlier venture could not claim. There followed several demonstrations and militant rallies in support of *Diwan*, with some international politicians publicly speaking in *Diwan*'s favour. Emergency finance was offered by the department and region, and the possibility of a *contrat simple* (such as that accorded to private schools) emerged as the most likely possibility of state integration. One important sticking point was the number of hours of French taught at the primary level. *Diwan* had already decided formally to teach the French language, but not to teach any in the first class. (This was felt to be especially important for those children coming to school with little Breton, if any at all.) Only in the top two classes of the primary schools did *Diwan* teach the same number of hours of French as the mainstream schools, and technically fulfil the terms of a *contrat simple*. *Diwan* remained inflexible on its policy and the government on its own terms for handing out a contract. This apparent confirmation of the Republic's 200 years of unmitigated genocide inevitably rallied militants into action again. By April 1988, the contract had been signed.

What has happened in Plounéour?

In Part four of this book, we focused on the commune of Plounéour-Ménez in Finistère. We saw, on the one hand, the local people who pursued French and education and, on the other hand, the educated newcomers who pursued Breton and the oppositional values invested in it. Each group had very different attitudes to the languages and culture of their daily lives, and Part four suggested some of the ways in which each group dealt with the contradictions posed it by the other.

The *Diwan* school at Le Relecq was ultimately forced to close, in 1984, due to municipal opposition and lack of recruitment. Three years later, however, discussions were under way for opening another school – in Morlaix, opened in 1988. In the meantime, changes were occurring within Plounéour itself. In keeping with the wider upheavals of the 1986 elections, three politically 'white' inhabitants were elected, for the first time, to the municipal council. So, too, was one member of the UDB who was voted in on the list of the mayor, to which he had gained entry after it had become clear in the pre-election campaigns that the newcomers were threatening to set up their own collective list in opposition. (One newcomer had actually joined, as part of this threat, the list of the 'whites'.) Since these elections, the mayor and his followers have been faced with an articulate opposition within the council, from people who do not work the land. The municipality eventually began payments to the private school, the *école libre*. In 1987, however, the long fight for the College paid off, and a new building was opened adjacent to the old prefabs. The leader of this fight was the new UDB councillor, and he simultaneously gained some Breton teaching in the College, which his own children and those of other newcomers were by now attending.

The population of Plounéour has begun to increase slightly, and the commune is having to come to terms, as the old agricultural sector within it recedes further, with a changing and sometimes confusing self-image. Urban/rural differences have themselves changed and can no longer be so neatly aligned. Plounéour is becoming self-consciously 'modern' just as the peasant and rural world is morally transformed, as an object of value and contemplation. Education, rural/urban population movements, and media intervention are commonly seen as the factors which destroy minority languages, but they are also the forces which create minority or ethnic identity, as an economic commodity and a persuasive and fashionable option. Distances which, in similar British contexts, might be measured in several generations or 200 years can here be counted in decades or in one or two generations; with car and telephone, these town-village distances can be driven and talked. The traditional world important to the modern construction of minority identity can readily be found. That world is now, with increased media intrusion and tourism, coming into self-conscious existence in inland Brittany.

History, culture, ethnicity, gender, and language

Clearly, there are several issues in this book which are of direct concern to the social sciences and the theory or assumptions with which they work. Such themes or issues would include (among others) history, culture, ethnicity, gender, and language. On the question of *history*, a good deal has already been said (e.g. in the Introduction, Chapters five and six, and Chapter thirteen). On the question of *culture*, it remains to stress that anthropology has often worked with ideas of 'culture' which nationalism – and ethnicity – have constructed. However, 'Breton' takes its meaning or reality within different systems of values, as we have seen, and these systems, which we might call cultural systems, are not neatly coincident with the boundaries that nationalism or ethnicity would construct. Rather than seeking other *a priori* categories of cultural boundary and difference it seems more interesting and fruitful to leave the boundaries of difference to those under study, and to watch them in action. In the process, other related matters of interest present themselves. For example, we have seen how a distinct 'Breton culture' was constructed in the spaces of conceptual opposition, and its character and homogeneity imposed from without. The spaces of conceptual opposition which this culture has inhabited have, in some contexts, distinguished it from material matters of the economy or from the domain of politics. Breton culture shares, in this respect, many of the features and the problems of the notion of 'culture' with which the social sciences have worked. However, material matters of the economy (those touched on here include what peasants produce and how, differences and changes in their relative wealth, or the economic value of bran, cider, and Breton, say, or the tourist industry and where and why it spends its money) are irreducibly conceptual, spilling out of wider structures of cultural evaluation. All the economic aspects I have described, including relative salary levels or gross economic and demographic changes, are inextricably linked with, compounded by, and a part of, other aspects of taste and ambition – areas which, in a more traditional anthropology, some have liked to see as a residual or ephemeral world of the 'symbolic' or 'semantic'. Any division of 'cultural' (or 'symbolic' or 'semantic') matters on the one hand and the politico-economic on the other, a division which is still common within social anthropology as in other social science disciplines, invites versions of the definitional problems which the Breton militants have faced.

Ethnicity is another topic discussed in these chapters – explicitly so in the Introduction and Chapter six – but present, in action, throughout. In the social sciences, the gradual shift which has occurred since the Second World War, and especially since the 1960s, from the biologism and essentialism of 'race' to the issues of definition and self-definition, in time and space, which 'ethnicity' involves, has also meant a move from a category ('race') which could include everyone to a concentration on one half of majority/minority ('ethnic') relations. The majority has long constructed oppositional identities at its frontiers (with the attribution and loss of minority identity becoming, in the nineteenth century, two sides of the same coin: see Chapter six), but the development of 'ethnic' studies has placed increased pressure on the minority to be conscious of its identity in a way that the majority is not required to be (cf. p. 143 on the contextual emptiness of the majority category). In some social psychology, which has become part of the equipment of ethnic or minority movements such as the Breton movement in France, the identity which language and culture represent has become an allegory for individual and collective mental health: human groups are deemed to have one essential identity to the loss or damage of which are attached repression, trauma, alienation, complexes, mental blocks (and so on), and other pathologies to its troubling. The social anthropologist, however, can find little sense in talking of the loss of an identity which, in the absence of popular account, people might not even know they had. We know from ethnographies that individuals and groups are unproblematically involved in multiple identities, constructed through relativities (and most clearly in opposition), and changing according to context (see the ethnographies cited – e.g., Chapter six, p. 108; also Cohen 1985). Ethnicity is one kind of identity, and identity or identification is one aspect of classification. 'Classification' has, in one form or another, been a common topic of study for anthropology, a discipline with a special interest in the way human beings construct the realities in which they live. However, the result has often been a detailed but inert taxonomy set out on the one hand, leaving problems of 'action' or 'social change', or some reified 'power' on the other. In everyday life, we know, however, that there is no such gap between classification and reality. We have seen in these chapters that definition and action, symbolism and reality exist simultaneously in the same apperceptions and events. Power resides in the ability to have one's definitions accepted by others, and I have tried to suggest in this book wherein both the problems and self-limitations and the power and persuasiveness of the militants' world reside.

Just as there has been a move away from talking of 'race' to talk of 'ethnicity', so too there has been, over the same period, a move away from biologistic and essentialist understandings of sex differences towards an understanding of *gender*. The categories 'man' and 'woman' find their meaning within the systems in which they exist. The biological or physiological differences tell us nothing about the varying cultural meanings of those differences, about their possible social significance or interpretations. Moreover (a point sometimes overlooked) the biology and physiology themselves are inevitably cultural. We know that we cannot unearth any rock-bottom or essential reality of the 'Breton' or 'Celt'. Similarly, we cannot get behind the meaning of 'man' or 'woman' in any system in order somehow to get at what men or women are *really* like. I have outlined in this book an important and pervasive system of thought in which an essential and inherent 'masculinity' and 'femininity' have been forged from recensions of the dichotomies of positivism and romanticism (dichotomies which also commonly construct majority/minority relations: see the Introduction, p. 21, and Chapters six and fourteen; also Husband 1982). The 'femininity' so constructed, although common in many parts of Europe and beyond, will always find different meanings in different cultural systems. Within France itself, there would seem to be differences between north and south, for example, with women's domestic power appearing more diffident in the south and with responsibility for familial and social propriety and order largely invested in the men (for commentary on Mediterranean gender constructs, see Herzfeld 1980; see also McDonald 1986c).

Around ideas of 'femininity' have developed common ideas of home, family, mother, and father (see e.g., Coward 1983) – with each of these categories requiring inverted commas, and always finding its meaning according to the system in which it is placed. Although in the area of inland Finistère that I described in Part four, there might seem to be a general trend towards a 'family' structure consisting of the common purse and separate household of a couple and their children, the strong networks of kinship reciprocity in which these units are embedded should themselves make us wary of imagining that there has been any simple shift from an 'extended' to a 'nuclear' family (cf. Ségalen 1984). We cannot posit any general consonance of the development of the nuclear family with increased commercialization and industrialization, and typologies of the 'family' are, in any case, unhelpful (see Flandrin 1979; Laslett 1972). Similarly, with the category 'mother', we need to accept that this will find different meanings in different systems (if it is translatable at all) and that common ideas about home and hearth, households, or domestic units of any kind being built up around biological mothers and their children, and ideas of maternal instinct, love, or daily maternal child-care, cannot be generalized (see e.g., Stack 1974). I have suggested at various points in these chapters (e.g., Chapter four, p. 53, Chapter ten, p. 177, Chapter twelve, p. 207, Chapter fourteen, pp. 243–56) that mother-child relationships as the more educated in France understood them have come relatively recently to the rural agricultural milieu, and the moral imperativeness which informs the 'mother tongue' imagery draws particularly on milieux in which it is the mother who has responsibility for the children. This responsibility has been strongly felt in the agricultural milieu, as part of the new sense of 'femininity', just as feminism, amid its own contradictions, has started to place such responsibilities in question. The 'femininity' I described developed along with commercialization, increased education, wage labour, demographic changes, and changes in urban-rural relations. We cannot say that such developments have had a deleterious effect on the position of women in the rural world described (where there has, in some respects, been an inversion of the 'feminization' of agriculture described for some of these developments elsewhere: see e.g., Lewis 1984), and there has been no 'relegation' of women to the domestic sphere (to use a moral language common to several versions of feminism in both Britain and France) in this world where 'liberation' takes its own meaning. Modern feminism itself developed, as I have suggested, as one aspect of a much larger process of contestation and rethinking which has occurred particularly since the 1960s. Within anthropology, feminism has been one aspect of an important rethinking, strongly influenced by new theories of language and of meaning, which stresses – whether explicitly citing the linguistic analogy or not – the structural arbitrariness of *all* the categories or classifications we use. Given that anthropology has not always seemed able or willing to apply such insights to the category of 'woman' (and associated ideas of 'mother', 'family', and so on), then it is perhaps not surprising that 'feminist' has remained a sometimes strident self-ascription among some (predominantly) women anthropologists. However, it is to be hoped that anthropology is approaching the point where it can confidently declare such inability or omission simply *bad* anthropology. Some feminist scholarship – while it has undoubtedly drawn attention to a few important areas of rethinking and provided its own important compendia of 'goods to think with' – still contains, perhaps through its concentration on 'women', its own apparent inability or unwillingness to extend its insights to other categories which it invokes (including 'class' or the still common 'race') as part of the analysis. Moreover, 'feminism' itself has a history which requires re-examination (rather than simple continuities), always finding its meanings within different systems. I have tried to give some indication in this book of one system of thought in which 'feminism' finds a particular meaning or reality, in consonance with the 'Breton' aspirations of the movement. I am painfully aware that, on femininity and feminism, as on so many related topics, a good deal more could be said here. However, I hope that it is clear enough that if anthropology is able now to integrate ethnographic aspects of itself, then 'feminism' should not – as part of the ethnography rather than as analysis – be invisible.

Finally, *language* has clearly been an important topic in these chapters. The discussion has some bearing on ideas of 'language' in anthropology, both in its nationalist legacy and in more traditional ideas of 'going native'. These chapters have touched on the creation and definition of 'language', on historical linguistics, bilingualism, socio-linguistics, orthography, and dialectology, and suggest, I hope, how an ethnographic approach to such questions might proceed. Throughout this book, there has been discussion of the values invested in language. The values invested in French and those invested in Breton largely determine, for the speakers involved, what French or Breton is. We cannot somehow sweep away these values to get to the language underneath, or get behind the obstacles or the socio-linguistic evaluations to find the language in its true or pristine form and value. The language does not exist external to socio-linguistic structures of the kind I have described. There is no language external to the social context of its evaluation and use. The language *is* the values invested in it or the values woven into it by its speakers. This point is important not only for Brittany, but for an understanding of sensitive language situations elsewhere, and in a consideration of any 'mother tongue' policy.

Much scholarly interest in Breton, both militant and Celtic, is un-doubtedly well intentioned, and there is sincere concern at many levels, from the regional to the international, for the fate of Breton. However, in the Breton context or elsewhere, if we talk of the 'decline', 'corruption', 'impoverishment', or 'death' of a language, then we may seriously mis-represent the social reality of the language-speakers implicated in such metaphors of decay. They might well have imagined themselves to be flourishing. Languages do not 'die'. Rather, people stop speaking them or they simply change the way they speak. It is the linguists and the educated, however, who hold the dominant definitions of what is sophistication and what is deformation, of what is enrichment and what is impoverishment. The militant intellectuals may have to get used to the idea that they are privileged and educated, and get used to the directive moral influence that they exercise, and stop pretending to be peasants or powerless or oppressed.

Persuasion and disgust

I have tried to give some indication in these chapters of the persuasive argument, and the moral tyrannies, of both the French Republicans and the Breton movement. It can take some imaginative effort to conjure up the enduring fear and loathing which 'federalism', 'superstition', counter-revolution' – and 'Breton' – have had the capacity to evoke in the making of the Republic. It is generally very much easier to capture and appropriate the sense and sentiment of militant argument in the Breton movement. Clearly, it would be no solution to the worries of the modern Republic for it to send in the riot troops. The French government, in seeking to oppose minorities in the name of national unity, nurtures the very nightmare it wishes to dispel. Movements such as the Breton movement grow and blossom on opposition. There are still many in the government, however, for whom Breton-language education makes them fear for the future of France, and more than one official has told me with horror of how *Diwan* introduces French in its primary schools 'as a *foreign* language!' One is tempted to respond, in chorus with the militants, that the government asked for it.

The persuasiveness of the militants' arguments is such that it is easy to be won over before you are sure what it is you are arguing about. The entire range of modern thinking can pass through the divides within which their arguments are constructed – heaping every virtue of modern liberal thinking on one side, and all the warts and sores of modernity, capitalism, and imperialism on the other. Opposition easily withers on the tongue. Any attempt to resist the easy grooves of the militants' position, to hold it up and examine it and watch it in action, can readily make the ethno-grapher feel that, with every word, she is saying how disgusting she is. Inevitably, much of the ethnography in this book will seem, in this sense, to be told against myself. Writing an ethnography of well-educated people is not easy. It is not easy because the ethnographer inevitably ends up outlining, as interesting theories that people have of themselves and the world, certain practices, prejudices, and ideas which we, as anthropologists or as members of a post-imperial, self-castigating, intellectual milieu, may share and hold dear.

This book is not in the vein of books and articles generally written on the topic of Celtic minority identity. It would have been simpler, in many ways, to have presented a customary view of Breton and Brittany, beginning with the genocidal enthusiasm of the French Republic and moving on to Plounéour-Ménez, over which would be cast the dying glow of traditionality. Such a presentation would have allowed readers to nestle down comfortably in their seats, and would have allowed us all a cosy virtue. I think it is generally true in anthropology, however, that the greater concern is with the native realities rather than with customary, external perceptions of them. I have tried to follow this bias and, at the same time, to show the complex relationships between the realities involved. It is difficult, however, in the resultant work, to please all the parties involved. Neither of the obvious options of publishing only material which would please everyone concerned, or not publishing at all, would do much to further the cause of human understanding. Certain militants of the movement and individuals in Plounéour have had occasion to discuss or peruse the relevant contents of this text. Between the material to which I had access and the material presented here, a negotiated discretion has been exercised (and the importance of contextual detail simultaneously emphasized). Where Plounéour-Ménez is concerned, I have not tried to disguise the commune by a change of name. People in Plounéour felt cheated by the very thought of any such strategy. Its location has, in any case, been very much a part of the ethnography. Moreover, the commune has already, through an earlier version of this work, been cited in the media and in public discussion.

During 1983, an earlier thesis version of this book came to the attention of the French press, and from that time onwards debate has continued, beginning as passionate discussion in a French newspaper and settling into passing swipes in militant journals by 1987. It is perhaps worth noting that those militants who have been the sharpest and most enduring critics have not actually read the work. A published bibliography of some of the discussion, largely composed of militant attacks and responses thus far, appeared at one stage (see Broudic 1984). The starting point of the whole debate was a French newspaper headline in June 1983, which read, in translation: 'Breton peasantry accepted French with open arms'. The article claimed to offer a summary of my archival findings. The rest of the work was ignored. It was enough, however, to spin the movement into action. Over the next few months, I was redefined by the movement as an outsider. Where I had once been a 'Celt' I was now, inevitably, 'English' once more, and a 'fascist'. I was 'reactionary' and working for figures and bodies as diverse as Thatcher and Marchais, the CIA and the KGB. I was also 'royalist', or, rather *royaliste*, which is insult indeed. My own public debate with the movement seemed to consist much of the time in me restating what I had actually written, and in pointing out that every militant attack, in its structure and the categories used, was predictable and might be seen as confirmation of the authenticity of my work. The Breton movement, for its own part, was caught up in its own autonomous discourse of oppression and tried to use every occasion to make me yet another instance of it. Militants penned articles and voiced opinions likening their own oppression (of which I, along with the Republic, was now a perpetrator) to that of Poland under the Soviets and of the blacks in South Africa. That of the Jews in the Holocaust was not far behind. The debate advanced little. Within the movement, I was appropriated by the metaphorical Gauls, and members of both the UDB and *Skol an Emsav* each sought at one point to use me against the other. From outside the movement came letters from *députés* of the French National Assembly asking for copies of the thesis. At my request, the thesis was made unavailable for reading or loan at the Bodleian, Oxford, where a copy had been deposited. In the meantime, reactions within Plounéour-Ménez were nervous but supportive (see also McDonald 1985 on local reaction). A copy of the thesis had been placed in Plounéour's town hall, but, at the height of the debate, it was gently hinted that perhaps I should remove it, so I did. There were fears that the town hall might go the way of part of the Palace of Versailles. In general, there was a mixture of mischievous amusement and genuine perplexity among inhabitants of Plounéour that things which they had themselves told me, or which I had found in their archives, should have the capacity to generate such a stir. Within Kerguz itself, I was offered the electric fences commonly used around the fields: I could use them, it was suggested, to keep away any threatening characters. For a while, it was woe betide anyone who might try to visit me in the village. Any stranger was one of 'those people', and the whole affair gave a special edge to the assertion of a 'local' identity. Militants were incorporated, for a while, into an insulated discourse of sorcery, and cited as the cause of anything from the breakdown of agricultural machinery to the rebelliousness of sons and daughters. For all I know, I, too, am part of that discourse or might become so with the publication of this book.

This published version appears after much discussion and waiting. With some militants, dialogue has been re-established and they have generously awaited this book as a context in which thinking might be resumed. Certain people who appear often in these pages and now know the contents well, notably Thérèse and her son in Kerguz, have awaited the published text with an eagerness that was only momentarily stayed by the disturbing and confusing vigour of the wider Breton movement's earlier reactions. I should stress that I am fully in support of the movement's ambitions to see Breton learnt and taught. The task which these enthusiasts have set themselves is not easy, and this may have been especially clear in my account of *Diwan*. I hope that all that I have said does not detract from their determination, or the valour of their efforts. The movement has helped to create a new space of glamour that the ordinary Breton-speaker can occupy, and that in itself is laudable. It remains the case, however, that it is the militants who have appropriated the virtues of the Breton-speaking minority, and who dress themselves in its history, and who reap much of the benefit of the modern minority cause. It is they who are at the centre of things, it is they who do the defining, it is their story that the world is inclined to believe, and it is their struggle that the world is likely to applaud.

Appendix

Revolutions and Republics: some dates

1789   'The French Revolution': fall of Bastille; abolition of feudal rights.

1790–: Grégoire launches nation-wide enquiry on the 'idioms of France' (Chapter one).

1792   First Republic declared.

1793: Education laws of *vendemaire* and *brumaire an II* (Chapter one).

1794: Report and law of Barère, Committee of Public Safety (*pluviôse an II*; Chapter one)

Report of Grégoire on his enquiry (*prairial an II*; Chapter one).

Education law of *brumaire an III* (Chapter one).

1799   Consulate: Bonaparte First Consul

1801: The *Concordat*.

1802: Education law: elementary schools the responsibility of communes, and parents contribute (Chapter two).

1804   The First Empire: Napoléon Bonaparte Emperor.

1805: *Académie Celtique* established in Paris (Chapter six).

1808: Organization of the *Université*, to mean all state educational establishments; from this developed the Ministry of Public Instruction, later the Ministry of National Education.

1814   First abdication of Napoléon I; restoration of Louis XVIII.

1815   Waterloo; second abdication of Napoléon; second restoration of Bourbons.

1824   Charles X succeeds Louis XVIII.

1830   Revolution in Paris; abdication of Charles X; accession of Louis-Philippe and the 'Charter'.

1831: Proposal of Montalivet, Minister of Public Instruction, for bilingual schooling in Brittany (Chapter three).

1833: Education law of Guizot (*Loi Guizot*): communes obliged to have boys' school (Chapter two). Guizot was Minister of

Public Instruction from 1832 to 1837; Salvandy took over from 1837 to 1839, and 1845 to 1848.

1836; Ordonnance encouraging girls' schools.

1838: La Villemarqué goes to Wales (Chapter six).

1848   February Revolution; Second Republic proclaimed: Louis Napoléon President.

1850: Education law of Falloux (*Loi Falloux*): more say of clergy in education and religious orders encouraged to open communal schools; ambiguities of articles 13, 28 and 29 concerning Breton (Chapter two); communes to have a girls' school if over 800 inhabitants. Falloux was Minister from 1848 to 1849, and his law was promulgated in March 1850. Falloux himself was royalist and Catholic.

1851   *Coup d'état* by Louis Napoléon.

1852   Second Empire proclaimed; Emperor Napoléon III.

1867: Education law of Duruy: communes obliged to have girls' school if over 500 inhabitants; more help from State to make elementary schooling free.

1870   Franco-Prussian war; Second Empire collapses.

Third Republic proclaimed.

1871: Franco-Prussian Armistice.

1871   Revolutionary Commune in Paris.

1879: Republican victory in Senatorial elections: 'Republican Republic'.

1881 & 1882: Education laws of Jules Ferry: education compulsory, free to all, and *laïque*. No religious education in schools. Clear division of *écoles libres/écoles laïques*.

1881: Finistère Council for Public instruction accepts article 14 of 1880 decree, no translational footnote added (Chapter two).

1887: Educational legislation of Goblet, reiteration of much of Ferry laws; article 14 of 1880 decree becomes article 13 of Goblet law (Chapter two).

1889: Teachers paid by State (as *fonctionnaires* or 'civil servants'). General Inspector Carré visits Brittany (Chapter three).

1901: Law on Associations; closure of many schools run by religious orders.

1902 & 1903: Debates in Senate and Chamber of Deputies regarding closure of religious schools, and French and Breton in the churches (Chapter two).

1914–18   First World War.

1919: Treaty of Versailles.

Breiz Atao founded (Chapter six).

1924–6: *Cartel des Gauches* in power.

1925: *Gwalarn* launched (Chapter six).

1936: Victory of left-wing Popular Front.

1939–45 Second World War.

1940–44: France occupied; Vichy regime.

1944: Liberation; Provisional government (De Gaulle).

1945: Referendum vote to end Third Republic.

1946 Constitution of Fourth Republic accepted by referendum.

1949–50: Debates on Deixonne's law for 'local languages' in the schools; 1951: *Loi Deixonne* (Chapter four).

1946–58: Over twenty changes of 'government' in France, under two Presidents: Auriol (1947–54) and Coty (1954–58); Algerian war breaks out in 1954; De Gaulle recalled in 1958.

1958 Fifth Republic accepted by referendum; De Gaulle elected President.

1968 'May 1968'.

Large victory for government in June elections.

1969: De Gaulle resigns as President, after defeat of referendum on regional reforms. Pompidou elected President.

1972: twenty-two 'regions' of France established as '*établissements publics*'.

1974: Giscard d'Estaing elected President.

1975: Haby Law on education (some mention of regional languages; Chapter four).

1977: A Cultural Charter for Brittany; signed in 1978.

1979: Breton launched as second modern language option in schools (Chapter four).

1981 Mitterrand elected President (May); Socialist victory in legislative elections (June).

1986 Return of right-wing government (under Chirac) but Mitterrand still President.

1988 Return of Socialists. Government of Rocard.

Table 1 Total population, urban and rural, of Brittany and France, 1851–1975 (figures given in thousands)

Year	BRITTANY Population Total	Rural	Urban	% of rural population[a]	FRANCE Total	Population Rural	Urban	% of rural population[a]
1851[1]	2,303	1,916	367	84	35,783	26,648	9,135	74
1856	2,283	1,923	360	83	36,039	26,194	9,845	73
1861[2]	2,327	1,923	404	83	37,386	26,596	10,790	71
1866	2,397	1,973	424	82	38,067	26,472	11,595	70
1872[3]	2,345	1,943	402	83	36,103	24,868	11,235	69
1876	2,406	1,990	416	83	36,906	24,929	11,977	68
1881	2,446	1,985	461	81	37,672	24,575	13,097	65
1886	2,493	2,008	485	81	38,219	24,452	13,767	64
1891	2,517	2,031	486	81	38,343	24,032	14,311	63
1896	2,530	2,006	524	79	38,517	23,491	15,026	61
1901	2,559	2,057	502	80	38,962	23,005	15,957	59
1906	2,592	2,030	562	78	39,252	22,715	16,537	58
1911	2,602	2,007	595	77	39,541	22,096	17,445	56
1921[4]	2,425	1,863	562	77	39,108	21,004	18,104	54
1926	2,411	1,852	559	77	40,581	20,759	19,822	51
1931	2,384	1,805	579	76	41,524	20,413	21,111	49
1936	2,396	1,751	645	73	41,502	19,935	21,567	48
1946	2,337	1,642	695	70	40,503	18,951	21,552	47
1954	2,339	1,559	780	67	42,777	18,830	23,947	44
1962	2,397	1,374	1,023	57	46,520	16,690	29,830	36
1968	2,468	1,189	1,279	48	49,781	14,239	35,542	29
1975	2,595	1,196	1,399	46	52,656	14,252	38,404	27

Source of figures: Daucé and Léon 1978: 29
a as a % of the total population
1 France: 86 *départements*
2 France: 89 *départements*
3 France: 87 *départements*
4 France: 90 *départements*

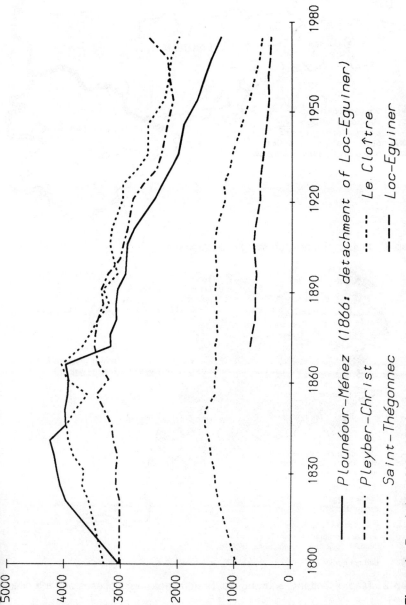

Figure 1 Population 1800–1975 for the canton of Saint-Thégonnec (including Plounéour-Ménez)

Plounéour-Ménez (1866: detachment of Loc-Eguiner)

Pleyber-Christ

Saint-Thégonnec

Le Cloître

Loc-Eguiner

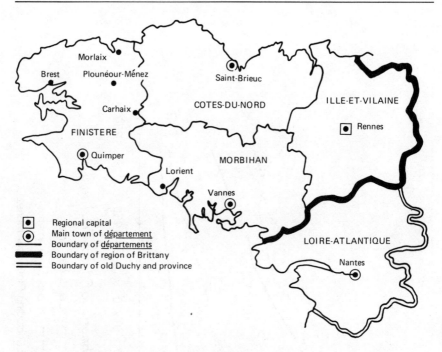

Map 1 Map of Brittany, showing *départements*

Map 2 Map of Brittany, showing old 'Breton-speaking' dioceses and the dialect areas

Meurvor
Atlantel

Inbhir Nis

Bro-Skos
Scotland
Ecosse

ALBA

Glaschu

Dùn-Eideann
(Edinburgh)

Mor an
Hanternoz

Béal Feirste

Iwerzhon
Ireland
Irlande

EIRE

MANNIN

Doolish

Manav
Man
Ile de Man

Baile Átha Cliath
(Dublin)

Corcaigh

Kernev-Veur
Cornwall
Cornouailles

Abertawe

CYMRU
Wales
Pays de Galles

Kembre

Caerdydd
(Cardiff)

KERNOW

Truro

Mor Keltiek

Mor Breizh

Brest

Roazhon (Rennes)

An Oriant

BREIZH

Brittany
Bretagne

Naoned
(Nantes)

BROIOÙ KELTIEK
CELTIC COUNTRIES
PAYS CELTIQUES

Versions of the above map are common in Inter-Celtic conferences
and congresses and in Celtic literature. This example dates from the
mid-1970s.

Map 3 Map of the 'Celtic countries'

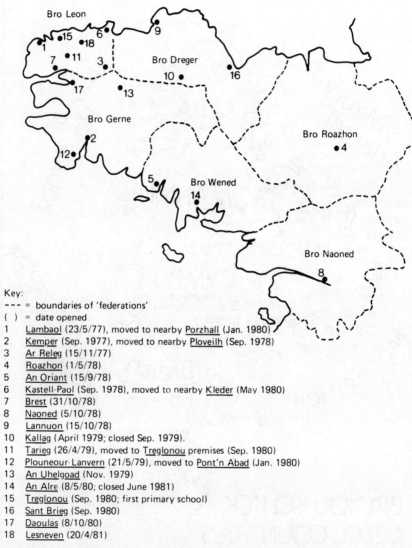

Key:
- - - = boundaries of 'federations'
( ) = date opened
1 Lambaol (23/5/77), moved to nearby Porzhall (Jan. 1980)
2 Kemper (Sep. 1977), moved to nearby Ploveilh (Sep. 1978)
3 Ar Releg (15/11/77)
4 Roazhon (1/5/78)
5 An Oriant (15/9/78)
6 Kastell-Paol (Sep. 1978), moved to nearby Kleder (May 1980)
7 Brest (31/10/78)
8 Naoned (5/10/78)
9 Lannuon (15/10/78)
10 Kallag (April 1979; closed Sep. 1979).
11 Tarieg (26/4/79), moved to Treglonou premises (Sep. 1980)
12 Plouneour-Lanvern (21/5/79), moved to Pont'n Abad (Jan. 1980)
13 An Uhelgoad (Nov. 1979)
14 An Alre (8/5/80; closed June 1981)
15 Treglonou (Sep. 1980; first primary school)
16 Sant Brieg (Sep. 1980)
17 Daoulas (8/10/80)
18 Lesneven (20/4/81)

All localities are given their Breton names here; in French, the names would
be as follows: 1. Lampaul/Portsall. 2. Quimper/Plomelin. 3. Le Relecq. 4. Rennes.
5. Lorient. 6. Saint-Pol-de-Léon/Cléder. 7. Brest. 8. Nantes. 9. Lannion.
10. Callac. 11. Tariec/Tréglonou. 12. Plounéour-Lanvern/Pont-l'Abbé. 13. Huelgoat.
14. Auray. 15. Tréglonou. 16. Saint-Brieuc. 17. Daoulas. 18. Lesneven.
Note: Bro Gerne (the Cornouaille) was sometimes written in Diwan's literature
as Bro Kerne, without the mutation; and Kerne was occasionally given the final,
mute -y of the 'ZH' (optional in the O.U.), or -w of the 'Interdialectal'.
Gwened after Bro can mutate to Wened, hence Bro Wened, the usual form employed
in Diwan.

Map 4 Map of Brittany, showing *Diwan* schools, 1977–81

KEY:-
—·—·—·— Boundary of département
————————— Boundary of arrondissement
□ Main town of arrondissement
○ Main town/bourg of canton
● Commune (site of bourg)
===== Boundary of canton of Saint-Theǵonnec (with the boundaries of its 5 communes also marked).

⠐⠂⠄ Geographical relief area of Monts d'Arrée range
(minimum altitude 220 metres)

ap 5 Map of Finistère, showing the canton of Saint-Thégonnec

325

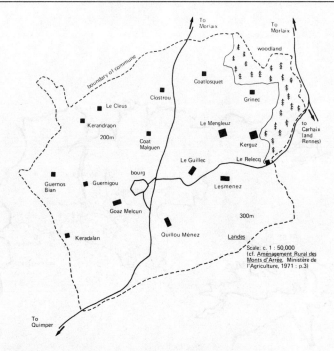

Map 6 Map of the commune of Plounéour-Ménez

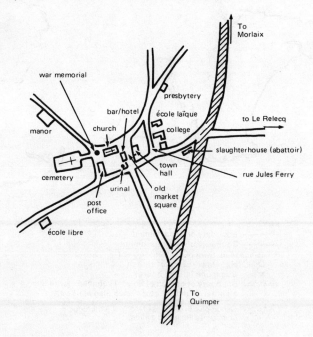

Map 7 Diagram of the bourg of Plounéour Ménez

The *symbole* on sale, 1980s

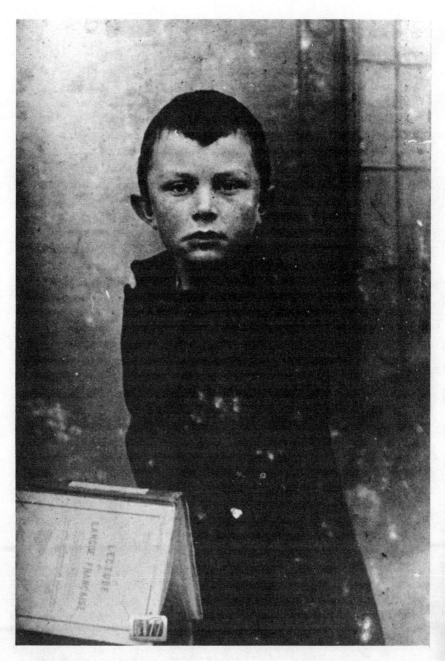

A pupil of the Le Relecq *école laïque* (Plounéour-Ménez), 1940s

Notes

General note

Unless otherwise qualified by the context of my discussion, I have generally used the 'ZH' orthography of 1941 when writing Breton words in the text in their fullest, literary forms. The convention 'ZH' is used to denote the name of the 1941 orthography; *zh* denotes the orthographic sign from which the orthography has gained its name.

Introduction

1 'Urban' and 'rural' populations have been distinguished in the French census by counting as 'urban' every commune with 2,000 inhabitants or more at its centre (see INSEE 1973:14). By comparison with the UK this has seemed a low figure by which to classify a population as 'urban' (see J. & M. Lough 1978:13). Some of these general politico-demographic differences were suggested in a preliminary seminar paper given by Malcolm Chapman in Oxford in late 1980, and their implications given attention in McDonald 1982 and Chapman and McDonald 1982.
2 The 1972 region, and the 1982 one which consolidated it, have been contentious in some circles because of the delimited area of historical Brittany they have covered. The Breton region is composed of four *départements*: Ille-et-Vilaine, the Morbihan, the Côtes-du-Nord, and, on the western tip, Finistère. Many would claim that Brittany should have a fifth *département*, the Loire-Atlantique, which is currently part of another region, the 'Pays de la Loire'. The Loire-Atlantique has been represented in the Cultural Council of Brittany, but otherwise had never formed part of an official region of 'Brittany' in earlier regional plans, and has long developed its own commercial and industrial links elsewhere (see Pléven 1961).

Part one

Chapter one

1 The laws cited here can be found in Gréard (1873) 1891–1902 (2nd edition). Where Gréard's compilation of French educational legislation does not include laws I cite, other references are given in the text.
2 *Dictionnaire et colloque françois et breton, traduits du françois en breton par*

G. Quiquer de Roscoff; cited in Ogès 1937:28. This *colloque* may have been an adaptation, into a Breton context, of a Flemish model of the sixteenth century; polyglot works of this kind were common at the time. A summary discussion of these '*colloques*' can be found in Le Goaziou 1950.

3 During the period of the Revolution, and on into the nineteenth century, visitors commonly reported that this was a situation that the clergy deliberately sought to maintain in some areas. In 1815, for example, a visitor to Finistère was told that the clergy were trying to impede the spread of French 'in order to keep their flock from the contagion of Enlightenment ideas and to keep them in an enduring state of vassaldom' (B. de la Pilae (1850) *Etudes archéologiques et géographiques*; cited in Ogès 1945–6:81). Similar sentiments about the injustice of a peasantry dependent on intermediaries had come from several local republicans in the 1790s (e.g., the would-be teacher cited in note 7 below).

4 The *domaine congéable* is one example. Many Bretons had explicitly asked for the abolition of this 'unjust' system of land tenure in their *Cahiers de Doléances* of 1789, but it was a regime which managed to persist in parts of the Breton countryside well into the nineteenth century, in spite of the fact that the Revolution had passed a law against it in 1792. The *domaine congéable* was peculiar to parts of Brittany. The *domainier* (or tenant) owned the buildings and all on the surface, and the land itself was owned by a *seigneur*, or wealthy bourgeois. The *domainier* was reluctant to invest in the amelioration of his own living conditions, or to improve his farm, since he could be *congédié* (or evicted) at any time. This helped to constrain agricultural development in Brittany over a long period (see Ogès 1949:34).

5 Grégoire: *Rapport sur la nécessité et les moyens d'anéantir les patois et d'universaliser l'usage de la langue française: 16 prairial an II*, in Gazier 1969: 292. In the text, these *patois* are given as follows: 'le bas breton, le normand, le picard, le rouchi ou wallon, le flamand, le champenois, le messin, le lorrain, le franc-comtois, le bourguignon, le bressan, le lyonnais, le dauphinois, l'auvergnat, le poitevin, le limousin, le picard, le provençal, le languedocien, le velayen, le catalan, le béarnais, le basque, le rouergat et le gascon . . . '. Grégoire talked of thirty *patois*, but twenty-five are listed here, with 'le picard' given twice.

It is significant that this text was published at the beginning of the Third Republic, and then again, with different significance, in the late 1960s (for which see Chapter four and, especially, Chapter five).

6 The seven-day week, seen as a religious institution, had been replaced by the ten-day period of the *décadi*. The new metric system was also much in prominence in the educational programmes of the Revolution.

7 These letters can be found in ADF: 8L 105. The bilingual letter is from a Jean Nédélec, written *16 pluviôse*. It seems he did get a post, without trouble, in Finistère. In his letter, he emphasizes his 'patriotism' and his hatred of the clergy, of 'prejudices', and of 'fanaticism'. The Breton would appear to be a translation of the French for the most part, and would suggest that, in such domains at least, the author was more at home in French than in Breton (although he emphasizes that he has spoken Breton since childhood). It is interesting, too, that *La Republique* in the French remains *a(sic) republic* in the Breton (and *la raison* is *raison*, and so on). There are times, however, when he has obviously either found direct translation difficult or is expressing a sentiment commonly and easily said in Breton in another way; instead of word-for-word equivalence, he has sometimes opted for a different phraseology. For example, the letter opens with the statement, in French: '*Les français vont enfin jouir des bienfaits d'une éducation Republicaine*' ('Frenchmen are at last going to enjoy the benefits of Republican education'); in the Breton version – set out on the same page, like

parallel text – this sentence reads: '*Ar-francisien a zo vont erfin da jouissa eus an deskadurez convenabl da eur Bobl libr*' ('Frenchmen are at last going to enjoy an education befitting a free people'). In general, the influence of French on the Breton vocabulary is manifest throughout, and not simply in the new political terminology.

Chapter two

1 At the beginning of the Empire, about half the mayors of Finistère were deemed to be illiterate: see Ogès 1945–6:33.
2 Cited in Decap *et al.* 1914:138; this explanation came from the Morbihan, but is not untypical of other areas where Breton predominated as the daily language. Some of these statements were, in fact, replies to a national enquiry into the local school situation, launched *21 floréal an XI* (11 May 1803). We note that, during the summer months, when agricultural work demanded a greater labour force, many children did not go to school. This situation lasted, in some areas, into the twentieth century, even though schooling was by then free and compulsory.
3 This figure is cited in Weber 1977: 499. Finistère was composed of 284 communes by 1863, and had a total of 534 schools. It is a matter of interest that while twelve of the communes were, in an official report of the time, classified as 'French-speaking' and the remaining 272 as those where Breton predominated, only thirty-three schools wholly in Breton were known to exist. The total population was estimated at 627,304, and the total population in school (7–13 years) at 72,112; of this latter number, 23,814 were considered able to speak French, and another 18,615 able both to speak and to write it (ibid.).
4 The text gave only *éléments de la langue française* in a list that otherwise included 'moral and religious instruction, reading, writing . . . arithmetic, the legal system of weights and measures . . .' (art. 1).
5 *Circulaire du Ministre de l'Instruction publique, relative aux élèves des Ecoles primaires qui parlent un idiome local* (Signed: Salvandy), 25 October 1838. In 1829, a Breton member of the national *Société pour L'Instruction élémentaire* based in Paris had already affirmed that translation was the best method, and indicated that translation had been the dominant method in Finistère schools for some time (see Ogès 1931:136–43). He also reported that a local teacher, who used this method, was pleased to see its effectiveness in teaching French and that this meant, for the teacher, that at last Bretons were no longer cut off from the rest of France (ibid.).
6 Correspondence on this issue, between diocesan and secular education authorities, and the Prefects, can be found in ADF:T:1:79.
7 The *Loi Falloux* dates from 15 May 1850; a '*modèle de règlement*', dated 17 August 1851, was then sent out to all *départements*, containing the outline of the school programmes. The *Conseil Académique* of Finistère discussed this text on 7 October 1852, the law requiring these departmental councils of education to give their views and make any necessary amendments. The bishop was in the council and a priest took part in the special commission that the council delegated for the discussion of the text. The text, amended in minor detail only (including the Breton clause, and the insertion of religious holidays), was then returned to Paris, where it was ratified by the Ministry of Public Instruction on 23 March 1852. The relevant texts can be found in *BAIP* 1851:2:20:367–75; and ADF:CAF:1852.
8 Letter from the Inspectorate of Brest to the Academic Inspection of Finistère

(Quimper), 3 September 1863, in ADF:T:1:79 (no. 847, Brest reference). This letter also suggested that perhaps priests could be persuaded to give religious instruction in the churches in French, and then it could also be introduced in French in the schools.

9 Letter from the Inspectorate of Morlaix and Quimper *circonscriptions* to the Academic Inspection of Finistère (Quimper), 31 October 1863, in ADF:T:1:79 (no. 1755, archive reference).

10 See: Letter from the Prefect of Finistère to the Ministry of Public Instruction (marked 'Confidential'), regarding the commune of Ergué-Armel, February 1877; in ADF:T:1:79 (1877 file).

11 See letter from Anselme, Bishop of Quimper and Léon, to the Prefect of Finistère, 9 March 1877; in ADF:T:1:79 (1877 file).

12 These were principally the laws of 16 June 1881 (education was to be free to all), and 28 March 1882 (schooling was made compulsory and *laïque* or secular and 'neutral'); a law of 19 July 1889 accorded a state salary to teachers. Once again, moreover, the ecclesiastics were barred from the public schools altogether.

13 The national regulation was an *arrêté* of 7 June 1880: *Règlement scolaire modèle pour servir à la rédaction des règlements départementaux aux écoles primaires publiques* (Signed: Jules Ferry, *Ministre de l'Instruction Publique et des Beaux Arts*); see *BOSIP* 1880, no. 42:643–6. The language ruling involves article 14 of this *règlement*. The Finistère 'Departmental Council for Public Instruction' adopted this ruling on 1 April 1881 (with article 14 unamended). See: *BOSIP* 1881, no. 45:750–3. An account of the general philosophical and political background to the Ferry laws can be found in Singer 1971.

14 The national regulation (*Règlement scolaire modèle ...*) dates from 18 January 1887; the Finistère 'Departmental Council for Primary Instruction' adopted this (as *Règlement spécial des écoles publiques de garçons, de filles et mixtes du Finistère*) on 23 April 1887. It was ratified in Paris on 5 April 1888. See: *BPIIF* 1888, no. 17:44–9.

15 In the 1890s, for example, the 1887 ruling seems to have been a source of flexibility, but then its 'article 13' was cited, alone and unqualified, as late as 1936, by the Minister of Education himself, when asked for clarification by a right-wing Breton politician (see Rees 1939:206). The Popular Front Government of the 1930s had its own battles to fight.

16 The full debate, from which I am quoting here, can be found in *JO, Sénat: débats*: 31 October 1902, pp. 1069–1088.

17 Combes followed this point by noting that enquiries undertaken, separately, by government and church authorities, concerning the numbers of children able to understand catechism in French, did not tally, and that the church figures were insidiously and deliberately lower than they might be. According to the statistics of the Bishop of Quimper, said Combes, there were 110 communes (which is, in fact, well under half) in Finistère where French catechism could not be understood. According to the Prefect, however, 80 per cent of children in Finistère's schools were deemed able to follow catechism in French. The diocesan figures often relied on the estimates of local priests, and the Prefect's figures took much from local Inspectors and teachers in the schools. All the citations from this 1903 debate can be found in the full text published in: *JO, Chambre: débats* (16 January 1903), 1903, 1:24–34. The figures can be found on p. 29.

18 De Monzie, A. *Circulaire du 14 août 1925 relative aux idiomes locaux*; in *JO*, 1 September 1925:207–10; the last quotation can be found on p. 210.

19 On these points, see Ogès 1934:134;56; Taldir 1935, and, for earlier periods, Ogès 1937, and Albistur and Armogathe 1977, I.

20 Ferry had spoken in 1870 of women's 'secret and persistent support' for the *ancien régime*, of which he was determined to rid France for ever. He went on:

> The Bishops know full well that he who holds sway over the women holds all because he has influence firstly over the children and secondly over the husbands ... That's why the Church wants to hold on to the women [but] democracy has to choose on pain of death: either the women belong to science or they belong to the Church.
>
> (Cited in Prost 1968:268–9)

A further discussion of women and education in Brittany is offered in McDonald 1986b, and in Chapter fourteen below.

21 The population of Finistère, living off small parcelled plots of land in most instances, fell by 8 per cent from 1911 to 1931; the higher rate of births over deaths was absorbed and overtaken by emigration. Thereafter, the Finistère population showed no more striking decrease, in spite of a falling birth-rate, but this was primarily due to the (related) attraction of the coastal areas, and increased activity there in all sectors (on this general point, see Ariès 1948).

22 See *La Semaine Religieuse du diocèse de Quimper et de Léon*, January 1930:141–2 (Circular of 24 January 1930).

23 See *La Semaine Religieuse du diocèse de Quimper et de Léon*, 13 December 1935 no. 50:819–21 (Circular of 3 December 1935).

Chapter three

1 The results of this enquiry can be found in ADF:1.N:192. The categories of the enquiry are unclear, however, and some of the figures are contradictory. The figure of 50 per cent, I would stress, is only a rough calculation which I have myself estimated from the manuscripts available, and with a heavy reliance on a category entitled *'ne parlant que le breton'*. The figures of this latter category do not always correlate with another category entitled *'parlant français'*. The figure of 50 per cent does not seem unlikely, however, as an indication of the minimum proportion of Breton monolinguals for the rural areas at this time. Another official enquiry, in 1864, carried out mostly by school inspectors, suggested a figure nearer 80 per cent in Finistère *'ne parlant pas français'* (see Certeau *et al.* 1975:270–1). The standards demanded by inspectors (in order to classify people as 'French-speaking') may well have been higher than those of the people themselves. The 1831 figures were supplied by local municipalities. In some instances they seem to have wanted both to urge more education (hence a high percentage *'ne parlant que le breton'*) and also to boast some local progress (hence a significant number *'parlant français'*); these two categories sometimes overlap, or add up to more, or to less, than the overall population of the commune, small children excluded. There are obvious variations and contextual subtleties involved in any definition of who speaks what.

2 Montalivet proposed that the first two years of schooling for all the Breton-speaking areas should run as follows: in the first year, the children would be taught through Breton, using one of the four established dialects, according to area, and learning from abridged versions of elementary texts translated into Breton; in the second year, they would begin to look at the other dialects of Breton, compare them, and effectively bring them closer together. After this, they would begin to learn French (using grammars written in Breton) and to

learn to read French from unabridged textbooks in use elsewhere (including, incidentally, the catechism). It was hoped that pupils taught in this way would later be able to go out and teach in other areas, using the same programme, for other Breton-speakers. Source: Circular from the Minister of Public Instruction to the Prefects of the Côtes-du-Nord, Finistère and Morbihan, dated 15 October 1831; see ADF:T:I:79 (no. 1054, administrative reference). Some account of this project, and the responses, can be found also in Bernard 1917.

3 See Bernard 1917:4. The full text of the Committee's report can be found in a communication from the Prefect of Finistère to the Minister of Public Instruction (1831): ADF:T:I:79; there is also a covering note from the Prefect, attached, in the same file.

4 The Prefect of the Morbihan replied to the Prefect of Finistère, stating the views I summarize here, on 26 October 1831; see ADF:T:I:79, and Bernard 1917: 5–7.

5 The reply of the Côtes-du-Nord Prefect to the Minister is cited, briefly, to this effect in Bernard 1917:9. The letter from the Prefect of the Morbihan to the Minister can be found in ADF:T:I:79, and is cited in Bernard 1917:8.

6 Dufilhol's report can be found in ADF:IT:27 (*Fonds de l'Inspection Académique; Rapports des Inspecteurs*): 1833, *arrondissement de Brest*.

7 There are indications that some form of the *symbole* originated in church-run or private establishments, and may have been inherited from a similar Jesuit device used, before the 1789 Revolution, to encourage the use of Latin in the colleges (see Guieysse 1936; Weber 1977:315).

8 See Letter from the Primary Inspector (Quimper and Morlaix) to the Academic Inspection (Quimper), 31 October 1863; no. 1755 (archival reference), ADF:T:I:79.

9 For a general discussion of the development of the category of 'childhood', and some of its changing perceptions in France, see Ariès (1960) 1979; Crubellier 1979; and, on more specific points, Weber 1977:62, 171, 173, 175.

10 A full outline of Carré's detailed instructions and suggestions can be found in Carré 1888:222–36; Boucheron and Nonus 1890:39ff.

11 The correspondence concerning Carré's method and its effectiveness can be found in *BOSIP* 1893:105 and in the pages of *BPIIF*, in 1896 especially (see Cariou 1896; Le Bris 1896; Mme 'X' 1896; Mercier 1896; also Canévet *et al.* 1899).

12 This was said in reply to a query from the right-wing Breton politician, Inizan; a few right-wingers who were particularly keen on the use of Breton in Brittany at the time took this as meaning that the use of Breton was therefore clearly permitted (see Le Berre 1935:33).

13 It is interesting that one very small group of Breton enthusiasts of the 1930s, who were supporters of *laïcité*, agreed with the government on the harm that Breton might do to French in this way, although they were also keen to see Breton in the schools (see *Ar Falz* 1935 (December):314). Earlier, Dosimont (1897), and Breton teachers' correspondence towards the end of the nineteenth century, had clearly expressed the dominant view that any Breton, even a Breton accent, was doing harm to the clarity of French (e.g., Le Bris 1896). The equation of French linguistic purity with clarity of ideas and ideals was, by then well established. In the 1902 debate in the Senate, a Republican had suggested that perhaps there was no confusion of nationality involved in the use of Breton unlike, he said, in the Flemish case (Delobeau, in *JO, Sénat: débats*, 31 Octobre 1902:1077). This was swiftly taken up by the right-wing Breton, Lamy, in the 1903 debate in the Chamber, and thus became a right-wing argument in a debate specifically about Breton. In this same debate, De l'Estourbeillon also

pleaded for Breton in the schools, saying that France was now allowing some use of local languages in the schools of (French) India, Madagascar, and the Congo, so 'why', he asked, 'inflict on 1,500,000 good Frenchmen a treatment of pariahs from which the lowest savages of our colonies are kept immune ...?' (Lamy, in *JO, Chambre: débats* (16 January 1903) 1903:1:26,33). In 1925, De Monzie declared that: 'when we are making an effort to give to all the children of France the same, clear and well-defined language, in which words and sentences translate, without ambiguity or uncertainty, the ideas or sentiments of each, would it not be self-contradictory to give dialectal words and expressions the possibility and temptation of coming into the French of our schools?' (De Monzie 1925:208). He repeated the views of Carré, and added that the situation in Belgium would not encourage any bilingual policy in France, anyway: he had no desire to encourage any nascent *'flamingantisme'* which was never without its dangers, for, he said, 'France, unified as she might be, can never be too much so' (ibid.:209).

14 See, for example, *Ar Falz* 1935 (December):314; and citation of Desgranges in *Ar Falz* 1939 (July):6–7; also *Voeu du Conseil Général du Finistère*: 20 September 1923 (in ADF:T:1:79); the Prefect of Finistère, Collignon, had earlier, in 1905, also urged the use of both languages for this reason (see *Ar Falz* 1939 (July):9); also Guieysse 1925:23.

15 Such views had generally come from the pro-clerical right wing, however: for example, from those arguing for Breton in the 1902 and 1903 debates in the Chamber and Senate, referred to above in Chapter two (see Chapter two, note 16). They became more explicit in a report produced for the Chamber by M. le Chanoine Desgranges in 1937, which reiterated the propositions contained in a 1936 bill of law put forward by the right-wing Breton Trémintin (see *Ar Falz* 1937 (July):3; 1939 (July):8). The *Commission de l'Enseignement et des Beaux Arts* unanimously converted it from a *proposition de loi* into a *proposition de résolution* on 30 June 1937, and asked the government to study the question (see *Ar Falz* 1948 (September):3). The same bill had also asked for some study of Breton in the *Ecoles Primaires Supérieures*, the *Lycées*, the Colleges, and the *Ecoles Normales* (or teacher-training colleges), and had also asked for an examination in Breton, as second language, at the *baccalauréat* level.

16 See, for example, Desgranges in 1937, in *Ar Falz* 1937 (July), and 1939 (July); and, earlier, *Rapport du Comité de Préservation du Breton*, 1903:24, 28 (published Saint-Brieuc: Prud'homme).

Chapter four

1 These include, in their French versions: *Déclaration Universelle des Droits de l'Homme* (UN 10 December 1948; especially articles 2, 7, 22, 26, 27, 29); *Convention Européenne de Sauvegarde des Droits de l'Homme et des Libertés fondamentales* (4 November 1950; ratified 1973; art. 14); *Convention de l'UNESCO, concernant la lutte contre la discrimination dans le domaine de l'enseignement* (14 December 1960; arts. 1, 2, 5); *Convention Internationale sur l'élimination de toutes les formes de discrimination raciale* (or relating to national or ethnic origin: 21 December 1965; art. 1); *Pacte International relatif aux droits civils et politiques* (UN 16 December 1966; arts. 1, 2, 13); *Déclaration des principes de la coopération culturelle internationale* (UNESCO: 4 November 1976; arts 1, 6); *Déclaration sur la race et les préjugés raciaux* (1967); *Acte final de la Conférence sur la sécurité et la coopération en Europe*, Helsinki, 1 August 1975 (Part 1, paragraph VII, concerning respect for the Rights of Man and

fundamental Liberties); *Pacte international relatif aux droits civils et politiques* (June 1980; art. 27).

I have cited here some of the principal texts used since the Second World War to persuade the government to give a greater place to Breton in the schools, and have singled out the articles generally referred to. Their interpretation as directly related to the issue of Breton, however, was not necessarily shared by those who were signatories to such agreements on France's behalf.

2 In June 1949, Deixonne's report, which was both a synthesis and a new bill of law, was adopted by the *Commission de l'Education Nationale* of the National Assembly, and voted by the National Assembly itself in December of that year. After this first vote, in the National Assembly in December 1949, the text passed back via the *Commission de l'Education Nationale* in March 1950 to arrive for debate by the *Conseil de la République* a few days afterwards. Two more meetings of *Commissions*, and one more debate in the *Conseil* then followed, before the vote on the final text in the Assembly in the December of 1950.

3 The texts of the reports and debates and of the final law can be found in:

(1) *JO: AN: Docs. Parls. Annexe 7777*: 6 July 1949:1302–1304 (CEN).

(2) *Ar Falz* 1950 (April):7 (15 June 1949: adoption by CEN).

(3) *JO: AN: Débats*: 29 December 1949; *2e séance*: 7538 (29 December 1949: acceptance on agenda of AN 'providing there is no debate').

(4) *JO: AN: Débats*: 30 December 1949: *1ère séance*: 7576 par. 6 (vote of text, no debate).

(5) *JO: CLR: Docs. Parls. Annexe:no. 6*: 10 (10 January 1950: AN sending text to CLR, to pass via CEN).

(6) *JO: CLR: Docs. Parls. Annexe:139*: 146–147 (2 March 1950: CEN: Lamousse report, revised text).

(7) *JO: CLR: Débats*: 7 March 1950: *2e séance*: 709–721 (CLR: Lamousse report and debate).

(8) *JO: CLR: Docs. Parls. Annexe:178*: 174–175 (16 March 1950: CEN: Lamousse: supplementary report).

(9) *JO: CLR: Débats*: 23 March 1950: 940–959 (CLR debate on last CEN text).

(10) *JO AN: Docs. Parls. Annexe 9616*: 535 (23 March 1950: CLR sending text to AN, to pass via CEN).

(11) *JO: AN: Docs. Parls. Annexe 10815*: 1666 (28 July 1950: CEN: Deixonne: brief report and text).

(12) *JO: AN: Débats*: 22 December 1950: *1ère-séance*: 9471 (AN: vote of text of CEN).

(13) *JO*: 13 January 1951: 483 (11 January 1951: Promulgation of law: *Loi no. 51–46 du 11 janvier 1951 relative à l'enseignement des langues et dialectes locaux*).

The text of the two post-war bills of law which concerned Breton and which informed Deixonne's initial report in 1949, can be found in:

(a) 1947: *Proposition ... de M. Pierre Hervé et al.* ('groupe communiste et apparentés, députés'): in *JO: AN: Docs. Parls.: 16 May 1947: Annexe no. 1326* (pp. 917ff.; this bill, although often cited subsequently as a '*proposition de loi*', was, in fact, a '*proposition de résolution*'). See also *Ar Falz* 1947 (December) 2–3.

(b) 1948: *Proposition de loi sur l'enseignement de la langue bretonne*,presented by Vourc'h, Henry, Le Coënt, and Trémintin (a group of four *Conseillers de la République*, from both right and left): in *JO: AN: Docs. Parls.:27 July 1948: Annexe no 5071*: (pp. 1667ff.) and *JO: CLR: Docs Parls:27 July 1948: Annexe no:748* (pp. 573ff.).

4 Discussions were particularly heated in the *Conseil de la République*, and it was here that Delbos always stepped in authoritatively to save the text (see especially texts nos. 7 and 9, note 3 of this chapter).

5 Before Carré, there would seem already to have been a definitional problem at the official level. In 1875, an army manual stated: '1. We call mother tongue the tongue that is spoken by our parents, and in particular by our mothers; spoken also by our fellow citizens and by the persons who inhabit the same *pays* as us. 2. Our mother tongue is French' (cited in Weber 1977:311).

6 *Ar Falz* 1975, 9–10:21.

7 Report and *proposition* of Le Duc (*Commission des Affaires Culturelles*), 25 April 1961: see *Ar Falz* 1961: 31.

8 *Proposition* of Le Pensec-Alduy-Bayou (Socialists and *Radicaux de Gauche*), 1974; see *AEB* 1974:3 (October). The Education Law of Haby, of 11 July 1975, talked of 'regional languages', however (*Titre 1ère*, art. 12), and it seems that Haby said that 'in a national community, there is neither majority nor minority' (cited in *AEB* 1976 (January–February), 8:3).

9 See, for example, Amouret 1977 and Fichou (1977) 1981; both of these works, emanating from the Inspectorate and teachers of Finistère, deal with the question of 'Bretonisms' in French.

10 It was made optional principally because the Minister felt that those teachers who did not know Breton should not be penalized. This was very variously interpreted, however. For example, one Finistère circular in November 1951 limited this article 3, without central directive, to those classes where at least two hours of 'directed activities' were available and 'in principle' to those pupils over 11 years of age. This seemed to limit article 3 only to those pupils in their final year of what was still called 'primary' education. (See 'Dialectes locaux: circulaire ministérielle du 23 November 1951', in *Bulletin Officiel de l'Enseignement Primaire du Finistère*, 1951 (December), 35:136–8. 'Primary' education still involved pupils up to 14 years of age. The total *activités dirigées* time that existed in each class was as follows: *C.P.* (preparatory class): two and a half hours per week; *C.E.* (elementary class): one hour; *C.M.* (middle class): one hour; *cours supérieur*: one hour; *classes de fin d'études*: two hours. The situation was further confused by the fact that the 'directed activities' regime was scrapped for the two lower levels of the primary schools in 1956. In 1961, a report stated nevertheless that teachers who had been teaching Breton in this way were simply continuing to do so (see Le Duc report, 25 April 1961, in *Ar Falz* 1961 (April–June), 3:7). The Finistère circular of 1951 mentioned above seems to have had little effect and was, in any case, withdrawn. Obviously, official instructions did not always determine what happened in the schools. Even during discussions of this article 3 of the law as early as 1950, the Minister of Education had stated that some schools were offering this option already, at least in other parts of France (see CLR: 2 March 1950, note 3 above).

11 See *Ar Falz* 1950 (May–June), 9; 1950 (August–September), 3; 1950 (November–December), 1:3.

12 In the report of 1949, the first report informing the Deixonne law, the optional Breton oral examination had begun as one that would count towards the overall passing of the *baccalauréat*. In discussions of this text, some members of the *Conseil* did not see the point of this oral Breton test at all, and there were worries about who might competently examine it; however, the Minister was insistent, and the final text instituted the examination. It was only to count, however, for a special '*mention*', and not actually towards passing, in order, principally, to maintain overall standards. In July 1970, however, a decree removed the clause that had limited the value of this oral test, and another

decree of October that year stipulated that it was to count towards passing the whole examination as well as for a *mention*; see *Décret no. 70–650* (10 July 1970) and *Décret no. 70–933* (5 October 1970). Breton had a place, too, as an optional, oral exam at the lower level of the BEPC from 1953 to 1958, until this exam framework itself was re-organized, and the optional tests abolished (see *Ar Falz* 1959–1960 (December – January): 13 n. 3). Breton remained, however, at the higher level of the *baccalauréat*, surviving reorganizations of this examination.

13 This dissent was published in the Bulletin of the Finistère section of the National Primary Schoolteachers' Union (*Syndicat National des Instituteurs*, generally known as the 'SNI'), and it was written in the name of the Union's local *Commission des Classes Primaires*.

14 It is not at all clear that any of these measures received any great degree of popular approval or support. In February 1942, the Prefect of Finistère reported that only one parent had asked for Breton courses in the primary schools. At the beginning of 1943, only a few student-teachers in the *Ecole Normale* of Rennes were studying some Breton as an option (cf. Halls 1981:243; Morgan 1979:323). At the end of 1943, the Ministry also allowed pupils to do an optional Breton test in the *certificat d'études*, then the main school-leaving certificate. This lapsed with Liberation, but in 1953, after the Deixonne law, a new measure instituted the possibility of an optional Breton test at the level of the BEPC, which came to replace the old certificate.

15 A fuller account of the wartime situation, as summarized here, can be found in issues of the Breton magazine *Arvor* of the time (e.g., of 5 January 1941; 24 August 1941; 11 January 1942; 1 March 1942; and 12 December 1943: '*Ar Brezhoneg er Sertifikad*'), and in Morgan 1979:321–6 and Halls 1981:241–5; see also Chapter seven below.

16 Finistère had 40.2 per cent of its schoolchildren in private establishments in 1939 and 49.1 per cent in 1943, an increase of almost 9 per cent. In the Morbihan, 68.3 per cent of the children were in private schools by 1943, an increase of 11.5 per cent over the same period (see Halls 1981:409–10).

17 This was so even when requests for some Breton in the schools came from the elected *Conseils Généraux* of the Breton *départements*, sometimes with moderate local republican backing, and even when the requests themselves were moderate by later standards. The *Conseil Général* of Finistère, for example, voted a *voeu* for the teaching of Breton to aid French, and for Breton as a second language at the *baccalauréat*, in 1921; the *Conseil* repeated this request in 1923. Breton at the *baccalauréat* level was necessary, it was felt, to supply the teachers who would then use Breton competently to teach French. These requests were made in response to a standard petition circulated by Breton right-wing groups of the time (and the relevant papers can be found in ADF:T:1:79). The Prefect of Finistère supported the *Conseil*'s vote, but was away from his post, it seems, when the vote was tra smitted to the Ministry, and so it did not receive his official backing (see Taldi 1935:160). The local Inspectorate did not agree with him anyway, and the main outcome was in the form of the circulars of Albert in 1924 and De Mon ie (1925) that I have already cited. Later motions, of similar content, came again from the *Conseil* in 1935 (joined here by the *Conseil* of the Côtes-du-Nord, and in 1938, when Desgranges' report was being presented at the national level (see Le Berre 1935:11). The war ended that debate, however. After the war, in 1946, the *Conseils* of Finistère, and the Morbihan, and the Côtes-du-Nord, asked for Breton at the higher levels of the *Lycées* and *Ecoles Normales*, and repeated this request in 1947 (see Fleuriot 1981:6; *Ar Falz* 1951 (January–February):iv).

In 1948, optional Breton ('facultative') was allowed officially in the *Lycée* of Quimper and Brest, and the *Conseil* of Finistère voted money to pay the teachers. They continued to pay, it seems, at the beginning of the 1950s, awaiting state funds following the 1951 law (*Ar Falz* 1951 (May–June):2). In general, the few post-war *voeux* were more effective than any requests before the war.

18 An account of this bill of law, entitled *Proposition de loi du PCF relative à la langue et la culture bretonnes*, can be found in *AEB* 1976 (January–February), 8:4–7.

19 Some instances of confusion at this level were reported in the Breton journal *Ar Falz* (e.g., 1963, 5:4). In 1964, the government set up a special Commission (*Commission Mixte de l'Etude de l'Enseignement Régional*) to clarify some of the legislation and issues concerning regional languages and their teaching. The Commission met five times during the period 1964–5, and had the active participation of members of the Ministry and the Inspectorate (including Haby, then a General Inspector) and teachers of all levels from the regions concerned (see the journal *Skol Vreiz* 1967:11, for the Commission's texts). A report was produced in November 1965, and this, in turn, generated further confusion, in the form of yet more reports, circulars, and bills of law. Ultimately, the 1975 *Loi Haby* (see note 8 above) revised the whole of French education, and firmly gave 'regional languages' a guaranteed place 'throughout schooling' (*Loi Haby*, or *Loi Sur l'Education*, 11 July 1975: *Titre 1*, art. 12, in *JO* 12 July 1975:7181 (*Loi no. 75–260*; 7180)). The 'regional languages' were now, for the first time since the 'local idioms' of the Revolution, explicitly referred to in a full educational law. This did not end the matter, for more decrees and circulars followed the law, along with yet more bills of law, and more debates. The period leading up to the 1981 elections was a busy time. In the period 1977–80 alone, there were five further bills of law (which remained only bills of law) on the regional languages issue, all of them dealing with the languages in relation to education. Among these, two came from the Socialists (PS), one from the Communists (PCF), one from a Centrist group of Senators, and one from the centre-right (UDF: Lower-Rhine). One of the Socialist bills and the bill from the Centrist group were retablings of earlier texts.

20 Sources in the *Rectorat*, where private and state figures are now collated, insisted that figures provided by private authorities were suspect and that 'we do not know what really goes on in private schools' and 'we hardly dare go in there'. The public authorities have the right of inspection, but it is generally the private authorities who give the figures to the state bodies who ask. Mutual dismissal of the two sectors is common: state schools were said to exaggerate their figures 'to make believe they are doing something for Breton', and similar comments came from the state sector about the private schools. From 1979, closer inspection of figures for Breton in private secondary schools was begun by a state employee, although this has not necessarily ruled out disagreement.

More generally, the right of public authorities to inspect private schools is not as contentious as it was a hundred or more years ago. (See, for example, Mourier (1889), who recounts his experiences as *Recteur d'Académie* at Rennes under the Second Empire. He tells of the uncertainties of the State Inspectors, who were not sure whether they were allowed to inspect private schools, and of the obstructions posed by the private establishments, which sometimes barely let the Inspector past the door anyway.) Nowadays, where private schools have contracts with the State, as the great majority do in Brittany (and all at the secondary level in Finistère, with the primary schools following suit), they can, in theory, be subject to inspection like the state schools, but with reservation of certain liberties. Previously, State Inspectors could enter only to check sanitary conditions or to see that 'morality, the law and the constitution' were not contravened (*Loi Falloux*: art. 21; see also Godfrey 1974:57–60; ADF:L1:1851). The emphasis, however, was on questions of morality and hygiene. In 1886, the private schools clearly emerged from the new legislation with total educational liberty (law of 30 October 1886: art. 35); this has only been surrendered through the system of contracts set up since the end of the 1950s (1959: 20 per cent of the syllabus can differ from that of state schools (*contrat simple*); 1977: schools must follow the state syllabus, with the possibility of some educational freedom and extra activities, including religious instruction (*contrat d'association*); several interpretations of this latter contract would seem to exist.) In practice, many State Inspectors still inspect only buildings and books; the private sector has, furthermore, its own Diocesan Inspectorates.

21 All population figures here are from the published counts of INSEE (1973; 1980).

22 The level of the *Lycées* here has seen conflicting official figures, and I have given the most generous estimate (619 pupils). Similarly, at the College level, I have calculated according to the highest figure given (689 pupils).

23 I have not obtained figures for the *département* of Loire-Atlantique, in the region of the 'Pays de la Loire', with its own *Rectorat* at Nantes.

24 Figures have varied considerably here. Original official figures suggested a drop from 55 Colleges (1978–9) to 41 (1979–80). After protest and argument some sources agreed to reduce this gap to that between 51 and 48, respectively, thereby contradicting earlier figures for the number of Colleges doing Breton. Following discussion with sources inside and outside the schools, and inside and outside the *Rectorat*, I was given figures suggesting a decline from at least 55 Colleges (1978–9) to 48 (1979–80). It is not so much the exact number here, as the decline itself that has caused great contention.

25 The final text was somewhat abridged and changed from earlier drafts of 1977, when discussions had first begun, although where Breton in the schools was concerned, the text remained substantially unchanged. Details of the numerous meetings in which the text(s) were discussed can be found in Letertre 1977 and 1978. An indication of some of the differences between earlier and final texts was given in *Ar Falz* 1978:23. The Regional Council (*Conseil Régional*) of Brittany was, at the time, predominantly right-wing; Communists abstained at the vote, Socialists refused to take part, and one member (UDB) voted against, partly because of curtailments in the text. The text was accepted none the less.

26 For details, see *Ar Falz* 1975, 9–10:21–22; *AEB* 1975, 7:13 and 1976, 8:1–15; Haby made several promises in 1975 and effected certain measures for the promotion of Breton in the context of the 1951 legislation, subsequent circulars, and his own 1975 law. Many of the promises were not realized until the advent of the Charter.

27 *Charte Culturelle de Bretagne*: 'Préambule': 1. (Text available from *Mission Régionale*, Rennes.)

28 Accusers pointed out that a copy of the Cultural Charter was circulated to the *Lycées* at the beginning of 1978–9, but not to many of the Colleges until the beginning of 1979–80, followed by a circular, after the school year had begun.

29 On this point, see Singer 1971, especially Chapter 5. Singer interviewed Ogès while preparing a general historical thesis on education in Finistère, and looked at some of the exercise books of his past pupils.

30 All citations here are from the letter entitled '*Témoignage d'un professeur de Lycée, fils d'instituteur du Finistère*' (*Musée de l'école*, Tregarvan); the letter i

undated but had, I was told, been written during 1979–80, specially for the required additions to the exhibition.

Part two

Chapter five

1 Beer's list of named groups, with their estimated dates of foundation, runs as follows, and I quote:

> Brittany – Ar Falz (1945); Ar Skol Dre Lizer (1945); Bodadeg Ar Sonerion (1946); Kamp Etrekeltiek (1948); Kamp Yaouankiz Vreizh (1948); Kamp Al Leur Nevez (1948); Kamp Breuriezh Sant Erwan (1948); Bleun-Brug (1948); Committee for the Study and Liaison of Breton Interests (1950); Confederation of Breton Cultural, Artistic, and Folklore Societies (1950); Movement for the Organization of Brittany (1957); Breton Student Youth (1963); Breton Democratic Union (1964); The Call (1964); Committee of Free Brittany (1965); Breton National and European Federalist Movement (1966); College of Druids, Bards, and Ovates (1966); Breton Organizing Committee for Progressive and Regional Action (1967); Breton Front (1968); Youth of New Brittany (1968); Breton Liberation Front (1968); Office of Documentation and Information for Local Breton Officials (1969); Committee of Action for the Breton Language (1969); European Committee for the Defense of the Breton People (1969); Adsav 1532 (1971); Group for Breton and International Political Studies (1971); Breton Communist Party (1971); Survival in Brittany (1972); Breton Action Committees (1972); Breton Cultural Centers (1973); For the Breton Language (1973); Party of the Land (1973); Presses of Breton Anger (1973); Breton Resistance (1974). In addition, there are approximately forty-four minor groups for which no dates of foundation have been established.
>
> (Beer 1977:148)

There is not space here to comment on all these names and dates but one should note that several groups now of some importance are not listed, and some of the above no longer exist (e.g., the 'Breton Communist party', a grouping now rarely mentioned in any history of the movement, oral or written).

2 See especially *CNB* 1981a; *Galv* 1969; Lebesque 1970; Le Menn 1975; Morvannou 1980; *Le Peuple Breton (PB)*, esp. 1973, 117:14 and 118:14; Piriou 1971; *Pluriel* 1976, 5:78; *Les Temps Modernes* (special issue) 1973, 324–66.

3 See, for example, Gwegen 1975:38–40; *Evid ar Brezhoneg* ('For Breton', a bilingual journal for learners of Breton), 17 May 1974.

4 For such citations, see, for example, *Le Peuple Breton (PB)* 1973, 117:14; Gwegen 1975:34; *Pluriel* 1976, 5:78. In oral citation, this misattribution regularly occurs. Some militants do not seem to know that the government ever offered bilingual schooling, and not all those who quote – or misquote – the Prefect in this respect show any awareness of the project in response to which these comments were made (by, in fact, the local Quimper Committee – see Chapter three).

5 For some details of the UDB's past electoral history, see J. and M. Dayries 1978:94; Hechter and Levi 1980:44; Stephens 1976:386. The greatest victory ever, and wholly exceptional, was a claim of 12 per cent of the votes in Auray (Morbihan) in 1970, on a 'United Left' ticket. Profiting from the 'Union of the

Left' in 1977, the party gained thirty-two seats for municipal councillors in twenty-seven communes in Brittany, and one of these, from Brest, became a Regional Councillor. All this, however, was not gained on a lone UDB ticket. The UDB presented candidates in fifteen (out of a total of thirty-three) Breton *circonscriptions* in 1981, in the first round of the legislative elections, and gained an overall average, in these areas, of 2.15 per cent of the votes; in 1978, this average had been 1.87 per cent (see PB 1981, 211 (July):12).

6 A full account of the CELIB, its history, plans, and decline, can be found in Berger 1977; J. and M. Dayries 1978; Hayward 1969, 1976; Pléven 1961; Plunier 1979.

7 For some histories of the Breton movement, see Déniel 1976; Fouere 1977; Nicolas 1980; the works of Déniel and Nicolas are the most detailed; see also the special issue of *Pluriel* 1979, 18.

8 Further details of this coming together of the left and regional causes can be found in Berger 1977; J. and M. Dayries 1978: esp. 108–24.

9 For a pre-election text which promised this, see 'Proposition de loi portant décentralisation de l'Etat' in *AN, Annexe no. 1557, séance: 20 December 1979*; text registered with AN on 10 December 1979.

10 Details of France's colonizing process, and its relationship to language, can be found in Gordon 1978.

11 A common citation in support of the colonial interpretation comes from a Sub-Prefect of Quimperlé in 1831, who said that Brittany should be subjected, in its rural areas, 'to a sort of colonial regime' (cited in *PB* 1973, 117:14, for example). The Sub-Prefect in question was responsible for an area of Finistère that was particularly lacking in schools (Ogès 1931; 1934:143–6).

12 For details of some problems and comparisons, see, for example, Berger 1972; J. and M. Dayries 1978:64, 81; Le Guen and Pors 1980; *PB* 1979, 186:12; *Skol Vreiz(h)* 1976.

13 Salaries in many jobs in Brittany in the 1960s were coming closer to general French norms. Strikes in the 1970s narrowed the gap further, as well as providing publicity which the Breton movement exploited, with many militants active in trying to give the strikes a 'Breton' dimension. If the average national salary is taken as index 100, then Brittany had 80 in 1963 and 85 in 1973 (or 20 per cent and 15 per cent, respectively, below the national average). When the influence of the Paris region is eliminated from the last figure, then Brittany goes up to 94 (or 6 per cent below the national average) for 1973. The gap then closed further during the 1970s (see Bertrand *et al.* 1978; Hayward 1976: 56; Krier and Ergan 1976; and Philipponneau 1970:200–1, for details). Part of the difference lies in the lower proportions of *cadres* and highly skilled workers in Brittany compared with France overall, although there has been some difference of salaries at these levels also. For details of strikes in the early 1970s the most notable of which was at the St Brieuc factory of the *Joint Français*, see O' Callaghan 1983:87–9; Lovecy 1982; Philipponneau 1972.

14 Beer's Breton sample brought only ninety-five replies, and he excluded student from his occupational analysis. Even so, he found that almost 70 per cent of hi respondents were in professional, white-collar, or 'intellectual' occupations. These occupations make up, in the total active population of Brittany, only 19 per cent. Beer notes that an especially high proportion of his Breton sampl were 'professors' or teachers of some kind (over 29 per cent), and that only on was a 'farmer'. We are not told what kind of 'farmer' (his term) this solitary figure was, and Beer tentatively suggests that perhaps there were more 'farmer who did not reply (Beer 1977:152–3). My own experience in Brittany, howeve makes me confident that his proportions are not misleading as they stand.

15 There had, in the past, been other attempts to create a united 'Breton' front (see, for one example, *Galv* ('Call') 1969), but all these had consisted only of movement members, and were broken apart by internal feuding.

16 *Sossialism* is the Breton form generally used by proponents of the Interdialectal orthography, including *Ar Falz* and the UDB. Upholders of the 'ZH' orthography, including *Skol an Emsav*, would normally use the terms *sokialegezh* or *sokialourezh* (see also Chapter seven). Such issues were generally avoided in the Front, and French was, in any case, the usual language.

17 According to a report presented to the Regional Council of Brittany in February 1979, the Breton language could be heard for a total of 251 ¾ hours per year on radio, and little more than 22 ¼ hours per year on television. Although these totals are (especially for television) nearly double what they were before the Cultural Charter, they remain meagre when compared (as they regularly are in the movement) with the Welsh situation.

18 The following is a list of the organizations that were formally co-signatories of the Front's tracts by January 1980; by no means all of the bodies named were physically represented in the meetings of the Front, however, during the period in question, and the PSU, for example, was hardly ever seen by the core of six to twelve members who did attend. Sometimes more than one representative from the same union was present. The list of co-signatories, printed on the tracts, ran as follows: *Ar-Falz*, GERIB, *Parti-Socialiste* (PS), *Parti Socialiste Unifié* (PSU), RTB, SGEN-CGT, *Skol an Emsav*, SNETP-CGT, SNRT-CGT, SFRT, SFRT-CGT (*Sections Bretagne-Pays de Loire*), *Union Démocratique Bretonne* (UDB). The 'SNRT-CGT' and the 'SFRT-CGT' were the television unions from FR–3. The 'CGT' affix indicates affiliation to the national *Confédération Générale du Travail*, the largest French trade union, and a 'CFDT' affix indicates affiliation to the national *Confédération Française Démocratique du Travail* (for some details of French trade unions and their relative size, see Safran 1977; Geledan 1978). The 'GERIB' organization mentioned was represented, in theory at least, by the president of *Les Amis du Parler Gallo* (see Chapter eight); in practice, he rarely attended. By March 1980, the SNI-PEGC of the Morbihan (or SNI-PEGC 56, with '56' being the code number of the *département*), had formally consented to membership of the Front, although a representative had appeared at only one of the meetings I attended during the previous months.

Chapter six

1 The *Académie Celtique* held the ambition of 'studying and publishing the etymologies of all the languages of Europe, with the help of Celto-Breton, Welsh, and of the Erse language which is still spoken in its primitive purity, so to speak, in the mountains of Ireland' (*MAC* 1808, I:4). The insular connection was well established: in the 1790s, for example, one Breton respondent to Grégoire's questionnaire on the idioms of France said he had visited 'Wales, in *Angleterre*' and had heard Welsh, which led him to suggest that the Bretons had peopled Wales (cited in Gazier 1969:281). Long before this, in the sixteenth century, 'French antiquaries argued cogently that Britain had acquired its name from the Britons in Brittany' (Hay 1955:64).

2 As Chapman summarizes it, the 'Celt' took

much of his shape in opposition to rationality, intellectuality, and a materialist world of scientific and political manipulation. Instead of these the

Celt has an artistic capacity beyond the ordinary, a religious instinct of unusual depth, a strength and profundity of thought and feeling but a weakness in the external world of action, a ready emotionality and an easy communion with nature, a strength in domesticity but a weakness in a wider political sphere, and a femininity.

(Chapman 1978:86)

3 Direct inspiration had been found in the Ossianic poems, and also in the *Myvyrian Archaiology* and the much celebrated works of Walter Scott. La Villemargué was also influenced by a visit he made to Wales, in 1838, just one year before the first appearance of his poems, and where he was a guest at the *Eisteddfod* and was made a 'Bard'. La Villemarqué had gone to Wales looking for traces of old, imperial Gaul, and, benefiting from French nationalism and a contemporary wave of enthusiasm for romantic, liberal history, he was supported by a government scholarship and the Ministry of Public Instruction (see Gourvil 1960:67; Trénard 1968). On his return to France, however, the political career of his own ideas and writings favoured an image of the Breton as Welshman. (For a discussion of La Villemarqué, his followers, and the various editions of the *Barzaz Breiz*, see Gourvil 1960; Laurent 1974; Tanguy 1977.)

4 Anyone who was a 'true Breton in his heart' would, he said, 'have laughed with all his might to see the green grass reddened by the blood of the accursed Gauls' (Arthur de la Borderie, cited in Tanguy 1977:326).

5 Gildas, the British monk (from Wales), writing in the mid-sixth century (or thereabouts), clearly identifies in his writings with the Romans against the invading armies in the island; and he talks of '*nostra lingua*' ('our language'), meaning Latin (see Gildas in Winterbottom, M. (ed. and trans.) 1978:26–8). In summary, there is a long tradition in the literature of embarkations from the island, with Maximus (or 'Maxim'/Macsen Wledig) in the fourth century, by a youth that 'never returned', who are said to have settled in Armorica; and of numbers setting sail for Armorica in the face of invading armies at home, and the fall of the Empire and its values; and of a number of emigrant scholars (or 'saints': *sancti*), usually dated from the mid-sixth century onwards. There is also evidence that Armorican Gaul was densely populated in parts, encouraged by the fact that it was relatively untouched by the more evident troubles of the fall of the Empire elsewhere in Gaul. I am grateful here to the participants in a 'Brittany and Britain' conference held in Oxford in January 1981; and especially to Edwin Ardener for his help in researching sources and in discussion. Further details of the literature, and of relations between Gaul and Britain at this time, can be found in the works of Chadwick and Fleuriot cited in the text, and in Jarman and Hughes 1976.

6 See Le Goffic 1902:325, 327. Worries about this were evident in the 1903 Chamber of Deputies debate concerning Combes's measure. A right-wing Breton Deputy cited, as if to bolster his opposition to the measure, the interest and support of some Irish and Welshmen – but a Breton republican, who feared Combes's excessive zeal, was then quick to point out that Breton and British Celt had only ever met in war, and were, if anything, enemies (see Lamy and Louis Hémon, in *JO Chambre: Débats* 16 January 1903:24–31; see also the debates cited in Guieysse 1925:21–2 and Taldir 1935:158).

7 For a linguistic discussion of the mechanisms involved, see especially Hewitt 1977:39ff; Morgan 1979:271–82. The domestic source involved chiefly composition and derivation from native elements, with an elaborate system of prefixes and suffixes, some of them wholly new and others already unproductive in the popular language. The second source, the use of older texts, usually

meant the resurrection of obsolete terms from the two eras (divided according to accepted linguistic convention) of Old Breton (mainly glosses up to the end of the eleventh century) and Middle Breton (a few texts up to the mid-seventeenth century), but antiquity was no guarantee of un-Frenchness. Some of the older Breton terms intended to replace French were soon discovered themselves to be derivations from French (see Morgan 1979:251–3 and issues of *Buhez-Breiz* ('Breton Life') 1922–3).

8 Hemon (1964:71) went on to recommend the Breton word *arnevez*. *Arnevez* is preferred, in such circles, because it is felt to be older Breton, and closer to (pure) Welsh. Popular Breton, on the other hand, uses *modern*, and has taken it from French, not Welsh; *arnevez*, when it is understood locally, is taken, in my experience, to be a funny way of saying 'new' (*nevez*).

9 Previously, Breton terms such as *oual* or *wall* had been used for 'Wales', in learned eighteenth-century dictionaries, and by Le Gonidec (see Le Menn 1980:9). Such terms were used to describe both Cornwall and Wales; the term *gallois* (which now means 'Welsh') was sometimes used, in French at this time in Brittany, to describe the people of Upper Brittany. Standard Breton now has *Kembraeg* ('Welsh language') *Kembread* ('Welshman'), and *Kembraeger* ('Welsh-speaker'), for example.

10 Previously, terms such as *Irland* and *Islandr* had dominated, with a confusion between Iceland and Ireland long shared by Breton and French (see Le Menn 1980:7–8). A single text of the fifteenth or sixteenth century, which became of interest only in the eighteenth and nineteenth centuries, contains terms such as *Hybernia, Hibernia, Hiverdon,* and *Ynerdon*, all in the same text. *Ynerdon* is now felt to have been an error for *Yuerdon*, and a learned borrowing from Welsh (*Iwerddon*) at that time (Le Menn 1980:7–8). Terms used in the new standard Breton include *Iwerz(h)on* ('Ireland'), *Iwerz(h)oneg/k* ('Irish language'), *Iwerz(h)onad* ('Irishman'), and *Iwerz(h)oneger* ('Irish-speaker') See Hemon GIAB:1399–1400.

11 For instance, one earlier invention, by Hemon's colleague Vallée, had been a term for 'calorie': *tommderenn* (lit. *tommder*, meaning 'heat', plus *-enn*, a singulative suffix, giving something like 'a (passing) heating' or 'heat-maker'; *-enn* is not as common in popular speech as it is in standard literary vocabulary). In later dictionaries of his own, Hemon replaced *tommderenn* with *kalori*. His own translation of *tommderenn* into French suggests that he had realized that there was a problem: he translates it as '*femme d'humeur galante*' (see Hemon 1973:793; cf. Morgan 1979:262). I have found that the term *tommderenn* causes great amusement among local Breton-speakers. *Tommderenn* (sometimes understood as *tommderez*) is taken to mean variously 'hot stuff' or a woman who is a 'tease'.

Hemon felt that some of the more curious inventions of earlier years could be replaced with international terms, particularly 'scientific' terms, providing these were 'Bretonized', which effectively meant using the same Bretonized derivational system by which other new words had been formed (see *Hor Yezh* ('Our Language') 1956–7:12–16; Hewitt 1977:45). On this basis, some broadly 'international' terms were not accepted into standard Breton. As an example of this, we can take one term widely taught and used in the modern movement to mean 'electricity': *tredan*. *Tredan* is a neologism from Welsh, and the only term reported in popular Breton usage is *elektris(s)ite* (/elɛK'tRisite/); cf. *électricité* in French. Modern scholars, followers of Hemon, have explained to me that this popular term is not acceptable because, whereas *tredan* could generate Breton derivatives (such as *tredaner* or *tredanour*, 'electrician'; and *tredanerezh* or *tredanadur*, 'electrification') *elektris(s)ite* could not. In popular speech, *elektris(s)ite* can and does generate related terms, but using suffixes shared with French (*-ien*, *-(ifica)tion*, and so on), passed through a Breton phonological grill. Such terms are not, in general, used in militant vocabulary and are not considered 'Breton'.

12 *Gwalarn* 1934, 72:54; Hemon 1947:81, 1964:70. A fuller idea of the changes that Hemon and his colleagues effected can be found in Hemon 1947:78–80.

Chapter seven

1 In the departmental archives in Quimper there are counter-circulars, of unknown source, but seemingly emanating from teachers and the political left of the time, arguing against any Breton in the schools at all, some in terms similar to those used by the 1831 Quimper Committee over a century before (see Chapter three; these ideas are explicit in the 1938 vote of the commune of Tourc'h, *arrondissement* of Quimper, for example: see ADF:T:1:79). In 1938, several municipalities seem to have used model counter-circulars to register their vote against (for model examples, see the 1938 votes of Ploujean, near Morlaix, and of Fouesnant, in ADF:T:1:79).

2 La Villemarqué felt it was the least 'Celtic' of the dialects. In Vannetais, he said,

> words have lost most of the finer qualities of language. They contract, are obliterated, and lose lustre the further one gets from the Léon and the mountains of Cornouaille, the areas where the language is richer, more melodious, and more regular than elsewhere. When one gets to Vannes, the words are completely truncated.
>
> (La Villemarqué (1847) 1977:99)

3 *Iwerzhon*, a neologism from the Welsh *Iwerddon*, is not 'historically' correct in the terms of the etymological framework which the *zh* is now widely held to demonstrate. This framework can be diagrammatically summarized in the following way:

Late *Brittonic*:

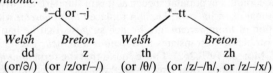

Welsh	*Breton*	*Welsh*	*Breton*
dd	z	th	zh
(or/ə/)	(or /z/or/–/)	(or /θ/)	(or /z/–/h/, or /z/–/x/)

Iwerddon should, within this framework, have stayed as *Iwerzon* in Breton, rather than becoming *Iwerzhon*. Critics of the 'ZH' have not been slow to point out 'historical' errors of this kind (see Hewitt 1977, ch. three; Merser 1980). *Barzhaz*, a nineteenth-century neologism from the Welsh *barddas*, suffers from error here also, although this was soon recognized by 'ZH' proponents, and the *Barzaz Breiz* usually remains as such; this is partly for reasons of literary authenticity, since it was under this title that La Villemarqué first published his work. *Iwerzhon* has not been (re-) 'corrected' to *Iwerzon* in the 'ZH'.

4 Argument and counter-argument leading up to the 1941 'solution' can be found in Hemon 1929b; Vallée 1935; and Hemon 1936; 1938; 1942. Some of the post war arguments over orthography can be found, in chronological order, in Falc'hun 1953, 1956; Hemon 1956; Denez 1958; Kalvez 1977; Kergoat 1975; Denez 1975; Hemon 1976; Merser 1980.

Chapter eight

1 The Breton term *Gouel* is normally reserved, in popular usage, for religious festivals or holy days: e.g., *Gouel an Ollsent*, meaning 'All Saints' in English or *La Toussaint* in French. In the militant world, *Gouel* (cf. Welsh *Gwyl*) came to signify, above all, this annual celebration of the Breton language.

Part three

Chapter ten

1 The first of these earlier ventures was a Breton-medium primary school, active during the Occupation from 1942 to 1944, at Plestin-les-Grèves in the Côtes-du-Nord. It was called *Skol Blistin* ('Plestin school') and had at most nine pupils, from six families, some from Rennes; all were boarders, and three already spoke the Breton of their militant parents. The school was *laïque* but private (i.e., fee-paying), and used the orthography of Hemon. The teacher, a member of a contemporary Breton nationalist group, was disappointed to find that many militants who had encouraged the project did not send their children. Their 'excuses' were various – fear of politics at school, concern over academic standards, dislike of *laïcisme*, and political or literary rejection of the 'ZH'. Recruitment proved difficult, and the school closed for ever when, with the Allies advancing, fighting threatened the children's safety (see Kerlann 1980). The second venture, in the 1950s, was inspired by contemporary Welsh projects. A militant priest established *Skol Sant Erwan* ('Saint Erwan School') at Plouézec, also in the Côtes-du-Nord. This school was independent and bilingual. About twenty children studied some subjects (including arithmetic, history, and geography) in Breton, totalling eight hours a week. This was again a primary school, used the 'ZH', and took in boarders (most from Quimper, Rennes, and Paris). It had problems of finance, local support, and recruitment, and lasted from 1957 to 1960 (see *Skol* 1959, 6). Two of its pupils, Breton-speakers from militant families (one in Paris), helped to create *Diwan*.

2 During the first ten months of 1980, money from the Charter and employment schemes made up over forty per cent of the income of *Diwan*'s central treasury. The first departmental awards (which offered a sum amounting to over half that of these other two sources together) were granted at the end of 1980 and the beginning of 1981. *Diwan* members later calculated that almost twenty per cent of the overall income of the central treasury and of the schools for 1980 came from public subventions alone (see *An Had* July 1981, 4:5).

3 Within this new structure, the federations, rather than *Diwan Breizh*, became the legal employers of the teachers in their area, and money from individual schools was now to be sent to a treasury established in each federation. The central treasury of *Diwan Breizh* was to continue paying the salaries of the office staff, for the running of the office, for trainee-teachers, and the expenses of the board. Besides the capacity to limit the possible consequences of a local crisis, the federations brought other financial advantages: e.g., certain taxes due from any association with over ten staff, could be avoided by technically splitting up the teachers (although these taxes had amounted to only two per cent of their total salaries). A legal limit of four fund-raising events per year could also, in theory, be respected.

Chapter eleven

1 These figures were arrived at through questionnaires collectively constructed and filled out in meetings with teachers and parents in each school; the results became accepted social fact within the *Diwan* organization, where the request for 'exact figures' had frequently been made.

2 Conjugated prepositions, for example, such as *din, dit, dezhañ* ('to me', 'to you', 'to him', respectively) were understood, for the most part, but were regularly reproduced as *da me* (or even *da moi*; cf. *à moi* in French), *da te/toi*, and *da lui (toi* and *lui* being French), respectively. This ran right through the prepositions (e.g., *ganin*, meaning 'with/by me', became *gant me* or *gant moi*; and *evidon*, meaning 'for me', was often *evid/t me* or *evid/t moi*, and so on). The children regularly had trouble with mutations also. Interestingly, a very common difficulty was to replace lenition by spirantization: thus, for example, a child might more easily acquire the transition from *(va) penn* ('(my) head'), with no mutation, to *(va) benn* ('(my) head') with a mutation of lenition effected in some contexts; however, the mutation by spirantization, demanding *(va) fenn* ('my') head'), which is the mutation of standard or literary Breton, was less common – and the teachers who were concerned about this found it difficult to elicit; other teachers would simply accept *(va) benn*, either because it was at least a step better than *(va) penn* (no mutation at all) or because they worried about the child's spontaneity, or did not wish to 'impose' any standard; or because they felt it a perfectly acceptable localism anyway.

3 Two such instances occurred in the Le Relecq school discussed in Part four. One little boy, who heard no Breton at home, would often try to translate the teacher's statements into French, seemingly in order to be sure he had understood. At meal-times, for instance, the teacher would usually say: *'Ouzh daol!'* (lit. 'To table!'), and this four-year-old boy would always ask *'à table?'* Similarly, *'ket da gerc'hat da vantell'* ('go and get your coat') was often heard from this teacher at home-time, and the same boy would first ask *'je dois aller chercher mon manteau?'* According to the teacher, the ambivalence of this boy's parents about his presence and their own involvement in *Diwan* were implicated in the son's apparent insecurity. The second, and very different, example in Le Relecq was the five-year-old girl cited in the text, p. 199.

4 As just one example, there was a well-prepared game that involved a large cardboard house with windows and entrances cut out at different heights and in different shapes (e.g., circle, triangle, and square or oblong). The teacher called out a shape in Breton, and, at the same time, gave a child a small cardboard cut-out of the same shape. The child then had to enter the house by the appropriate shape, matching the small card to the larger opening. Each child did this in turn, and several times, with different shapes. Then the teacher drew the shape on the blackboard, instead of giving the piece of card, and the children eagerly went to the appropriate entrance. Finally, the teacher only called out the shape, without visual representation, and the game continued. Such a game would be spaced out over several days, and returned to later on. It was interspersed with musical activities in which relative distinctions of low/high notes were made (and represented by simple lines/circles), and with body movements, involving down/up, and so on, and gestures reproducing some of the shapes already learnt. Some children could easily reproduce the shapes themselves on paper.

Chapter twelve

1 *Pellgomz* is a term which militants have pasted on telephone boxes in many parts of Brittany. I found that, although local Breton-speakers could come to understand it after some prodding, it remained laughably metaphorical for them. One kindly peasant in the north of Finistère explained to me: 'You can speak from afar (*komz a-bell*) if you want, but it wouldn't be the same as telephoning (*telefoniñ*), would it? You'd really have to shout!'

2 The main suggestion for a name for the primary level was *Greun*, meaning 'Seeds' or 'Berries'. Although this name was felt to be metaphorically apt, many sensed that it would be obvious that this was *Diwan*'s enterprise anyway, and that such timidity did not augur well for recruitment or success.

3 For example, the 'ZH' *evit* ('for') would occur along with the Interdialectal *ewid*, or even be written as *ewit*; the OU *leor* ('book', *levr* in the 'ZH') would occur in an article otherwise written in the 'ZH'; and so on (for such instances, see *Kannadig* 1979, 4:4; 1980, 15:25).

4 This parent had long experience in the hard-core of the *emsav*, where the '*tch-tch*' or Vannetais militant is still sometimes suspected of merely 'covering up mistakes in Breton'. The fact that research from the OU camp of Brest University proudly linked Vannetais with Gaulish in the 1950s and 1960s (e.g., Falc'hun 1963), and continues to do so, has confirmed suspicion of it. The 'mistake' which was corrected by the 'ZH' parent in this Commission involved the Breton for 'to draw', which had been written *tressañ*, and which was 'corrected' to *tresañ*. It was pointed out, however, that *tressañ* was Interdialectal and *tresañ* 'ZH', and that the text had been consistently written in the Interdialectal throughout. The Interdialectal orthography had introduced an –*ss*– sign, using an *s/ss* distinction where the 'ZH' uses *z/s*, and with the –*ss*– sign often indicating words of obvious French origin (see Hewitt 1977:22). No staunch 'ZH' militant likes to see 'French' words pointed up in this way, and, for some, the –*ss*– sign has become almost as contentious as the *zh*.

5 This bill of law, first registered at the National Assembly in December 1980 and officially distributed on 16 April 1981, was entitled as follows: '*Proposition de Loi* relative à la place des langues et cultures des peuples de France dans l'enseignement, dans l'éducation permanente, dans les activités culturelles, de jeunesse et de loisir, dans les émissions de la radio et de la télévision et dans la vie publique' (AN, no. 2269). The article of this bill concerning *Diwan* runs as follows:

> Les écoles de création privée et non-confessionelles utilisant la langue de la région comme langue véhiculaire principale peuvent être intégrées au service public de l'éducation, au titre d'écoles expérimentales, sur demande de leurs initiateurs et après enquête et avis des assemblées régionales ou départementales, des conseils départementaux de l'enseignement public et des autorités académiques. Chaque école ainsi intégré au service public fait l'objet d'une convention qui lui guarantit de poursuivre son expérimentation pédagogique. Les enseignements des ecoles ainsi intégrées doivent satisfaire aux critères habituels de qualification des maîtres du premier degré et leur enseignement doit répondre aux exigences de neutralité de l'école publique'.
>
> (article 7–j; page 32)

This bill formed part of the Socialist government's general plans for decentralization. The Commission discussed several specific points of concern. The status offered by the Socialist bill was that of 'experimental school' – 'as if education in Breton and leading the Breton people to a recovery of their true identity were not normal'; moreover, *Diwan* teachers would require formal qualifications, which several did not possess; and there were fears that 'the Socialists cannot be trusted', with past experience in local municipalities seeming to confirm this. A permanent Commission was set up to negotiate terms of integration which would guarantee *Diwan*'s autonomy within the wider system. In *Diwan*'s own first revision of the text, the phrase '*au titre d'écoles expérimentales*' was deleted; also, the requirement that *Diwan* teachers should have the same qualifications as those in the mainstream system came out; by early 1982, *Diwan* and the authorities were agreed that a minimum of five children was necessary in each school, at nursery and primary levels; the text had not yet been debated at the national level.

Part four

Chapter thirteen

1 Plounéour attracted and sustained more than one of these 'French language teachers' in the mid-1790s, and the municipality was careful to accredit only candidates of proven Republican sympathies, refusing a certificate to at least one who seems to have wanted the job mainly because he had lost his fortune in the upheavals and confiscations of the Revolution. For some details and documents, see ADF: 26 L 147.

2 See the *Enquête* of Le Briol, 1820, in ADF: 1T 27. The Abbé Le Briol (the *Recteur d'Académie*) launched this enquiry, encouraging teachers to denounce others in their neighbourhood who were undeclared to the new, higher authorities. Saint-Thégonnec's teacher, a M. Cocaign, promptly denounced a M. Olier teaching in Plounéour-Ménez, adding comments about his behaviour. The behaviour of some rural schoolmasters certainly gave substance to the worries of the clergy and, later, of men such as La Villemarqué (see Chapter six). Balzac's Fourchon was a common image of schoolmasters, and one which received confirmation in the apparently drunken and disorderly behaviour of some rural teachers, especially since some liked to express their political zeal thus, in defiance of the clergy; the authorities were concerned that the local population might, as a result, reject the education offered them, and disciplinary measures and sackings were not unknown in Finistère (see Ogès 1934; Weber 1977:305–15).

3 See ADF: 1T 27. In 1830, a M. Nicholas (Charles) was teaching in Plounéour; he taught at least twenty-eight children, six of them attending free.

4 See the *Enquête* of Guizot, 1833, in the National Archives (Paris): reference F 17 104. Plounéour's teacher named here is a M. Richard. The pupils were aged from seven to fourteen years; only about fifteen of them attended during the summer months. The teacher used the 'simultaneous' method (i.e. teaching the class as a whole), rather than individual tuition; in this, he was quite advanced in comparison with many other teachers at the time. Plounéour seems never to have had a 'mutual' school. In Pleyber-Christ in this year, there were slightly more children at school (in the winter months at least); about a third of them attended free. In Saint-Thégonnec, the number of children at school was also higher. In Le Cloître, however, there is no record of any school at this time.

5 For details of the municipal council discussions, see AM 3 July 1887; 7 August 1887; 14 April 1903; 21 June 1903; 15 November 1903; 21 February 1904; 28 February 1904; 3 March 1904; 9 June 1904; 2 October 1904. Also, for correspondence with higher authorities on the matter, see ADF: series 0

(Plounéour-Ménez): 1:1–7 (Mairie-Ecole), reference 783–44; and ADF: 0–11 2–0 784.

6 From 1938 to 1980, the *école libre* made nine requests to the municipal council for aids and grants, sometimes only for fuel for heating or for Christmas presents for the children. Each time the request was refused. See AM 4 June 1938; 23 February 1941; 7 March 1954; 10 December 1954; 11 December 1960; 21 September 1977; 13 December 1977; 29 April 1979; 11 May 1980.

7 In the late 1830s, for example, Thomas Trollope (brother of Anthony) visited Brittany, his enthusiasm fired by Emile Souvestre; his walk into the interior took him near the abbey of Le Relecq, and he was surprised to hear very similar stories about the old monks, told him in fluent French by a peasant he met on the road. Trollope was shocked to hear this peasant say that the ransacking of the buildings of the abbey had been 'no more than they deserved', and that the 1789 Revolution had been just judgement on the behaviour of the monks and local clergy (T. A. Trollope 1840, 2:141–2; Trollope felt that, in all, 'M. Souvestre' had been far too 'romantic', I:v–vi).

8 See AM 26 August 1917; 8 September 1928; 15 February 1931; 11 June 1935; 12 February 1937; 19 December 1937; 13 June 1939; 20 January 1948.

9 See, for example, *Rapport Pastoral: Paroisse de Plounéour-Ménez, doyenné de Saint-Théonnec, Diocèse de Quimper et de Léon*, 22 April 1963 (available in the presbytery of Plounéour-Ménez, and in the diocesan offices at Quimper).

10 Numbers increased more or less steadily through the 1960s, reaching the highest ever figure of 182 pupils in 1972. By 1970–80, there were 143 pupils in the College, and in 1980–1 it became necessary to close a class. The College was nationalized in 1977, making the major burden of the College's upkeep the responsibility of the State, although the commune still pays a proportion of its upkeep, as do the other communes of the canton.

11 Not all the sixteen couples remained in the Le Relecq *Diwan* throughout the year, some leaving to establish or join the Huelgoat *Diwan*, on the other side of the mountains, and some leaving due to internal quarrels or general disappointments. The occupations of the thirty-two parents involved were as follows:

Fathers: one 'Celtic' artist; five 'alternative' peasants; two students; one teacher (*professeur*, in a Morlaix *Lycée*); two psychologists (in a Morlaix clinic); one journalist; three 'alternative' artisans (carpenters/ wood sculptors); one doctor.

Mothers: one 'Celtic' artist; five 'alternative' peasants; one housewife/former accountant; one drawing social security benefits/former accountant; one student nurse; two nurses; one teacher; one speech therapist; one housewife/'artisan'; one former teacher, re-qualified as carpenter; one 'Celtic' folk-singer.

Not all of the above-mentioned stayed together as couples, and four were unmarried. The 'peasants' and 'artisans' include former teachers or students, a former nurse and an ex-engineer.

Chapter fourteen

1 We find this metaphor, for example, in the work of Emile Souvestre (a writer much influenced also, in his depiction of the Bretons, by Fenimore Cooper). Although a French-speaker himself, Souvestre turned from Paris to invest his native Brittany with an untouched and disappearing, rural traditionality – a pure 'virginal beauty', he called it, that he loved as he 'could have loved a woman' (Souvestre 1971:xiv–xv).

2 Each village seems to have had, at some stage, its *vieille famille*, or 'old family' of some relative landed wealth with whom others might find work. Some of these families quite deliberately avoided the official rule of shared inheritances, often producing several generations of single heirs. Nearer the plain, and further into the Léon, such families were known (and are still known) as *ar chuloded* (Br.) or *les Julots* (Fr.; see Le Gallo 1982).

3 In 1967, for example, over forty-five per cent of men in their thirties were unmarried in a central area including Plounéour-Menez (see R. Simon 1974:95ff.). By 1968, over a third of the farms in Plounéour were worked by men alone, and in 1980, three out of the eight local men over thirty-five years of age in Kerguz were unmarried.

4 Generational differences in language use could perhaps be summed up schematically in the following way:

	Age
Generation 1 great-grandmother	c. eighty years
Generation 2 grandmother and grandfather	c. fifty years
Generation 3 mother and father	c. twenty-five years
Generation 4 child	c. five years

This might be in itself a fictional, but none the less typical, agricultural family inhabiting rural Finistère. Nearer the coast, French may intervene earlier. (I am grateful to Malcolm Chapman, Institute of Social Anthropology, Oxford, for confirming this picture from his own research experience on the southern Breton coast.)

Generation 1: Great-grandmother feels more at home in Breton than French, and Breton is usually a more appropriate language, in any case, for much of her daily round. She knows that her French is not as good as that of her descendants, and she also knows that French is the polite language to speak to strangers or to important visitors. However, she does tend to use Breton more than she did, as her grasp of socio-linguistic proprieties begins to wane with age. Usually, she speaks Breton to her daughter and her son-in-law (generation 2), and they commonly respond in Breton.

Generation 2: Grandmother and grandfather use both Breton and French among themselves. Breton is often used when they are alone together, and talking privately or of private adult matters (and do not want the children to hear), or when they are in informal situations with friends or relatives of their own age. They normally speak French to their children's generation (generation 3). They use only French to their young grandchildren (generation 4).

Generation 3: Mother and father speak French between themselves, and to grandmother and grandfather (generation 2). They have heard a good deal of Breton spoken around them over the years, but it has not usually been spoken to them. Their parents (generation 2) have made every effort to bring them up as French-speakers, and have never wanted or expected them to speak anything but French. This generation (generation 3) is, therefore, able passively to understand much Breton, but does not really speak it. They might, however, use a limited amount of Breton in communication with great-grandmother (generation 1).

Generation 4: The child, and the brothers and sisters if there are any, do not speak anything other than French. They are normally addressed by everyone in French. Should great-grandmother (generation 1) forgetfully address them in Breton, they might just, if alone with her, muster some sense from her words, and respond in French. Their confusion is usually enough to jolt great-grandmother back into French, and propriety, herself. If parents (generation 3) or grandparents (generation 2) are present (a presence more likely to cause, or contribute to, great-grandmother's own confusion in the first place) then the children are likely to look to them for help. The children will reply through these older generations.

There are several qualifying factors and complications that one could introduce here – including, for example, the fact that generations 1 and 2 will usually have cohabited while generations 2 and 3 will not; and if generation 2 is living in the family home of the male partner (the 'grandfather' here) then the different uses of Breton and French between generations 2 and 3 may well have an extra edge of rivalry and exclusion and affect also the language used within generation 2. It is not uncommon for mothers-in-law to use Breton to exclude daugters-in-law, for instance, and it has also been known in the past for daughters-in-law to use French, and only French, with everyone in the household to mark themselves off from mothers-in-law with whom they do not get on.

The kinship terms used here are, obviously, those of a British system. The appropriate Breton system is one in which both gender and educational level are important, and age more important than generation, in determining the terms used in kinship designation and, especially, address. Significantly, where the female gender is involved, and also when one moves nearer the coast, there is less lateral generalization of terms and a more obviously 'French' terminology (see, on some of these points, Izard (1965), although he finds 'impoverishment' and a disappointing unCelticness here – where local women would, no doubt, find sophistication).

5 The total of ninety-eight existing farms is well under a third of the number that existed at the end of the Second World War. These details can be found in Le Gall 1958; RGA 1979–80, and SEMENF 1971.

Chapter fifteen

1 Such confusion was not limited to the environment of the Le Relecq *Diwan* school, and was poignant when, at the level of Brittany more generally, *Diwan* set up a Recruitment Commission (see Chapter eleven, p. 195) to try to get a new and different intake of teachers. Some early candidates to this Recruitment Commission were housewives, responding to advertisements, and hoping to earn extra money. They had little idea of the values of *Diwan*. They were on their best behaviour in their 'interview', spoke in French, and were not offered jobs.
2 Some Welsh importations have been rather unhappy – in one instance, quite literally so. Militants enjoy a bit of *keuz* ('cheese'; cf. Welsh *caws*); in Plounéour, some *fromage* (Fr.) is eaten, or some *fromaj* or *fu(/y/)rmaj* (Br.), but *keuz* means 'regret'. Another instance comparable to that of *liorzh/jardin* is offered by the term *gouest*, in regular use by militants to mean 'able', 'capable', or 'clever'. In Plounéour, and in many other areas, a distinction exists between *gouest* ('able', in a physical sense of being strong enough) and *kapabl* ('able', 'capable', or 'clever', as opposed to 'stupid'). Also, the term *straed* is widely used in the movement to mean 'street' or 'road' (translating the French *rue*) and, in correspondence with *emsaverien*, envelopes are expected to bear *straed*, not *rue*. In attempts to erect Breton or bilingual street signs and sign-posts, the movement is trying to have many a *rue* renamed *straed* in Brittany. However, in Plounéour, *straed* does not mean *rue*. A *rue* (or *ru*, if we were to render it into Breton orthography) is a street or road tarmacked and kept up by the commune; a *straed* is a dirt track, usually on private land. If the movement has

its way, many a posh urban *rue* in Brittany will become, somewhat incongruously to local native-speakers, a *straed*, or dirt track. In the militant world, I and others drove around in *ur c'harr-tan* (Br. 'a car'); many peasants in Plounéour are now the proud owners of *un auto* (or *un oto*, Br. 'a car') and I soon learnt that it was better for me to offer lifts in my *voiture* (Fr.) or in my *auto* (Br.), rather than in my 'fire-cart' (which is how the standard neologism *c'harr-tan* might translate literally). Similarly, local peasants may talk of *un avion* (Br.) while militants will talk of *ur c'harr-nij* (Br. 'an aeroplane'); the latter means, literally, 'flying-cart'.

3 In the militant world, the mismatch between *glas*/*gwer* in Breton and *bleu*/*vert* ('blue/green') in French is well known, and a favourite instance of the un-French and Celtic nature of Breton. In the teaching and learning of Breton in the movement, the difference between the Breton *glas* and the Breton *gwer* has been positivized in explanation. *Glas*, it is said, is used for the colour of 'natural' things (thus peasants can seem to see trees as *bleus* (Fr.), or 'blue', and, through French, offer an excitingly relativistic and poetic world); on the other hand, *gwer*, generally deemed to be an intrusion of the French *vert*, is said to be used only for 'artificial' things. This explanation, widespread in the movement, confirms a picture of Breton (*glas*) as speaking a 'natural' world, and French (*gwer*; cf. *vert*) an 'artificial' one. However, in Plounéour, the uses of *glas* and *gwer*, whether finding their relative meaning within Breton, or in the translational mismatches with French, did not wholly comply with this moral syntax. I noticed that a bright blue, plastic bucket in one village house was sometimes described as *glas*. It was quite distinctly *glas* in relation to another, light blue bucket, and also a very pale blue-greyish, plastic table-cloth, both of which were *gwer*. *Gwer* is often used to denote a relatively light, or greyish, or virtually transparent colour (and one local etymology likened *gwer* to *verre* ('glass' in French) and also to *gwerenn* or *ur werenn* in Breton ('a (drinking) glass')). In contrast, a bright solid blue (whether 'natural' or not) is often *glas*. Thérèse was one person who had heard militants explaining the proper difference between *glas* ('natural') and *gwer* ('artificial'), but to this difference itself she gave a different moral association. *Glas*, she told me, should 'really' only be used for 'nature – for things outside', and *gwer* for 'modern things'. Other people in Kerguz had a go one day at trying to sort this out for me, and became amused at the novelty of Breton/French translation it involved: 'It's true – in Breton we say *glas* for trees, and in French we say *vert*. Are trees blue (*bleus*) then ...?!' There was also a conviction of some genuine deficit in Breton: 'Trees, grass and sky – all that is *glas*; it's only in French we can make the difference.' One lady, however, summarily tidied it all up for me, to her own satisfaction: '*Glas* is *bleu*, and *gwer* is *vert*'.

4 For example, I acquired a whole new set of past tenses in Breton (involving a double compound or indefinite perfect): these forms are very common in local speech, but I had never learnt to use them in Rennes, and they have been omitted from the most well-known Breton-learning manual altogether (for some details of these forms, see Hewitt 1977:30–1). Some associated with the 'Brest' camp in the movement have been especially critical of this omission, particularly because the double compounds have no equivalent in educated French. However, scholars of the 'Rennes' side in the movement have also had their misgivings about their Breton. They have noticed, for example, that they have, in their own models and manuals, asserted a grammatical difference between certain verbal particles, a difference which simply does not pertain in much local speech (see Urien and Denez 1975). Such a difference, I found, does pertain in Plounéour, but the verbal particles are themselves different from

those of standard texts. In standard Breton, there is also a distinction between present and past conditional tenses, which is not made or recognized in Plounéour.

5 People in Plounéour were amused and intrigued to watch me writing down Breton words when I took notes. 'We don't write Breton', I was told. Thérèse had one day told me of how her father-in-law in Kerguz (who had also been able to read some Breton, from the catechism) had been unable to speak at all when very ill on his death-bed. When asked questions (in Breton), he would scribble replies on a piece of paper. He was regularly asked if he wanted to eat, and his very last word was a large, if shaky, French '*NON*'. There was surprise at my surprise that this man had never written a single word in Breton, or even attempted to do so. The Breton orthography to which Thérèse had been accustomed, in the catechism and *Buez ar Zent* ('Lives of Saints'), approximated to the KLT (see Chapter seven, p. 130).

6 When opening conversation with new acquaintances in Plounéour, it is important to answer a common first question: 'Who are you?' Some answer such as 'Well, actually, I am a researcher doing ...' (etc.) means automatic exclusion from the category of 'local', in the mode of expression alone. Usually, the answer would be in the form of kin relations (e.g., 'I am the daughter of so-and-so's first cousin ...', or its equivalent 'I am the cousin of so-and-so') and/ or with the commune, village, or hamlet of residence tagged on to the end of one's name. My own answer to such queries, within Plounéour, became 'I am the friend of Thérèse of Kerguz', or I was '*l'Anglaise Kerguz*'. Thérèse herself, often 'Thérèse Kerguz' (where she had her immediate family and land) within Plounéour, changed when she visited relatives in the plain, taking on the name of her late father's family and the village they inhabited there (and in which she was still heir to a small share of land).

7 This was evident when one well-respected peasant told me he had heard that 'a long time ago' some *Anglais* had come over the Channel and settled in Brittany; he then proceeded to collapse this into some more of them – pirates, he said – coming in the Middle Ages, and yet more coming on Brittany Ferries, on weekend shopping trips; and he linked this all up to the British imperial presence and exports in the EEC. 'You are always invading and colonizing us – it's still going on!' With the entry of Spain in the EEC, the axis may now change, and the peasantry of the northern Breton coast in particular (competing, as they do, with Spanish vegetables for the British market) may well discover their Celtic roots.

Conclusion

1 After the Socialist victory of 1981, *Diwan* had expanded fast, imagining that all its schools would be funded by the promised 'integration' scheme (see Chapter twelve). This funding was not immediately forthcoming and it became clear that certain conditions had to be met: only schools of at least two years of age, for instance, would be integrated. In late 1982, *Diwan* took matters into its own hands and stopped paying employers' taxes to the State. In 1983, a '*Convention*' was signed awarding *Diwan* state funding for three years. This did not cover all *Diwan*'s expenditure. The possibility of full integration was still under discussion. Militant protest at the delay, and *Diwan*'s debts, grew. In 1985, the fact that the National Assembly had voted in the framework of finance (rather than education) law for *Diwan*'s financial integration into the national education system held things up further within a web of legal and constitutional

discussion. In January 1986, the Ministry of Education proposed another possibility: the phased integration of the number of *Diwan* teachers previously negotiated (thirty-one of them), but as assistant teachers. In virtual desperation, *Diwan* agreed. Then came the election of March 1986, and a change of government. *Diwan* waited. By October 1986, representatives had managed to speak to the new Minister of Education, Monory. The terms now on offer involved integrating only twelve of the teachers, backdated to January 1986 (and with little compensation for the seventeen posts not integrated). *Diwan*, in increasingly difficult financial straits, agreed, but urged the government to sort things out for the coming year, according to the terms of the old 1986 agreement. By this time, few beyond *Diwan*'s own representatives seemed to know what those terms were, or the status of that agreement. At the end of 1986, *Diwan* approached the *Recteur* in Rennes, who in turn requested clarification from the Minister. The response came in January 1987: the agreement made between *Diwan* and the Minister of the previous government, just prior to the elections, was the 'fruit of particular circumstances' and not binding on the new government of Chirac.

Bibliography

Abjean, R. (1975) *La Musique Bretonne*, Châteaulin: Jos Le Doaré.
ADI–V (1979) *Bretagne XVIIIe. Etats ou Intendance?* Rennes: Archives
d'Ille-et-Vilaine.
Albistur, M. and Armogathe, D. (1977) *Histoire du féminisme français*, 2 vols,
Paris: Editions des Femmes.
Amouret, M. L. (1977) 'Bretonnismes', *Ar Helenner* 1 (January), Brest.
Anderson, B. (1983) *Imagined Communities*, London: Verso.
Anderson, R. D. (1975) *Education in France. 1848–1870*, Oxford: Oxford
University Press.
Anon. (1895) See F. Vallée 1895, below.
Ar C'halvez (Abbé) (1959) 'Daou Vloavezhiad E Skol St. Erwan: Danevell Rener
ar Skol', *Skol* 6 (July).
Ardener, E. (1967) 'The Nature of the Reunification of Cameroon', in A.
Hazelwood (ed.) *African Integration and Disintegration*, Oxford: Oxford
University Press.
—— (1971a) 'Introduction' to *Social Anthropology and Language*, E. Ardener
(ed.) ASA Monographs 10, London: Tavistock.
—— (1971b) 'Social anthropology and the historicity of historical linguistics', in
Social Anthropology and Language, E. Ardener (ed.), ASA Monographs 10,
London: Tavistock.
—— (1971c) 'The new Anthropology and its critics', *Man* 6: 449–67.
—— (1972a) 'Language, ethnicity and population', *JASO* 3 (3).
—— (1972b) 'Belief and the problem of women', in J. La Fontaine (ed.) *The
Interpretation of Ritual*, London: Tavistock.
—— (1974) 'Social anthropology and population', in H. B. Parry (ed.) *Population
and its Problems*, Oxford: Clarendon Press.
—— (1975a) 'Further problems: the analysis of events', Munro Lecture, Edinburgh
University.
—— (1975b) 'The problem revisited' in S. Ardener (ed.) *Perceiving Women*,
London: Dent.
—— (1978) 'Some outstanding problems in the analysis of events', in
E. Schwimmer (ed.). *The Yearbook of Symbolic Anthropology*, vol. 1, London:
Hurst.
—— (1982) 'Social anthropology, language and reality', in D. Parkin (ed.)
Semantic Anthropology, London: Academic Press.
Ardener, S. (1975) *Perceiving Women*, London: Dent.
Ariès, P. (1948) *Histoire des Populations Françaises*, Paris: Editions Self.
—— (1979) *Centuries of Childhood*, Harmondsworth: Peregrine Books, (first
published in 1960).

Audic, R. *et al.* (1934) 'Pour les langues provinciales. Fédéralisme. (Enquête)', *Cahiers de la Quinzaine*, 6 July 1934.

Balibar, R. and Laporte, D. (1974) *Le français national*, Paris: Hachette.

Banton, M. and Harwood, J. (1975) *The Race Concept*, Newton Abbot: David & Charles.

Barère, P. B. (1794) *Rapport et projet de decret présentés au nom du Comité de Salut Public, Sur les idiomes étrangers et l'enseignement de la langue française. (8 pluviose an II)*, Convention Nationale, Imprimerie Nationale (ADF: E186).

Barth, F. (1969) 'Introduction' to *Ethnic Groups and Boundaries*, London: Allen & Unwin.

Beauvoir, S. de (1949) *Le Deuxième Sexe*, 2 vols, Paris: Gallimard.

Beer, W. R. (1977) 'The social class of ethnic activists in contemporary France' in M. J. Esman (ed.) *Ethnic Conflict in the Western World*, Ithaca, NY: Cornell University Press.

Berger, S. (1972) *Peasants Against Politics: Rural Organization in Brittany 1911–1967*, Cambridge, Mass.: Harvard University Press.

—— (1975) *Les Paysans Contre la Politique*, translation, by J. -P. Huet, of Berger 1972, Paris: Editions du Seuil.

—— (1977) 'Bretons and Jacobins: reflections on French regional ethnicity', in M. J. Esman (ed.) *Ethnic Conflict in the Western World*, Ithaca, NY: Cornell University Press.

Bernard, D. (1911–12) 'Deux écrits de propagande en langue bretonne', *Annales de Bretagne* XXVII.

—— (1912–13) 'La Révolution Française et la Langue Bretonne', *Annales de Bretagne* XXVIII.

—— (1917) 'La Langue Bretonne et l'Ecole Primaire: un projet officiel d'enseignement bilingue, en Basse Bretagne en 1831', *Annales de Bretagne* XXXII.

—— (1921) 'Le Breton dans les Actes Publics', *Annales de Bretagne* XXXV.

Bernard, L. (1976) *Les Ecoles Sauvages*, Paris: Vivre/Stock 2.

Berstein, S. (1977) 'Le Parti Radical et le problème du centralisme (1870–1939)', in C. Gras and G. Livet (eds) *Régions et régionalisme en France du XVIIIe siècle à nos jours*, Paris: PUF.

Bertho, C. (1980) 'L'Invention de la Bretagne: Genèse sociale d'un stéréotype', *Actes de la Recherche en Sciences Sociales* 35.

Bertrand, Y. and Caro, G. (1977) *Alcoolisme et Bretagne*, Rennes: CIRREES.

Bertrand, Y., Jégou Y., and Potet-Kergoat, M. (1978) 'Fresque historique de l'économie de la Bretagne (1950–1975)', *Cahiers Economiques de la Bretagne* 2–3.

Black, G. F. (1926) *MacPherson's Ossian and the Ossianic Controversy*, The New York Public Library.

Bonneton, C. (ed.) (1979) *Bretagne*, Le Puy: Bonneton.

Boucheron and Nonus (1890) 'Compte-rendu des Conférences d'Octobre 1889 (Carré I.)', in *BOSIP* (*Acad. de Rennes: département du Finistère*), (first published in 1889).

Bouët, A. and Perrin, O. (1970) *Breiz-Izel ou Vie des Bretons de l'Armorique*, Paris: Tchou, (first published in 1844).

Bourdieu, P. (1975) 'Le fétichisme de la langue', *Actes de la Recherche en Science Sociales* 4.

Brekilien, Y. (1972) *Le Livre des Vacances en Bretagne*, Quimper: Nature et Bretagne.

—— (1976) *Le Breton, Langue Celtique*, Quimper: Nature et Bretagne.

—— (1977) *Histoire de la Région Bretagne*, Paris: Hachette.

Broudic, F. (1984) 'Bibliographie des publications consacrées à la langue et à la littérature bretonnes', *Bulletin de la Société Archéologique du Finistère* CXII (2): 253–91.

Broudig, F. (1968) 'Mouvement de Mai et culture bretonne', *Ar Falz* 5 (October).

Brousmiche, J. F. (1977) *Voyage dans le Finistère en 1829, 1830 et 1831*, 2 vols, Morvran, (first published in 1829–31).

Burguière, A. (1977) *Bretons de Plozevet*, Paris: Flammarion.

Calvet, L. J. (1974) *Linguistique et Colonialisme*, Paris: Payot.

Cambry, J. de (1801) *Voyage dans le Finistère, ou état de ce département en 1794 et 1795*, 3 vols, Paris.

Canévet, R. *et al.* (1899) 'La rédaction à l'école primaire' (letters from 3 teachers: R. Canévet, P.M.N., and 'X'), *BPIIF* 36:193–7.

Carioù, A. (1955) 'L'Instruction dans le Département du Morbihan à la veille de la Révolution de 1789', *Mémoires de la société d'histoire et d'archéologie de Bretagne* XXXV.

Cariou, J. (1896) 'Le breton et l'enseignement du français', *BPIIF* 8:303–5.

Carré, I. (1888) 'De la manière d'enseigner les premiers éléments du français dans les écoles de la Basse-Bretagne', *Revue Pédagogique* XII (3): 217–236, 15 March 1888.

Certeau, M. de, Julia, D., and Revel, J. (1975) *Une politique de la langue: La Révolution française et les patois*, Paris: Gallimard.

Chadwick, N. (1965) *The Colonization of Brittany from Celtic Britain*, Proceedings of the British Academy LI, Oxford: Oxford University Press.

—— (1969) *Early Brittany*, Cardiff: University of Wales Press.

Chapman, M. (1978) *The Gaelic Vision in Scottish Culture*, London: Croom Helm.

Chapman, M. and McDonald, M. (1982) 'Bretons and Scottish Gaels: a comparison of two Celtic minorities', research paper.

Charency, Le Comte de, Gaidoz, H., and Gaulle, Charles de (1903) *Pétition pour les Langues Provinciales au Corps Législatif de 1870*, Paris: Picard et fils.

Charpy, J. (1972) 'Dénombrements de la population des communes du Finistère', *BSAF* XCIX.

Chédeville, A. (1974) 'L'immigration bretonne dans le royaume de France du XIe au début du XIVe siècle', *Annales de Bretagne* 81.

Chervel, A. (1977) *... et il fallut apprendre à ecrire à tous les petits français. Histoire de la grammaire scolaire*, Paris: Payot.

Chevallier, G. (1934) *Clochemerle*, Presses Universitaires de France.

CNB (1981a) 'La Langue Interdite; La Licence en Rade; Un Siècle de Pétitions', *CNB* 106 (10–17 June 1981): 8–9. ·

—— (1981b) *La Bretagne, Fille Bâtarde de la République*, Special issue of *CNB* 1981, 107–8 (July–August).

Cobban, A. (1969) *The Nation State and National Self-Determination*, London: Collins.

Cohen, A. (1985) *The Symbolic Construction of Community*, London and New York: Tavistock/Horwood.

Cohen, M. (1973) *Histoire d'une langue: le français*, Paris: Editions Sociales, (first published in 1947).

Contamine, P. (1976) *La Vie Quotidienne Pendant La Guerre de Cent Ans. France et Angleterre*, Paris: Hachette.

Coornaert, E. (1977) *Destins de Clio en France depuis 1800*, Paris: Les Editions Ouvrières.

Coward, R. (1983) *Patriarchal Precedents*, London: Routledge & Kegan Paul.

CRDP (1976) *Le Finistère 1800–1914 (les hommes)*, Rennes: CRDP.

—— (1978) *La Révolution dans Le Finistère. 1789–1799*, Rennes: CRDP.

Cressard, J. C. (1979) '"Aux Origines du Nationalisme Breton" . . .', *Pluriel* 18: 91–7.

Creston, R. Y. (1978) *Le Costume Breton*, Paris: Tchou.

Crick, M. (1976) *Towards a Semantic Anthropology. Explorations in Language and Meaning*, London: Malaby.

Croix, A. (1981) *La Bretagne aux 16e et 17e siècles*. vol. 1, Paris: Maloine.

Crubellier, M. (1979) *L'enfance et la jeunesse dans la société française 1800–1950*, Paris: Colin.

Cuisenier, J. and Ségalen, M. (1986) *Ethnologie de la France*, Paris: PUF.

Daucé, P. and Léon Y. (1978) *L'Evolution de la Population Agricole en Bretagne de 1850 à Nos Jours*, document de travail (February), Rennes: INRA.

Daucé, P. and Roze, B. (1975) *Le retard de la préscolarisation dans les campagnes*, Rennes: INRA.

Dauzat, A. (1930) *Histoire de la langue française*, Paris: Payot.

Davis, J. (1977) *People of the Mediterranean. An Essay in Comparative Social Anthropology*, London: Routledge & Kegan Paul.

Dayries, J. and M. (1978) *La Régionalisation*, Paris: Presses Universitaires de France, '*Que sais-je?*' series.

Decap, de la Martinière, and Bideau (1914) *L'Instruction primaire en France aux XVIIIe et XIXe siècles*, Paris: F. Rieder.

Decaux, A. (1979) 'La Charte culturelle . . . et après?', *Autrement* 19:211–13.

Delaporte, R. (1977) *Brezhoneg . . . Buan hag aes. A beginner's course in Breton*, translation of Denez 1972, Cork: Cork University Press.

Denez, P. (1958) *Au Sujet de l'Orthographe Breton – Aide-mémoire rédigé pour Kuzul ar Brezhoneg*, typescript.

—— (1972) *Brezhoneg . . . Buan hag aes*, Paris: Omnivox.

—— (1975) 'Hag adarre . . . an doare-skrivañ!', *Hor Yezh* (supplement) 99 (May).

Déniel, A. (1976) *Le Mouvement Breton, 1919–1945*, Paris: Maspero.

—— (1979) 'L'évolution politique du mouvement breton durant les années vingt', *Pluriel* 18: 5–22.

Denis, M. (1977) 'Mouvement breton et fascisme. Signification de l'échec du second emsav', in C. Gras and G. Livet (eds) *Régions et Régionalisme en France du XVIIIe siècle à Nòs Jours*. Paris: Presses Universitaires de France, (first published in 1974).

Dosimont, J. (1897) 'Le breton et l'enseignement du français', *BPIIF* 11 (1 February): 361–5.

Droixhe, D. (1978) *La Linguistique et l'appel de l' histoire (1600–1800). Rationalisme et révolutions positivistes*, Geneva: Librairie Droz.

Dubois, C.-G. (1972) *Celtes et Gaulois au XVIe siècle: Le Développement Littéraire d'un Mythe Nationaliste*, Paris: J. Vrin.

Duclos, P. (1980–1) 'Les "ismes" de l'Emsav', *CNB* 80 (December–January).

Duigou, S. (1979) *La Bretagne Ayant Dansé Tout l'Eté*, Le Guilvinec: Le Signor.

Dujardin, L. (1949) *La Vie et Les Oeuvres de Jean-François-Marie-Maurice-Agathe Le Gonidec. Grammarien et Lexicographe breton, 1775–1838*, Brest: Imprimerie Commerciale et Administrative.

Dumville, D. (1983) 'Ekiurid's *Celta Lingua*: an ethnological difficulty in Waltharius', *Cambridge Medieval Celtic Studies* 6: 87–93.

Dupuy, A. (1888) *L'Enseignement Supérieur en Bretagne avant et après la Révolution*, Rennes: Oberthur.

Durand, R. (1912) 'La question de l'Ecole du Breton dans le Département des Côtes-du-Nord sous la Monarchie de Juillet', *Annales de Bretagne* 1912, November.

—— (1912–13) 'Le Collège de Saint Brieuc en 1763', *Annales de Bretagne* XXVIII

Duranton, H. (1969) '"Nos ancêtres, les Gaulois". Genèse et avatars d'un cliché historique', *Cahiers d'Histoire* XIV.

Elegoët, F. (1979) 'Prêtres, Nobles et Paysans en Léon au début du XXe siècle. Notes sur un nationalisme breton: *Feiz ha Breiz* 1900–1914', *Pluriel* 18.

Ellen, R. F. (1984) *Ethnographic Research. A Guide to General Conduct*, London and Orlando, USA: Academic Press.

Emgleo Breiz (1972) 'The Situation of the language and culture of Brittany', *Brud* 41b (July).

Epstein, A. L. (1978) *Ethos and Identity*, London: Tavistock.

Ernault, E. (1935) 'Le Breton et L'Enseignement' (Extrait des *Mémoires de la Société d'Emulation des Côtes-du-Nord*), St Brieuc: Les Presses Bretonnes.

Esman, M. J. (ed.) (1977) *Ethnic Conflict in the Western World*, Ithaca, NY: Cornell University Press.

Etiemble, R. (1964) *Parlez-vous franglais?*, Paris: Gallimard.

Evans-Pritchard, E. (1941) *The Nuer*, Oxford: Clarendon Press.

Fahy, D. (1964) 'When did Britons become Bretons? A note on the foundation of Brittany', *Welsh Historical Review (Cylchgrawn Hanes Cymru)* 2(2).

Falc'hun, F. (1953) 'Autour de l'Orthographe Bretonne', *Annales de Bretagne* LX (1–2).

—— (1956) *L'Orthographe Universitaire de la Langue Bretonne*, Brest: Emgleo Breiz.

—— (1962a) 'Le Breton, Forme Moderne du Gaulois', *Annales de Bretagne* LXIX (4, December).

—— (1962b) 'Une controverse sur les origines de la langue bretonne', *Les Cahiers de l'Iroise* October–December: 178–84.

—— (1963) *Histoire de la langue bretonne d'après la géographie linguistique*, Paris: PUF.

—— (1970) *Les Noms de Lieux Celtique*, Rennes: Editions Armoricaines.

Favereau, F. (1981) 'Le Breton et son Enseignement', *Ar Falz* 34.

Fichou, M. (1981) *Bretonnismes*, CRDP (Finistère), (first published in 1977).

Fishman, J. (1972) *Language and Nationalism*, Mass.: Newbury House.

Flandrin, J. -L. (1979) *Families in Former Times*, Cambridge: Cambridge University Press.

Flatrès, L. (1920) *Contribution aux efforts d'amélioration de l'Enseignement du Français et en particulier de la Composition Française dans les Ecoles Rurales Bretonnes*, Quimper: Jaouen.

Fleuriot, L. (1980) *Les Origines de la Bretagne*, Paris: Payot.

—— (1981) *Les Réformes du Breton*, typescript.

Fleuriot, L. and S. (1972) 'Studies of Celtic Languages in France', *Word* 28 (1–2).

Foucher, J.-P. and Ar Floc'h, L. (1977) *Le brasier des ancêtres. Poèmes populaires de la Bretagne*, Paris: 10/18.

Fouere, Y. (1935) *Nous Devons Obtenir l'Enseignement du Breton. (Conférence du 5 septembre 1935 au Congrès de l'Union Régionaliste Bretonne)*, Rennes: Imprimerie Provinciale de l'Ouest.

—— (1938) 'Le Combat D'Ar Brezoneg er Skol pour l'enseignement du breton' in *Ar Brezoneg er skol; Union pour l'enseignement du breton*, Rennes: Imprimerie Provinciale de l'Ouest.

—— (1977) *Histoire Résumée du Mouvement Breton du XIXe siècle à nos jours*, Quimper: Nature et Bretagne.

Frankenberg, R. (1957) *Village on the Border*, London: Cohen & West.

—— (1966) *Communities in Britain: Social Life in Town and Country*, London: Penguin.

—— (1982) 'Participant observers', in R. Burgess (ed.) *Field Research: A Sourcebook and Field Manual*, London: Allen & Unwin, (first published in 1963).

Freinet, C. (1977) *Pour l'école du peuple*, Paris: Maspero, pre-1968 title: *L'école moderne française*, (first published in 1948 and 1968).

Frémy, D. and M. (1980) *Quid*, Paris: Laffont.

Fréville, H. (1979) *La Presse Bretonne Dans La Tourmente. 1940–1946*, Paris: Plon.

Galv (1969) *Livre Noir et Blanc de la Langue Bretonne*, special issue of *Ar Falz* 9, Brest.

Gaulle, C. de (1865) 'Mouvement de renaissance de la littérature bretonne', *Revue de Bretagne et de Vendée* VIII.

Gazier, A. (ed.) (1969) *Lettres à Grégoire sur les patois de France. 1790–1794*, Geneva: Slatkine Reprints, (first published in 1880).

Geertz, C. (1973) *The Interpretation of Cultures*, New York: Basic Books.

—— (1983) *Local Knowledge*. New York: Basic Books.

Geledan, A. (1978) *Les Syndicats*, Paris: Hatier.

Gellner, E. (1983) *Nations and Nationalism*, Oxford: Blackwell.

Gendre, C. and Javelier, F. (1978) *Ecole, histoire de France et minorités nationales*, Lyons: Fédérop.

Giacomo, M. (1975) 'La Politique à propos des langues régionales: cadre historique', *Langue Française* 25 (February).

Gildea, R. (1976) 'Education in nineteenth-century Brittany: Ille-et-Vilaine, 1800–1914', *Oxford Review of Education* 2 (3).

Giordan, H. (1982) *Démocratie culturelle et droit à la difference*, Paris: La Documentation Française.

Girardin, J.-C. (1971) 'Célestin Freinet: pédagogue révolutionnaire', *Les Temps Modernes* August–September.

Glazer, N. and Moynihan, D. P. (eds) (1975) *Ethnicity*, Cambridge, Mass.: Harvard University Press.

Godfrey, R. J. (1974) *Primary Education in France between 1879 and 1914, with special reference to the 'department' of Finistère*, D.Phil. thesis, University of Exeter.

Gordon, D. C. (1978) *The French Language and National Identity*, The Hague: Mouton.

Gourmelon, I. (1976) 'Gerioù galleg er brezhoneg komzet', *Skol Vreiz* 45 (April–June).

—— (1977) 'Quelques données quantitatives sur les différences dialectales du vocabulaire breton', *Skol Vreizh* 50 (January–March).

Gourvil, F. (1960) *Théodore-Claude-Henri Hersart de La Villemarqué (1815–1895) et le 'Barzaz-Breiz' (1839–1845–1867)*, Rennes: Imprimerie Oberthur.

Grall, X. (1977) *Le cheval couché*, Paris: Hachette.

Gras, C. and Livet, G. (eds) (1977) *Régions et régionalisme en France du XVIIIe siècle à nos jours*, Paris: PUF.

Gréard, O. (1891–1902) *La Législation de l'Instruction Primaire en France depuis 1789 jusqu'à nos jours*, Paris: Delalain, 7 vols, (first published in 1873).

Gregor, D. B. (1980) *Celtic: A Comparative Study*, Cambridge, UK/New York: The Oleander Press.

Groult, B. (1975) *Ainsi soit-elle*, Paris: Grasset.

Guieysse, M. (1925) *La Langue Bretonne*, Hennebont: Méhat.

—— (1936) *La Langue Bretonne*, Quimper: Nouvelles Editions Bretonnes.

Guilcher, J.-M. (1976) *La tradition populaire de danse en Basse Bretagne*, The Hague: Mouton, (first published in 1963).

—— (1979) 'La danse traditionelle en Basse Bretagne', in C. Bonneton (ed.) *Bretagne*, Le Puy: Bonneton.

Gunther, R. T. (1945) *Early Science in Oxford*, vol. XIV, Oxford: Oxford University Press.

Guyonvarc'h, C-J. (1973) *Dictionnaire Etymologique Du Breton Ancien, Moyen et Moderne: Introduction*, Rennes: Ogam-Celticum, Supplement, vol. 24.

Gwegen, J. (1975) *La Langue Bretonne Face à Ses Oppresseurs*, Quimper: Nature et Bretagne.

Haagerup, N. (1984) *Report, drawn up on behalf of the Political Affairs Committee, on the situation in Northern Ireland*, European Parliament Working Documents, Document 1–1526/83.

Haas X. and Caouissin, H. (1969) *Breizh. Visions d'Histoire*, Fontenay-aux-Roses: Melezour Breizh.

Halimi, G. (1973) *La Cause des Femmes*, Paris: Grasset.

Halléguen, E. (1872–4) *Armorique et Bretagne*, 2 vols, Paris: Didier, Librairie Académique.

Halls, W. D. (1976) *Education, Culture and Politics in Modern France*, Oxford: Pergamon Press.

—— (1981) *The Youth of Vichy France*, Oxford: Clarendon Press.

Hardie, D. W. F. (1948) *A Handbook of Modern Breton (Armorican)*, Cardiff: University of Wales Press.

Harris, R. (1980) *The Language Makers*, London: Duckworth.

Hay, D. (1955) 'The use of the term "Great Britain" in the Middle Ages', *Proceedings of the Society of Antiquaries of Scotland* 1955–6: 55–66.

Hayward, J. (1969) 'From functional regionalism to functional representation in France: the battle of Brittany', *Political Studies* 1969 (March).

—— (1976)*Institutionalized Inequality within an Indivisible Republic: Brittany and France*, paper presented at the Edinburgh Conference of the International Political Science Association, August 1976, typescript.

Hechter, M. and Levi, M. (1980) *The Rise and Decline of Ethnoregional Political Parties: Scotland, Wales and Brittany*, typescript, University of Washington.

Hélias, P. J. (1971) 'Brezoneg ar re vianna', *Skol Vreiz*, 26.

—— (1975) *Le Cheval d'Orgueil. Mémoires d'un breton du pays bigouden*, Paris: Plon.

—— (1977) *Le Savoir-Vivre en Bretagne*, Châteaulin: Jos Le Doaré.

Hemon, R. (1925) 'A-enep ar Gelannadurez Diouyezek', *Breiz Atao* 78 (June).

—— (1928a) *L'Instruction du peuple breton par le breton et l'oeuvre de Gwalarn*, Brest: Gwalarn.

—— (1928b)'Lizer d'ar Vreudeur Tramor' *Gwalarn* 13 (spring).

—— (1928c) 'Hon enklask diwar-benn stad ar Brezoneg', *Gwalarn* 14 (summer).

—— (1929a) 'Enklask diwar-benn stad ar Brezoneg e 1928', *Gwalarn* 17 (spring) and 19 (autumn).

—— (1929b) *L'Orthographe du Breton/Reizskrivadur ar Brezhoneg*, Brest.

—— (1930) 'Notenn diwar-benn levezon ar C'hembraeg war ar Brezoneg', *Gwalarn* 23 (autumn).

—— (1931) *Eur Breizad Oc'h Adkavout Breiz*, Brest.

—— (1936) 'Peurunvani', *Gwalarn* 94 (September) and 95–6 (October–November).

—— (1938) 'Kredenn "Gwalarn" e-keñver kudenn an doare-skriva', *Gwalarn* 119–20 (October–November).

—— (1939) 'Eur yez hepken', *Gwalarn* 122.

—— (1942) *An doare-skriva nevez*, Rennes: Imprimerie Centrale de Rennes.

—— (1947) *La Langue Bretonne et Ses Combats*, La Baule: Editions de Bretagne.

Hemon, R. (1953) 'Ur Yezh Etrekeltiek', *Ar Bed Keltiek* 49 (January).
—— (1956) 'Un Doare-skrivañ Fall Du', *Ar Bed Keltiek* 134 (November).
—— (1957) 'Adembann Barzhaz Breizh', *Ar Bed Keltiek* 1957 (January).
—— (1964) 'Ur yezh c'hlan', *Ar Bed Keltiek* 64.
—— (1972a) 'A-enep ar gelennadurezh divyezhek', in R. Hemon *Ur breizhad oc'h adkavout breizh*, Brest: Al Liamm, (first published in 1925 and 1931).
—— (1972b) *Ur breizhad oc'h adkavout breizh*, Brest: Al Liamm, (first published in 1931).
—— (1973) *Nouveau Dictionnaire Breton Français*, fifth edition, Brest: Al Liamm.
—— (1974) *Dictionnaire Français Breton*, Brest: Al Liamm, (first published in 1947).
—— (1975a) *Grammaire Bretonne*, eighth edition, Brest: Al Liamm, (first published in 1940).
—— (1975b) *Cours de Breton élémentaire*, eighth edition, Brest: Al Liamm.
—— (1976) 'Yezh komzet ha yezh skrivet', *Al Liamm* 175.
—— (1959–78) *Geriadur Istorel ar Brezhoneg*, special issues of *Preder*, Rennes.
Hemon, R. and Mordrel, O. (1925) 'Premier et Dernier Manifeste en Langue Française', *Gwalarn* 1 (spring).
Henson, H. (1974) *British Social Anthropologists and Language*, Oxford: Clarendon Press.
Heppenstall, R. (1958) 'The Children of Gomer', *The Times Literary Supplement* 17 October 1958: 600.
Herrieu, M. (1974) *Gwenedeg. Le Breton du Morbihan. Vannetais*, Paris: Presses de la Néogravure.
—— (1981) *Dictionnaire Français Breton. Vannetais*, Bro-Gwened: Editions Bleun-Brug.
Hervé, P. (1981) *Maisons Rurales de Bretagne*, Morlaix: Skol Vreizh.
Hervieu, B. and Leger, D. (1979) *Le Retour à la nature. Au fond de la forêt . . . l'Etat*, Paris: Editions du Seuil.
Herzfeld, M. (1980) 'Honour and shame: problems in the comparative analysis of moral systems', *Man* 15(2).
Heusaff, A. (1970) 'Currents in the Breton Movement', in *'The Celt in the Seventies': Celtic League Annual*, special issue.
Hewitt, S. M. (1977) *The Degree of Acceptability of Modern Literary Breton to Native Breton Speakers*, Linguistics diploma thesis, University of Cambridge.
Houée, P. (1979) *Bretagne en mutation*, 2 vols, Rennes: INRA.
Husband, C. (ed.) (1982) *'Race' in Britain: Continuity and Change*, London: Hutchinson.
Illich, I. (1974) *Une société sans école*, Paris: Editions du Seuil.
Imbourc'h (1980) *Geriadur Ar Brezhoneg Arnevez*, special issue of *Imbourc'h* 125–6 (15 September 1980).
INSEE (1973) *Annuaire Statistique Régional: Bretagne*, Rennes: INSEE.
—— (1980) *Annuaire Statistique Régional: Bretagne*, Rennes: INSEE.
Izard, M. (1965) 'La terminologie de parenté bretonne', *L'Homme* 1965, V (3–4): 88–100.
Jackson, K. H. (1967) *A Historical Phonology of Breton*, Dublin: Dublin Institute for Advanced Studies.
JAC–MRJC (1979) *50 ans d'animation rural*, Paris: Promo.
Jacob, Y. (1981) *Les Conflits A Propos De La Langue Bretonne Dans Le Diocèse de Quimper et de Léon au Début du XXe Siècle*, unpublished TER thesis, Université de Bretagne Occidentale, Brest.
Jarman, A. O. H. and Hughes, G. R. (1976) *A Guide to Welsh literature*, vol. I, Swansea: C. Davies.
Jégouzo, G. (1979) 'Le Célibat Paysan en 1975', *Population* 1: 27–41.

Jégouzo, G. and Brangeon, J-L. (1976) *Les paysans et l'école*, Editions Cujas.

Johnson, D. (1986) 'French identity: the historian's view', paper presented to ASMCF Annual Conference on 'France: Image and Identity', Newcastle Polytechnic, September 1986, in J. Bridgford (ed.) *Image and Identity in France*, Association for the Study of Modern and Contemporary France, 1987.

Johnson, D., Bédarida, F., and Crouzet, F. (eds) (1980) *Britain and France: Ten Centuries*, Folkestone: Dawson.

Jones, D. (1706) *The Antiquities of Nations: More particularly of the Celtae or Gauls, Taken to be Originally the Same People as our Ancient Britains*, London: Janeway.

Jones, D. M. (1971) 'Left-Wing Nationalism in Brittany', *Planet* 7 (August–September).

Jones, M. (1970) *Ducal Brittany. 1364–1399*, Oxford: Oxford University Press.

—— (1975) 'L'enseignement en Bretagne à la fin du Moyen Age: quelques terrains de recherche', *Mémoires de la Société d'histoire et d'archéologie* LIII.

—— (1976) '"Mon Païs et ma Nation": Breton identity in the fourteenth century', in C. T. Allmand (ed.) *War, Literature and Politics in the Late Middle Ages*, Liverpool: Liverpool University Press.

—— (1978) 'Education in Brittany during the later Middle Ages: a survey', *Nottingham Mediaeval Studies* xxii.

Kalvez, T. (1977) 'Pour un quatuor de dialectes', *Ar Falz* 18, (first published in 1974).

Keating, M. (1985) 'The rise and decline of micronationalism in mainland France', *Political Studies* XXXIII: 1–18.

Kedourie, E. (1960) *Nationalism*, London: Hutchinson.

Keravel, A. and Thomin, J- P. (1981) 'La Charte Culturelle de Bretagne', *Bretagne. Mode d'emploi* (supplement to the journal *Autrement* 32), Paris.

Kergoat, L. (1975) *Reolennoù an Doare-Skrivañ Nevez*, Skol an Emsav, cyclostyled, Rennes/Quimper.

—— (1980) *Istor ar Brezhoneg, Kevredigezh ha Politikerez*, Skol an Emsav, typescript.

Kerhervé, J. (1986) *L'Etat Breton aux 14e et 15e siècles. Les ducs, l'argent et les hommes*, 2 vols, Paris: Maloine.

Kerlann (1980) 'Skol Blistin 1942–1944', *Skrid* 22 (1980): 33–44, (first published in 1959).

Kohn, H. (1962) *The Age of Nationalism*, New York: Harper.

Krier, H. and Ergan, L. (1976) *Bretagne de 1975 à 1985. (Informations et conjoncture)*, Paris: SOCEDIT Press.

Kuter, L. (1981) *Breton Identity: Musical and Linguistic Expression in Brittany, France*. Ph.D. thesis, Indiana University, USA.

Laslett, P. (1972) 'The history of the family', in P. Laslett and R. Wall (eds) *Household and Family in Past Time*, Cambridge: Cambridge University Press.

Laurent, D. (1974) *la Villemarqué, collecteur de chants populaires. Etudes des sources du premier 'Barzaz Breiz', à partir des originaux de collecte (1833–1840)*, 4 vols, Brest: Université de Bretagne Occidentale.

Laurent, J. (1972) *Un Monde Rural en Bretagne du XVe siècle. La Quevaise*, Paris: SEVPEN Press.

Laurent, L. (1969) *En Faveur de la Langue Bretonne*, Brest and Redon: Editions Kendalc'h.

La Villemarqué, Th. H. de (1850) *Dictionnaire breton-français de Le Gonidec, précédé de la Grammaire bretonne et enrichi d'un avant-propos, d'additions et des mots gallois et gaéliques correspondant au breton*, St Brieuc: Prud'homme.

—— (1963) *Barzaz Breiz. Chants Populaires de la Bretagne*, Evreux: Perrin, (edition first published in 1867).

La Villemarqué, Th. H. de (1977) *Essai sur l'histoire de la langue bretonne*, vol. 2 of B. Tanguy (ed.) *Aux origines du nationalisme breton*, Paris: 10/18, (first published in 1847).

Leach, E. (1954) *Political Systems of Highland Burma*, London: Bell.

Le Berre, L. (1935) *Rapport du Comité de Préservation de Langue Bretonne*, 3 July 1935, St Brieuc: Prud'homme.

Lebesque, M. (1970) *Comment peut-on être Breton?*, Paris: Editions du Seuil.

Le Braz, A. (1980) *La Légende de la Mort chez les Bretons Armoricains*, 2 vols, Marseille: Lafitte Reprints, (first published in 1902).

Le Bris (1896) 'L'accent breton', *BPIIF* 3 (1 May).

Le Du, J. and Le Berre, Y. (1979) *Textes Choisis dans Feiz ha Breiz*, special issue of *Studi* 11 (April), UBO.

Le Gac (1896) 'Le breton auxiliaire du maître', *BPIIF*, 8 (1 November): 301–3.

Le Gall, Th. (1958) *Commune de Plounéour-Ménez*, manuscript *mémoire*, September 1958.

Le Gallo, Y. (1982) 'Une caste paysanne du Haut-Léon', *Mémoires de la Société d'Histoire et d'Archéologie de Bretagne* LIX: 53–74.

Léger, D. (1979) 'Les utopies du "retour"', *Actes de la Recherche en Sciences Sociales* 29 (September): 46–63.

Le Giouron *et al.* (1980) *Plogoff. La Révolte*, Le Guilvinec: Le Signor.

Le Gléau, R. (1973) *Syntaxe du Breton Moderne*, Editions La Baule.

Le Goaziou, A. (1950) *La longue vie de deux 'Colloques François et Breton' (1626–1915)*, Quimper: Librairie Le Goaziou.

Le Goffic, C. (1902) *L'âme bretonne*, Paris: Honoré Champion.

Le Gonidec, J.F.M.M.A. (1807) *Grammaire Celto-Bretonne*, Paris.

—— (1821) *Dictionnaire Celto-Breton ou Breton-Français*, Angoulème: François Trémeau.

Le Guen, G. and Pors, H. (1980) 'Une Autre Bretagne', in *La Région Bretagne*, Rennes: Ouest France.

Le Menn, G. (1972) 'Les linguistes et la connaissance de la langue bretonne', *BSAF* XCIX (2).

—— (1975) 'Le Breton et Son Enseignement', *Langue Française* 25 (February).

—— (1980) *La Grande-Bretagne A Travers La Littérature Bretonne (XVe–XVIIe s.) Et Le Vocabulaire Breton*, typescript.

Lemm-e-bluenn (1981) 'Kendalc'h Keltieg Etrevroadel', *CNB*, 13–20 November 1981: 11.

Le Roux, P. (1924) *Atlas Linguistique de la Basse Bretagne*, Rennes.

Leroy, M. (1967) *The Main Trends in Modern Linguistics*, Oxford: Blackwell.

Le Roy Ladurie, E. (1974) *Les paysans du Languedoc*, 2 vols, Paris: Ecole Pratique des Hautes Etudes.

Le Sann, A. and Ferec, G. (1973) *Breiz Atao et le nationalisme breton entre les deux guerres mondiales*, 3 vols, Mémoire de Maîtrise (Histoire) Rennes.

Le Scouëzec, G. (1968) *Histoires et Légendes de la Bretagne Mystérieuse*, Paris: Tchou.

—— (1979) *Guide de la Bretagne Mystérieuse*, Paris: Tchou, Editions Princesse.

Le Solliec, P. (1970) 'For an Alternative to Politics', in *'The Celt in the Seventies': Celtic League Annual*, special issue.

L'Estourbeillon, Le Marquis de (1919) *Le Droit des Langues et de La Liberté des peuples*, St Brieuc: Prud'homme.

Letertre R. (1977) 'Assemblées Régionales de Bretagne: Chroniques de septembre 1976 à août 1977' *Armor* (supplement) 95 (December).

—— (1978) 'Assemblées Régionales de Bretagne: Chroniques de septembre 1977 à septembre 1978', *Armor* (supplement) 104 (September).

Lévi-Strauss, C. (1955) *Tristes Tropiques*, Paris: Plon.

Lévi-Strauss, L. and Mendras, H. (1981) 'Rural community studies in France', in J. L. Durand-Drouhin *et al.* (eds) *Rural Community Studies in Europe*, Oxford: Pergamon Press.

Lewis, B. (1984) 'The impact of development policies on women', in M. Hay and S. Stichter (eds) *African Women South of the Sahara*, London: Longman.

Lhuyd, E. (1707) *Archaeologica Britannica*, vol. I, *Glossography*, Oxford: Oxford University Press.

Loréal (1897) 'Les idiomes locaux', *BPIIF* 12 (1 March): 499–500.

Loth, J. (1898) 'Les Etudes Celtiques, leur importance, leur avenir', *Revue Internationale de l'Enseignement* XXXV (5), May.

—— (1911) *Les Etudes Celtiques. Leur Etat présent, leur avenir*, Librairie Général de Droit et de Jurisprudence, Paris.

—— (1926) 'Les Langues Bretonne et Française en Bretagne (d'après un travail récent: Dauzat, A., 1926: 'Le breton et le français', *Nature*, 1 May 1926: 273)', *Revue Celtique* 43.

Lough, J. and M. (1978) *An Introduction to Nineteenth Century France*, London: Longman.

Lovecy, J. (1982) 'Protest in Brittany from the Fourth to the Fifth Republics: from a regionalist to a regional social movement', in Cerny, P. G. (ed.) *Social Movements and Protest in France*, London: Frances Pinter.

Luzel, F. M. and Souvestre, E. (1982) *Contes des Landes Bretonnes*, Rennes: Ouest France.

Lyotard, J. (1986) *The Postmodern Condition: A Report on Knowledge*, translated by G. Bennington and B. Massumi, Manchester: Manchester University Press, (first published in 1979).

McDonald, J. R. (1978) 'Europe's restless regions', *Focus* XXXVIII (5), May–June.

McDonald, M. (1982) *Social Aspects of Language and Education in Brittany, France*, D. Phil. thesis, University of Oxford.

—— (1984) 'Tourism: chasing culture and tradition in Brittany', paper presented to RESSG (British Sociological Association), October 1984, in M. Winter and M. Bouquet (eds) *'Who From Their Labours Rest?' Conflict and Practice in Rural Tourism*, London: Gower, 1987.

—— (1985) 'The politics of fieldwork in Brittany', paper presented at ASA 'Anthropology at Home' Conference, Keele University, March 1985, in A. Jackson (ed.) *Anthropology at Home*, ASA 25, London and New York: Tavistock, 1987.

—— (1986a) 'Celtic ethnic kinship and the problem of being English', *Current Anthropology* 27 (4): 333–47.

—— (1986b) 'Brittany: politics and women in a minority world', in R. Ridd and H. Callaway (eds) *Caught Up in Conflict: Women's Responses to Political Strife*, London and New York: Macmillan.

—— (1986c) 'Drinking and social identity in Western France', paper presented to Anthropology Research Seminars at Oxford University and the London School of Economics, forthcoming.

MacFarlane, A. (1977) 'History, anthropology and the study of communities', *Social History* 5: 631–52.

Mme 'X' (1896) 'Le Breton en dehors de l'école', *BPIIF* 5 (1 July) 186–7.

Malmanche, T. (1903) 'Bezomp "ni hon-unan"', *Spered ar Vro* 1 (August).

Markalé, J. (1977) *Histoire secrète de la Bretagne*, Paris: Albin Michel.

—— (1980) *La Bretagne racontée aux enfants*, Rennes: Ouest France.

Martin, H. (1855) *Histoire de France*, vol. I, Paris: Furne.

Maurois, A. (1969) *A History of France*, London: Cape (first published in 1949).

Mauss, M. (1966) *The Gift*, translated by I. Cunnison, London: Routledge & Kegan Paul, (first published in 1925).

Meirion-Jones, G.-I. (1978) *La Maison Traditionelle. Bibliographie de l'Architecture Vernaculaire en France*, Paris: Centre National de la Recherche Scientifique (Centre de Documentation Sciences Humaines).

—— (1980) 'L' Architecture Vernaculaire en Bretagne', *Mémoires de la Société d'Histoire et d'Archéologie de Bretagne* LVII: 31–62.

Mendel, G. (1974) *Pour décoloniser l'enfant*, Paris: Payot.

Mendras, H. (1970) *The Vanishing Peasant*, translated by J. Lerner, Mass.: MIT Press.

Mennell, S. (1985) *All Manners of Food, Eating and Taste in England and France from the Middle Ages to the present*, Oxford: Blackwell.

Mercier, U. (1896) 'Les exercises de langage', *BPIIF* 7 (1 October): 241.

Merser, A. (1980) *Les Graphies du Breton*, special issue of *Ar Helenner* 15, Brest.

—— (1981) *Précis de Prononciation du Breton*, special issue of *Ar Helenner* 25, Brest.

Meyer, J. (1966) *La Noblesse Bretonne au 18e siècle*, 2 vols, Paris: Ecole Pratique des Hautes Etudes.

—— (1974) 'Alphabétisation, Lecture et Ecriture. Essai sur l'Instruction populaire en Bretagne du XVIe au XIXe siècle', Congrès National des Sociétés Savantes (Reims, 1970), in *Histoire Moderne*, vol. 1. Paris, (first published in 1970).

Michel, J. (ed.) (1975) *Enfances de Bretagne*, Paris: Magnard.

Ministère de l'Education (1977) *L'Ecole Maternelle*, Centre national de documentation pédagogique.

Ministère de l'Intérieur (1979) *Associations. Régime Général*, *JO* (no. 1068), Paris, (first published in 1977).

Monnier, J. J. (1981) 'D'où Viens-tu Breton?', *CNB* 27 February 1981–6 March 1981: 4.

Montfort, E. (1941) 'L'Instruction à Pleyben sous l'Ancien Régime', *BSAF* LXVIII.

Monzie, A. de (1925) 'Circulaire du 14 août 1925 relative aux idiomes locaux', *JO* (1 September 1925): 207–10.

Mordrel, O. (1973) *Breiz Atao. Histoire et actualité du Nationalisme breton*, Paris: Moreau.

—— (1975) *La Voie Bretonne. Radiographie de l'Emsav*, Quimper: Nature et Bretagne.

Morgan, S. J. (1979) *Roparz Hemon and the Breton Cultural Movement in the Twentieth Century*, D.Phil. thesis, University of Oxford.

Morin, E. (1967) *Commune en France: La Métamorphose de Plodémet*, Paris: Fayard.

Morvannou, F. (1975) *Le Breton Sans Peine*, Paris: Assimil.

—— (1980) *Le breton, la jeunesse d'une vieille langue*, Brest: Presses populaires de Bretagne.

Mourier, A. D. (1889) *Notes et souvenirs d'un Universitaire*, Orléans: Imprimerie Jacob.

Mouvement laïque des cultures régionales (1959) 'Les Langues de France et l'Ecole Publique', special issue of *Ar Falz* 1 (January–February).

Needham, R. (1962) *Structure and Sentiment*, Chicago: University of Chicago Press.

Neill, A. S. (1972) *Libres enfants de Summerhill*, Paris: Maspero.

Nicolas, M. (1980) *L'Emsav: politique et thématique du mouvement breton*, Doctorat d'Etat, Université de Haute-Bretagne (Rennes).

—— (1982) *Emsav: Histoire du Mouvement Breton*, Paris: Editions Syros.

Nordmann, J-T. (1977) *La France Radicale*, Paris: Editions Gallimard/Julliard.

O'Callaghan, M. J. C. (1983) *Separation in Brittany*, Redruth, Cornwall: Dyllansow Truran.

Ogès, L. (1919) *La Langue Bretonne*, Quimper: *BSAF*.

—— (1931) 'Les Ecoles d'enseignement Mutuel dans le Finistère sous la Restauration.' *BSAF* LVIII.

—— (1934) 'L'Instruction primaire dans le Finistère sous le régime de la Loi Guizot (1833–1850)', *BSAF* LXI.

—— (1936) 'L'Instruction sous l'ancien régime dans les limites du Finistère actuel', *BSAF* LXIII.

—— (1937) 'L'Instruction sous l'ancien régime dans les limites du Finistère actuel (suite)', *BSAF* LXIV.

—— (1939) 'L'Instruction dans le Finistère pendant la Révolution (à suivre)', *BSAF* LXVI.

—— (1940) 'L'Instruction dans le Finistère pendant la Révolution (suite; à suivre)', *BSAF* LXVII.

—— (1941) 'L'Instruction dans le Finistère pendant la Révolution (suite; à suivre)', *BSAF* LXVIII.

—— (1942) 'L'Instruction dans le Finistère pendant la Révolution (suite et fin)', *BSAF* LXIX.

—— (1945–6) 'L'Instruction dans le Finistère sous le Consulat et l'Empire (1799–1815)', *BSAF* LXXII.

—— (1949) *L'Agriculture dans le Finistère au milieu du XIXe siècle*, Quimper: Le Goaziou.

Okely, J. (1983) *The Traveller Gypsies*, Cambridge: Cambridge University Press.

Olier, Y. (1960) 'Istor ar yezh Peurunvan', *Hor Yezh* 11.

—— (1972) 'Emsav 1972', in *Celtic League Annual* 1972.

Olivier, F., Keginer, K., and Guilloux, J-M. (1978) *Bretagne. Breizh. Une nouvelle prise de conscience*, Verviers, Belgium: Marabout Flash.

Ossian (1760) *Fragments of Ancient Poetry Collected in the Highlands of Scotland and Translated from the Gaelic or Erse Language*, 2nd edition, Edinburgh.

—— (1762) *Fingal, an Ancient Epic Poem in Six Books composed by Ossian the son of Fingal*, translated from the Gallic language by James Macpherson, Dublin.

—— (1763) *Temora, an Ancient Epic Poem in Eight Books*, translated from the Gallic language by James Macpherson, Dublin.

Ozouf-Sohier, M. (1970) 'Deux langues, deux cultures', *Le Pays Breton* 149 (March): 7.

PB (1980) 'Qui parlera breton en l'an 2000?', debate, in *PB* 193 (January–February 1980); 4–8.

Peabody, D. (1985) *National Characteristics*, Cambridge: Cambridge University Press/Paris: Editions de la Maison des Sciences de l'Homme.

Pelletier, W. (1970) 'L'Enfance Indienne', *Soirées* 32 (November 1970), translated from *This magazine is about schools*, spring 1969.

Pérennès, H. (1932) 'Une Vieille Abbaye Bretonne. Notre Dame du Relec en Plounéour-Ménez', *BSAF* LIX: 55–154.

Person, Y. (1973a) 'Présentation', *Les Temps Modernes* 324–6 (August–September).

—— (1973b) 'Impérialisme Linguistique et Colonialisme', *Les Temps Modernes*, 324–6 (August–September).

Peyre, H. (1933) *La royauté et les langues provinciales*, Paris: Les Presses Modernes.

Pezron, Dom P. (1703) *Antiquité de la Nation et de la Langue des Celtes, Autrement appelez Gaulois*, Paris: Marchand & Martin.

Philipponneau, M. (1970) *Debout Bretagne!* St Brieuc: Presses Universitaires de Bretagne.

—— (1972) *Au Joint Français: les ouvriers bretons*, St Brieuc: Presses Universitaires de Bretagne.

Pichavant, R. (1980) *Les Pierres de la Liberté*, Douarnenez: Morgane.

Piette, J. R. F. (1973) *French Loanwords in Middle Breton*, Cardiff: University of Wales Press.

Piggott, S. (1967) *Celts, Saxons and the early Antiquaries*, 1966 O'Donnell lecture, Edinburgh University Press.

Piriou, Y-B. (1971) *Défense de cracher par terre et de parler breton. Poèmes de combat (1950–1970)*, Paris: Oswald.

Plaine, Dom P. (1899) *La Colonisation de l'Armorique par les Bretons Insulaires*, Paris: Picard et fils.

Pléven, R. (1961) *Avenir de la Bretagne*, Paris: Calmann Levy.

Plunier, J. (1979) 'Une innovation politique, le C.E.L.I.B.' in *'Bretagnes, les chevaux d'espoir . . .'*, special issue of the journal *Autrement* 19 (June), Paris.

Poisson, H. (1967) *Alain Barbe-torte, Libérateur de la Bretagne*, Bretagne et Culture, St Brieuc: Les Presses Bretonnes.

Prost, A. (1968) *L'Enseignement Primaire en France, 1800–1967*, Paris: Colin.

Quellien, N. (1889) *Chansons et danses des Bretons*, Paris: Maisonneuve & Leclerc.

Quéré, L. (1979) 'Les militants ont toujours les yeux bandés!', in *'Bretagnes, les chevaux d'espoirs . . .'*, special issue of the journal *Autrement* 19 (June), Paris.

Quéré, L. and Dressler-Holohan, W. (1978) '"Vivre au pays", généalogie d'un slogan', *Autrement* 14 (June).

Quiniou, A. (1973) *Images de la Bretagne Dans la Littérature Française du XIXe Siècle*. Mémoire de maîtrise, UBO.

Quiniou, F. (1929) *Saint-Thégonnec. Une Paroisse Bretonne Sous la Révolution*, Brest: Presse Libérale.

Radcliffe-Brown, A. R. (1968) *Structure and Function in Primitive Society*, London: Cohen & West.

Reader, K. A. (1984) 'The intellectuals: notes towards a comparative study of their position in the social formation of France and Britain', *Media, Culture and Society* 4 (1984):263–73.

Reece, J. E. (1979) 'Internal colonialism: the case of Brittany', *Ethnic and Racial Studies* 2 (3), July.

Rees, W. H. (1939) *Le Bilinguisme des Pays Celtiques*, thèse de Doctorat d'Université, Rennes, Rennes: Imprimerie M. Simon.

Rex, J. and Mason, D. (eds) (1986) *Theories of Race and Ethnic Relations*, Cambridge: Cambridge University Press.

RGA (1979–80) *Recensement Général de l'Agriculture, 1979–80. (Département du Finistère, Direction Départementale de l'Agriculture.)*

Roberts, H. (1986) *Northern Ireland and the Algerian Analogy*, Belfast: Athol Books.

Rochefort, C. (1976) *Les enfants d'abord*, Paris: Grasset.

Rogers, V. (1984) 'Ethnicity, inequality and integration: ethnic activism in post-war Brittany', in P. Morris (ed.) *Equality and Inequalities in France*, Association for the Study of Modern and Contemporary France.

Ross, G. and Jenson, J. (1985) 'Pluralism and the decline of left hegemony: the French left in power', *Politics and Society* 14 (2): 147–83.

Rothney, J. (ed.) (1969) *The Brittany Affair and the Crisis of the Ancien Régime*, Oxford: Oxford University Press.

Roudaut, F. (1975) *La Prédication en Langue Bretonne à la fin de l'Ancien Régime* thèse de 3e cycle, 2 vols, UBO.

Roudaut, R. (1973) 'Histoire du Mouvement Breton', *Les Temps Modernes* 324–6 (August–September).

Royer, A. (1980) *Meubles et objets des provinces de France. Bretagne*, Paris: Hachette.

Safran, W. (1977) *The French Polity*, New York and London: Longman.

—— (1984) 'The French left and ethnic pluralism', *Ethnic and Racial Studies* 7 (4): 447–61.

Saizieu, T. B. de (1984) 'Les formes actuelles de l'entraide agricole dans une commune de Basse Bretagne', *Ethnologie française* XIV (4): 363–76.

Sancier, R. (1952) 'L'Enseignement primaire en Bretagne de 1815 à 1850 (à suivre)', *Mémoires de la Société d'histoire et d'archéologie de Bretagne* XXXII.

—— (1953) 'L'Enseignement primaire en Bretagne de 1815 à 1850 (suite et fin)', *Mémoires de la Société d'histoire et d'archéologie de Bretagne* XXXIII.

Saunders, G. (1980) 'Adding a second native language in the home', *Journal of Multilingual and Multicultural Development* 1 (2).

Schlemmer, H. (1936) *Le Collège de Morlaix (Fondé en 1597)*, Morlaix: Imprimerie Nouvelle.

Ségalen, M. (1980) 'Le Nom Caché', *L'Homme* XX (4): 63–76.

—— (1984) 'Nuclear is not independent: organization of the household in the Pays Bigouden Sud in the nineteenth and twentieth centuries', in R. Netting *et al.* (eds.) *Households: Comparative and Historical Studies of the Domestic Group*, Berkeley, Ca.: University of California Press.

SEMENF (1971) *Aménagement Rural des Monts d'Arrée. Commune de Plounéour-Ménez*, Morlaix: SEMENF.

—— (1973) *Le Pays de Morlaix. Evolution et Perspectives*, Morlaix: SEMENF.

Servat, G. (1979) Une voix en avant, deux voix en arrière', in '*Bretagnes les chevaux d'espoirs . . .*', special issue of the journal *Autrement* 19 (June), Paris.

Seton-Watson, H. (1965) *Nationalism, Old and New*, Sydney: Sydney University Press.

Siegfried, A. (1964) *Tableau Politique de la France de l'Ouest Sous la IIIe République*, Paris: Colin, (first published in 1913).

Simon, P.-J. (1978) 'Le Mouvement Breton, Expression ou Créateur de la Question Bretonne?', *Pluriel* 15: 27ff.

—— (1979) 'Racisme et Anti-Sémitisme dans le Mouvement Breton des Années Trente', *Pluriel* 18.

Simon, R. (1974) *Tourisme Rural en Bretagne. Les Gîtes Ruraux du Nord Finistère*, Mémoire de Maîtrise (géographie), Brest: UBO.

Singer, B. B. (1971) *The Village Schoolmaster in Brittany, 1880–1914*, Ph.D. thesis (modern history), University of Washington.

Skol Vreiz(h) (1974) *Histoire de la Bretagne et des Pays Celtiques. De la Préhistoire à la Féodalité*', special issue *Skol Vreiz* 39, Morlaix.

—— (1975) *Histoire de la Bretagne et des Pays Celtiques. L'Etat Breton de 1341 à 1532 et Les Pays Celtiques au Moyen Age*, special issue *Skol Vreiz* 42, Morlaix.

—— (1976) *Géographie de la Bretagne*, Morlaix: Skol Vreiz.

—— (1978) *Histoire de la Bretagne et des Pays Celtiques. La Bretagne Province (1532–1789) et les Pays Celtiques du XVIe à la fin du XVIIIe siècles*, special issue *Skol Vreizh* 54–7, Morlaix.

—— (1980) *Histoire de la Bretagne et des Pays Celtiques de 1789 à 1914*. Morlaix/Rennes: Skol Vreizh, Imprimerie Commerciale.

mith, A. (1979) *Nationalism in the Twentieth Century*, Oxford: M. Robinson & Co.

—— (1981) *The Ethnic Revival in the Modern World*, Cambridge: Cambridge University Press.

Smyth, R. (1979) 'French speak up for their language', *Observer* 16 December 1979.
—— (1981) 'Mitterrand gives power to provinces', *Observer* 19 July 1981: 10.
Souvestre, E. (1971) *Les Derniers Bretons*, vol. I, Le Portulan: Bertout, (first published in 1835–7).
Spence, K. (1978) *Brittany and the Bretons*, London: Gollancz.
Stack, C. (1974) *All Our Kin: Strategies for Survival in a Black Community*, New York: Harper & Row.
Stéphan, L. and Sèité, V. (1978) *Lexique Breton-Français et Français-Breton*, Edition F.C.B., Brest: Emgleo Breiz.
Stephens, M. (ed.) (1973) *The Welsh Language Today*, Llandysul: Gomer Press.
—— (1976) *Linguistic Minorities in Western Europe*, Llandysul: Gomer Press.
Stone, J. (1985) *Racial Conflict in Contemporary Society*, London: Fontana.
Strathern, M. (1984) 'The social meaning of localism', in T. Bradley and P. Lowe (eds) *Locality and Rurality: Economy and Society in Rural Regions*, Norwich: Geo Books.
Taldir (1935) 'Genèse de la campagne en faveur de l'enseignement du breton', *Le Foyer Breton* 52.
Tanguy, B. (ed.) (1977) *Aux origines du nationalisme breton*, 2 vols, Paris: 10/18.
Thierry, A. (1828) *Histoire des Gaulois*, vol. 1, Paris: Sautelet.
Thomas, G. M. (1954) 'Pas de Breton à l'école Primaire', *BMSELF* 1954 (March): 30–1, on behalf of *Commission des Classes Primaires*, Quimper.
Tilly, C. (1976) *The Vendée*, Cambridge, Mass.: Harvard University Press.
Tourneur, V. (1905) *Esquisse d'une Histoire des Etudes Celtiques*, Liège: Vaillant-Carmanne.
Trégouët, B. (1978) 'Agriculteurs: le dépeuplement des campagnes', *Octant* 3 (September).
Trellu, D. (1954) 'A propos de l'enseignement du breton à l'école primaire', *BMSELF* 1954 (March): 31–5.
Trénard, L. (1968) *Salvandy en son temps. 1795–1856*, Lille: Giard.
Trollope, T. A. (1840) *A Summer in Brittany*, 2 vols, London: Colburn.
UDB (1972) *Bretagne = Colonie (Avec l'UDB pour que ça cesse!)*, Rennes: UDB/ Imprimerie commerciale.
Urien, J.-Y. (1981) *Réflexions socio-linguistiques sur le concept de langue*, typescript, Université de Haute- Bretagne, Rennes (U.E.R. de langage).
Urien, J.-Y. and Denez, P. (1975) *Essai d'Analyse Sémiologique du Mot Verbal et du Syntagme Verbal en Breton Contemporain*, typescript, Bibliothèque de langage, Université de Haute-Bretagne, Rennes.
Vallée, F. (1895) *La Langue Bretonne et les Ecoles*, St Brieuc: Prud'homme.
—— (1935) 'Conseils aux Ecrivains Bretons', in L. Le Berre *Rapport du Comité de Préservation de Langue Bretonne*, 3 July 1935, St Brieuc: Prud'homme.
—— (1980) *Grand Dictionnaire Français-Breton, suivi du 'Supplément'*, in collaboration with E. Ernault and R. Le Roux, second edition, St Brieuc: Les Presses Bretonnes, (first published in 1931).
Van Tieghem, P. (1967) *Ossian en France*, 2 vols, Geneva: Slatkine Reprints.
Vermeulen, H. (1984) 'Introduction' in H. Vermeulen and J. Boissevain (eds), *Ethnic Challenge. The Politics of Ethnicity in Europe*, Gottingen: Edition Herodot.
Wardhaugh, R. (1986) *An Introduction to Sociolinguistics*, Oxford: Blackwell.
Weber, E. (1977) *Peasants into Frenchmen*, London: Chatto & Windus.
Weill, G. (1899) 'Les Républicains et l'Enseignement sous Louis-Philippe', *Revue Internationale de l'Enseignement* 37.
Williams, R. (1981) *Cyflwyno'r Llydaweg*, Caerdydd/Cardiff: Gwasg Prifysgol Cymru.

Winterbottom, M. (ed.) (1978) *The Ruin of Britain, and other works*, Gildas, edited and translated by Winterbottom, London: Phillimore.

Zeldin, T. (1973) *France 1848–1945*, vol. 1, *Ambition, Love and Politics*, Oxford: Clarendon Press.

—— (1977) *France 1848–1945*, vol. 2, *Intellect, Taste and Anxiety*, Oxford: Clarendon Press.

Zernatto, G. (1944) 'Nation: the history of a word', *Review of Politics*, 6: 351–66.

Name index

Subject index

Upper Brittany 16, 28, 112, 125, 141, 142, 200

Vannes, Vannetais 15, 16, 45, 49, 129–31, 159, 163, 211–12, 215
Vichy regime: and education 55, 123; and Breton *see under* Breton
villages 19
Villers-Cotterêts *ordonnance* (1539) 5

Wales, the Welsh 2, 97, 112, 114, 117, 121, 146–7, 153, 163, 164, 196, 218,

295, 296, 344n, 345n; *see also* Gaul, Gauls
Welsh education 179, 197
Welsh language 12, 97, 100, 110, 111, 113, 114–16, 120, 121, 127, 132, 138, 145, 160, 163, 166, 179, 205, 206, 346n, 353n; teaching of 157, 197
women 170, 310–12; in Plounéour-Ménez 243–56, 267–8; *see also* under Breton; gender; girls; feminism
word order *see* syntax, Breton
World War I *see* First World War
World War II *see* Second World War